Boundless Faith

The publisher gratefully acknowledges the generous support
of the General Endowment Fund of the University of
California Press Foundation.

Boundless Faith

The Global Outreach
of American Churches

Robert Wuthnow

UNIVERSITY OF CALIFORNIA PRESS
Berkeley · Los Angeles · London

University of California Press, one of the most
distinguished university presses in the United States,
enriches lives around the world by advancing
scholarship in the humanities, social sciences, and
natural sciences. Its activities are supported by the
UC Press Foundation and by philanthropic
contributions from individuals and institutions.
For more information, visit www.ucpress.edu.

University of California Press
Berkeley and Los Angeles, California

University of California Press, Ltd.
London, England

Library of Congress Cataloging-in-Publication Data

Wuthnow, Robert.
    Boundless faith : the global outreach of American
    churches / Robert Wuthnow.
        p.   cm.
    Includes bibliographical references and index.
    ISBN 978-0-520-25915-7 (cloth : alk. paper)
    1. Missions, American.   I. Title.

BV2410.W88   2009
266'.02373—dc22   2008026283

Manufactured in the United States of America

18   17   16   15   14   13   12   11   10   09
10   9   8   7   6   5   4   3   2   1

This book is printed on Cascades Enviro 100, a 100%
post consumer waste, recycled, de-inked fiber. FSC
recycled certified and processed chlorine free. It is acid
free, Ecologo certified, and manufactured by BioGas
energy.

Contents

124832

Preface

The United States is one of the richest nations in the world and arguably the strongest militarily. It is also a nation with deep religious values and tens of thousands of flourishing churches. In the past, powerful countries spread their religious values to far corners of the world. Spanish priests accompanied the conquistadors. British missionaries and colonists followed the traders. Is the United States now playing a similar role in promoting global Christianity? Or have times changed?

We citizens of the United States have never liked to think of our nation as an imperial power. The colonial adventures of the Spanish and British empires over several centuries and our own brief expansionist forays at the end of the nineteenth century presumably taught us that there is a better way. Encourage freedom and protect our interests, but respect the autonomy of other nations. If we had to intervene militarily in Vietnam or Afghanistan or Iraq, our leaders told us, it was not to gain territory but to promote democracy.

Yet it is undeniable that America's power has also shaped the world. The litany of influences is familiar—from oil tankers in the Persian Gulf to reruns of American sitcoms in Thai villages. Indeed, it is easy to side with critics who predict that historians in the future will gauge American influence more in terms of pop culture and consumerism than anything else.

Where in all of this are those tens of thousands of flourishing churches? Have they played a significant role in giving the United States a different image than purveyor of soap operas and consumer of world oil? Does the average churchgoer contribute to international relief efforts? Does he or she think differently about world events than the person whose outlook is shaped only by CNN or Fox News? Or are American Christians so focused on themselves that their religious practice is irrelevant to the larger world?

These were the questions that prompted me to write this book. They have been with me for a long time. As a teenager, I read war journals and missionary biographies and wondered about the people who had gone on exotic journeys to fight enemies and save souls. Later, I studied European history and colonialism with similar questions in mind. In the books I have written about American religion, I have found it necessary to focus on the small details of how people make sense of their lives and where they seek for meaning in their congregations and families. I have also been consistently mindful that these small details take shape in larger contexts composed of power arrangements and institutions. Increasingly, these contexts lie outside local communities and even outside the United States itself.

My central argument is that American Christianity has been significantly influenced in recent years by globalization and is, in turn, playing a much larger role in other countries and in U.S. policies and programs abroad. The evidence supporting this argument is both quantitative and qualitative. Increasing globalization is directly apparent in the growth of U.S. support for missionaries and churches in other countries and in the large number of American Christians who participate in short-term volunteer efforts abroad. The influences of globalization are also evident in the extent to which American churchgoers value being part of the global Christian community and in the changing ways in which U.S. religious organizations have become involved in such diverse activities abroad as building orphanages, encouraging small-scale local businesses (also called micro businesses), and setting up computer networks.

The research was guided by two key assumptions. First, I am methodologically indifferent to whether or not American Christianity *should* influence the rest of the world. I have my views of course about the kinds of influence that might or might not be desirable, but as a social scientist my aim is solely to describe and understand what Americans are doing in this respect. Second, I am old enough to know better than to try to write a book about all the ways in which American Christianity is being globalized (let alone about global Christianity itself). Rather, my interest is in understanding better what ordinary people are doing through their congregations and other religious organizations or by themselves. To do this, I have spent a great deal of time learning about the more specialized activities of government bureaus and nongovernmental organizations, too. However, my central concern is with the outlooks and activities—here, transcultural—in which individuals themselves might be engaged. It also goes without saying that this is a book about Christians in the United States, not about Christians in other countries.

Broadly speaking, all the various religions represented in the United States are diversely transcultural. Members of a synagogue who give money for Hadassah's hospital work in Israel would be one example. A community of Laotian immigrants who maintain their ethnic and cultural traditions by attending services at a Buddhist temple in Dallas or Omaha would be another example. This book, however, is about the transnational activities of America's majority faith community. The Christian population makes up about 80 percent of the total U.S. population (and better than 90 percent if those with no religious affiliations are excluded). Christianity is an evangelistic religion whose adherents believe variously in sharing their faith and putting into practice the ethic of love expressed in the life of Christ. I am thus interested in describing the activities through which American Christians are engaged in such sharing and practice beyond their own borders.

To focus on such activities as expressing one's faith in an international context puts me in the scholarly domain that has traditionally been occupied by missiologists. I am not one and this book is not intended as a contribution to that field. Missiology is an interdisciplinary endeavor that draws on biblical studies, theology, history, and the social sciences. Some of the questions about statistics, finances, and congregational programs that interest me are also of interest to missiologists. Where we differ is with respect to our normative assumptions. Missiological studies begin with the assumption that Christians *should* be engaged in spreading the good news of their faith. As a social scientist, I understand my task to be that of learning as objectively as I can what is happening and why.

Social science is never as dispassionate as those of us who practice it might like it to be. In fact, some biases are built into the enterprise itself. Here are some of mine. I am bothered by ideas that have become trendy. Not all trends are bad, of course, but if it is trendy to send missionaries to "convert the heathen," I want to know why people are jumping on the bandwagon, and if it is trendy to go on short-term mission trips to deepen one's spiritual life, I want to pose hard questions about that as well. I have been trained to study the influences of culture on religion. Thus, I am sensitive to how the secular consumer orientation of our culture may be shaping how we think about such transnational religious activities as missionary trips and humanitarian aid. I do not assume that these activities spring simply from first principles found in the Bible. Another bias of mine is that social life is composed of groups and organizations rather than only autonomous individuals. For this reason, I am inclined to emphasize that beliefs and preferences are produced by groups and organizations rather than rising unassisted from the human heart. At the same time, I am deeply critical of simple "supply-side" perspectives in the social sciences. If religious practice does not spring full blown from the heart, it doesn't arise just from free markets, either.

These biases mean that my arguments will perhaps seem more critical than they are intended to be. As I have done in previous books, I try to be candid about things that work the way people hope and about things that do not work. For instance, if churchgoers think their congregations are doing more to support relief efforts in other countries than they really are, then a balanced assessment requires being honest about what is not happening as well as what is happening. I know from reactions to previous books that boosters of particular programs do not often want to hear balanced assessments. To them I say, if your mind is that made up, then don't bother reading this book. To readers who are more open-minded, though, I must add that even tacitly critical remarks do not come easily for me. For instance, in writing about the social conditions that make it easier for people to engage in international humanitarian work, I in no way mean to detract from the fact that they *are* doing such work. Indeed, the dangers such people frequently face inspire nothing but admiration.

The research for this book was conducted with generous support and assistance from a large number of organizations and individuals. It includes information from a nationally representative survey of 2,231 members of local churches. I also commissioned in-depth qualitative interviews with approximately three hundred pastors, church leaders, and members who had been involved in transnational ministries. This part of the research was supported by the Lilly Endowment in Indianapolis, and I am grateful to Chris Coble and Craig Dykstra for their interest and encouragement. Chintan Turakhia and Robert Magaw at Schulman, Ronca, and Bucuvalas, Inc., supervised the fieldwork for the survey, and

Karen Myers, Libby Smith, Jennifer Kang, Peter Mundey, and Steve Offutt conducted most of the qualitative interviews. I am especially grateful for the many rank-and-file church members and leaders who took part in the survey and interviews. I have also drawn on the World Christian Database at Gordon-Conwell Seminary and on numerous surveys and international data files generously made available through Firestone Library at Princeton University. I am grateful to Alicia Juskewycz, Matthew Parker-Lavine, Mariana Kim Huh, and Tim Callahan for assisting me with the library research and to Valerie Lewis for help in analyzing the survey.

No scholar works in a vacuum, and, although I work well by myself, I have been the recipient of particularly valuable advice, both direct and indirect, from a number of colleagues and students. I wish especially to thank Neil Ahlsten, Wendy Cadge, Elaine Ecklund, Jim Gibbon, Conrad Hackett, Becky Yang Hsu, Michael Lindsay, Katherine Marshall, Mark Noll, Janet Parker, Amy Reynolds, Robert Seipel, Drew Smith, and Larry Stratton. The literature that contributed valuably to shaping the ideas for this book is vast and much of it is referenced specifically. I want to single out several scholars whose work has been especially helpful: David Barrett, Joel Carpenter, Mark Chaves, Darrell Guder, Dale T. Irvin, Philip Jenkins, Todd Johnson, Lamin Sanneh, Immanuel Wallerstein, and Andrew Walls. Finally, I thank my family, not only for their continuing encouragement and support, but also for their growing personal interest and involvement in transnational endeavors.

Introduction

In recent decades U.S. Christianity has significantly extended its activities abroad and is quietly redefining itself at home. Spending by American churches on overseas ministries has risen to nearly $4 billion annually, an increase of almost 50 percent after inflation in a single decade. The number of full-time missionaries serving abroad has increased steadily over the same period and is significantly larger than a half century ago when the missionary movement was at its presumed all-time high. During the past two decades, nearly every international faith-based relief and development agency has expanded dramatically, and the supporters of these organizations have become more actively engaged in foreign policy initiatives. By all indications, the number of Americans who do short-term volunteer work abroad as church builders, evangelists, religious teachers, technical advisors, and relief workers has also risen to a record high. A majority of U.S. congregations are currently involved in overseas ministries—through special offerings for humanitarian causes, supporting missionaries, hosting foreign speakers, forming committees, and sending out volunteers.

Although the globalization of American Christianity is not entirely recent, it represents a new phase in the history of American religion. During the eighteenth and nineteenth centuries, a mosaic of denominations and creeds largely of European origin developed in the United States, increasingly accompanied by indigenous churches, all reflecting the cultural, ethnic, regional, and racial divisions in which they were instantiated.

In the twentieth century, a national faith was forged from these diverse strands—a tripartite faith of Catholics, Protestants, and Jews, and later of religious liberals and conservatives—whose unifying principles and governing movements transcended the earlier divisions and struggled to express themselves as a kind of civic religion. In the current phase, American religion has moved significantly beyond these domestic concerns, broadening its scope not only through the sporadic missionary efforts of the past or in expressing itself about government policies but also through direct partnerships with overseas congregations, engaging in faster and more efficient transcultural communication, interacting with a sizable population of refugees and immigrants, and contributing to large-scale international humanitarian and relief organizations.

The globalization of American Christianity is part of the nation's wider participation in the international economic, political, and cultural community. Because of foreign trade and finance, travel, and the mass media, the typical church member in the United States participates daily in this wider community. He or she wears clothing produced abroad, consumes food from overseas suppliers, and interacts with neighbors and co-workers who grew up in other countries. The day's news includes stories about foreign investments, bombings, trade agreements, poverty, and international trafficking in drugs and sex. As a nation, the United States is deeply involved in these processes of globalization. Our way of life depends on being able to import goods from countries where labor is cheap and on finding investors abroad to finance the considerable trade deficits we incur. We participate indirectly in global networks whenever we shop, vote, pay our taxes, or consume news about the larger world in which we live.

No congregation, even in the most isolated corner of America, is exempt. The new Bibles in that congregation's pews stand a good chance of having been printed in China. The paper plates for its monthly potluck dinner may have come from Guatemala, and if they were purchased by credit card, the transaction may have been processed in India. The pastor's clerical garb may have been woven in Peru. The building and grounds may be maintained by a contractor who hires workers from Central America. Were that not enough, the church's members would have to be exceptionally closed-minded not to recognize that the troops they pray for on Sunday are deployed on foreign soil, that members of their own congregation may be recent immigrants to the United States, that the fellow Christians they claim to be in community with are scattered across the globe, and that many of these fellow Christians are living in abject poverty or dying from starvation or AIDS. They certainly will have heard that Christianity is not just for Americans.

Globalization intersects with faith on many different levels. Theologians and Christian ethicists have begun to emphasize the ways in which globalization challenges Western assumptions about God, prosperity, suffering, social justice, the environment, military intervention, and a host of other issues.[1] Globalization, concludes the study committee of one ecumenical body, affects the work of churches everywhere by advancing international networks, promoting communication, diminishing the boundaries separating nations and cultures, generating in some instances a corresponding backlash of nationalism and xenophobia, undermining the traditions and lifestyles of local communities, transferring power and wealth, fueling border conflicts, and creating large populations of refugees and immigrants. Although the scale of these developments is immense, globalization challenges people of faith where they live and where they worship. Thus, as this committee urges, "the local church must seek to interact creatively with the global" not only by strengthening itself locally but also by redefining itself in relation to its larger geographical context.[2]

International communication, including actually spending time in other countries, is one of the key factors driving the globalization of American Christianity. As one indication of how much such communication has increased, international telephone traffic quadrupled between 1991 and 2004.[3] Another indication is that the number of air passengers traveling from the United States to other countries grew from about ten million in 1975 to nearly sixty million in 2000.[4] Nearly two-thirds (62 percent) of active church members in the United States have traveled or lived in another country. One in seven (14 percent) has lived in another country for at least a year. More than four in ten (43 percent) have friends or relatives who live outside the United States. Vacations, foreign study, military service, and business all contribute to these international connections. Eleven percent of active church members have served in the armed forces. Among church members currently working, 37 percent say they routinely interact with people from other countries at work. Immigration is another source of transnational ties. Although the United States is historically a nation of immigrants, the pace of immigration in the past three decades has been considerably greater than it was during the preceding half century. Approximately twenty-two million immigrants arrived during this period and as many as twelve million more came as undocumented workers. The impact was especially evident among young males in their twenties, the percentage of whom were foreign born jumping from 4 percent in 1970 to 18 percent in 2000. Currently, 8 percent of active church members are immigrants, 14 percent are children of immigrants, and 74 percent attend congregations in which recent immigrants are present. Besides having personal ties and experiences abroad, most Americans regularly consume information about the wider world through the mass media. Among active church members, 38 percent claim to be "very interested" in news about other countries. Three-quarters watch news about other parts of the world on CNN, MSNBC, Fox News, or other channels at least once a week; a quarter read about international news at least once a week in a major national newspaper; and four in ten obtain information about foreign events at least once a week from the Internet.[5]

Another important factor in the globalization of American churches is the growing number of foreign congregations and religious organizations with which partnerships and cooperative relations can be initiated. According to one source, the number of local worship centers in Africa grew from 282,000 to 603,000 between 1970 and 2000; in Latin America, from 131,000 to 462,000; and in Asia, from 234,000 to 1,146,000.[6] Equally important, the number of international nongovernmental organizations (INGOs) and the countries in which they work has increased. For instance, figures compiled in 1966 and again in 1988 show that the total number of INGO memberships in Africa grew from 76 to 264 and in Asia from 129 to 407.[7] One of the largest of these is World Vision International, a Christian organization specializing in humanitarian assistance in more than a hundred countries and with annual cash and in-kind donations of nearly $1 billion.[8] World Vision and similar organizations, such as World Relief and Catholic Relief Services, work closely with congregations in the United States to forge links with churches and local projects in other countries.

A third factor contributing to the globalization of American Christianity is its sheer preponderance of resources. If Christianity was ever the faith of downtrodden people, it is by no means that in the United States. Nearly half (47 percent) of active church members earn family incomes of at least $50,000 a year, and more than a quarter (28 percent) have incomes in excess of $75,000. On a per capita basis, church members' incomes are roughly the same as the national average, which in inflation-adjusted dollars doubled during the last three decades of the twentieth century.[9] During the 1990s alone, philanthropic giving to religion grew by 70 percent and donations to international organizations tripled.[10] Even though few Americans donate more than 1 or 2 percent of their income to religious causes, the nation's affluence and its large percentage of churchgoers make it possible for U.S. Christians to play an important role in the wider world. The Southern Baptist Convention, for example, spends nearly $300 million a year on international ministries.[11] The much smaller Assemblies of God denomination spends almost $200 million annually supporting more than 2,500 Christian workers abroad. Compassion International, a nondenominational organization founded in 1952, raises nearly $250 million annually, which it uses to assist more than 500,000 children worldwide.

Not only are U.S. churches replete with resources, but these resources are also increasingly concentrated in megachurches—a fourth significant factor in the globalization of American Christianity. Megachurches, defined as congregations of at least two thousand members, make up fewer than 2 percent of all congregations in the United States, but these churches already include one of every six active churchgoers and their numbers are growing.[12] Although congregations of all sizes encourage members to pray for overseas programs and provide small contributions, megachurches amass enough resources in one place to engage directly in global outreach rather than working through intermediaries. Most megachurches are in fact heavily involved in global ministries. At Willow Creek Church in suburban Chicago, for instance, the congregation raised almost $2 million the first time it took up a special offering for international ministries in the early 1990s and this amount has been growing ever since. Nationally, 60 percent of the members of megachurches report that their congregation focuses "a great deal" or "a fair amount" on people living outside of the United States, 53 percent say their congregation emphasizes helping people who live in other countries a lot, and 44 percent say their congregation emphasizes international ministries a lot.

A fifth factor influencing globalization might be termed the "saturation effect." During much of the nation's history, the resources church leaders could muster beyond those needed to support their own congregations went into church expansion within the United States itself. The nineteenth century witnessed a huge investment in church building as the population spread westward and then at the end of the century into the nation's large cities. This expansion continued until after World War II, when construction of church buildings and high birth rates led to a temporary upsurge of religious involvement in the 1950s and in some denominations fueled significant growth well into the 1970s. In the past decade, though, even the denominations that had been growing the most appear to have reached a saturation point. For instance, the Southern Baptist Convention, which registered annual gains of 2.3 percent in the 1970s, grew by only 0.6 percent annually between 1996 and 2003, not quite half the rate of increase in the U.S. population as a whole. The Church of Jesus Christ of Latter-Day Saints, which had previously experienced enormous growth, increased by only 0.4 percent annually during the same period, and the Assemblies of God dropped from an annual growth rate of 9.2 percent in the 1970s to 1.8 percent in the late 1990s.[13] Faced with declining growth, church leaders have redoubled their efforts to provide attractive ministries in the United States, but increasingly they also seek opportunities elsewhere. For instance, the Southern Baptist Convention, having grown by about a third since the early 1970s in total U.S. membership, has more than doubled its foreign missionary staff.[14]

As the world becomes increasingly interdependent, Christianity in the United States is becoming transcultural, responding to the realities of globalization by actively and intentionally engaging in activities that span borders. Transcultural congregations give priority to programs that honor their commitments at home but also seek to be engaged in the lives of others around the world. A transcultural orientation connects local commitments with churches, communities, organizations, and individuals in other countries. Church leaders increasingly stress having a vision that transcends the interests of those who gather for worship each week at the local church building. They contend that a congregation that focuses only on itself becomes insular. They want their members to understand that the Christian gospel is for all of humanity, and they encourage members to become informed about and engaged with the full range of conditions to which Christian teachings apply, whether this involves evangelization, feeding the hungry, ministering to the sick, serving as peacemakers, caring for children, or showing hospitality to the stranger.

Transcultural Christianity poses new challenges that are only now coming into view. In the past, congregations worked best when they provided a safe, homelike community. The experience of home is nurtured through worship and fellowship, through the mundane intimacies of living in a familiar place and interacting with friends and neighbors. Theologically, a homelike congregation incarnates the mysterious indwelling of God. In the best-case scenario, though, transculturalism dislocates this sense of security. Being not at home results in the troubling awareness that the security of home is fragile, not shared by those who have no homes, and even dependent on arrangements of power and exploitation that are inconsistent with the spirit of divine love. Living transculturally is thus to acknowledge the precariousness of being and the possibility of hope. The divine indwelling that manifests itself at home radiates outward. As theologian Cynthia Moe-Lobeda writes, "The presence and power of God, living in and loving in creation, will lead those who dare to know that presence more intimately *and* to see the realities of globalization more clearly, along life-saving and life-savoring paths."[15]

U.S. churches are currently attempting to strike an appropriate balance between the local and the global in a wide variety of ways, many of which are broadening the horizons of their members. A nondenominational megachurch in southern California sends teams of technical advisors to help start micro businesses in Kenya. A Baptist church in suburban Atlanta takes in a refugee family from Honduras and helps its members learn English. A Methodist youth group in Oklahoma spends a week in Guatemala painting an orphanage. A Roman Catholic parish in Philadelphia takes up a special offering to help its sister parish in Lithuania. The vestry at an Episcopal church in Chicago formulates a resolution about debt relief for countries in Africa. An independent evangelical congregation in Texas trains and supports overseas missionaries in more than a dozen countries.

Examples like these suggest that U.S. congregations are increasingly trying to reach beyond their local communities and do so with whatever resources they can muster. Conversations with pastors and church members who have become involved suggest that the experiences are genuinely beneficial. However, thoughtful reflection on these conversations also suggests a need for closer and more critical scrutiny. For instance, the anecdotes are almost always rosy, implying that efforts inevitably have positive results. The refugee family all learned English, found jobs, and are now pillars of the church. The youth group not only painted the orphanage but installed a new septic tank and made lasting friends. Its members reported that the week in Guatemala had been life transforming. The sister parish in Lithuania is eternally grateful for the financial assistance it receives. International debt relief is perhaps moving more slowly than the vestry would like, but just formulating the resolution has brought a new sense of togetherness and commitment to its members. The overseas missionary sends heartfelt e-mails about the wonderful people she has been meeting. In these distillations, transcultural experiences are easy and uncomplicated, too uncomplicated.

Anecdotes are inspiring, but they are no substitute for hard facts. And the truth is, good evidence has been almost nonexistent until recently. Nobody has been able to say for sure whether the typical congregation is going out of its way to be involved in ministries abroad. The sparse evidence that has been available yields mixed conclusions: some of it suggests that international ministries make up only a small fraction of congregations' overall programs, while other reports point to massively well-financed overseas efforts. When a teenager returns from Guatemala claiming to have had a life-transforming experience, it has been impossible to know if this is typical or atypical. It is thus difficult to know if the time and money Americans spend on short-term mission trips is well spent or if these programs are poorly conceived. It is equally difficult to know if congregations should be focusing more of their attention on overseas programs, or less. Who gets involved in supporting these ministries? Why? And with what consequences?

These questions are compounded by the fact that there is a huge debate at present among church leaders themselves about the very nature of so-called overseas ministries and about reasons for supporting them. In some accounts, Christianity is doing just fine in other parts of the world without intervention from the United States and indeed, U.S. efforts abroad may be inadvertently reinforcing a kind of cultural imperialism by spreading Western values. It may be time for Americans to sit back, hunker down, focus on their own communities, and, if anything, learn from the indigenous leadership of churches in developing countries. In other accounts, congregations in the United States need to redouble their efforts to help with ministries overseas, but leaders disagree about how to focus these efforts. Some argue that congregations should work directly with missionaries, others favor working through denominational agencies, and still others argue that the most effective programs are now being run by large parachurch agencies and relief organizations.

Were congregations simply in a position to support as many different ministries as they wanted and to do so thoughtfully, questions and debates like these would perhaps be unimportant. Each congregation would do what it could and be happy if anything beneficial came from it. But congregations make difficult choices about which ministries to support. The demands of local programs are considerable, and spending time or money on programs in some other part of the world usually has to be weighed against these demands. The same is true for individual church members. Many are heavily invested in church activities that benefit themselves, their families, and their neighbors. All are faced with significant responsibilities in their jobs, their homes, or their neighborhoods. When it comes to thinking about programs concerned with spreading the faith or helping the needy in other countries, they may well be tempted to say they can do no more. One is reminded of Serepta, the faithful church-woman portrayed in Marietta Holley's popular late-nineteenth-century novel, *Josiah Allen's Wife,* who complains, "I must be all the time away from home a workin' for the heathen and missionary societies. And I must at the same time be to home all the time a workin' and a takin' care of my family."[16]

Serepta's complaint underscores the important point that church programs abroad always begin at home. They take place within the local congregation, as Serepta's activities do when she participates in the ladies' missionary society that was so much a part of the nineteenth-century congregation. They are supported through special offerings and organized by local pastors and lay committees. They also require that time and energy be diverted from taking care of oneself and one's family. The transcultural church that becomes significantly involved in activities and concerns beyond the borders of its own nation is still fundamentally a local church operating in a local community and constrained by local needs and resources. If it is interested in motivating its members to be more engaged with such global issues as hunger, economic development, evangelism, war and peace, refugees, immigrants, and the environment, it must do so by connecting these issues with the lived experiences of its members within their local communities.

My treatment of U.S. Christians' responses to globalization includes the views of pastors and members and emphasizes what congregations and individual churchgoers are doing and thinking. To make sense of these transcultural activities, though, we must have a broader grasp of what is at stake. Transcultural programs, whether concerned with supporting or engaging in missionary work or encouraging church members to think more deeply about environmental and economic development issues, take place amidst pressures to devote time and energy only to activities of benefit to local congregations themselves. These international efforts are guided by longstanding assumptions about foreign missions and evangelism, but they are also shaped by the changing landscape of global Christianity itself.[17]

Although much has been written in recent years about the shifting dynamics of global Christianity and about globalization, the very abundance of this writing has resulted in a great deal of confusion. Some of the confusion is unimportant except to academic specialists with esoteric interests in the topic, but much of it is of wider significance as well. For instance, it is difficult to assess what Christians and Christian congregations in the United States are doing transculturally if one believes, as some writers apparently do, that the United States is simply irrelevant to the future of global Christianity. Similarly, it is difficult to sort out the meanings of American Christians' responses to globalization without considering the highly contested claims that globalization is a sea in which all boats are rising, that it is an exploitative system in which poverty is increasing, that it is promoting a universal monoculture, and that it is revitalizing local diversity.[18]

An aspect of globalization that has become trite because it is so often mentioned is the fact that international transportation and communication have become quicker and easier. Naturally, faster and more efficient transportation and communication make it possible for local churches to become more actively and directly involved in ministries abroad. The same is true for individual church members who may wish to do volunteer work in another country or whose exposure to international news heightens their interest in foreign affairs. But the idea that transculturalism consists mainly of church members doing things overseas is wrong. From their inception in the nineteenth century, missionary and relief organizations had to figure out sustainable ways to conquer the challenges of distance. The resulting organizations were a curious hybrid of centralization and decentralization. They had to maintain control over a far-flung and dedicated group of frontline workers while also connecting effectively enough with the local home churches to raise money and recruit personnel. But during the twentieth century two developments began to alter these organizational strategies. One was the growing role of government not only in shaping foreign policy in general but also as a direct source of funding for international humanitarian organizations. The other was the development of a more professionalized—and more highly specialized—cadre of personnel. Even Christian organizations concerned mainly with evangelism became involved in a wide variety of new endeavors, including water conservation programs, sanitation efforts, health screening, vaccinations, sustainable agriculture programs, and emergency disaster relief. How local congregations fit into this larger and more complex pattern of international organizations is an important part of what we must consider in order to understand the transcultural church.[19]

These broader matters provide the context in which to think about the specific activities in which congregations and individual church members engage. New national data make it possible to consider how many congregations support missionaries, how many church members go abroad on short-term mission trips, how much of the average church member's financial contributions are devoted to international ministries, whether congregations hold meetings to talk about war or environmental justice, and whether church members think their congregations should or should not be interested in questions about international trade. The evidence suggests that congregations and individual church members are more actively involved in transcultural issues than most observers would have guessed. However, the available data also show wide variation in levels and kinds of involvement, which are in turn influenced by denominational tradition, church size and location, and members' beliefs and values.[20]

The globalization of American Christianity poses significant questions about the changing role of Christianity within the United States itself. One of these is whether being part of a church makes any difference to the way Christians think about America's role in the world, particularly on questions of international policy. It is widely assumed in discussions of international relations that religion simply does not matter, at least compared to economic and political interests. That assumption has been challenged by events in other countries, such as the conflicts between Muslims and Christians in Sudan or between Shiite and Sunni Muslims in the Middle East. But it has been unclear whether religion in the United States matters much to U.S. policies. On the one hand, it might be supposed that religious convictions make a difference in the same way they do about abortion or gay and lesbian issues. On the other hand, American Christians and Americans more generally are known for favoring individualistic solutions to problems and believing that private voluntary efforts are the only way to deal with humanitarian issues. If that is the case, then we need to understand the assumptions that discourage church members from being a more distinct voice when it comes to major issues of international policy.[21]

The goal of this book, then, is both to illuminate the relatively neglected global aspect of American Christianity and to broaden the framework in which we customarily think about the successes, failures, and variations among faith communities. The central need is to reorient our perspective in such a way that the chronology of religious events in our particular national location is understood in a wider, more diverse, and interconnected cultural context. As globalization increases, that task becomes ever more urgent.

CHAPTER I

At Home and Abroad

The Changing Contours
of American Religion

Throughout most of our nation's history, religion in America has conjured up images of local activity. "Church" means a church building with a local address. People gravitate to these homey places of worship because their friends and neighbors do. The pastor or priest knows them and cares about their problems. The church is part of the local community. Few images capture this sense of proximity better than Norman Rockwell's 1953 *Walking to Church*. Mom, dad, and the three kids stroll happily past the barber shop and the Silver Slipper Grill, with the church steeple rising in the background no more than a block away.[1] Half a century later, the church may be further from one's neighborhood, but its orientation is still local.

The local focus of American religion comes through loud and clear when people talk about their congregations. Jack Mitchell, a member of a Presbyterian church in suburban Chicago, illustrates how prominently local considerations leap to mind as people discuss their places of worship. Mr. Mitchell is now in his sixties and has been attending the same church for more than thirty years. It is a typical middle-class congregation of about 350 members. He and his wife attend worship services every Sunday, except when they are traveling, and both have served on various committees, including the congregation's board of elders. When they first started attending, their children were young. He says they were "looking for a family-oriented church." The pastor, he recalls with muted enthusiasm, was "a capable man." What drew them was mainly the congregation, "the people." And over the years, through good times and bad, including some tensions in the congregation that resulted in families leaving, it has been this sense of family that has kept him involved. He does of course have loyalties beyond the congregation itself. For instance, he says he is proud to be a Presbyterian and holds no particular grudges against the denomination. He notes in passing that the congregation sponsors "a girl who was a missionary over to Africa." But his voice is most animated when he talks about what is happening locally. He tells a long story about the church's roof and why it is more "handsome" now than in the past. He relates another story about a decision the church made to build a nursing home on an adjacent property. The church building and the nursing home next door give him a tangible sense of what it means to be part of a congregation. The congregational singing, the weekly sermons, and the familiar flow of the worship services do too. Above all, it is still the people who gather there from week to week who make the church his home. It is "this feeling of congregational togetherness" that he likes best, "this one big family type of thing."

Mr. Mitchell's perspective is not unusual among American churchgoers. Although he has been involved more actively and over a longer period in one congregation than have many people, his emphasis on family and community is no different from the language newcomers typically use to describe what they like about their congregations. A recent newcomer at a Baptist church in Saint Louis says she especially appreciates the "small family-like atmosphere." A member of a Catholic parish in an older urban neighborhood in Milwaukee stresses the "spirit of community here," adding that "people know each other and like each other." A couple who recently joined a downtown Methodist church in Dallas describe it as "very friendly" and note that it was actually a homemade pie from the church that showed just how friendly it was.

Church, family, and homemade pie. Congregations pride themselves on being friendly. The best ones do function like caring families. Members talk about community because it is a manifestation of Christian ideals. Knowing one another and supporting one another is what it means to be the body of Christ. They also talk about community because it seems to be missing in other parts of their lives. They do not feel emotionally close to people in their sprawling, anonymous neighborhoods or at work. For American Christians, the local church is thus special precisely because it is local. It is a secure and familiar space composed of people who gather there regularly and form bonds as strong and as enduring as those in one's own family.

Research demonstrates the extent to which U.S. congregations are locally oriented. Finances are a telling indication of this orientation. Although most congregations are affiliated with a denomination or some denomination-like entity, the typical congregation expends less than 5 percent of its income supporting that larger organization.[2] Nearly all congregations own their own building and have at least one clergy person, and these items account for the biggest items in the typical congregation's budget. Weekly worship services are the centerpiece of most congregations' activities, and, although it is possible to watch religious services on television or listen to religious radio programs, it is still the norm for American churchgoers who participate in religious services to attend in person. At a majority of churches, most of those who do attend live within a ten-minute drive of the church.[3] Among all church members, 80 percent claim that at least three of their closest friends are fellow members of their congregation.[4] Between half and two-thirds of congregations help sponsor various service activities, such as soup kitchens or tutoring programs, and these are generally local or at least in the same community.[5] Ethnographic studies show that people think of their congregations as places of warmth, acceptance, and friendship.[6] Members typically identify more closely with a particular congregation than they do with such remote entities as denominations, and few know much about the national offices of their denominations.[7] Even if they are newcomers to their congregations, they will have shopped for one that is convenient and seems likely to provide them with friends similar to themselves.[8]

To say that American congregations are locally oriented is not to say only that most of their activities happen at a particular place. Researchers have also found that church members often hold what might be called a "localistic" worldview. For instance, in a study of North Carolina church members, sociologist Wade Clark Roof found that the more active churchgoers preferred local news to national or international news and expressed greater loyalty to their local communities than less active church members did, and these differences remained when Roof took account of differences in age and levels of education.[9] In another study, researchers found similar patterns among Jews.[10] A national study of Episcopal churches using ethnographic methods and qualitative interviews documented a striking emphasis among clergy and members alike on "local loyalty" and an equally notable sense that the "linkages between local congregations and wider structures are . . . ineffectual and growing weaker."[11] Drawing on statistical data from a national study of congregations from a range of denominations, sociologist Nancy Ammerman demonstrated that congregations do have linkages but that these are usually with other local organizations instead of with national or international bodies. For instance, of more than 1,200 such linkages involving human services, 83 percent were with local partners while only 17 percent were with national or international organizations.[12] "Overwhelmingly, interorganizational involvement is aimed at assisting the needy and providing services that enhance the general well-being of *local communities*," Ammerman observed.[13] "Local" did not mean the immediate neighborhood of the church itself. But it did mean the general environs of the congregation, such as the town or suburb in which it was located, as opposed to activity concerned with helping people in another region or part of the world.

Besides the obvious fact that it is convenient and perhaps more interesting to focus religious energies on nearby instead of faraway activities, several features of contemporary life in the United States contribute to this emphasis on local activities. One is the entrepreneurial ethos from the business world that infuses American culture and that increasingly encourages a managerial style among clergy and other church leaders. The managerial style emphasizes numeric growth as the premier sign of congregational success. It links clergy salaries, promotions, and prestige with attaining this kind of success. It elevates congregational autonomy as a facilitator of such success, while identifying larger denominational structures as impediments. With potential congregants characterized by fewer denominational loyalties and greater tendencies to engage in denominational switching, the autonomous congregation that focuses on its own programs and local priorities is thus in the best position to succeed.

A related factor is the widely noted tendency for churchgoers to adopt the same consumerist mentality that they do in negotiating commercial transactions. The watchwords of this consumerist mentality are personal gratification and efficiency. Gratification means focusing first and foremost on satisfying one's personal needs and desires, including those of one's immediate family. Efficiency means doing so by incurring the least possible cost. Faced with making a decision among the various churches available in one's community, the religious consumer will thus choose the one that offers the best Sunday school program for one's children, the greatest chances of finding a suitable mate if one is single, the most convenient location, the most inspiring sermons, the clearest moral guidelines, or some other attractive feature, while avoiding such costs as having to spend money on programs from which there is no immediate personal benefit. Of course the calculations involved are never quite this crass or explicit. On balance, they nevertheless favor congregations that supply the most attractive incentives, secure the greatest commitment from their members, and keep the resulting resources in-house for the congregation's own growth and development.

Another aspect of American life that reinforces a localistic emphasis in congregations is what some observers refer to as alienation from large bureaucratic structures, or simply anti-institutionalism. Although it is difficult to establish the precise nature and sources of this alienation, it is perhaps evident in the large proportion of Americans who tell pollsters they are concerned about the alleged breakdown of community. If not exactly demonstrated in books claiming to document the collapse of community in America, it is at least expressed in the widespread popularity of such books.[14] In the face of seemingly intractable economic forces and large impersonal governmental structures run by politicians with little apparent interest in the common person, the warmth and security of the local congregation becomes especially appealing. Devoid of linkages or obligations beyond its own walls, the local church is a private space, an extension of one's home in which familial relationships prevail. It is, in Victor Turner's words, a manifestation of *communitas,* a protected place of "anti-structure."[15] Within this sheltered enclave, a person weary of the travails of the bureaucratized world can find solace and comfort.

This desire to retreat from the wider world fits handily with yet another feature of contemporary life: the experiential legitimation of truth. There is no evidence that Americans have abandoned such core tenets of religious doctrine as belief in the existence of God or the divinity of Jesus. Yet, when asked if they find biblical teachings or personal experience more credible for spiritual guidance, nearly half opt for personal experience.[16] Truth is validated not by tradition or institutional authority but by firsthand knowledge gained from personal experience. Clergy and other religious leaders have by no means given up on truth claims rooted in tradition or institutional authority. But they do increasingly play into the desire for authenticated individual experience. The congregation becomes a therapeutic community. The love of Christ is felt directly as people gather in small support groups or participate in sharing the Eucharist. To be a member of the church means primarily being part of the gathered community, *koinonia* (fellowship) taking precedence over dogma. The experience of worship becomes the hallmark of the Sunday service. All this of course happens most effectively in a local setting. The experience is more intense and authentic when it is shared with the believers who make up one's local congregation.

The fact that congregations encourage—and are encouraged in—a local emphasis in these various ways does not mean that Christianity in the United States is weak. The view that American churches are faltering is often a starting point in discussions of America's role in the wider arena of world Christianity. If American churches are weak, then hope for the future lies chiefly in sitting back and learning from the more vibrant churches that exist elsewhere. But that view is too simple. It runs contrary to the fact that American churches remain considerably stronger than those in most other wealthy nations of the world and, indeed, have shown remarkable resilience even in comparison with their American predecessors of a generation or two ago.[17]

The point is rather that any consideration of the transnational role of American churches must acknowledge the overwhelming predisposition of congregations to be local. This predisposition is by no means unique to the contemporary period, but it does mean that churches' activities abroad are always conceived in relationship to their ministries at home. It means, too, that the recent globalization of American Christianity is all the more interesting because it has occurred at a time when many factors have encouraged congregations to retreat into their own local programs.

TRANSCENDING THE LOCAL

The mandate for Christian congregations to engage in ministry beyond their immediate locale is expressed most clearly in the New Testament teaching known as the Great Commission (Mark 16:15): "Go ye into all the world, and preach the gospel to every creature." Acts 1:8 emphasizes the same mandate: "You shall be my witnesses in Jerusalem, Judea, Samaria and unto the uttermost parts of the earth." The early church established a pattern of congregations commissioning and financially supporting apostolic ministries. Paul and Peter, along with Mark, Thomas, and others, traveled widely, spreading the gospel through Asia Minor, to Rome and Alexandria, and as far as India. However, the subsequent diffusion of Christianity was not accomplished primarily through local congregations' supporting ministries abroad. The spread of Christianity came in large measure from conquest and territorial rule as individual leaders, particularly Constantine, converted to Christianity and declared it the official religion. Christianity spread through persecution, as congregations fled and became diasporic communities in new locales. It also spread through the witness of itinerant evangelists and traders. By the sixth century, the Western church was sufficiently organized that ministries abroad were centrally commissioned under papal authority, much like ambassadors and emissaries sent by secular authorities. In 597, for instance, Pope Gregory sent Augustine and forty other monks to evangelize the British Isles. This pattern expanded during the Middle Ages through the establishment of monastic orders, including the Benedictines, Franciscans, and Jesuits, who took on the responsibility of representing the church abroad. These religious orders played a significant role in carrying Christianity to the New World during the Spanish imperium of the fifteenth and sixteenth centuries. Local parishes were involved in these efforts, but their role consisted largely of paying mandatory tithes. The Protestant Reformation did not greatly alter this pattern, although the religious conflicts of the sixteenth and seventeenth centuries resulted in a new diaspora of religious dissenters, such as the Huguenot community that fled to Brazil and the Puritans who settled in North America.[18]

Local congregations assumed a more direct role in overseas evangelistic and humanitarian efforts during the nineteenth century, especially in Great Britain and the United States, where missionary societies emerged as voluntary organizations. Prior to this time, local congregations had mostly assisted in founding and supporting new congregations within the American colonies themselves by sending itinerant preachers and taking up special collections. Catholic leaders and the heads of Protestant denominations increasingly provided supervision and funding for new congregations. As the European population in North America increased, congregations of immigrants often sent money directly to other congregations seeking to provide places of worship for immigrants of similar ethnic or national origin. Precedent was thus established for congregations to consider needs beyond their own communities. The arrival of large numbers of immigrants in urban areas at the end of the nineteenth century further established this precedent, as congregations contributed to settlement house projects, relief chests, and other urban ministries.

The earliest missionary societies in the United States raised money by finding ways to do so without compromising the budgets of local churches. During the first decade of the nineteenth century, what became known as female cent societies raised money by asking women to save a penny a week by tightening household budgets in small ways.[19] These societies, organized by churchwomen, led within a few decades to the development of hundreds of ladies' associations that raised funds for foreign missions and gradually drew their congregations into a more sustained supporting role. Whereas the larger organizations for missions, such as the American Board of Commissioners for Foreign Missions, developed centrally coordinated programs, the ladies' associations adopted specific missionaries and supported specific projects, thus anticipating the direct congregational support that was to become popular during the last third of the twentieth century.[20]

Local churches balanced ministries abroad with ministries at home primarily by cooperating with governing boards that transcended specific congregations, such as missionary societies, church councils, conferences of bishops, synods, presbyteries, and the like. Each congregation paid an "apportionment" to this larger body, which in turn allocated funds for evangelistic and relief work in other domestic locations and in other countries. During the course of the twentieth century, numerous other ways of linking local congregations with wider ministries gradually emerged. Independent mission boards assisted congregations in working directly with missionaries. Some congregations developed partnerships with congregations in other countries. A large number of humanitarian, relief, and economic development agencies also came into existence during the last half of the century.

As a result of these developments, congregations and individual members now have ample opportunities to initiate activities that extend beyond the local community and even to other countries. Church members have a broad range of options for supporting these wider ministries, such as taking short-term mission trips sponsored by congregations, doing individual volunteer work abroad, and sending letters or e-mails. Besides direct expenditures of money or time, church members also routinely make choices about difficult issues involving the wider world through indirect means, such as working for legislation to promote or restrict free trade, helping refugees, or protecting the global environment. What is also evident from the historical record, though, is that purely voluntary programs organized only at the local level have seldom been the preferred pattern for addressing wider needs. Congregations participated in wider efforts because political arrangements or leaders at the highest levels of church authority required them to or because they could do so in small ways through church boards and parachurch organizations. Apart from this, congregations' record of translocal involvement was until recently spotty, either helping other congregations when there was some direct affinity or pitching in because an occasional leader with exceptional charisma encouraged them to do so. If congregations are currently engaged in wider activities, it is because these activities have become more firmly grounded in sustainable institutional practices.

GLOBAL REALITIES

The situation in which American church members now find themselves is one of unprecedented opportunities for engagement in the experiences of people whose lives are quite different from their own. A large minority of the churchgoing public has traveled abroad, witnessing firsthand the diversity of lifestyles and cultures. A growing minority of American church members are immigrants, and for them, transnationalism has literally meant crossing borders and adapting to cultural differences. Television makes it possible to visualize, say, a street in Marrakech or a refugee camp in Somalia more vividly than ever before. The Internet further expands these possibilities. The resulting potential for awareness about human needs beyond the borders of one's own community or nation is thus greatly increased. This is not to say that the typical church member is necessarily cognizant of these needs at a deep level or is particularly mindful of them from day to day. It is to say that newspapers and television bring daily reports of suffering, hunger, and violence from around the world.

It is a truism to say that suffering has always been the plight of the human condition; moreover, there is usually enough suffering close to home so that people in the United States do not have to look abroad to find it. Yet the realities of global media, travel, trade, and economic interdependence make it difficult to ignore the extent to which suffering prevails in the wider world. Figures compiled by the United Nations, for instance, suggest that more than 800 million people in the world are malnourished. More than a billion lack access to clean water. Six million children under the age of five die annually as a result of hunger. Three million children die each year from waterborne disease. More than twenty-two million people have died from AIDS, leaving at least thirteen million children without mothers.[21] The people who suffer most have been helped very little by the expansion of global trade, and by some indications their situation has worsened. That expansion has, if anything, increased the huge discrepancies between the rich and the poor. Currently, the amount of money that the richest 1 percent of the world's people make each year equals that of the poorest 57 percent. More than a billion people worldwide struggle to survive on less than a dollar a day.[22]

In addition to these manifest physical needs, the church's historic mission of preaching, teaching, and making disciples of all nations remains far from being fulfilled, at least to those who interpret this mission in terms of numeric gains for Christianity. Some 2.6 billion of the world's 7.8 billion people are estimated to be adherents of Christianity, meaning that nearly two-thirds of the world's population belong to some other religion or none. Opinions differ, of course, about how to interpret such figures and about whether they are meaningful at all. Some authorities, for instance, point to rapid growth among Christian groups in Africa or Latin America and conclude that Christianity is clearly on the ascendancy. Others are not so sure, especially when sagging participation rates at churches in western Europe are considered. But from the number crunchers themselves, the best estimates are that adherents of Christianity have hovered at 33 to 34 percent of the world's population for the past century and that this level is likely to remain steady for at least another half century.[23]

Whether Christianity expands or remains constant, many observers of the international scene point to the growing possibilities of religious conflict and the need for sustained interreligious dialogue and creative theological reflection. Political scientist Samuel P. Huntington's prediction of escalating tensions between Christians and Muslims has been particularly notable.[24] Religion and religious conflicts have thus reentered debates among international relations specialists and experts on economic development in ways that would have been inconceivable a few decades ago. "At a time when the notion of a global 'clash of cultures' is resonating so powerfully—and worryingly—around the world," writes United Nations Human Development Programme administrator Mark Malloch Brown, "finding answers to the old questions of how best to manage and mitigate conflict over language, religion, culture and ethnicity has taken on renewed importance."[25] International relations scholar Daniel Philpott emphasizes that people across the globe seek "to worship and submit to their God, to protect and defend their mosques, temples, shrines, synagogues, and churches, to convert others to their faith, to reside in a realm governed by *sharia,* to live under a government that promotes morality in many spheres of society, to draw on their faith to extend civil rights to minorities and women, and to practice forgiveness and reconciliation in the wake of decades of injustices."[26] Is it any wonder, he asks, that these activities have a profound impact on societies and the relationships among societies?

Discussions of the physical needs and spiritual quests of the world's population invariably raise thickets of arguments and counterarguments, proposals, and questions. For instance, an influential segment of America's business and political elite believes that the world's problems can best be solved by the spread of free market capitalism. Others believe the solution lies in propagating American-style democracy, while still others anticipate that only the imminent return of Christ will put an end to the current state of affairs. In these scenarios, the average church in the United States has such a small role to play that playing any at all hardly matters. However, the extreme cynicism represented in these views appears not to be widely shared. Religious leaders generally agree that churches should be involved in ministries to the wider world. The questions, rather, are what is being done and what can be learned from these efforts?

WHAT ARE CHURCHES DOING?

Researchers have paid so little attention to the transcultural activities of American churches that it has until recently been difficult to answer even the simplest questions about what is currently being done. Although countless studies of church leaders and church members have been conducted, hardly any of these have ventured into topics involving programs outside the United States. Those that have included such topics provide only scant evidence, and this information has evoked more questions than answers. For instance, sociologist Mark Chaves's National Congregations study found that only 8 percent of Americans attend congregations that sponsor or participate in "programs explicitly mentioning beneficiaries outside the United States, including Crop Walk."[27] But it is likely that the reference to Crop Walk directed respondents' thinking toward social service or fund-raising activities and discouraged them from considering the foreign missionaries their congregation might have been sponsoring. A national study of individuals conducted by political scientist John C. Green also suggested that congregational support for international ministries may be relatively rare. When asked if they had given time or money to support "international programs," only 11 percent of those surveyed said they had done so through a religious venue, while another 13 percent said they had through a secular venue.[28] However, no questions were asked about informal programs or other forms of individual involvement that may have been influenced by congregational participation. These national results must also be weighed against evidence that in some settings congregations are more likely to be involved in international ministries. For instance, social scientist Ram Cnaan's research among Philadelphia churches (which are larger, more urban, and more involved in other social ministries than congregations nationally) found that nearly a quarter of congregations (22.3 percent) claimed to be involved in helping provide "international relief" services—about the same proportion that helped sponsor soup kitchens or prison ministries locally.[29]

If existing surveys have provided little information about international programs, other evidence suggests that American churches in the aggregate are doing quite a lot to support missionary work and humanitarian ministries abroad. Figures collected by Protestant mission agencies and denominations in 2001 showed that there were 42,787 U.S. citizens working full-time as missionaries in other countries, representing an increase of approximately 16 percent over the previous decade, and significantly higher than the comparable number in the 1950s, at the often assumed height of overseas missionary endeavors. In addition, approximately 65,000 non–U.S. citizens and foreign nationals were working in other countries under full sponsorship by a U.S. agency. Besides this, as many as 350,000 Americans had spent between two weeks and up to a year abroad serving as short-term mission volunteers, and an estimated one million (a number that may have been considerably higher) had served for less than two weeks. In total, U.S. churches contributed more than $3.7 billion for overseas ministries, an after-inflation increase of 45 percent over the previous decade.[30]

It is worth underscoring what these figures suggest about the involvement of American churches in ministries abroad because they run counter to a popular view about such ministries. In the popular view, ministries abroad began to falter in the 1960s, at which time they were left largely in the hands of independent evangelical agencies, and even these efforts began to diminish by the 1990s. In contrast, the numbers of Americans engaged in both short- and long-term foreign missions efforts and the amount of money spent suggest that the United States still plays a very significant and increasing role. Other evidence also supports this view. For instance, World Vision International, Catholic Relief Services, and the Salvation Army are among the world's largest international relief and development organizations, and each, while thoroughly international in organization and administration, secures a large share of its revenue from individual donors within the United States and, for that matter, depends increasingly on the U.S. government for funds.[31]

The fact that American churches provide substantial assistance to foreign missionary efforts and to humanitarian agencies does not mean that these programs necessarily stand high on the list of financial priorities of most congregations. Nevertheless, American churches are able to sponsor these global programs because the United States is a rich country and because U.S. churches continue to be generously supported by a large share of the population. Scholars generally agree that there are between 300,000 and 350,000 local congregations in the United States and that as many as 60 to 65 percent of the adult population claims membership in at least one of these congregations. Between 40 and 45 percent of the adult population are estimated to be active members of a religious congregation, meaning that they participate in religious services at least a few times a month, while between a quarter and a third of the public participate regularly in services at their congregations. Figures reported in *Giving USA 2006* showed that Americans gave a total of $260.3 billion to various kinds of charities and voluntary organizations, of which $93.2 billion went to religion.[32] Thus, if churches set aside even 5 percent of that amount for international programs, the amount available would be in excess of $4 billion.

Further perspective on the resources of American religion can be gained by comparing the United States with the second-most populous Christian country in the world—Brazil. With a population (in 2000) of 170.1 million, 91 percent of whom are Christian, Brazil figures prominently in discussions of how the center of gravity in global Christianity is shifting to the Southern Hemisphere. In raw numbers, the 155 million Christians living in Brazil and the 192 million Christians living in the United States give an appearance that the two countries are nearly equivalent. But differences need to be considered as well. In the United States the average Christian receives an annual income of $26,980, whereas the average annual income of a Christian in Brazil is $3,640. Not surprisingly, Christian organizations are much more numerous and better supported in the United States than in Brazil. For instance, Brazil has more than twice as many Catholics as the United States, but the United States has more than twice as many Catholic parishes as Brazil does, and the ratio of priests to parishioners is six times higher in the United States than in Brazil.[33] Overall, Catholic and Protestant churches take in approximately nine times as much money annually as churches in Brazil. According to one estimate, there were at least 2,300 Christian service organizations in the United States, compared with 250 in Brazil.[34] Other reports have suggested that at least 1,200 missionaries from the United States are currently working in Brazil.[35] The point of such comparisons is not to diminish the importance of indigenous churches in Brazil, many of which have experienced explosive growth in recent decades. It is rather to emphasize that churches in the United States have enormous capacity to support ministries both at home and abroad. Were a family in the United States to pledge a tenth of its annual income to foreign missions, for instance, that pledge would cover the annual salary of a missionary in Brazil for nearly a year; in contrast, a similar pledge in Brazil would have to be made by seventy-five families to support a missionary in the United States.

Besides providing assistance to international programs, American congregations also have the capacity to influence their members' attitudes toward international policy and other government programs. In a previous study I found that 81 percent of the American public claimed to be "quite" or "fairly" interested in "international human rights issues" and 68 percent expressed the same level of interest in "relief and development programs for people in Third World Countries." Three-quarters (74 percent) of the public said religious organizations should become "more active" in "making Americans aware of hunger and poverty in other countries." Regular churchgoers were more interested in these issues and supportive of church involvement than were infrequent attendees. At least a quarter of churchgoers said they had heard sermons in the past year on such topics as poverty and the environment.[36] In another study, three-quarters of self-identified Christians said the United States should be actively involved in world affairs, and their theological orientations were related to their views of just exactly how the nation should be involved. Theological "moderates or liberals" were more likely than were religious conservatives (defined as "fundamentalists, evangelicals, charismatics, or Pentecostals") to favor economic involvement, whereas the reverse was true for military involvement. When asked if they thought globalization was mostly good or mostly bad for the United States, a majority of both groups thought it was mostly good (but religious conservatives were almost twice as likely as moderates or liberals to say that globalization was mostly bad).[37]

On balance, the evidence that has been collected in previous studies, while inconclusive, does suggest that American churches are engaged in transcultural ministries and have the potential to be even more engaged. The issue is not that congregations and other religious organizations are doing nothing. It is rather one of understanding more precisely what they are doing and the factors that are currently influencing congregations' decisions about these ministries. American churches may be only one small part of larger economic, humanitarian, and evangelistic efforts. Yet these congregational efforts hold enormous potential not only for what they may contribute to the rest of the world but also for how they affect the lives of church members.

THE DISAPPEARING OTHER

One other aspect of the present situation must be introduced as background for considering the global outreach of American churches. *New York Times* columnist Thomas Friedman provides a way of bringing this issue into focus. Friedman is a gifted writer whose work has given him the opportunity to travel widely and rub shoulders with interesting people in many parts of the world. His insights often serve better as sound bites than as in-depth analysis, but his writing raises interesting questions about how the world is changing. In *The World Is Flat* Friedman argues that people everywhere—and the places where they live and work—are increasingly becoming interchangeable.[38] A journalist can play golf in India just as easily as in California and in either location meet people who work for Microsoft or IBM. It makes no difference to Microsoft's Bill Gates if his employees are in Fresno or Bangalore. Friedman's image of a flat world captures this sense of interchangeability. It matters little to Wal-Mart's customers if the toaster oven they purchase was manufactured in Caracas or Shanghai so long as it is cheap. The Bank of America customer is probably not even aware that his or her account may be kept in Delhi or that a direct marketing call from the bank may be routed through Bangladesh.

Of course people in different parts of the world are not truly interchangeable, any more than the globe is literally flat. But the idea of an emerging sameness or homogeneity has become increasingly popular. In the literature on globalization, for instance, writers point to the homogenization of tastes that comes about through fast food chains, such as McDonald's, and specialty franchise shops, such as Starbucks, or through the global economic clout of such businesses as Microsoft and the Bank of America. Inexpensive clothing produced in China or Guatemala, resulting in hordes of teenagers around the world dressed interchangeably in T-shirts and blue jeans, is another example. Yet another is the diffusion of a common culture centered in Western music, television programs, and motion pictures. The argument is not that people everywhere are becoming exactly the same or that they no longer have freedom to make their own choices. It is just that the choices are more likely to fall within a certain range of options dictated by a kind of global shopping mall.

Analysts of religion have been making a very similar argument. In *The Next Christendom* historian Philip Jenkins has popularized the idea that Christianity is now a truly global religion, centered increasingly in Africa and Latin America, where population growth rates are much higher than in Europe and North America.[39] Jenkins's argument is not that the entire world is Christian (or will be anytime soon). Indeed, he emphasizes the differences and potential conflicts between Christian and Muslim populations and within Christianity itself. Yet his book underscores an important point that mission specialists and church leaders at the grass-roots have been observing for a long time: when Christians from the United States go abroad or think about helping people in other countries, they more easily see these people as being no different from themselves than at any time in the past. People elsewhere are no longer Serepta's heathen, marked by radical superstition and paganism that places them outside the fold. They are now fellow Christians who share the same beliefs and practices, though inflected with some cosmetic ethnic differences, just like the person in an adjacent pew at one's own church.

This emerging sense of global oneness, as it is sometimes called, has resulted in a dramatic reorientation in academic thinking about Christian missions. In their widely read *Missional Church,* Darrell Guder and his associates describe both a "radical shift" in the way society views the church and a "paradigm shift" in scholarly thinking about missions. They call for local congregations to rededicate themselves to being "missional" and to move beyond the traditional "sending-receiving mentality" that engaged congregations in raising money to be sent to mission enterprises elsewhere. As part of this shift, they observe that "local congregations are beginning to see their own context as their mission."[40] Although a superficial reading of this argument might lead to the conclusion that local churches should simply pull back from supporting transnational endeavors, the larger point is that churches can no longer rely on familiar practices or models of mission. The world has in this sense become flat. There is no longer a distinctly American Christendom from which to engage in activities aimed at spreading the gospel to those in other parts of the world who are outside the fold.

In the social sciences, an erosion of distinctions between "us" and "them" is generally regarded as a positive development. Such distinctions are often the basis for misunderstanding and prejudice. In the case of American Christianity, it is easy to see that historic distinctions between the Christians here at home and non-Christians abroad were often tinged with a paternalistic attitude that diminished the full humanity of those living in other parts of the world. Few would deplore the erosion of markers distinguishing the "other" in this way. A flat earth is more consistent with research showing that a genuine spirit of compassion is nurtured not by feeling superior to an other but by emphasizing one's common humanity.[41]

But there is a wrinkle. Disappearance of the other also signals an erosion of identity. It becomes harder to know who "we" are in the absence of an other who differs from us. Communities nearly always establish their identity by symbolically or ritually demarcating themselves from others (initiation rites, insignia, mascots, loyalty oaths, and membership fees all serve this purpose). Historically, the other has always been important to the identity of religious communities. The stranger might be welcomed but was clearly in a different category from blood members of the tribe. Laws prohibiting usury applied to dealings with insiders but not to outsiders. "We" were the chosen people, the elect, the saved, and others were not. Christians set themselves apart from Jews in this way, as did Protestants from Catholics, and in other instances one Protestant denomination from another. Small denominations and minority religious groups distinguished themselves as outsiders to the dominant culture, while larger and better-established groups kept their distance from what they called "cults." None of this cultural posturing necessarily involved overt discrimination or conflict, although it often did. It was done subtly and in good faith as people met for worship, picked up implicit signals about who they were and who they were not, and interacted differently with insiders and outsiders.

In *Outside the Fold* the comparative literature scholar Guari Viswanathan documents the fascinating story of what happened in nineteenth-century England with the disappearance of the religious other. At the height of Britain's colonial empire it became economically and politically expedient to imagine that all religions were interchangeable, at least if those who practiced them in the colonies no longer took them very seriously and behaved as civilized people were expected to behave. She writes that "in the expectation that Indians were more acceptable if they were no longer practicing Hindus or Muslims, it was considered profitable to make good Englishmen of them, even if it was unlikely or even undesirable for them to be good Christians." But once it became the empire's official practice to turn "Hindus into non-Hindu Hindus, or Muslims into non-Muslim Muslims" in the colonies, the same logic came home to roost in attitudes within England itself. "A nation of good Englishmen was a more realistic goal than a nation of good Anglicans."[42] Contrary to the familiar charge that Anglicanism declined simply because it was an established state church, then, this argument emphasizes a transcultural perspective that associates the diminishing strength of the church at home with the way in which the "other" was perceived abroad.

A flat-earth perspective in which American Christians view themselves simply as an indistinguishable aspect of global Christianity may not suggest an outcome resembling that of nineteenth-century Britain. It is interesting, though, that some of the strongest proponents of the paradigm shift implied by the rise of global Christianity have little to say about the continuing role of churches in the United States. For instance, Jenkins devotes more attention to the possibility of other countries sending missionaries to the United States than the reverse and hardly mentions the humanitarian and relief work of American churches at all. In the absence of a clear vision of the "other" abroad, it is also interesting that the various branches of American Christianity seem to be shoring up their identities by experimenting with "others" of their own, whether through likening themselves to an exile-like community, as some writers suggest, or by identifying themselves through the symbolic politics of popular social and moral issues as an embattled minority of true believers.[43] For our purposes, the main implication of this new flat-earth perspective toward global culture and global Christianity is the uncertainty it produces for local churches as they consider their role in missions and service work abroad.

TRANSCULTURAL CHURCH

The globalization of American Christianity is becoming evident in the extent to which congregations and individual Christians in the United States are engaged in transcultural activities, such as supporting overseas missionaries and relief workers or sending medical teams abroad, and registering interest in U.S. policies and the work of humanitarian agencies in other countries. It is also measurable in the degree to which the self-identity of American Christianity includes a normative commitment to the wider world, as expressed in the idea of a transcultural church. "Transcultural" is of course an ambiguous word. Its connotations are similar to those of "transnational," because the activities at issue take place outside of or are concerned with people who live outside of the national boundaries of the United States (such as doing volunteer work in another country). However, "transnational" has two meanings that limit its usefulness in the present context.

One connotation, suggested by the common phrase "transnational corporation," points to something massively large and existing as a significant economic presence in several countries (such as Microsoft or Exxon). That connotation may well apply to an entity such as the Roman Catholic Church or the Anglican Communion, but otherwise is hardly the most suitable phrase for the sporadic, small-scale, border-spanning activities in which U.S. congregations are engaged, let alone attitudes and beliefs that are not truly located in other countries at all. The other connotation of "transnational" is emphasized by scholars of immigration, who restrict its meaning to a category of immigrants that travels back and forth between two countries, perhaps maintaining residences in both, and is at least bicultural enough to be quite different from the kind of person who lives only in one place.[44] This, too, fails to capture the variety of ways in which congregations and church members engage in boundary-crossing activities.

It is important to understand the special sense in which I use the term here. Transcultural does not mean simply being exposed to different ethnic or regional customs within the United States, and it does not mean that a person enjoys getting out once in a while, for instance, to eat at an ethnic restaurant. Transcultural means being involved in or interested in activities that take place outside of the United States and holding attitudes about such issues as international trade or military intervention that affect people in other countries besides the United States. In this sense, most Christians in the United States are indeed transcultural, although the degree to which they are varies, as does the character of their activities and attitudes.

I refer to "transcultural church" in the singular to emphasize the deliberate ambiguity that has always surrounded discussions of the Christian church. Christians understand the church to be the earthly and historical manifestation of the body of Christ. It is thus one body, a singular entity, diverse in functions and united in spirit, although geographically dispersed. This is not the same thing as "Christendom," a term that connotes more internal organization and political recognition than is currently the case and for that reason has rightly been criticized and largely rejected by scholars of Christianity. To speak of the church, singular, serves as a reminder that Christians within the United States and around the world do bear an affinity with one another, even though this affinity is sometimes overshadowed by huge differences in local customs, practices, and beliefs. At the same time, the fact that "church" takes on its primary and most significant meanings within local congregations also points to the fundamental plurality of church and hence to the common sentiment that "my church" is one of "many churches" in the community, nation, and world. To be a transcultural church is thus to be the church in both this singular and plural sense—to understand that the local congregation of which someone is a member is also part of the global church that spans local and national boundaries.

CHAPTER 2

The Global Christianity Paradigm

*From Cultural Connection
to Demographic Distance*

The recent globalization of American Christianity cannot be understood or fully appreciated until a huge conceptual obstacle is removed. Ironically, this inhibiting factor is squarely concerned with globalization and Christianity. It is the popular notion that Christianity's center of gravity has shifted to the point that it may no longer matter very much what Christians in the United States do or think. Christianity is flourishing on its own in other parts of the world and will continue to do so whether Christians in the United States are involved or not. However one interprets it, this paradigm shift has become such a massive feature of contemporary discussions about world Christianity that it is simply impossible to avoid considering it.[1]

The notion that the real action in Christianity is now taking place outside of the United States certainly cannot be taken lightly. The idea is nevertheless perplexing. Consider, for instance, the parallel notion that the economic powerhouse of the world is no longer the United States but China. That may or may not be true, but if it were, people living in both countries would still need to understand the role of the United States. Or consider the view that globalization is an abstract development that has no more to do with the United States than it does with Thailand. Critics might concede that a particular kind of decentering is at work, but they would also be right in arguing that the United States is still an economic force and that its role in globalization needs to be understood. The same is true of Christianity. Globalization should encourage more—not less—

interest in the connections between the United States and the rest of the world.

A new paradigm, as Thomas Kuhn contended in his influential work on scientific revolutions, makes sense of facts that have come to be seen as anomalies in the prevailing wisdom, but the new framework is in turn a political act, a simplification that brings its own distortions.[2] The paradigm shift that has occurred in recent years in understandings of global Christianity has correctly emphasized the numeric increases in population in certain parts of the world outside of the United States and Europe and thus has drawn attention to the vitality of new churches in those regions. However, in making their claim, proponents of the new paradigm have oversimplified the complexity of these developments. They have relied too heavily on population projections and used categories that are ambiguous at best and misleading at worst. Instead of focusing on the cultural connections among different parts of the world, they have emphasized demography to the exclusion of these connections. The emerging formulation has been influenced by two interesting background stories—one about secularization and one about colonialism—that have made it attractive but also problematic. Most germane to the globalization of American Christianity, the new approach has paid insufficient attention to the interconnections among Christian communities on the various continents. The failure to emphasize these linkages is not merely an oversight but stems from assumptions central to the new paradigm itself.

QUESTIONING THE NARRATIVE
OF GLOBAL CHRISTIANITY

In her *Invention of World Religions,* historian Tomoko Masuzawa assembles an impressive array of historical evidence to develop the startling conclusion that the great religions we commonly think of today as world religions—Hinduism, Buddhism, Islam, and Confucianism, among others—did not simply emerge over the long course of human history but were cultural constructions that came about during the nineteenth century at the hands of philologists and other scholars who were deeply influenced by the imperial contexts in which they were working.[3] It would perhaps seem far-fetched to say that global Christianity is a similar invention, especially in view of the fact that Christianity was never located in only one country, spread quickly across several continents, and has been considered a world religion for a long time. Despite this history, the concept "global Christianity" is in fact a fairly recent invention, and usage of this rubric has become almost synonymous with the new paradigmatic thinking about Christianity's shifting center of gravity.

According to Todd Johnson and Sandra Kim, the term "global Christianity" was first used by missions statistician David Barrett in his 1982 preface to the first edition of *World Christian Encyclopedia*.[4] In reality, a prior claim could be made for Methodist pastor Walter A. Graham, who gave a lecture in Baltimore on "Global Christianity at Work" in 1943.[5] Still, the point that the term came into popular usage only recently is valid. Other than the brief reference to Graham's lecture, the *Washington Post* did not use the phrase until 1979, when it was mentioned in passing in a story about the papal visit of that year.[6] The phrase did not appear in the *New York Times* until 1994.[7] And the first book bearing "global Christianity" in its title was not published until 1995.[8]

The kindred phrase "world Christianity" has a longer lineage, and it is significant that "global Christianity" has come into prominence in recent years as a replacement for that phrase. However, "world Christianity" itself is a newer concept than might be imagined. The first book title carrying this phrase appears to have been Francis John McConnell's *Human Needs and World Christianity*, published in 1929.[9] Prior to 1930, the phrase appeared in the *New York Times* only 19 times and then was used 122 times by 1996. It appeared in the *Washington Post* only 11 times prior to 1930 and 33 more times by 1996.[10]

The most popular rendition of the new paradigm is Philip Jenkins's *The Next Christendom: The Coming of Global Christianity*.[11] The thesis of Jenkins's book is that "by the year 2050 only one Christian in five will be non-Latino and white, and the center of gravity of the Christian world will have shifted firmly to the Southern Hemisphere."[12] Although there is much more in Jenkins's rich treatment of global Christianity, it was this assertion about a shifting center of gravity that captured the attention of most reviewers and came to be emphasized in subsequent discussions.[13] The idea that Christianity was changing its central location was clearly an idea whose time had come. It resonated with discussions of globalization and with concerns about the role of religion in world affairs. In the aftermath of the September 11, 2001, attacks on New York and Washington, it was easy for reviewers to connect the shifting location of Christianity with questions about possible conflicts with Islam. If nothing else, it was a novel enough idea that it made for good news stories and editorials.

In retrospect, it is difficult to overestimate the significance of Jenkins's contribution to the idea that a new paradigm was required for understanding Christianity. Reviews of *The Next Christendom* appeared in the *New York Times, Wall Street Journal, Christian Century, America, Commonweal,* and in numerous scholarly publications. The book received several awards, including being named Top Religion Book of 2002 by *USA Today.* After numerous printings in English, it was translated into a number of other languages, including German, Chinese, Korean, Portuguese, and Italian. Jenkins was an indefatigable lecturer, appearing at conferences and on television programs, speaking at churches and seminaries, and giving public lectures at such venues as Harvard University, the Foreign Policy Research Institute, Trinity National Leadership Round Table, and the influential Washington-based Witherspoon Fellowship. Besides the book, Jenkins also wrote a widely read *Atlantic Monthly* article that was nominated for a National Magazine Award and excerpted in magazines throughout North America and Europe.[14] At church colleges and seminaries, and especially among missions experts, it was soon hard to find anyone who was not familiar with the book and did not have strong opinions about its main thesis.[15]

But if Jenkins popularized the new paradigm, he did not invent it, at least not single-handedly. Almost two decades earlier, missiologist Andrew Walls observed that "we seem to stand at the threshold of a new age of Christianity, one in which its main base will be in the Southern continents, and where its dominant expressions will be filtered through the culture of those countries."[16] Jenkins himself credits Walls, Edward Norman, Walbert Buhlmann, and David Barrett with having originated the idea of featuring the rising prominence of Christianity throughout the Southern Hemisphere. He might also have listed Leslie Newbigin, David Bosch, Kwame Bediako, Samuel Escobar, and Lamin Sanneh. Many of these writers have lived in Africa or elsewhere in the developing world. As missionaries, professors, or church leaders, they witnessed firsthand the vitality of churches outside of Europe and North America. The fervor of these churches, their numeric growth, the passion of their preaching, the healing services, and the apparent miracles stood in stark contrast to the flagging zeal of parishes in London and Liverpool, New Haven and New York. As Newbigin remarked in his 1984 Warfield Lectures at Princeton Theological Seminary, "In great areas of Asia, Africa, and Oceania, the church grows steadily and even spectacularly. But in the areas dominated by modern Western culture . . . the church is shrinking and the gospel appears to fall on deaf ears."[17]

David Barrett played a particularly important role in the emergence of the new paradigm by providing hard numbers and statistical projections.

His figures showed that in 2000 there were 1.9 billion Christians in the world, 59 percent of whom lived in Africa, Asia, or Latin America, compared with 28 percent in Europe and only 11 percent in North America. By 2025, Barrett estimated that Christians in Africa, Asia, and Latin America would represent 68 percent of the world total, with only 30 percent living in Europe and North America.[18] Other social scientists contributed to the new paradigm as well. David Martin's sociological account of Pentecostalism in developing countries pointed to significant vitality, as did Kurt Bowen's ethnographic research in Mexico, Elizabeth Brusco's in Colombia, Paul Gifford's and Birgit Meyer's in Ghana, David Maxwell's in Zimbabwe, and Julie Hearn's in Kenya, among others.[19] The qualitative and quantitative research underscored a single conclusion: "The heartlands of the Christian faith are no longer found in the Western world, not in the northern continents, but in the southern continents of Latin America, Asia and particularly Africa."[20]

Had these sources offered only a description of Christian growth in the Southern Hemisphere, the scattered observations of missiologists and social scientists and even the popularity of Jenkins's book would hardly have constituted a new paradigm. It was rather the larger story that came to be told about this growth that necessitated and indeed defined a new way of thinking about global Christianity. In propositional form the new Christendom narrative can be summarized in a few simple assertions: Christianity on a global scale has experienced significant growth during the twentieth century and this growth will continue. The majority of Christians now reside outside of the United States and Europe. The growth of Christianity in these other parts of the world has been exceptionally strong and will remain so. This growth is happening primarily through the efforts of indigenous Pentecostal and other Spirit-filled churches, and for this reason Christianity in the global South is especially vibrant and authentic. During this same period Christianity has been weakening in the global North and as a result countries in the South are now sending missionaries to the North.

But the new paradigm is not simply a set of propositions. It is also a story about how things were and how they have changed.[21] As narrative, the new paradigm takes on additional drama and becomes more intellectually compelling and emotionally engaging. The story goes like this:

> Once upon a time (indeed, not very long ago), Christendom was located in Europe and the United States. The rest of the world was not Christian and needed to be saved. To save the world, the United States and Europe made heroic efforts for a long time to send missionaries. These efforts, while laud-

able, never worked quite as well as expected and often caused resentment. Europeans especially were guilty of combining missionary activities with imperialism and colonialism (Americans were largely uninvolved in this problem). After World War II, many colonies became independent nations with nationalist and even communist regimes causing doors to be closed to missionaries. All hope seemed gone. But then a surprising thing happened. Once left to themselves, people all over the non-Christian world began to discover Christianity on their own. Soon Christianity was flourishing everywhere. That is, everywhere but the United States and Europe, where it was declining in influence. As a result, the center of gravity of Christianity was now located in the global South. In those countries, especially in Africa and Latin America, evangelical and Pentecostal churches were growing at a furious pace and a new Christendom was being born. In this new heartland of Christianity faith was more vibrant, more authentic, and closer to that of the early church than it had been for a long time. In an ironic historical twist, this new Christendom in the global South would probably be the source of hope for the decadent people living in the United States and Europe. It would send them missionaries and challenge their secular assumptions. It might also have to wage war against the historic antagonists of Christianity, especially Islam.

The narrative form of the story will seem familiar to readers schooled in Christian teachings. It is a before-and-after story of dramatic change, even of conversion or rebirth, of transition from apparent death to new life, and thus of synergy and hope. The narrative tension in the story moves from despair to salvation. "The recession of Christianity among the European peoples appears to be continuing," Walls laments, but through the vitality of Southern Hemisphere churches "once again, Christianity has been saved for the world."[22] Little wonder that the new paradigm is attractive and little wonder that it challenges old ways of thinking. No longer are Europe and the United States at the epicenter of the Christian world. However, their displacement does not give reason for despair. Christianity has found defenders elsewhere. Jesus was despised in Judea but is now preached in Samaria. The stone that builders rejected has become the cornerstone after all. A phoenix has risen from the ashes.

The power of a new paradigm is evident in the variety of uses to which it is put. Scholars extended and applied the global Christianity narrative even when they sometimes questioned its assumptions. Missiologists argued that it necessitated a fundamental shift from an emphasis on sending missionaries, or even talking about missions, to viewing the church everywhere as being God's witness in the world.[23] Some suggested that evangelism, liberation, healing, and the role of the local church would need to be rethought in light of the vitality of non-Western Christianity.[24]

Church historians argued that the history of Christianity needed to be rewritten to show more clearly the non-Western locations of the earliest Christian communities—and major efforts were invested in producing a new history.[25] Some likened the current realignment to the Protestant Reformation, arguing that the new paradigm reflected a major shift that would have as long-term theological, political, and economic consequences as the Reformation did.[26] Some scholars drew parallels with other historic watersheds: the new paradigm was a Copernican shift, like the discovery of the New World, the dawn of a new dispensation.[27] Journalists cited the new framework in reporting on churches in Africa or Latin America or in telling stories about missionaries to the United States from these continents.[28] Meanwhile, ideas that had been promoted by missions experts a few years earlier, such as "unreached peoples" and the "10–40 window," diminished in popularity, while dozens of church-related colleges and seminaries institutionalized the new paradigm by redefining courses about missions and initiating professorships in "world Christianity."[29]

A new paradigm always leaves questions unanswered, though, and the global Christianity story is no exception. To the cautious observer, it is difficult not to entertain a number of questions: Why, given the obvious decentering of the United States, has the new paradigm been embraced so warmly by scholars in the United States? Were theologians, as Bosch had warned, erroneously making the truth of Christianity contingent on its numeric success?[30] What exactly do writers mean when they say the center of gravity has shifted to the global South? Where is the global South? Is there really such a thing as global Christianity or does the term convey more unity than is warranted? For Christians in the United States, the most important unanswered question is whether or not U.S. churches have any significant role to play in the further unfolding of global Christianity. Should they retreat into their own communities, perhaps to replicate the vitality of the Spirit-filled churches that are growing abroad? Should the American church pull its 40,000 foreign missionaries from the field, viewing their efforts as inconsequential? Are the million or so church members who go abroad on short-term mission trips helping themselves instead of serving others? How about the $3.7 billion that U.S. churches are spending on overseas ministries? Should it be invested directly in indigenous churches and, if so, invested quietly so as not to give an appearance of foreign intervention, or would it be better spent salvaging what is left of Christianity in North America and Europe? And what about the economic resources of the United States and the way its multinational corporations intervene in local communities around the world? Should these simply be ignored (or applauded?) since Christianity seems to be doing so well in the global South? Do Christians in the United States have a continuing obligation to think about such global issues as poverty, health, international debt relief, the environment, and social justice?

To answer questions like these we must take a closer look at the new paradigm. Some of these questions were being voiced in mission circles several decades ago, but the new paradigm has brought them into sharper focus. Viewed critically, the current narrative does not hang together quite as neatly as might be supposed. Although it makes sense of some of the facts, it does not make sense of all of them. The emerging story about global Christianity must be deconstructed to see the extent to which its fabrication has been influenced by unexamined presuppositions. Qualifications and nuances need to be added. Parts of the narrative are not entirely accurate and other parts could have been—indeed, were—interpreted in different ways.

COUNTING CHRISTIANS

Although the new paradigm is not simply a story about numbers, its credibility depends very largely on the availability of numbers and on how we construe those numbers. To anyone whose theology teaches that true Christianity is a secret covenant between the believer and God, the very idea that 1.9 billion of the world's population can be enumerated as Christians is likely to evoke suspicion. How, one would ask, is it possible to be so confident about who is a Christian and who is not? If the Good Shepherd cares more for one lost sheep than the other ninety-nine, the idea of massive numbers in the Christian fold is likely to seem beside the point. Isn't the message that Jesus cares about each person more than he does about statistics?

Nonetheless, the current interest in numbers should not be surprising. From its inception, the modern missionary movement has shown a penchant for quantitative information, even when this penchant was appropriately hedged with ambivalence. William Carey—a founder of the foreign missionary movement in England—wrote an eighty-seven-page manuscript in 1792 entitled *An Enquiry into the Obligations of Christians to Use Means for the Conversion of the Heathens*. This document played an important role in setting the agenda for the Particular Baptist Society for the Propagation of the Gospel Amongst the Heathen. More than a quarter of the manuscript consists of tables in which Carey lists each of the world's countries (including provinces and other political subdivisions for many countries), estimates the approximate length and breadth of each, provides a total population figure for each, and indicates whether its religion is Christian, Papist, Greek Christian, Mahometan, Pagan, or some combination of religions. Carey follows this tabular information with several pages of summary observations, concluding that 174 million of the world's 731 million inhabitants are Christian (Catholic, Protestant, or Greek Christian), 130 million are "followers of Mahomet," 7 million are Jews, and 420 million are "in pagan darkness."[31] By Carey's calculations, nearly all the Christians in the world were concentrated in Europe and North America (although it is notable that he emphasized promoting greater understanding of the Bible among people on these continents as much as he did spreading the gospel to pagans elsewhere).

Subsequent missionary leaders continued to be fascinated with numbers. For instance, in 1818 Gordon Hall and Samuel Newell wrote a widely circulated pamphlet entitled "The Conversion of the World, or the Claims of Six Hundred Millions, and the Ability and Duty of Churches Respecting Them" in which they estimated how many missionaries were needed and how their efforts should be distributed for maximum effectiveness.[32] A half century later, Rufus Anderson, the renowned leader of the American Board of Commissioners for Foreign Missions, wrote that he had "ceased to place much reliance on such calculations" but nonetheless offered his own calculations about how many of the world's inhabitants remained in need of evangelization.[33] During the 1880s and 1890s, as missions boards became better organized, statistical reports became more frequent. In 1902, James S. Dennis, serving as chair of the Committee on Statistics for the Ecumenical Conference on Foreign Missions, produced the *Centennial Survey of Foreign Missions,* a comprehensive compendium of facts and figures showing how many missionaries were deployed by each organization, their level of financial support, the kinds of activities in which they were engaged, the number of churches they had organized, and how many communicant members had been added during the previous year.[34] As part of this effort, Dennis also drew on the latest social science methods to conduct one of the first systematic surveys concerning religion by soliciting detailed information from approximately three hundred missionaries about their impressions of those to whom they were ministering.[35]

The work of David Barrett and his collaborators falls squarely in this lineage of statistical scholarship. Barrett and Johnson in fact argue that their efforts at enumeration descend from some two hundred previous surveys, atlases, and encyclopedias, and their figures for years prior to about 1970 are taken directly from these earlier sources.[36] The import of this lineage is twofold. It means that the idea of collecting statistics has the kind of legitimacy that comes from long years of experience. It also means that Barrett's particular set of statistics comes as close to being "official" as any such statistics could be. The credibility with which Barrett's estimates are regarded would be quite different were he the first person to have thought up the idea of collecting such information. The weight of his efforts are more similar to that of the U.S. Census, being not only a longstanding enterprise but also the most authoritative source.

When proponents of the new paradigm cite figures concerning the geographic distribution of Christianity, therefore, the quibbles and disclaimers that arise are similar to the ones scholars might entertain when referring to the U.S. Census. For instance, Jenkins makes a point of distancing himself from Barrett's statistics by questioning whether Barrett may have under- or over-represented the Christian population in a few countries where there may have been political pressures associated with data drawn from government reports.[37] Jenkins nevertheless accepts Barrett's overall conclusions about the shifting location of global Christianity. Similarly, Gerald Anderson writes of "gross discrepancies between information reported [by Barrett] and other reliable sources," citing a couple of statistics that are obviously wrong, but concludes that the compilation is an enormous achievement.[38] Mark A. Noll's thorough and judicious review also calls mainly for additional "fine tuning" of the data.[39]

An independent analysis by Becky Hsu, Amy Reynolds, Conrad Hackett, and James Gibbon compared Barrett's statistics with figures derived from other sources, such as the U.S. State Department, the Central Intelligence Agency, and various polls and surveys. This analysis largely confirmed the validity of Barrett's statistics. There were a few notable differences between Barrett's figures and those reported in other sources. There were also a dozen or more countries for which care needed to be taken in comparing figures because of different geographic boundaries being used (for instance, whether Taiwan, Hong Kong, and Macao were or were not included with China). But apart from these concerns, the analysis showed very high overall correlations between Barrett's data and the other sources.[40]

Insofar as one wishes to make descriptive claims about the geographic distribution of the world's population that can more or less be officially identified as "Christian," Barrett's data can be used, and these data provide a basis for describing shifts in the location of this population. However, the notion of a shift of influence (as expressed in the ambiguous phrase "center of gravity") cannot be inferred from such evidence. To do so is to assume a one-person-one-vote logic that serves no better as a measure of influence in the religious sphere than it does in the political or economic sphere. For instance, prior to the death of Pope John Paul II, countless journalists speculated that the next pope would be from Africa, using the fact that a growing share of the world's Catholic population was from Africa as support. The election of German cardinal Ratzinger as Pope Benedict XVI demonstrated the weakness of that argument.

The question of influence can be taken in several directions. To proponents of the new paradigm, the influence of Christianity in Europe and the United States is declining not only in numbers but also in ability to shape politics and mass culture. Others would question that view, especially in the United States, where just the opposite seems to have been the case in several recent presidential election campaigns. Critics would also point to the need to consider the economic and military power of the United States in assessing its influence within global Christianity. Proponents and critics alike, though, might heed Douglas John Hall's words in reference to Jenkins: "In religion, as in politics, statistics are useful for some limited purposes, but by themselves they convey little of analytical, to say nothing of historical and theological, significance."[41]

The point about influence can be further illustrated by considering some of the other numbers Barrett provides. For instance, the United States in 2000 had just 10 percent of the world's Christian population, yet in that year the United States accounted for approximately a quarter of the world's foreign missionaries and a quarter of the total amount spent on foreign missions, the publication of a quarter of all Christian books and periodicals, and a third of all church and parachurch revenue. By Barrett's calculations, the United States alone had more local worship centers than all of Latin America, more mission agencies than all of Africa, and more church revenue than Latin America, Africa, and Asia combined.[42] Such figures underscore the possibility of considerably greater U.S. influence in global Christianity than membership trends alone would indicate.

It is perhaps understandable that architects of the new paradigm have emphasized population trends in charting the changing geographic location of global Christianity. These figures are based on national censuses and are thus readily available. They are consistent with the idea that God counts all persons equally. In some instances, they also affect the representation of various countries at church councils. The problem is not that numbers are used but rather which numbers are used. Growth or decline in the Christian population of a particular country is largely a function of growth or decline in the overall population of that country and is in turn shaped by local conditions that affect longevity, morbidity rates, and decisions about fertility.[43] In this respect, population is quite different from economic transactions, communication flows, armed conflicts, political alliances, or cultural exchanges. Those connections foreground the possibilities of one country influencing another and are in this way consistent with globalization theory's emphasis on interdependence, whereas a focus on population underemphasizes those possibilities.

Besides its neglect of influence, the new paradigm poses problems about categories and definitions. Its framers have vacillated between referring to the part of the world where Christianity is ostensibly weak as "Western" or "Northern" and areas of Christian strength as "non-Western" or "Southern." Both pairs present more than terminological difficulties. For instance, in arguing that Christianity in the West is weak, writers lump Europe and the United States together, whereas in fact religious patterns in the two are quite different. For instance, from 1947 to 2001 belief in God declined by 34 percent in Sweden, 22 percent in the Netherlands, and 20 percent in France, but held steady (at 94 percent) in the United States.[44] Trends in church attendance have been harder to assess but also appear to have declined in many western European countries while holding nearly constant in the United States and, in any case, are considerably higher in the United States than in western Europe.[45] Putting all of Europe in a single category is also problematic. Earlier discussions of Christianity's decline in Europe usually included the ill effects of communism in eastern Europe, but in recent years Christianity has been growing in former Soviet countries while continuing to decline or holding steady in other parts of Europe. The distinction between West and non-West also falters by placing Latin America in the category that is supposedly declining. Yet if a North-South distinction is drawn, observers describing church growth in the global South have trouble fitting in China, Korea, Mexico, or even large parts of Africa on the basis of location. The global South becomes an ambiguous term that does not mean the Southern Hemisphere at all but anything that lies south of the United States—or perhaps east or west as well, depending on one's predilections.[46]

Just as geographic boundaries do, religious categories also prove more complex than numbers alone suggest. For instance, the claim that Christianity in the global South is particularly vibrant fails to distinguish two quite different observations. One is that Pentecostalism is growing. The other is simply that the overall Christian population is growing because of high fertility rates. If only Pentecostalism is considered, then the rate of growth appears to be high, but the total number involved is considerably smaller than if all Christians are considered. But if all Christians are considered, then the rate of growth is less impressive and, in fact, amounts to little more in some countries than natural increase. For instance, Ghana is one of the countries that on the surface best illustrates the growth of Southern Hemisphere Christianity (at least if it were actually in the Southern Hemisphere). Between 1990 and 2000, the number of Pentecostals in Ghana swelled by 44 percent. Yet Pentecostals account for only a quarter of the Christian population. Overall growth in the Christian population during the 1990s was 95 percent from natural increase and only 5 percent from conversions. In short, vitality outside of Pentecostalism has more to do with birth rates than anything else.[47]

The new paradigm's assumptions about the timing of change are also puzzling. If Barrett's figures are taken at face value, the majority of Christians in the world in 2000 lived outside the United States and Europe. Writers like to accentuate the significance of this fact by projecting trends into the future. Jenkins in particular casts an aura of futurology around his arguments by emphasizing what the world will be like in twenty or even fifty years. The futuristic quality of these projections gives the new paradigm a forward-looking, even prophetic, flavor but, as critics have noted, is a sleight-of-hand maneuver that uses the present to predict the future and then reinterprets the present in light of that future. Barrett is considerably more cautious, showing that demographers' predictions vary widely and mentioning that high death rates from AIDS, malnutrition, and war could greatly alter the predictions. The question of how recent the shift to the global South may have been is also perplexing. If it happened in 1990 or 2000, then it stands to reason that writers would have only recently begun announcing the need for a new paradigm. But in 1970, 49 percent of the global Christian population already lived outside of Europe and the United States. The literal geographic center of global Christianity had already migrated to northern Africa by that date.[48] And in terms of growth, the most spectacular increases in other parts of the world had taken place earlier instead of recently. For instance, the Christian population in Latin America grew by less than 3 percent annually between 1970 and 2000 but had grown by 5 percent annually between 1900 and 1970. The pattern for Africa was even more dramatic, with 3 percent annual growth from 1970 to 2000 but 17 percent annual growth between 1900 and 1970. Had it just been an issue of relative growth, therefore, it would have made more sense for the new paradigm to have been discovered much earlier than it was.

The upshot of these considerations is that the new paradigm is not as solidly grounded in empirical evidence as may first appear. Its neat depiction of a massive shift in global Christianity can be questioned on grounds that population figures alone tell little about resources and influence. The idea that Christianity is experiencing major vitality in the global South may say more about high birth rates than about conversions. Just what constitutes the global South becomes problematic when many of the countries said to be experiencing church growth are not in the Southern Hemisphere at all. The alleged decline of the North (or West) turns out not to characterize the United States or much of eastern Europe. And the dramatic growth assumed to be taking place in Africa and Latin America was actually more dramatic before 1970 than it is now.

One might concede that it is important to acknowledge these various concerns about numbers, categories, and timing, and yet argue that the main point of the new paradigm remains intact. After all, the growth of Christianity in many parts of the developing world seems considerable, and this growth seems to be happening largely on its own without intervention from the United States or Europe. The implication remains: Christians in the United States had better tend to their own gardens rather than thinking their efforts are of value beyond their local communities. It should not be surprising that Jenkins hardly mentions the continuing work of American missionaries, publishing houses, television ministries, seminaries, overseas volunteers, relief workers, humanitarian organizations, or foreign aid.[49] The arbitrariness of this perspective, though, can be seen clearly by considering an alternative paradigm. This narrative is especially interesting because it was proposed by none other than David Barrett. In Barrett's view, the numbers pointed to a very different story from the one that became inscribed in the new paradigm.

Barrett's interpretation is roughly as follows. Since 1900, the percentage of the world's population that can be considered Christian has remained static and is likely to continue to be static for the indefinite future. One should not be fooled by numeric increases. These are simply the result of overall population growth. If anything, it is Islam that has been growing, rising from about 12 percent of the world's population in 1900 to a projected 27 percent by 2200. The one hopeful feature about Christianity is that missionaries and evangelists have spread the word. In 1900 about 45 percent of the world's population had in some fashion been exposed to the gospel, but by 2000 that figure had risen to about 70 percent. The task now is to build on that momentum. To do this effectively, the world should be divided into three parts: World A consists of unevangelized countries, World B is the evangelized non-Christian world, and World C is composed of Christian countries. The Christian world that has been sending missionaries to the rest of the world should continue doing so. The major player in this effort has been the United States, and for at least the next twenty years the United States will continue to send more missionaries than any other country in the world. Meanwhile, such minor players as Mexico, Angola, Argentina, and Guatemala will become more important in sending foreign missionaries. Missionaries should work in partnerships with indigenous churches wherever possible. Agencies will continue to specialize, with some focusing on World A (especially important) and others on World B. Whatever the focus, careful planning and a variety of tactics will be needed, including distinguishing among the various opportunities that different mission fields provide and understanding the resources available in the Christian world, such as the relative wealth of these countries, their ability to train people, and their use of information technology.[50]

The main differences between Barrett's narrative and the one popularized by Jenkins and others should be clear. Barrett's paradigm sees greater continuity with the past and, despite the failure of many recent evangelistic programs, is cautiously hopeful about the future; it nevertheless downplays major growth or decline. Barrett does not deny that Christianity has grown in the so-called global South, but he does not emphasize a global shift or perceive it as the centerpiece of a new era in Christian history. His cartography focuses on an us/them distinction between the Christian and non-Christian world rather than on geographic distinctions involving West/non-West or North/South. Missionaries still play a critical role in Barrett's vision of the future, and strategic planning is required. Strategy necessitates resources, and resources point decidedly to the United States.

Despite Barrett's prominence as a scholar of world Christianity, his specific proposals were ignored by proponents of the new paradigm and on occasion explicitly repudiated. Barrett's perspective was tagged managerial missiology—the kind of old-style planning conducted by Western missionary organizations as opposed to the more authentic Spirit-filled Christianity of the global South. The basic tenet of this outmoded perspective was, in the words of one critic, "that Christian mission can be reduced to a 'manageable enterprise' thanks to the use of information technology, marketing techniques and managerial leadership."[51] Managerial missiology relied too heavily on science, research, and planning. It generated a bewildering array of concepts, such as "unreached peoples," "homogeneous units," and the "10–40 window," but had only succeeded in depersonalizing evangelism and diverting attention from the work of the Holy Spirit.

That Barrett's proposed paradigm did not catch on may have also been a function of its complexity. Its basic storyline must be pieced together from numerous maps and diagrams, none of which reinforce a single or simple picture of the world and in the end prove frustrating. For instance, Gerald Anderson confesses, "I gave up trying to understand [one central diagram] with its so-called aggregate categories, schemes, slices, building blocks, and vertical segments."[52] Barrett also posits a variety of future scenarios, rather than extrapolating one bold projection from the recent past. Nevertheless, his A, B, C categories are surely no more ambiguous than those involving West/Non-West and North/South. It is more likely that the new paradigm popularized by Jenkins, Walls, Escobar, and others gained popularity because it resolved—or appeared to resolve—underlying concerns about the fate of Christianity. One of those had to do with secularization. Understanding this background story helps not only to make sense of the new paradigm but also to see more clearly how this emerging narrative has influenced recent thinking about the international role of U.S. churches.[53]

BACK STORY I: SECULARIZATION

A well-known strand of historical and philosophical scholarship since at least the eighteenth century has held that the influence of Christianity is waning. In the social sciences, secularization theory, as it became known, was associated with the writing of Karl Marx, Max Weber, and Emile Durkheim and with more recent writers such as Peter Berger, Thomas Luckmann, and Bryan Wilson. Theorists of secularization variously attribute the waning influence of Christianity to such factors as scientific rationalism, urbanization, and economic development. Science presumably undermines faith by offering naturalistic explanations for the origins of the universe and the human species and by producing ways to cure illness and lengthen life.[54] Urbanization weakens faith by relocating people from a rural environment, where the hand of God may be perceived in the seasons or in natural disasters, to an artificial environment constructed by humans. In an urban context, faith may also be weakened by sheer diversity as residents mingle with people from different traditions and thus cease to believe as wholeheartedly in their own. Similarly, economic development gives people a greater stake in the present world and thus undermines faith in promises associated with a world to come. Whether these effects can be observed in the beliefs and practices of individuals is less the issue than the idea that Christianity's cultural authority is diminishing.[55]

The secularization story has found a receptive audience among church leaders. As they ponder the society around them, they see Christianity having too little influence and secular forces such as television and the entertainment industry having too much. Especially in affluent countries, these problems appear to be deepening. Church attendance is not as common as it used to be and Christian teachings seem to be less influential than ever before. Proponents of the new global Christianity paradigm have largely adopted the secularization story in this regard. "The churches of North America," write the authors of *Missional Church*, "have been dislocated from their prior social role of chaplain to the culture and society and have lost their once privileged positions of influence."[56] Not only have the churches been dislocated, but their idea of missions has also been clouded by secularity to the point of no longer being effective. "Western missions theology and practice has fallen captive to modernity," write James F. Engel and William A. Dyrness. "To make matters worse, the Western missionary outlook and practice has been infused with rationalism—a pattern of pragmatic and managerially motivated reasoning through which methods and techniques have come to drive both missions theology and strategy in many circles."[57]

For church leaders, though, the secularization story typically acquires a different meaning than it does for social scientists. Although they lament the dark cloud of Christianity's waning influence, church leaders generally look for a silver lining. For instance, the *Missional Church* authors write that the churches' declining social position actually presents a "great opportunity" for people of faith. "The same pressures that threaten the continued survival of some churches, disturb the confidence of others, and devalue the meaning of them all can actually be helpful in providing an opening for new possibilities."[58] These possibilities are already evident in younger churches outside of the West. These churches are now where the Spirit is actively working.

On this point, there has been a parallel development in the social sciences. Just as church leaders have refused on theological grounds to believe that Christianity's demise is inevitable, so social scientists have increasingly questioned the deterministic assumptions implicit in secularization theory. To some scholars, the secularization story is simply a faulty depiction of the facts. For instance, if the United States is a relatively scientific, urbanized, and economically developed society, then why does belief in God remain so pervasive and why in recent decades has church attendance not diminished more? Other scholars have posed more thoroughgoing theoretical critiques. Faith, they argue, is not so easily discouraged by science or by living in cities and earning a good income. People still need answers to life's enduring questions. They want to distinguish good from evil and they want solace as they face illness and bereavement. Insofar as secularization has happened anywhere, then, it must be an anomaly that can be explained by peculiar historical circumstances, such as oppressive regimes or monopolistic religions. If anything, Christianity should be growing as these historical barriers fall away.[59]

Neither the secularizationists nor the antisecularizationists, if they may be called that, have persuaded the other group to see the error of its ways. In the absence of compelling proof or conceptual agreement, the debate has actually intensified interest in the topic while narrowing the grounds on which it is discussed. Upticks and downswings in church attendance take on additional meaning in this context. So do statistics about the growth or decline of Christianity in various countries. Instead of the more subtle arguments advanced by Weber and others of his generation, recent debates hinge almost entirely on numeric trends and projections.[60] And Christian leaders, whose own success is increasingly measured by such metrics, naturally have a special interest in these discussions. If secularization is happening, it provides an occasion to criticize the secularity of contemporary culture and to decry the loss of faith. If secularization is not happening, its absence demonstrates the wrongheadedness of secular academics and the continuing appeal of Christianity.

The new paradigm is attractive because it offers a neat resolution to the secularization debate. It says in effect that both sides are right. Those who see waning influence in the global North are right, and those who argue that Christianity resiliently responds to fundamental human needs are vindicated by what is happening in the global South. Both sides can imagine that the future of global Christianity will lend further support to their position. Secularizationists look at the current vitality of churches in poor countries and argue that Christianity will weaken as these areas develop economically. In this view, the recent growth of Christianity is like retrograde motion. It represents a temporary backlash against the disruptions caused by economic development. Antisecularizationists look at the same evidence and see hope for the secular North (or West). Missionaries from the global South will evangelize the North. Or the North will simply recover from its temporary lapse of faith and become more like the South. As one writer observes, "The grand expectation that modernization and globalization would lead to secularization is being proven false." The rise of Christianity in the global South, he says, is calling into question all the "big ideas in modern social science" and is demonstrating that the "European pattern" is an anomaly, not "the paradigm shaper we have made it to be."[61]

A resolution this neat is too good to be true, though, and critics of the new paradigm have been quick to point out that its arguments about the Southern future of Christianity are still very much rooted in old categories bequeathed by the secularization debate. For instance, Dale T. Irvin writes of the "shadow of the European Enlightenment" that hangs heavy over Jenkins's book and criticizes it for applying Ernst Troeltsch's sect-church distinction to the global South. Irvin does not think Southern Hemisphere Christianity is sectarian or that it will follow the path predicted by Troeltsch of greater accommodation with the secular world.[62] Other critics reject any hint of secularization theory, pro or con, on grounds that Christianity in the global South should be understood in new terms that have never been used by scholars of Christianity in the global North.

What even the critics have not always recognized, though, is how the diachronic emphasis inherent in the secularization debate precludes thinking synchronically about religious developments.[63] Secularizationists and antisecularizationists have almost always viewed religious growth or decline as if it occurred within a single restricted space. Change occurs, as it were, within a temporal tube. What happens later may be compared with what happened earlier, but there is no room for influences that are truly from another space. For a story about the secularization of England, the tube is England. Religion is weaker than it was earlier and this weakness is because of factors within England, not because of mutual influences between England and India or the United States. For a story about the growth of American fundamentalism, the tube is American fundamentalism. It grows by preaching an appealing message and accumulating resources; its growth may be compared with that of other traditions; but the thought never occurs that fundamentalism might be interdependent with other traditions, cultures, or regions. The new paradigm adopts this logic. Christianity is declining in one part of the world; the tube is that part of the world. Christianity is growing in another part of the world; the tube is that other part of the world. There may be some hydraulic mechanism at work, such that Christianity always rises to a certain equilibrium level in the world. But this is a purely imaginary mechanism. It is not as if decline in one area causes growth in another area, or vice versa, or even that the two are systematically related.

But it is odd that this tubular way of thinking should still be compelling. The central logic of the globalization thesis is that different parts of the world are becoming more closely connected. The new paradigm enlarges the perspective from which global Christianity is viewed but does not pay sufficient attention to these connections. The key developments still happen in a tube. A sect appears in a given location and may or may not evolve into a church in that location. The fact that a sect emerges in the context of other sects or churches, and the high likelihood that it is influenced by these other sects and churches, is overlooked. Thus, what appears to be a resolution of the secularization debate turns out to be simply an affirmation of that debate. How it is possible to maintain such tubular thinking requires considering the other background story against which the new paradigm has emerged.

BACK STORY 2: POSTCOLONIALISM

Postcolonialism is the other cultural influence that has shaped the construction of the global Christianity paradigm. Postcolonialism is not only the geopolitical situation of the world after the end of the colonial era but also the desire to repudiate and correct the cultural biases associated with that era. This desire is evident in such fields as literature and anthropology, and it connects powerfully with Christian theology and the historical study of Christianity. Postcolonialism calls Christians to be attentive to the oppressed and is a reminder of the ambivalence that missionary endeavors have always evoked. In the extreme, it discourages efforts—or acknowledgement of efforts—that may be deemed paternalistic or conducive to dependence.[64]

Ambivalence about the paternalism of missionary endeavors has been an aspect of these endeavors in the United States almost from the start. Rufus Anderson was a strong advocate of what later became known as the indigenization principle. Indigenization meant that missionaries should plant churches abroad that would then become self-supporting, self-governing, and self-propagating. For Anderson, there was no question that American culture was superior to the "degraded mental condition of the heathen world" to which missionaries ministered.[65] To civilize the heathen, though, was beyond the scope of what missionaries could reasonably be expected to do, Anderson believed. It was a practical necessity, if nothing else, to start indigenous churches and then leave them to succeed or fail on their own. The very gifts that civilization conferred, he recognized, also posed barriers to communicating the gospel to other cultures.[66]

Indigenization was emphasized with increasing urgency at world missionary conferences during the twentieth century. Delegates to the 1910 conference at Edinburgh addressed members of churches in predominantly non-Christian countries, saying "the word that under God convinces your own people must be your word; and the life which will win them for Christ must be . . . set forth by you who are men of their own race."[67] An American observer wrote of the gathering that "it is a great assemblage of the church's greatest men. But all are on the same level. Germans, French, Americans, Englishmen, Scandinavians, Japanese, Chinese, Hindus, Africans—all are here and mingle together in an easy equality. It is an unparalleled confluence of the big men of the kingdom of God."[68] By 1928, when delegates met in Jerusalem, the call for indigenization was supplemented by an explicit pledge to "repudiate any symptoms of a religious imperialism."[69] Subsequent conferences gave further symbolic expression to the indigenization principle by allocating a growing proportion of official seats to delegates from predominantly non-Christian countries. At the Tambaram conference in 1938, these delegates constituted a slight majority of the delegates present. After World War II, the emphasis on so-called young churches continued. At the Conference on World Mission and Evangelism in Mexico in 1963 the concept of "foreign missions" was replaced by the more multilateral idea of "mission in six continents," and in Bangkok in 1973 representatives called for repentance on the part of rich Western churches and a greater commitment to eliminating economic injustice.[70] Among those who broke away to form the Lausanne Movement for a more deliberate focus on evangelism, the call for indigenization also remained strong. The Lausanne Covenant, adopted unanimously by evangelical leaders attending the Lausanne Congress of Evangelism in 1974, declared that "we rejoice that a new missionary era has dawned. The dominant role of western missions is fast disappearing. God is raising up from the younger churches a great new resource for world evangelization, and it is thus demonstrating that the responsibility to evangelize belongs to the whole body of Christ."[71]

The wider context in which recent discussions of postcolonialism have taken place includes an array of significant scholarly contributions during the last third of the twentieth century. Postcolonialism is not a single unified theory but a set of ideas about the continuing influences of the colonial era and about the relationships between former colonies and colonizers. As it has been formulated in literary studies and in the social sciences, postcolonialism nevertheless includes several common emphases or perspectives. One is skepticism about the applicability of Western conceptual categories and metanarratives, such as "underdeveloped" and "modernization." In place of such categories and metanarratives, proponents of postcolonialism argue for concepts that reflect the diverse geography and traditions of local cultures. In postcolonial missiology one must, for instance, be skeptical, as Dale T. Irvin writes, about "the distorting lens of Western Christendom" and instead emphasize the "diverse cultural formations that have shaped various communities throughout world Christianity."[72] A second tenet of postcolonialism is that Western assumptions about power and superiority should be rejected. The colonial view, in Edward Said's words, was that colonized parts of the world consisted of "lesser peoples, with lesser rights, morals, claims."[73] That view, proponents of postcolonialism argue, must be replaced by one in which all peoples are regarded as cultural and moral equals.

Given the historical ambivalence about missions and the scholarly prominence of postcolonialist criticism, it is not surprising that proponents of the new paradigm have implicitly and explicitly emphasized the autonomy, diversity, and internal vitality of indigenous churches in the formerly colonized world. Jenkins, for instance, writes that "it was precisely as Western colonialism ended that Christianity began a period of explosive growth that still continues unchecked."[74] Lamin Sanneh writes that "the end of the colonial era was also the end of the missionary era," an era of "toil and little gain" but one that, paradoxically, was followed by "large hauls of converts."[75] Jenkins, Sanneh, and others acknowledge that Christianity may have been spread by imperialism in an earlier time but argue that its current popularity has nothing to do with imperialism. The gospel in former colonies is authentic now, no longer tainted by Western power, attractive solely because of the power of the Holy Spirit. The gospel flourishes simply because it fulfills needs and works miracles.

The autonomous dynamism of Christianity in the global South provides a sharp contrast with—as well as a critique of—missionary endeavors rooted in old-style colonial thinking. "Imperial missiology," writes Samuel Escobar, "carried on missionary work from a position of superiority: political, military, financial, technological." He continues: "In the imperial missiology paradigm, Christianity is thus dependent on the prop and tutelage of another powerful partner." For Escobar, the recent "paradigm shift" is an explicit rejection of the imperial model.[76] Latin America and Africa are better positioned to evangelize their own people than missionaries from the outside ever were. Leslie Newbigin's view was similar. The European missionary enterprise was falling on deaf ears because it was importing Western values into an alien context.[77]

The relevance of postcolonialism to current understandings of U.S. missions is more significant than might at first be supposed. Because the United States was never as directly involved in colonialism as Britain, France, Spain, Germany, Belgium, and several other western European countries were, U.S. scholars have considered it less urgent to adopt an explicitly postcolonial perspective than scholars from those countries have. However, church leaders and scholars in the United States do not work in a cultural vacuum. Their ideas interact with the contributions of scholars from England, Africa, Germany, and elsewhere and are influenced by time spent in other countries as missionaries and teachers. In their view, it is essential to adopt a new paradigm that respects the distinctiveness and autonomy of Southern Hemisphere Christianity. Lamin Sanneh, for instance, writes that "the Western guilt complex hinders us from acknowledging the role of local agents in the story of the planting of the church in Africa. The West still looms so large in the standard accounts of Third World Christianity that there is little room for the men and women on the ground."[78] Local idioms and practices, Sanneh argues, need to be emphasized more. Doing so provides a way not only to understand the local diversity of Christianity but also to see it as it should be seen, without the biases imposed by American materialism, secularism, and militarism.

THE UNANSWERED QUESTIONS

The new global Christianity paradigm leaves unanswered the central question of how local churches in vastly different parts of the world are connected. It is one thing to acknowledge that Christianity is distributed among the various continents of the world and that there is vitality and diversity in many of these locations, including ones that a century ago had been mission fields. It is quite another thing to tackle the difficult questions of how these various local manifestations of the church influence one another. Yet the message of globalization is that they surely must. No corner of the globe is as isolated as it used to be. Local diversity may persist, even increase, but celebrating that diversity should not take the place of considering the flows of resources, information, and people that increasingly bring local expressions of Christianity into contact with other communities, traditions, and influences.

The new paradigm does posit one way in which Christianity's new center of gravity in the global South is connected with other parts of the world. This connection is the global South's potential for influencing theological discussions worldwide. Jenkins stresses the theological conservatism of the global South, especially in matters of sexual morality, and imagines that this conservatism could reinforce similar orientations in the United States.[79] Escobar notes the greater prominence of "uninhibited emotionalism" and interest in "dreams and visions" as a potential challenge to the "rationality" and "intellectual expression of biblical truth" that have been more common in the United States and Europe.[80] Kwame Bediako suggests that Christianity's new African center of gravity may require a "quite considerable" intellectual adjustment, much as did earlier shifts within the Greek and Roman empires or in Europe.[81]

To suggest that African Christianity may profoundly affect European or North American Christianity, though, assumes that the intermingling of transcultural ideas at the elite level, particularly among theologians, is somehow transmitted to the grassroots level of ordinary belief and practice. That is a hopeful assumption and is perhaps evident in the small ways that congregations in the United States have begun to incorporate African hymns into Sunday worship services or to discuss the work of Jenkins and others in Sunday school classes. However, an assumption of widespread influence is not entirely consistent with the counterpart argument that has been emphasized about the limits of Western influences in Africa or Latin America. If proponents of the new paradigm believe the global South has been resistant to outside influences and is becoming more thoroughly Christian only now that Christianity has become indigenous, then they would also need to argue that Europe and North America may be equally resistant to outside influences. This resistance might even be more pronounced because of the relative differences in power among these areas of the world. As Bediako observes, "The levers of global economic and hence political power are likely to be located in the post-Christian West [with the result] that Africa will be perceived as not significant."[82]

Another transcultural influence that the new paradigm highlights is the potential for Southern Hemisphere missionaries to evangelize the secular North. As of 2000, some 33,000 foreign missionaries were said to be working in the United States, for instance.[83] Churches in Africa and Latin America were sending workers to evangelize the United States, a phenomenon that so strikingly contradicted the old view of missionaries being sent *from* the United States that it captured the attention of nearly all the proponents of the new paradigm. Jenkins, for instance, writes that the current South-to-North missionary push is as ironic—and as potentially significant—as the Catholic church's efforts during the Counter-Reformation to reconvert vast segments of Europe's Protestant population.[84]

The potential for a kind of reverse missionary movement from South to North is certainly worthy of consideration, but its current scope should not be exaggerated. For instance, the 33,000 foreign missionaries said to be working in the United States could well describe nothing more than immigrant pastors ministering to immigrant congregations. Jenkins himself cautions that "when European and American Christians look South, they see what they want to see"—meaning that the possibility of foreign missionaries bringing the United States to a more biblical interpretation of Christianity may be little more than the wishful thinking of conservative Christians who would like their own views to be accepted by everyone.[85] A more likely scenario is what Escobar describes as the "transcultural witnessing" that takes place as people "move around as migrants or refugees."[86] Sociologist R. Stephen Warner, noting that the majority of recent immigrants to the United States are Christians, refers to their increasing presence as the "de-Europeanization" of America.[87] African and Asian immigration may also be producing a de-Europeanization of Europe.[88] However, it is by no means self-evident that immigration alone will fundamentally redefine the beliefs and practices of native-born Christians in the United States and Europe. Warner concedes that immigrant practices often converge with those of nonimmigrants, while studies of ethnic assimilation suggest that the proverbial "melting pot" is still operative for many immigrant groups.[89]

The continuing impact of the United States on Christianity in other parts of the world is perhaps the most difficult topic to consider accurately and with sufficient complexity. On the one hand, postcolonialism serves as an important reminder about exaggerating U.S. influence in world affairs and of perceiving connections with indigenous churches where none exist. On the other hand, postcolonialism itself has been criticized for neglecting the power differentials that do in fact exist between the United States and much of the world. "The situation of contemporary Africa and most other ex-colonies," writes Rita Abrahamsen, "is one of neo-colonialism, imperialism, and continued subservience in the international system as expressed, for example, in the debt crisis and the erosion of sovereignty implied by the imposition of structural adjustment programmes."[90] In her view, the global imbalances of power are too easily glossed over in postcolonial studies. For contemporary discussions of global Christianity, the challenge is thus to understand not only the limits of U.S. influence but also its considerable reach.

The most remarkable aspect of the new paradigm is that it is almost completely silent about U.S. influence in the current spread of global Christianity. Jenkins devotes an interesting chapter to the history of Christian missions in which he observes the importance of European and North American influences, but then he closes the story as if it ended with the colonial era and titles his chapter about churches in the global South "Standing Alone." Perhaps sensing that too much attention has been devoted to Northern missionaries in previous work, he concentrates more attention on Southern missionaries evangelizing the North. In similar fashion, Sanneh describes the "worldwide Christian resurgence" as one that is proceeding "without Western organizational structures"—a possible reference to the autonomy and organizational innovativeness of African and Latin American churches but clearly an overstatement if it is meant to deny the continuing role of U.S. evangelistic and humanitarian organizations.[91]

To go very far down the path of emphasizing U.S. influence, though, is to trod on treacherous ground. The work of anthropologist David Stoll provides an interesting case in point. Stoll is an accomplished anthropologist with considerable experience studying Pentecostalism in Latin America. His book *Is Latin America Turning Protestant?* provided one of the first comprehensive studies of the scope and sources of Latin American Pentecostalism.[92] Yet Stoll's treatment emphasized the convergence of U.S. military, economic, and political interests with those of U.S. and Latin American evangelistic agencies to the point that the role of local grassroots churches seemed to be diminished. His work and that of other writers emphasizing U.S. influence has largely been ignored by the chief architects of the new paradigm.[93] One writer has even suggested that depicting Latin American Protestantism as a "foreign" import has simply been "a favorite weapon of the Roman Catholic hierarchy against the inroads of Protestantism."[94] The more popular interpretation in missiological circles holds that Latin American Protestantism grew spontaneously once the Catholic monopoly was broken and a "shopping mall" favorable to all kinds of new religious movements emerged.[95]

If Stoll's emphasis on the manipulative role of U.S. churches is too simple, it serves as a reminder that this role needs to be considered, if only to understand how the image of a religious shopping mall gained resonance. The broader point is that globalization begs for a new paradigm that emphasizes not only the autonomous vitality of churches in the global South but also the cultural and organizational mechanisms through which Christianity in its scattered global locations has become more intricately connected. This point has both practical and theoretical implications. The practical implications concern especially the efforts of local churches to serve and be served by other ministries in other countries. The theoretical implications pertain to how we think about the new paradigm itself. Instead of a new paradigm that seems at once appealing and disappointing to both secularizationists and antisecularizationists, a new paradigm is required that focuses attention on the synchronic relationships between locations in which secularization may be happening and locations in which religion's influence is increasing. Similarly, a more satisfactory interpretation of postcolonialism moves beyond an emphasis on the autonomy of churches in the aftermath of colonialism to a perspective in which interdependence is acknowledged.

Edward Said called this emphasis on interdependence a contrapuntal approach. Contrapuntal music involves singing back and forth. A theme in one part of the chorale is played against and in relation to a theme in another part of the chorale. The privileged position that one occupies at any particular moment is provisional. The result is polyphony. Contrapuntal arrangement does not imply silencing any one set of voices completely. In less metaphoric terms, a contrapuntal perspective necessitates questions about the continuing power differentials that separate rich and poor countries, including questions about how the rich benefit from the poor as well as how the poor may benefit from the rich. In this respect, the problem, Said observed, "is how to connect the south, whose poverty and vast labor pool are inertly vulnerable to northern economic policies and powers, with a north that is dependent on it." And more broadly: "What we need to do is to look at these matters as a network of inter-dependent histories that it would be inaccurate and senseless to repress, useful and interesting to understand."[96]

I have argued that a new paradigm has emerged that brings the shifting center of gravity of global Christianity into focus but that also leaves important questions about the transcultural role of U.S. churches unanswered. The new paradigm emphasizes the autonomous growth of Christianity in parts of Africa, Latin America, and Asia, and the relative decline of Christianity in western Europe and the United States. Scholars who have written about the shifting heartland of Christianity foresee this as having far-reaching implications, probably as significant as the Protestant Reformation or other shifts that radically redefined the missional outreach of the churches. For the most part, the new paradigm is a hopeful story, suggesting that the end of the missionary era and the secularity of Europe and the United States have not spelled doom for the future of Christianity. But paradigms are always simplifications. They draw our attention to some aspects of the world and divert our eyes from others.

The reality of Christianity is much messier than the new paradigm has suggested. Whereas the idea of a global shift emphasizes changes in numbers of presumed Christians based on population projections, such projections tell us little about influence. No discussion of global political power could satisfactorily rest on population projections alone, and no discussion of Christianity should either. Despite Christainity's shifting population, a very significant share of its financial and organizational resources remains in the United States and Europe. The new paradigm also presents a distorted picture of church growth by not distinguishing more carefully between conversions and high birth rates. Some churches are growing because they are attracting new members who were not previously Christian at all. But much of the apparent growth of Christianity in certain parts of the world is simply the result of high fertility. Overall, the proportion of the world's population that can be considered Christian appears not to have changed much in the past century and is not expected to change much during the next century. As we have seen, a closer look at continent-specific trends casts doubt even on the idea that Christianity's shift southward is very recent. Moreover, the crude hemispheric distinctions that writers sometimes draw fail to depict accurately where Christianity has been growing and where it has been declining.

Because the realities of global Christianity are quite complex, the story that has been told in recent years is but one of several ways in which these realities could have been interpreted. For instance, David Barrett, the leading compiler of statistics about Christianity, proposed a rather different interpretation from the one that has gained currency. Why a particular interpretation catches hold, though, is not arbitrary. I have suggested two ways in which the new paradigm has been shaped by the intellectual context in which it appeared. The debate about secularization has had a significant impact. Writers who believed secularization was happening found evidence for their views in the apparent decline of Christianity in Europe and the United States, while antisecularizationists argued that their position was vindicated by the growth of Christianity in the global South. Arguments about secularization typically focused on diachronic developments within particular contexts and did not illuminate the synchronic interactions among these contexts. Postcolonialism also played a formative role in the new paradigm. In seeking to escape the biases of colonialism and imperialism, architects of the new paradigm emphasized discontinuities more than continuities and stressed the autonomy of Christian developments in formerly colonized parts of the world.

For church leaders in the United States, the new paradigm suggests a need to think differently than in the past but does not provide a clear message about the direction such thinking should take. I doubt that any of the writers who have contributed to the new paradigm would argue that churches in the United States should retreat from transcultural engagement. Writers know, though, that the conclusions they intend are not always the ones readers draw. A U.S. reader learning that Christianity is flourishing so well on its own in the global South could reasonably conclude that U.S. churches should mind their own business and focus on transcultural ministries only by engaging in self-examination. Upon realizing that the United States continues to send large numbers of missionaries and sizable amounts of humanitarian aid abroad, that reader might wonder if these efforts are simply ill-conceived. If anything, he or she might conclude that the mission of U.S. churches should be to their own communities, given the demise of Christianity in the global North. Were that person to reflect more broadly on the realities of globalization, he or she might well be left more puzzled than ever. On the one hand, arguments about globalization suggest that the world is becoming increasingly interconnected. On the other hand, the global Christianity paradigm seems to imply that Christianity in different parts of the world is simply growing or declining, largely on its own and in its own local contexts, without significant cross-national influences, especially from countries that are militarily and economically powerful.

A reformulation of the narrative about global Christianity that emphasizes the body of Christ would be truer to the Christian story itself. A body is organically connected. It functions best when the particular contributions of its various parts work together. A story that focuses on the withering of one appendage and the strengthening of another makes no sense. A better story acknowledges each limb or organ's dependence on others. In this story, global Christianity emerges less as a narrative about shifting centers of gravity and more about opportunities for mutual edification and interaction. A majority of the world's Christians live in Africa, Latin America, and Asia. Their numeric strength amplifies their importance in the overall work of the church as well as offering greater opportunities for international travel and communication. At the same time, financial resources and organizations remain disproportionately concentrated in Europe and North America. Poverty and severe health needs continue in much of the global South. Extreme differences in the power of nations also pose issues that people of faith cannot ignore, especially as nations compete for military and economic superiority.[97]

The challenge of globalization is to rethink how nations and the subunits of nations—corporations, nongovernmental organizations, churches, and individual citizens—have become interdependent. Contrary to the impression left by proponents of the new paradigm, the movement that sent so many missionaries abroad from the United States during the nineteenth and twentieth centuries is not over. It continues to be one of the most important ways in which U.S. congregations seek to play a role in the wider world. But this movement is not the only way in which U.S. influence is realized, nor should this influence be conceived only in narrowly religious terms or simply as a potential benefit to other parts of the world. The changing role of U.S. churches must be understood within the context of global interdependence, and globalization itself must be examined in order to understand those dynamics and implications.

Four Faces of Globalization

Debating Heterogeneity and Inequality

"Dear pastor, I thank Almighty Allah for giving you the wisdom and resources to spread your message to the whole nation. Pastor, I would urge
you to continue with your work and I am confident that Allah is using
you as an instrument to change our negative perceptions to the realization of the immense spiritual reality of Africa."[1] These are the words of
a Muslim in northern Ghana writing to one of his country's most influential Christian pastors. They contradict the much-heralded "clash of
civilizations" between Muslims and Christians. They coincide with "global
shift" arguments only to the extent that they are addressed to a Christian leader in Africa. They evoke more questions than answers. How
does a Muslim some distance away happen to know about a church in
Accra? What accounts for its rapid growth and national appeal? Why
does its ministry appear remarkably similar to ones in Texas and California?

To understand the growing linkages between U.S. Christianity and
other parts of the world, we must pay less attention to demographic
shifts and more to the complexities of global interdependence. The starting point is to recognize that globalization consists of international and
transregional flows of goods, money, services, power, information, and
people and thus is the larger arena in which to understand the changing
role of American religion. The present period of globalization, which
began in the 1970s and intensified during the late 1980s and 1990s, involves significant increases in the speed and volume of long-distance

communication, increasing numbers of people who travel abroad or migrate from one country to another, numerous free trade agreements, heightened foreign investment, and greater economic interdependence. The broadening scope of U.S. church activities in other countries takes place in the context of these other aspects of globalization and is shaped by them. Religious leaders respond to the challenges, constraints, and opportunities presented to them by these changing social conditions. A congregation in Akron does not decide to support a ministry in Accra simply because of demographic shifts in global Christianity that cause Ghana to appear larger on the map, although those considerations may be important. It also matters that Ghana, the United States, and the wider world are becoming more closely linked culturally, economically, and politically.[2]

The global flows that connect different parts of the world are particularly evident in the growing number of people who travel outside their home countries. Between 1980 and 2006 international tourism climbed from a world total of 278 million people to an estimated 843 million, and the tourism business grew from $104 billion to $735 billion.[3] These increases were fueled not only by affluence and free time among the residents of rich countries but also by lower costs. At the end of the twentieth century, airfares per passenger mile were about a third of what they were in 1960.[4]

Lower transportation costs not only have made it easier for people to travel but also have facilitated the burgeoning flow of long-distance commerce. Between 1980 and 2002, the cost of insurance and freight services in relation to the value of merchandise dropped from 4.7 percent to 3.3 percent globally and among developing countries from 8 percent to 4.8 percent. Over the same period, the overall value of merchandise and service exports tripled.[5] From 2002 to 2006, total exports grew at an annual rate of 16.7 percent, up from only 7.1 percent during the 1980s and 1990s.[6]

Had a traveler from Akron to Accra made the journey in recent years, he or she would therefore have not only flown for less and in less time but would also have been one of a much enlarged group of such visitors and part of an increasing flow of commercial transactions. In 1980 approximately 10,000 Americans and Europeans visited Ghana; by 2002 that number had swelled to 160,000 and, in turn, 16,000 Ghanaians visited the United States. During the same period the tourism industry in Ghana multiplied fivefold and the number of Americans actually living in Ghana grew to nearly 4,000. Since 1992, when military rule ended

and Ghana became a constitutional democracy, the country has become
the United States' third-largest trading partner in the region and is viewed
by the U.S. government as playing a pivotal economic and political role
among African nations. Although Ghana was still far less a part of the
global culture than many other countries, it was increasingly linked. Between 1980 and 2000, the proportion of Ghanaian households connected to the wider world by television grew from fewer than 1 percent
to more than 11 percent, and radio was available to a majority of the
population, judging from a national survey in which 69 percent claimed
to hear radio news at least once a week.[7] Imports increased significantly
in these years, doubling in value even when taking inflation into account.
Because of the large number of Ghanaians living in other countries, international remittances played an increasing role in the Ghanaian economy, rising tenfold from less than 0.1 percent of Gross Domestic Product in 1985 to nearly 1 percent by 2003.[8] Were the traveler from Akron
to arrive via London on Ghana International Airlines, he or she might
also have been interested to know that the airlines is part of a U.S.-based
consortium that took over the failing Ghana Airways and recapitalized
it in 2004.[9]

On a wider scale, international travel increasingly linked other countries to each other and especially to Europe and North America. As
China's borders became more open to foreign visitors and foreign trade,
international tourism from Europe and the Americas grew from a mere
233,000 in 1980 to 4.5 million in 2002. Other countries reachable from
Europe and the Americas only by long-distance travel also experienced
dramatic growth in international tourism. The number of Europeans and
U.S. residents who visited Indonesia grew from 245,000 to one million
in these years. On a smaller scale, the number who traveled from these
countries to Nigeria grew from 51,000 to 390,000 and to Zambia from
18,000 to 164,000. Closer to the United States, shifting political conditions encouraged tourism to the Dominican Republic among Europeans
and U.S. residents to rise from 297,000 to 2.2 million and to El Salvador
from only 115,000 to 900,000.[10]

Besides the growing number of tourists, globalization is evident in the
increasing flow across borders of long-term residents. During the 1980s
many countries saw large numbers emigrate because of civil wars, violent uprisings, purges, poverty, and natural disasters. Cambodia, the Dominican Republic, El Salvador, Ghana, Guatemala, Guyana, Iraq, Jamaica,
Kyrgyzstan, Laos, Lebanon, Mozambique, Nicaragua, the Philippines,
Sri Lanka, Tajikistan, and Uruguay all experienced at least 2 percent

annual population losses from net migration during this period, according to United Nations estimates. In the same years, rich countries attracted an increasing number of immigrants. By 2000, 25 percent of Australia's population was migrant stock as was 19 percent of Canada's, 12 percent of the United States', 11 percent of France's, and 9 percent of Germany's. Political unrest and oil resulted in the Middle East experiencing high rates of immigration. Forty percent of Bahrain's population at the end of the twentieth century were migrants as were 58 percent of Kuwait's, 40 percent of Jordan's, 37 percent of Israel's, and 27 percent of Oman's. The Soviet Union's dissolution resulted in increasing migration in parts of eastern Europe and Central Asia. The Estonian population in 2000 included 26 percent migrant stock, Latvia's included 25 percent, and Ukraine's included 14 percent. East Asian politics and commerce produced another migration stream. Nearly 40 percent of Hong Kong's population in 2000 were immigrants, and 66 percent of Macao's were, as were 34 percent of Singapore's.[11] Major economic and cultural centers in North America and Europe were especially affected. Foreign-born residents made up 28 percent of London's population, 36 percent of New York's, 41 percent of Los Angeles', 44 percent of Toronto's, and 59 percent of Miami's.[12]

Through increasing flows of goods and capital, globalization during the 1990s resulted in economic integration on a particularly wide scale. Among standard measures of integration into the global economy, trade in goods as a share of Gross Domestic Product rose significantly during the decade for sixty-seven countries for which records were kept while declining for only fourteen. For the United States, this share climbed from 44 percent to 68 percent of Gross Domestic Product. For developing countries in Africa and Latin America, it increased to even higher levels. During the same period, other measures of integration into the global economy also registered significant growth. For instance, private capital flows and foreign direct investment both doubled as a percentage of Gross Domestic Product for the world as a whole.[13] One estimate showed that foreign assets as a proportion of world Gross Domestic Product grew from 17.7 percent in 1980 to 56.8 percent in 1995.[14] Cross-border corporate mergers and acquisitions, bilateral investment treaties, and legal changes also contributed to the increases in international exchanges of goods and capital. Over a thirteen-year period, the United Nations tracked 1,885 changes in national regulations, 94 percent of which it regarded as having liberalized the flow of international trade.[15]

In significant measure globalization also consists of international flows of information. Telephone service continues to be an important means of communication, as indicated by the fact that international phone calls rose from a total of 38 billion minutes in 1991 to 145 billion minutes in 2004 while the per-minute cost dropped by about half.[16] Approximately a million transatlantic conversations occurred simultaneously via satellite and fiber optics, compared with fewer than a hundred transmitted at once in the 1950s.[17] Of course the Internet and e-mail have played an even greater role in spanning borders, with global Internet users multiplying from about 4 million in 1991 to 863 million in 2004.[18] By 2005, an estimated 14 percent of the world's population had become Internet users, an increase of 146 percent in the preceding five years. Much of this growth occurred in the richer, technologically advanced countries, leading to a digital divide largely excluding poor countries. For instance, 67 percent of U.S. residents and 36 percent of Europeans were estimated to have Internet access, compared with only 1.5 percent of Africans and 8.4 percent of Asians.[19] A 2001 report showed that personal computers were about 40 percent as numerous as people in developed countries but only about 2.5 percent as numerous as people in developing countries. However, even that small a percentage meant that more than 120 million computers were present in developing countries. Another indication of the global penetration of the Internet was the growth of electronic commerce, or e-commerce, which mushroomed from a world total of $2.3 trillion in 2002 to $12.8 trillion in 2006, with more than 90 percent being conducted among developed countries. Nevertheless, e-commerce among developing countries in Africa grew from nearly nothing to $6.9 billion in this period, and in Central and South America e-commerce grew from $7.6 billion to $100.1 billion.[20]

The United States is by no means the only driving force in the global economy, but alongside the European Union, Japan, and China, it is one of the most central and powerful players. As a market for the world's trade, the United States annually imports goods valued at more than twice those imported by Germany, the nation's closest competitor; nearly four times as much as Japan; twenty times as much as India; and more than the imports of forty other countries combined.[21] U.S.-based transnational corporations constitute a significant influence in the global economy. Three of the top five transnational corporations, ranked by foreign assets, were U.S. companies, according to a 2002 United Nations report, as were more than a quarter of the top hundred. During the 1990s, many of these companies moved up in the international rankings and significantly extended their operations in other countries. For instance, General Electric moved from nineteenth to first in terms of total foreign assets and, while its total employment grew by a mere 6 percent, foreign employment increased 140 percent and foreign sales climbed more than 400 percent.[22] In dollar value, the sales of the largest transnational corporations were larger than the entire Gross National Product of many countries. For instance, the revenues of General Motors were larger than Denmark's, and IBM's were larger than Ireland's. Overall, forty-nine of the largest economies in the world were countries and fifty-one were corporations.[23]

U.S. companies play an increasingly diverse role in world markets. In the 1980s, the most internationally invested corporations were primarily in petroleum (Exxon, Mobil, Amoco, Chevron, and Texaco), motor vehicles (Ford, General Motors), and electronics (General Electric, IBM). These are now accompanied by communications (Verizon, AOL Time Warner), pharmaceuticals (Pfizer, Johnson & Johnson, Abbott Laboratories), and purveyors of mass consumer items (Wal-Mart, McDonald's, Coca Cola). Wal-Mart, the largest retailer in the United States, holds a third of its assets and employs a quarter of its work force overseas. McDonald's added more than 200,000 employees and doubled its work force during the 1990s, nearly all in other countries, and increased its foreign sales by almost 50 percent despite a slight overall decline in total sales.[24] Among the more than 63,000 transnational corporations in the world, U.S.-based corporations ranked first in terms of total assets in advertising (Interpublic Group), media (AOL Time Warner), restaurants (McDonald's), tourism (Carnival), law (Baker & McKenzie), retailing (Wal-Mart), and banking (Citigroup).[25]

Overall, the United States ranks as the fourth "most globalized" nation in the world according to a composite index based on trade, travel, technology, and links to the rest of the world compiled by *Foreign Policy*. It ranks first on such measures of technological connectivity as Internet users and secure servers and first on memberships in international organizations, but falls below such small countries as Singapore and Switzerland on trade and foreign direct investment because of its large domestic markets.[26] Globalization is in no way simply another term for Americanization. Yet the United States holds not only a prominent position but also a pivotal one, for instance, as the central link through which economic exchange is channeled or as an influential voice in international diplomacy.[27] Beyond its economic and political roles, the U.S. cultural role must also be kept in mind. For example, in 2006 the number of foreign students enrolled at American universities totaled more than 564,000, up from only 154,000 in 1975.[28] As a very different cultural influence, the *Baywatch* television series is distributed in 140 countries and translated into thirty-three languages, and it reaches an estimated global audience of one billion.[29] To speak of the effects of globalization is thus to speak of processes in which the United States is significantly involved.

The perceived costs and benefits of globalization have made it a highly charged topic, with proponents "overselling" it, as economist Joseph E. Stiglitz has argued, and critics mobilizing against it.[30] Not surprisingly, a vast literature about the effects of globalization has emerged, much of it focusing on economic, political, and cultural processes that have no obvious or direct bearing on religion.[31] However, these are precisely the aspects of globalization that must be understood if we are to grasp the changing relationships between Christianity in the United States and other parts of the world. It is these larger economic, political, and cultural aspects of globalization that constitute the changing contexts in which the international outreach of U.S. churches takes place. In significant ways, these changing contexts also present the challenges that religious leaders face as they engage in international programs. At the risk of oversimplification, we can divide these effects into four broad categories. Two of the four concern the supposed cultural consequences of globalization—the prospect of an emerging global monoculture and the likelihood of continuing or increasing cultural diversity. The others emphasize hypothesized economic consequences of globalization—beneficent markets and immiserating dislocation—and thus not only represent competing perspectives but also pose questions about the social and political implications of globalization, which in turn define the conditions under which transcultural religious activities occur.[32]

THE SPREAD OF GLOBAL MONOCULTURE

The idea that everything becomes more and more alike over time is at first blush an odd notion. An observant person who has recently traveled to another country or walked the streets of any major city in the United States would surely be struck more by the seemingly endless variety of people and customs and tastes than by their sameness. Predictions of rampant homogeneity, though, are not new. Karl Marx and Max Weber wrote of the stultifying erosion of uniqueness and meaning that comes with the advance of capitalism (although they did not focus on sameness per se).[33] Decades later, social theorists Theodor Adorno and Herbert Marcuse predicted that aesthetic creativity would wither under the onslaught of mass consumption and modern bureaucracies' penchant for treating everyone as interchangeable parts.[34] More recently, writers observe that large-scale organizations, such as corporations, educational institutions, and national governments, often do business similarly whether they are in the United States, Europe, China, or Brazil, apparently because of worldwide models that are constructed and propagated through global cultural and associational processes.[35]

As globalization brings people from different corners of the world into closer contact with one another, the opportunities for mutual influences increase. These influences, though, are rarely entirely mutual. Nations and cultures with the most power and wealth disproportionately shape the decisions of those with fewer resources. They do so in at least three ways: requiring weaker decision makers to conform to their wishes, establishing expectations that decision makers realize might be in their best interest to follow, and simply setting themselves up as highly visible models that others imitate without necessarily thinking about it. A rich nation that pressures a poor one to govern more democratically in order to qualify for foreign aid illustrates the coercive means by which globalization generates uniformity. A developing country may open its borders for imports or sell goods cheaply on the export market because it considers these practices to be in its best interest. A Christian pastor in Guatemala and a Hindu cleric in Cleveland may organize their Sunday services very similarly because it seems to be the accepted custom everywhere one travels.[36] If global culture is indeed becoming homogeneous, this has powerful implications for the ease with which religious organizations in one country might interact with religious organizations in other countries.

In the global economy the influence of powerful transnational corporations is one of the ways in which behavior in remote parts of the world is presumed to become more and more alike. To maintain their competitive edge, corporate leaders look for workers who display the same qualities: loyalty, efficiency, and a willingness to do whatever they are asked for a modest wage. In their mutual dealings, corporate officials want to appear both reasonable and progressive, so they do similar things, such as advertise, host conferences, initiate personnel departments, and develop new products. Leaders of government bureaus and international nongovernmental organizations adopt similar strategies that emphasize rationality and efficiency.[37] The common culture that emerges is not necessarily the one that anybody planned. It results from small cues learned in small ways as people who have lived in local settings respond to the pressures of being workers in the global economy and the opportunities of being its beneficiaries.[38] Besides these inadvertent influences, diplomatic negotiations, educational institutions, and corporate cultures also promote common norms, languages, and understandings.

The spread of English and the erosion of folk languages are among the most compelling examples of rising cultural uniformity. According to a 2003 UNESCO report, 6,800 distinct vernacular languages currently exist worldwide, compared with about 15,000 in the sixteenth century and 10,000 at the start of the nineteenth century; the same study estimates that 97 percent of the world's population currently use only 4 percent of the existing languages, leading ethnolinguists to believe that many will become extinct within the next century.[39] Chinese, English, Hindu/Urdu, Spanish, and Arabic are the most commonly spoken languages, collectively representing 2.3 billion of the world's 4 billion people.[40] English is the first language of only 375 million people but is a second language for another 375 million people as a result of colonial histories and migration, and is estimated to be part of the repertoire of another 750 million people who have felt the need to learn English as a second language. First-language English speakers are concentrated among the world's richest nations, including the United States, England, Canada, and Australia, while second-language English speakers live in former British colonies that are among the most populous and rapidly growing parts of the world. For instance, 43 million English speakers live in Nigeria, 37 million live in India, 36 million live in the Philippines, and 10 million live in South Africa. Numerous countries in which English has previously been a foreign language are also thought to be moving into the category of second-language English speakers. These countries include Argentina, Costa Rica, Ethiopia, Honduras, Nicaragua, Somalia, and Sudan.

Globalization contributes to the spread of English in several ways. English is the dominant language in which scientific and diplomatic interaction occurs and thus earns desirability as a language to be taught in schools and universities. Upwards of 90 percent of all Web sites are in English.[41] Globalization also encourages the formation of large regional blocs united by common political and cultural ties. One example is the European Union in which an estimated 42 percent of citizens can communicate in English and 70 percent report being able to follow television news in English. Trade and mass communication, led by rich countries in the global North, contribute significantly to the spread of English as well. "In the 20th century," one British report concludes, "the role of the U.S. has been more important than that of Britain and has helped ensure that the language is not only at the forefront of scientific and technical knowledge, but also leads consumer culture."[42] It takes only a small leap of imagination to see how this growing dominance of English might affect the outreach of American churches.

Another much discussed effect of globalization occurs through the marketing of Western-based consumer goods and services. Using McDonald's fast food restaurants as an example, sociologist George Ritzer argues that tastes and eating practices have become increasingly homogeneous in the United States as a result of such chains and that this uniformity is destined to spread throughout the world as these organizations globalize.[43] Ritzer observes that McDonald's, which opened nearly a thousand restaurants outside the United States in 2002 alone and currently serves 46 million customers a day in 118 nations, is but one example of the growing international popularity of chain stores and franchises. Yum! Brands, which markets under the names Pizza Hut, KFC, Taco Bell, and A&W Root Beer, operates 33,000 restaurants in 100 countries. Subway has more than 19,000 outlets in 72 countries. Starbucks, Wal-Mart, Blockbuster, Home Depot, and Ace Hardware are examples of other rapidly internationalizing franchises. Among consumer goods, motion pictures are frequently cited as another industry in which U.S. influence is producing a single worldwide set of preferences. In 2000, for instance, the global market for films was estimated at $1 trillion, of which American content comprised slightly more than half.[44] Of the ten top-grossing films at the international box office, all originated in the United States. Only four films from other countries (one from Japan and three from England) were among the top hundred.[45] Although it is unclear how widespread these cultural influences may be, writers point to numerous anecdotal examples, such as "Amazonian Indians wearing Nike sneakers, denizens of the Southern Sahara purchasing Texaco baseball caps, and Palestinian youths proudly displaying their Chicago Bulls sweatshirts in downtown Ramallah."[46] If consumer products spread this easily, American religious messages may also be circulating with increasing facility.

U.S. domination of global culture has generated sufficient concern to prompt inclusion of "cultural exception" clauses in international free trade agreements. While these clauses seek protection especially for national film and music industries, they have generated considerable popular support as well from publics concerned about the erosion of traditional values. Bikini-clad *Baywatch* girls and the lyrics of gangsta rap are, to say the least, objectionable in many societies. Proponents of cultural diversity also worry that mass entertainment conveys consumer values that are potentially damaging to the symbols and images that constitute local identities. Yet American media conglomerates argue that free trade should be promoted in all realms and that small countries should somehow fight back, if they are able, by launching their own conglomerates.[47] The sheer popularity of foreign films and music also misses the larger point that McDonaldization involves not simply an emerging taste for high-fat hamburgers but also an implicit emphasis on convenience, fast and efficient service, low prices, predictability, and standardized selections. Although the choices consumers make are varied, the fact that they behave as consumers signals cultural homogenization.

The McDonaldization of culture may be less likely in religion than in sectors driven by marketing and consumerism, but religion is affected. Consider the worldwide spread of Pentecostal churches. Although it is important to be mindful of the local variation among congregations labeled as Pentecostal, observers argue convincingly that Pentecostalism is both a recognizable category and growing dramatically in many parts of the global South.[48] Pentecostal churches are certainly not franchises, like fast food restaurants, but they do impress scholars with their promotion of the diffusion of relatively homogeneous cultural norms. For instance, political scientist David Lehmann describes Pentecostal churches as "notoriously uniform across the globe" and notes their "radical similarity of practice."[49] Globalization, scholars contend, fits perfectly with Pentecostals' view of themselves as a "world-wide fellowship."[50] Other scholars suggest that Pentecostal churches are less oriented toward incorporating local traditions into religious services than the older churches established by mainline Protestant and Catholic missionaries are, and instead follow a common pattern that their leaders deem to be more modern.[51] "Charismatic churches celebrate their services according to a specific format," writes anthropologist Marleen De Witte. "This entails not only a more or less fixed sequence of practices and performances, but also a similarly, but more implicitly fixed pattern of bodily behavior and vocal utterances required of the congregation."[52] Apart from communicating implicit norms, Pentecostal churches also rely on Western media and thus stand to be accused of importing Western values in the same way that U.S. motion pictures and popular music are said to do. A study in Nigeria, for example, described a thriving consumer media industry consisting of approximately a thousand video-films being produced within the country, a disproportionate number of which featured Pentecostal religion, as well as popular "cross-over artists" catering to the Pentecostal music market, and "worship stores" selling gospel songs, video-tapes, musical instruments, religious magazines, and inspirational books.[53]

On the surface, locally produced media of this kind would appear to be examples of the very diversity that cultural exception clauses are meant to preserve. Yet the Nigerian author of this study argues that the popularity of Pentecostal video-films is an example of religious consumerism that is essentially creating a Westernized spiritual supermarket. The connections with globalization began in the 1970s as Nigerian traders introduced consumer goods and then increased as a result of oil-boom wealth in that period. During the subsequent economic crisis and civil unrest, television and video rentals provided safe in-home entertainment in the cities. During the 1980s, videotapes of television broadcasts by U.S. televangelists Jimmy Swaggart, Oral Roberts, Jerry Falwell, and Robert Schuller were imported in large quantities and subsequently mimicked by young Nigerian pastors. In borrowing and subsequently producing their own video technology, the Pentecostal churches have explicitly portrayed themselves as up-to-date, compared with the backwardness of other churches, and in so doing have implicitly contributed to the diffusion of a consumerist mentality that emphasizes purchasing goods, seeking material success and prosperity, and solving personal problems through participation in the marketplace.[54]

On a broader scale, another effect of globalization is simply the replacement of indigenous religious traditions by more universalistic religions, such as Christianity and Islam, or by secular worldviews. Just as languages become extinct, so religious heterogeneity may be decreasing, perhaps with some practices disappearing entirely, like Sumerian and Aztec beliefs did in the past. One indication of this possible reduction in diversity is the fact that 80 percent of China's population and 23.5 percent of the world's population in 1900 were assumed to be "Chinese folk-religionists," whereas in 2000 this proportion was estimated to be only 28 percent in China and 6.4 percent globally. If these estimates are valid, they reflect the assumption that Chinese communism rather than globalization militated against folk religions. Yet other so-called ethnoreligionists reportedly declined as well, from 7.3 percent of the global population in 1900 to 3.8 percent in 2000.[55] The more important relationship of religion to language, though, is probably that global communication among Christians becomes easier as more of the world speaks English.[56]

Research on religious transplants from one culture to another suggests another form of homogenization that in some respects seems very much akin to McDonaldization. This is the apparent tendency among otherwise diverse religious traditions to adopt a congregational style of organization. R. Stephen Warner observes among immigrants in the United States from widely differing cultural traditions and even religions, for instance, that there is a tendency to meet in congregations that resemble other voluntary membership associations, are led by an elected board of lay members, are financed by private donations, and use multifunctional gathering places for activities that benefit the members, such as classes and potluck dinners.[57] Within global Christianity the congregational style is not of recent origin, having been widely promulgated during the nineteenth century by missionaries. However, global communication technologies increase the likelihood of large numbers of people being aware of this aspect of commonality. Anthropologists report that Christians in rural parts of Africa and the Far East, for example, talk about worshipping in the same way and at the "same hour" on Sundays as Christians in the United States and Europe. The centralized mission boards of the nineteenth century provided uniform standards for worship services through lexionaries, prayer books, and liturgical guides. To those can now be added model prayers posted on Web sites and more frequent visits by denominational officials and leaders from partner congregations in other countries.

While the global diffusion of Christianity may be facilitated by uniformities of language and cultural expectations, concerns about Western influences also shape religion by prompting reactions against globalization. Wahabi Muslim groups, some Pentecostal churches that oppose modernization, and fundamentalist Protestants in the United States who ally themselves with antiglobalist movements are examples. While these groups differ from one another and cannot appropriately be lumped under any single heading, they represent another way in which the perception, if not the reality, of a dominant monoculture being spread by globalization serves as a social connection between religions in widely separated parts of the world.[58]

GLOCALIZED DIVERSITY

A counterargument to the view that global culture is becoming more and more the same is the view that diversity not only persists but actually increases. Globalization may preserve or promote diversity in at least three ways. One is by bringing goods and values from the outside world so that local cultures are presented with new opportunities. A second is to bring outside resources that make it possible for local cultures to resist change and maintain their distinctive customs. The third is to set in motion processes by which the external influences mingle with local practices to produce new and more diverse forms of behavior. The point of all three is that local diversity exists not in the absence of globalization but in its presence. Thus, globalization is a direct or indirect influence on the social conditions in which various religious responses emerge, even though these religious expressions display the distinctive traits of local decisions and traditions.

Studies of the effects of integrating local communities into wider markets reveal the ways in which this process itself increases the likelihood of the entry of diverse goods and values from the outside world. For instance, economists Christian Broda and David Weinstein show that product variety in U.S. imports between 1972 and 2001 increased by a factor of four. They also estimate that increases in imported varieties raised U.S. real income by about 3 percent during this period, thus supporting their view that the increasing globalization of trade has been beneficial. Their definition of product diversity includes information not only about the nature of the specific product (milk, wine), but also about its origin (U.S. milk, French wine). It stands to reason, therefore, that international trade would increase this kind of diversity. A grocery store that sold only locally grown produce would, with increasing access to foreign suppliers, provide apples from New Zealand, grapes from Mexico, and mangoes from Hawaii. Such diversity is attractive to consumers, economists argue, because it derives from competition that reduces prices and appeals to an assumed love of variety. Other examples of globalization leading to greater variety include immigrant-run ethnic restaurants in the United States, American hamburgers served by McDonald's in Beijing, and Disney films on Japanese television. What may appear as global monoculture from one perspective is in this view simply an increase in product variety.[59] Critics of course argue that an apple from New Zealand is still an apple and, for that matter, that the ostensible variety in one's supermarket may reflect an underlying uniformity. For instance, a study of one suburban store found 104 varieties of packaged bread, but none free of hydrogenated fat or diglycerides.[60]

The possibility that local diversity is unaffected or strengthened by globalization is illustrated by research on the spread of Starbucks coffee establishments. Some 30 percent of the 14,000 freestanding coffee houses in the United States are owned by Starbucks, with rapidly increasing numbers in Canada, China, Japan, Britain, and elsewhere. Although Starbucks coffee houses typically offer more than two dozen specialty coffee drinks, the diffusion of these establishments promotes the kind of standardization that worries proponents of the McDonaldization thesis. Starbucks's advertising, corporate size, "latte lingo," sanitized music, and upscale ambience also illustrate the potential for hegemonic companies to drive out local options the way Home Depot has replaced independent lumberyards and hardware stores. Yet when researchers conducted observations and interviews in a number of locations, they found that Starbucks actually reinforced local diversity. It did so by creating a market for coffee consumption, which was then fulfilled by independent coffee houses in the same vicinity. Customers flocked to these competing establishments because they were more distinctive, offered a different ambience, or simply were "not Starbucks."[61]

A closer look at the role of McDonald's restaurants also suggests that local customs can adapt to and even benefit from the resources provided by an external influence of this kind. An ethnographic study of McDonald's in several geographically and ethnically different communities, for instance, showed considerable diversity among these locations in décor and food selections. At one inner-city location in southern California, retired African American men congregated for coffee on Saturday mornings much like they might have in earlier times at an independent café. The inexpensive coffee and breakfast items, abundant space, and relaxed atmosphere were resources that facilitated camaraderie among the men.[62]

Instances of globalization bringing outside resources that strengthen local religious practices are not hard to find. In the San Juan de la Costa region of Chile adherence to the shamanic Mapuche religion has been revitalized by three aspects of globalization: Mapuche leaders' having acquired better education, often through Catholic schools; competition with Pentecostal churches that are perceived to be in league with external economic forces; and international environmentalist groups that have mobilized against the World Trade Organization and forged alliances with local leaders.[63] A second example, which has been described by historian David Maxwell, is the emergence of a clearer emphasis on the distinctive features of African Christianity as a result of Africa's expanding role in the global economy and greater resources for relevant theological and historical scholarship.[64] A quite different example is the rise in China of Falun Gong—which political scientist Patricia A. Thornton terms a cybersect because of its effective use of the Internet to attract followers.[65] Falun Gong included traditional meditation techniques and presented itself as having a scientific perspective but was suppressed by Chinese authorities, who, according to some interpretations, responded more aggressively because the movement was widely categorized in the Western press as a religious cult.[66] In each of these examples, globalization prompted local reactions that then followed their own course.

The idea that globalization interacts with local cultures to produce entirely novel adaptations is sometimes termed glocalization, a concept associated with the Japanese business strategy of selling products for a global market but customized for local traditions.[67] Glocalization can be illustrated in the aforementioned spread of English, which produces not only a linguistic monoculture but also numerous local variations involving different accents, hybrids (such as Creole), and code switching. Glocalized diversity is important because it belies the notion that cultural practices can simply be exported from one context to another and thus fits well with postcolonial emphases on the creativity and vitality of local practices. However, glocalization clearly takes account of the fact that these local practices are influenced by transcultural relationships. The outcomes, as anthropologist Ulf Hannerz observes, are the result of "variously accomplished efforts at striking a bargain between opposing metacultures."[68]

That external influences produce novel and varied local responses is hardly a new idea. In the nineteenth and twentieth centuries the arrival of European traders and missionaries often prompted such results. In Melanesia, for example, the cargo cults that anthropologists wrote about in the 1950s illustrate an interesting synthesis of folk beliefs, Christian messianic teachings, and expectations that material goods and good fortune like the Europeans embodied would arrive by airplane—or perhaps would have arrived had the missionaries not intercepted them.[69] The literature on "Africanized" Christianity similarly emphasizes the creative incorporation of traditional beliefs and practices into the teachings brought by Western missionaries, as does the concept of inculturation, which has long been emphasized in Catholic settings.[70] Yet the point of glocalization is to suggest that these dynamic interactions are increasing as trade and communication reduce the distances separating cultures. External influences, such as "armaments, advertising techniques, language hegemonies, and clothing styles," writes anthropologist Arjun Appadurai, "are absorbed into local political and cultural economies, only to be repatriated as heterogeneous dialogues of national sovereignty, free enterprise, and fundamentalism."[71]

Repatriation of this kind occurs increasingly in multilateral directions. Consider the fact that more than half a million Chinese have immigrated to the United States in recent decades and that the rate of conversion to Christianity among these immigrants has been high. This influx has not only enhanced the global diversity of religion in the United States but has also fed a growing stream of avocational missionaries to China—as tourists, exchange students, English teachers, and businesspeople. The result, writes political scientist Jason Kindopp, is an "extensive web of overseas Chinese Christian networks of individuals who conduct mission work in China or revitalize the church upon their return home." Christianity in China has grown both in numbers and in diversity, with official and unofficial congregations receiving support, humanitarian efforts gaining assistance, and religious literature and films proliferating.[72]

Ethnographic studies of global Christianity suggest that the synergy between new international influences and local traditions is generating an enormous variety of distinctive beliefs and practices. Writing about religious developments in Latin America, sociologist Bernice Martin says that Pentecostalism is producing a "riotous syncretism" of "beneficent, novel possibilities and massive new strains."[73] Anthropologist Paul Gifford describes an interesting example of syncretism from his research in Ghana. A distinct form of popular music called highlife emerged in the 1920s, already a period in which local and Western intermingling was evident. By the 1970s, highlife was still popular but was being challenged by so-called hip-life music, a fusion of hip-hop, rap, and highlife. However, a regime change in the 1980s that brought a curfew and heavy tax on the entertainment industry significantly depressed the availability of highlife. During the period, large churches grew and began importing sermons, evangelistic techniques, and music from the United States. "Overnight," Gifford writes, "the highlife artists . . . became the vocalists and instrumentalists and groups carrying charismatic worship. Highlife in its new setting became Gospel Life (or 'G-life')." Because churches were exempt from taxes, attendance at dance clubs diminished and audiences gravitated to gospel revivals where the same music was featured.[74]

The evolution of gospel life music illustrates both the reality of U.S. Christianity's global reach and the complexity of the resulting religious practices. The popularity of gospel life is partly attributable to the broader increase in Ghanaian media imports, which climbed to more than seven million music cassettes and CDs, according to a 1998 report.[75] Gospel life music continues to evolve as well, with Ghana now ranking among the top twenty international consumers of Atlanta-based "holy hip hop" music.[76] To say that American Christianity is globalizing its influence does not mean, therefore, that congregations in Africa or Latin America are singing the same music or watching the same videos as Christians in the United States (although they may be). It does mean that gospel songs and televangelists' preaching in the United States more easily become part of the raw material with which artists and pastors in other countries work, just as influences from abroad enter with greater frequency into the composition of a Sunday mass in San Antonio or a Pentecostal service in Detroit. Gospel life music may be aesthetically pleasing, but its popularity also depends on the economic circumstances that make musical imports from the West attractive and that lead a regime to tax secular entertainment.

BENEFICENT MARKETS

If globalization consists essentially of people and places being incorporated into a single large-scale market, then an obvious possibility is that this process creates new opportunities, rising expectations, and, perhaps for some, rising incomes. "Workers with the same skills—be they farmers, factory workers, or pharmacists—are less productive and earn less in developing economies than in advanced ones," writes World Bank economist David Dollar. "Integration through trade in goods, foreign investment, international telecommunications, and migration reduces these gaps by raising productivity in the developing world. In this way globalization can be a powerful force for poverty reduction."[77]

However, "can be" does not necessarily mean "is." Empirical support for the view that globalization reduces poverty is mixed. If poverty is defined as living on less than one dollar a day, then global poverty appears to have declined during the 1980s and 1990s over roughly the same period that international economic integration was occurring. Between 1987 and 1998 alone, the share of the world's population living in extreme poverty fell from 28 percent to 23 percent, according to one estimate. However, most of this decline occurred in China and India, whereas the number of poor people living in Africa increased. China's reduction in poverty is consistent with arguments about the beneficence of free markets insofar as it was a result of greater liberalization of trade. The fact that this liberalization was guided by a communist regime, though, runs contrary to the idea that free markets alone are the source of prosperity or that open markets simply happen.[78] Other evidence also provides a mixed picture. Gross Domestic Product among the richest countries rose significantly between 1970 and 1995, but gained only modestly among middle-income countries, and did not increase among the poorest countries.[79] Within developing countries, income inequality appears to have declined in some cases and risen in others.[80] Other measures of development, such as primary schooling and reductions in child mortality rates, show only modest gains during the recent period of globalization.[81] Some economists also question whether the reductions in poverty noted in statistical studies can be attributed directly to greater international trade.[82]

The important point is not that global economic integration lifts all boats but that it does improve the life chances of some (and not only those living in rich countries). China's middle class is estimated to have grown to 19 percent of the population by 2003 and is anticipated to include 40 percent of the total population in 2020. In China's rapidly growing cities, 13 percent of households were classified as middle class in one study, and this share was expected to increase to 25 percent by 2010. These changes are widely assumed to reflect China's growing role in global exports; as well, the many employees of firms specializing in foreign trade and technology may inflate the percentages.[83] Such employees are also thought to be fueling a growing taste for individual freedom, democracy, information, and entertainment. India's middle class is said to have tripled during the 1980s and 1990s, with the impoverished population declining by about 5 percent annually.[84] On a much smaller scale, Uganda's poverty rate declined by nearly 6 percent annually during the 1990s, during which the country's exports expanded at an annualized rate of 15 percent.[85] In the same period, the share of El Salvador's population living in poverty fell from 64 percent to 40 percent, Ghana's declined from 52 percent to 40 percent, and Brazil's decreased from 62 percent to 51 percent.[86]

Where globalization plays a role in lifting people from poverty, the consequence of greatest importance for religion is seldom that large numbers become affluent or that promoting trade becomes the solution to world poverty. It is rather that people who are now just above the threshold of poverty can imagine themselves being better off financially and in some cases have new opportunities for pursuing these dreams. As wages and aspirations rise, the role of religion also changes. Gifford's research in Accra illustrates these connections. With a population of 1.6 million and a total of 3.2 million in the greater metropolitan area, Accra is the hub of international trade and travel, the location of a majority of the country's government offices, the headquarters of many international nongovernmental organizations, and a place where people can aspire to work in the expanding support-services economy as security guards, truck and taxi drivers, receptionists, and clerks. It is also the location of numerous churches, which Gifford estimates to be one of the largest industries in the city. The pastors, many of whom are foreign trained, have close ties to U.S. televangelists, saturate the airwaves with their own programming and videos of American ministries, travel and sometimes have second residences outside the country, and regularly host foreign preachers. For the most successful of these pastors, revenues from book sales, videos, and contributions far exceed the average income of their members. Although a few of the churches cater to the poorest residents, most draw from strata above the official poverty line. Sermons emphasize the desire for economic success and suggest ways of attaining it through hard work and especially through generous giving to the church. "Money, money, money," one leader asked his congregation to repeat, "as you go into this offering bowl, return to me in USA dollars, in Yen, Euros, Swiss Francs, and Pound Sterling."[87] "In Ghana's new Christianity," Gifford writes, "the 'victory' is above all in the economic sphere." Economic success is more frequently discussed, he says, than healing, prophecies about the end times, or teachings about soul winning. Globalization has created new opportunities for these ministries by drawing potential church members to the city, giving them a taste for consumer goods, raising their hopes for success, and exposing them to wider economic and religious marketing.[88]

The International Central Gospel Church is one of Accra's most successful congregations. Its leader, the Reverend Dr. Mensa Otabil, is the pastor to whom the Muslim quoted at the start of this chapter was writing. Since 1992, Reverend Otabil has built the International Central Gospel Church into a congregation of more than seven thousand members and started hundreds of other churches throughout Ghana. Sunday evening broadcasts of his services reach an estimated audience of two million.

Although the ministry is "charismatic," meaning that full members are encouraged to receive such gifts of the Holy Spirit as speaking in tongues, the distinctive charismatic identity is evident only in Bible study groups rather than at the Sunday services or on television. Reverend Otabil, who is as often described as a "motivational speaker," regards his work as oriented to "message" rather than "miracle," and the message is tailored primarily for young, better-educated adults who either are or aspire to be upwardly mobile. Sermons, tapes, and books offer practical advice about personal morality, family relationships, work, money, and success. The leaders clearly think of themselves as being part of a global network and look favorably on the opportunities that liberalization of trade and communication have brought. They "transcend the nation and enter a global public sphere to engage with both religious and secular transnational movements," writes Marleen De Witte. "God himself wants profit," one of the lay leaders told her in explaining that the Bible is a book about good management. Telecasts intentionally mimic the performances of Billy Graham, Benny Hinn, Kenneth Hagin, and other televangelists from the United States and are underwritten by a member who runs a transnational corporation. In keeping with the ministry's emphasis on individual success, the church regularly hosts Christian trade fairs, and Reverend Otabil often criticizes the Ghanaian government for accepting poverty instead of doing more to promote economic development.[89]

Pentecostalism is by no means the only expression of Christianity that is attracting adherents among the upwardly mobile. In a study of the coastal province of Zhejiang, which borders Shanghai, sociologists have identified an emerging class of "boss Christians," composed of young, well-educated private business entrepreneurs and employees whose incomes and occupational opportunities have risen substantially with China's expanding export market. Boss Christians often travel to the United States, Europe, and Southeast Asia on business and regard themselves as global citizens. They give generously to their churches, which are officially recognized as Protestant or Catholic congregations, and are a significant reason for these churches' growth. One example is the Protestant Zhu'en church in Longgang, which began in a factory workshop in 1986 and currently occupies a worship center that seats eighteen hundred people, owns a six-story educational building, and has constructed a home for senior citizens.[90]

The role of American televangelists is considerably greater in Ghana than in China because of the differing political circumstances. Even in democratic societies, the role of televangelists is often limited to training indigenous pastors and providing them with materials and support or serving as role models. Yet these relationships sometimes go further. When free markets appear to be in the spiritual and economic interest of all concerned, American preachers are sometimes tempted to support the regimes to which these market relations are attached. An example of such support occurred in the 1980s, when televangelist Jerry Falwell condemned the imposition of sanctions on South Africa as a means of ending apartheid, applauded South African president Pieter Willem Botha, and encouraged his viewers to invest in Krugerrands. In the 1990s, televangelist Pat Robertson praised Zaire's president Mobutu Sese Seko on Zairian television as a fine Christian, despite Mobutu's soldiers having recently killed a large number of pro-democracy citizens. At the time, Robertson was engaged in diamond mining operations in the country as part of a contract with Mobutu. In 1999, Robertson signed another mining agreement with Liberia's president Charles Taylor, who was also accused of widespread slaughter, and defended him as a fellow Christian.[91] These are perhaps extreme examples but provide illustrations of the ideological affinities that sometimes develop between U.S. clergy and foreign leaders favorable to particular kinds of market relations.

A quite different connection between global markets and religion is evident in a study conducted by sociologist Amy Reynolds in rural Nicaragua.[92] With some 25 percent of the labor force involved in coffee production, the Central American economy has long been dependent on international trade. In recent years, rising global demand for coffee has increased market opportunities, but these have been dominated by large firms at the expense of local growers, whose share of total revenues has steadily decreased. If globalization was not directly beneficial to growers, it nevertheless offered new opportunities for religious and other humanitarian organizations to intervene. The most visible of these efforts was the so-called fair trade plan, which sought to influence markets by encouraging consumers to pay slightly higher prices for coffee distributed by firms that guaranteed a specified percentage for growers. Although the fair trade plan experienced some success and was widely supported by U.S. church leaders, it captured less than 3 percent of the total market. In Nicaragua, Reynolds found a different plan that brought together market opportunities and faith groups. Through a $1.5 million grant from the U.S. faith-based humanitarian organization World Relief, a Christian farmers' association emerged in 1998. Although most of the money was for loans and technical assistance, the grant also created

networks among the local coffee growers and relationships with a
Christian-owned milling business. Instead of joining the fair trade consortium, the growers and mill owners opted to work within the broader
parameters of free trade by specializing in premium-grade coffee. By
catering to this expanding market niche, the growers were able to increase their earnings by at least as much as those participating in the fair
trade plan.

World Relief's role in this enterprise is but one of hundreds of instances in which faith-based organizations in rich countries are seeking
to help the poor by taking advantage of expanding markets. The typical
strategy is to supply seed capital, loans, job training, and technological
assistance to help micro businesses emerge and compete more successfully in available markets. Enterprise Development International is a
nonprofit Christian organization headquartered in Virginia that has
successfully adopted this strategy since 1985. In 2005, it worked with
partner organizations worldwide to assist in issuing 192,000 micro-
enterprise loans, totaling $29.4 million. Recipients launch small busi-
nesses, such as sewing and weaving shops and restaurants, receive in-
struction in saving and borrowing, and are required to meet regularly for
Bible study. Nearly 48,000 recipients, including 6,000 Muslims, participated in the Philippines; more than 23,000 took part in Bangladesh;
about 5,200 did so in Mexico; and 3,200 were involved in India. Eighty-
five percent of the recipients are women.[93]

IMMISERATING DISLOCATION

Against the view that poor people benefit by being drawn into international markets is the argument that globalization uproots people from
stable kin networks and traditions and makes matters worse for others
by leaving them behind. Although poverty declined during the 1990s in
Uganda, El Salvador, Ghana, and several other countries, it did not decline, or actually increased, in others. For instance, the share of Zambia's
population living in poverty increased from 69 percent to 75 percent during the 1990s and Romania's grew from 20 percent to 29 percent.[94] Despite China's integration into global markets, Chinese farmers still make
up 70 percent of the country's population and most continue to live in
poverty. At least twenty million urban residents also suffer from extremely low incomes.[95] In China and elsewhere, health care, clean water,
secure housing, and access to schools are often inadequate in overcrowded
urban areas and impoverished rural areas alike. Globalization appears

to strengthen families in some instances but elsewhere contributes to the exploitation of women and children by separating them from families or drawing them into the market economy as low-wage service providers, maids, and sex workers.[96] Among smaller countries, globalization may also exacerbate poverty by exposing local economies to the vagaries of international markets and foreign loans.[97] In these ways, globalization shapes the conditions in which local religious practices occur, even in areas that are only indirectly involved.

Papua New Guinea, where more U.S. and other foreign missionaries still operate than in any country of similar size, is an interesting illustration of the complex spiritual dynamics involved in being absorbed into the global economy and of being left behind.[98] In Port Moresby the population has doubled since 1980 to nearly 200,000 and trade has become more active as a result of increasing foreign demand for coffee, rubber, timber, and manufactured goods since completion of the country's first oil refinery in 1999 as well as more than 150 mining exploration licenses having been granted to large multinational companies.[99] More of the rural population is connected with Port Moresby because of migration from the countryside and the growing trade in betel nut and coffee.[100] English is the official written language and is taught in the community's two preschools, two primary schools, and two high schools. Forty percent of the residents use English as their primary language at home, and a survey found that 73 percent think English should be learned at home.[101] The earlier mission efforts, which focused heavily on translating the Bible into the country's many vernacular languages, have now been supplemented by numerous short-term missionaries and lay preachers, many from fundamentalist and Pentecostal churches in the United States and Canada. For the new urban working class, which struggles to stay above those who live in shantytowns and are endangered by youth gangs and crime, the missionaries' message promises a new identity that is more Western, more individualistic, and more hopeful.

The situation in remote regions of Papua New Guinea is quite different but also bears the imprint of globalization. Research conducted by anthropologist Eric Hirsch among the Fuyuge in the early 1990s found that they were very aware of the economic opportunities in Port Moresby, about one hundred kilometers away, and among other groups that were linked to the city. Fuyuge stories and rituals increasingly portrayed themselves as being decentered and as having lost a way to make sense of themselves. Like earlier believers in airborne cargo cults, their hope for prosperity focused on rumors that a highway to Port Moresby was being planned. They looked to the local missionaries whose connections with the outside world were stronger than theirs to be the instruments through which this hope was fulfilled. Meanwhile, the missionaries operated a store that brought an increasing array of goods—metal for roofs, clothing, sugar, canned food—from the outside world and the local residents produced fewer of their own necessities. However, this transitional period proved to be short-lived. A decade later and following a national agreement with the World Trade Organization, mining in the area had commenced and some of the traditional rituals now incorporated disco steps and guitars with amplifiers. Local leaders worried increasingly about youth gangs ("rascals") from Port Moresby and the loss of a distinctive culture.[102]

A study among the Urapmin in another remote section of Papua New Guinea provides insight into a different way in which globalization affects local religion.[103] The Urapmin were never missionized, but in 1977 heard about Christianity from people in other villages, became convicted by the Holy Spirit, and soon after started their own indigenous church pastored by a local man who had attended a mission school in another community. This would seem to be a clear instance of the global South independently furthering its own intrinsic interest in Christianity. Yet in the early 1990s, when anthropologist Joel Robbins spent time in the community, he observed periodic rumors about the imminent Second Coming of Christ that sounded remarkably similar to ones among fundamentalists in the United States. These rumors, which betrayed a notable awareness of the outside world and were described colloquially as "world news," predicted Christ's return on grounds that the pope was the anti-Christ, the European Union was the harbinger of a world government, turmoil in the Middle East signaled the end times, a new world order was in the making, and Satan was behind the universal product code and the spread of ATM machines. Investigation traced the rumors through local networks among the villagers and their pastor to several outside sources, including a New Zealand–based evangelist who had become popular in Papua New Guinea and who, in turn, had been heavily influenced by the American writer Hal Lindsey, author of the best-selling *Late Great Planet Earth*. "Theirs is a globalizing apocalypticism," Robbins says, "in which heaven is a place where everyone participates fully in what the Urapmin imagine is Western culture."[104]

In Belem, a city of 1.3 million in northern Brazil, the effects of globalization have been primarily to create a class of low-wage service workers uprooted from their rural origins. The region remained relatively isolated until the Belem-Brasilia highway was built in the 1960s. As the national government sought to integrate the region into the global economy, iron, timber, ranching, and hydroelectric power drove subsistence farmers and agricultural workers to move to the city, causing its migrant population to swell and the shantytown population to grow between four- and eightfold. Historian R. Andrew Chesnut studied the area in the early 1990s to see how these changes had affected the residents' religious practices. He found that Pentecostal churches were most abundant in the poorest neighborhoods and that the members of these congregations were mainly women who worked as domestic servants and men unemployed or employed as security guards, janitors, or day laborers. Without health care or traditional family networks, the members were especially drawn to the healing services the churches offered.[105]

These examples from Papua New Guinea and Brazil provide stark reminders that globalization not only connects people in otherwise isolated areas to the wider world but also interacts with local conditions to benefit some and dislocate others. For many people in the world's poorest countries the influence of world markets began in the nineteenth century and transformed local subsistence economies into export sectors. Living conditions were thus increasingly dependent on the vicissitudes of the global economy. Abrupt declines in demand during times of war, failures to maintain prices against competitors elsewhere, and such natural calamities as droughts and cash crops being devastated by disease all contributed to economic difficulties that could not easily be overcome by more general processes of globalization. Religious patterns that may have arisen with colonization and in more prosperous times have been affected accordingly. Immiserating dislocation has created new challenges to which religious practices have had to adapt.

The Ewe in southeastern Ghana illustrate the complex ways in which shifting fortunes in the global economy shape the social conditions in which both local and transcultural faith communities function. The first Christian mission to the Ewe was established in 1847 by German Pietists. Although the area had already been influenced by European slave traders in the seventeenth century, its role in the world economy increased significantly in the final decades of the nineteenth century as trading companies bought cash crops, such as cotton and cocoa, from local wage laborers and in turn offered them European commodities. Cocoa exports proved increasingly profitable and until the 1940s permitted many of the Christian converts to purchase commodities unknown to previous generations and in this way to forge a strong symbolic connection between ideas about Christianity and prosperity. World War II severely interrupted the international trade in cocoa, and after the war a devastating plant disease brought cocoa cultivation nearly to a halt. When anthropologist Birgit Meyer studied the region in the early 1990s, the Ewe were experiencing severe poverty that contrasted sharply with the stories of better times in the past and with the lifestyles of elites in the nation's capital. Although cocoa exports were rising, two-thirds of the Ewe lived in poverty, more than twice the rate of those in urban areas. Christianity no longer provided credible hope of material gain as it had when missionaries and trading companies cooperated to draw producers into the cocoa market.

Christianity nevertheless flourished among the Ewe in the 1990s. Pentecostal churches were especially popular. They attracted young educated people and middle-aged women, both of whom were least protected economically by traditional patriarchal and gerontocratic social relationships. Material goods were common topics at the church services and prayer meetings that Meyer observed. Yet the relationship of faith to commodities was ambivalent. On the one hand, prayer raised expectations that God would provide goods or money—and some expectations were fulfilled as checks came from relatives and supporters in Europe and the United States. On the other hand, prayer protected people from being overcome by the demonic powers assumed to reside in material goods and from the broader wiles of Satan, who was waging a desperate struggle against God for control of the world. The world at issue was not merely an abstraction but the literal world of which church members felt very much a part. The Pentecostal pastors had often been trained abroad, used "global" and "worldwide" in naming their churches, described their congregations as being part of a global movement, and preached often about the political and spiritual state of the world.[106]

Pentecostalism among the Ewe was thus both a response to globalization and a means of reinterpreting and gaining control over it. For those to whom integration into the global economy had brought little in the way of material gain, Pentecostalism provided hope of divine intervention and a perspective from which to be critical of people who foolishly spent scarce resources on consumer goods. In rejecting and literally demonizing such commodities as jewelry, televisions, and Western clothing, the pastors encouraged an ascetic lifestyle that was conducive to self-sufficiency. As representations of a global market over which the Ewe had no control, commodities were rightly perceived as dangerous items.

Through the preaching and prayer services in which they participated, church members gained a way of understanding these dangers and acquiring control over them. At the same time, the Pentecostal churches were linked to the rich countries from which these goods came and benefited from being part of a worldwide movement.

Similar developments are evident in rural China, where faith healing has proven attractive in the absence of adequate health care and isolation from government monitoring has made it possible for so-called underground religious movements to flourish. Although Bibles and videos of U.S. religious television programs are far less available than in Ghana or Papua New Guinea, Chinese farmers and villagers are aware of the modernization taking place within China and have often been exposed to Christianity through indigenous churches and foreign visitors. The resulting religious movements produce innovative interpretations of Christian teachings under entrepreneurial local leadership. The Three Grades of Servants movement in Henan Province, for instance, emerged in the late 1980s and combines predictions of Christ's return to earth with heavy emphasis on the divine powers of the movement's leader. Another movement, Lightning from the East, was founded in 1990 and teaches that Jesus has returned as a Chinese woman. Both movements have attracted considerable attention not only among rival groups within China but also among Western missionary organizations and in the international press.[107]

The broader implication of the immiserating dislocation argument is that globalization often aggravates or ignores the worst suffering of many people around the world, meaning that religious organizations that claim to care about suffering have a role to play in criticizing the harmful effects of globalization and finding ways to channel resources from the rich to the poor. Trade and communication give religious leaders from the United States opportunities to interact more often and more easily with fellow believers in other parts of the world. Yet these contacts are far different from those inspired by a new Starbucks franchise. It is the underlying values of religion that also matter. The globalization of U.S. Christianity is less concerned with markets than with spreading the gospel and addressing human needs. Whether suffering is exacerbated by globalization or unaffected is less the issue than the fact that it remains widespread. The central point for religious leaders and policy makers, as economist Nancy Birdsall writes, is thus that "the global economy needs the civilizing hand of appropriate intervention if we are to see a reduction in global poverty and increased income convergence across countries."[108]

The occasional book or article that focuses specifically on globalization and religion usually approaches the topic as if it were part of the modernization story that emerged in the nineteenth century. As time progresses, religion becomes more rational, this-worldly, ascetic, and compatible with capitalism. Except for the view that religious people now think of themselves as citizens of the world, the story could have been written without specific consideration of globalization at all.[109] I have taken a rather different perspective here. I have emphasized evidence that shows in concrete ways how international flows of people, information, goods, and money have increased over the past quarter century. This evidence provides a tangible sense of what globalization is and how it might affect the relationships among people in places separated by distance. I agree with scholars who argue that these changes, while considerable, are by no means the first instances in history of cross-cultural contact and that they did not occur as an emanation of some ineluctable economic process. They happened because government planners in rich countries began formulating free trade policies at the end of World War II, altered monetary policies and set up international finance organizations (such as the International Monetary Fund and World Bank) in the decades that followed, and used diplomatic pressures to open markets. The global integration of people and places happened as well because of technological developments reducing the cost of travel and communication and because of wars and regime changes that drove people from their homes.[110]

Although the increasing connections that constitute globalization can be summarized fairly easily, their consequences are more complex. To sort out the effects that bear most directly on religion, I have suggested that we think about four broad categories: global monoculture, glocalized diversity, beneficent markets, and immiserating dislocation. For each of these, scholars have sometimes posed sweeping generalizations that are so implausible as to defy logic, but hard evidence has also been produced to test the limits of these assertions and to show how they may pertain in specific settings. What I have emphasized is that globalization has no singular effects that lead to simple conclusions about religion in general or American Christianity in particular. Yet globalization does forge direct and indirect links between people in different countries, and these connections serve to shape and facilitate the ties between U.S. Christians and communities abroad.

The idea that globalization is creating a worldwide set of standardized norms and practices is, on balance, less useful for understanding the transcultural processes in which religion is embedded than its prominence in the scholarly literature might suggest, although it does remain helpful. Where this argument provides insight is in the possibility that international communication within global Christianity is easier when more of the world speaks the same language and, for that matter, sees one another more frequently, consumes the same music, or attends the same conferences. The fact that English has become at least a second language in many parts of the world is particularly important for understanding the international activities of U.S. churches. Homogenization of other kinds, such as dress and styles of worship or beliefs about the Holy Spirit, are also likely to increase the sense among widely scattered congregations that they share a common destiny and bear responsibility for one another. These similarities of belief and practice may be further reinforced by common participation in consumer markets. To the extent that these uniformities are present among Christians in different countries, the idea of a flat earth composed of notable affinities makes sense. The global reach of U.S. Christianity is thus facilitated by the fact that people elsewhere speak English, eat at McDonald's, and watch Benny Hinn on television.[111] Religious leaders also express concerns about the spread of consumerism and the role of globalization in encouraging ministries that focus too much on prosperity and success.[112] In other respects, though, the global monoculture thesis proves limited. Conceived properly, it applies mainly to elites who have reason to imitate one another or conform to the same expectations. Scientists, government officials, and leaders of transnational corporations would thus conform to common norms to a greater extent than rank-and-file Christians living in Idaho or Zambia. The organizational forms that result from imitation and competition among elites may resemble one another superficially but be quite different in substance. For instance, the argument that immigrant groups in the United States develop a common congregational style of organization has been challenged with evidence showing high variability among immigrant groups.[113] Even among governmental units and businesses, research shows distinct national patterns instead of across-the-board homogeneity.[114]

The view that globalization preserves or increases local diversity is helpful because it acknowledges the persistence of regional, ethnic, and religious variations in the face of outside influences and thus gives religious leaders reason to think their outreach programs are not simply destroying local traditions. It is even more helpful in illuminating the fact that these traditions nevertheless respond to and are thus influenced by contacts with the wider world. Studies of these influences on religious practices in developing countries show that straightforward arguments about an American gospel being exported transnationally are too simple. Yet to deny these external influences is also simplistic. Globalized Christianity takes different forms that reflect its particular locations, but its local manifestations include preaching styles learned at a seminary in Dallas or by viewing American televangelists, music combining local lyrics with imported acoustical accompaniment, and buildings constructed with the assistance of foreign visitors or foreign funds.[115] Where observations that simply celebrate the fact of diversity fall short is in revealing much about why particular beliefs and practices emerge. Diversity is the occasion for choice, and choice in turn is shaped by structures of power and wealth. With easier global communication, the choices people make in one location are increasingly influenced by relationships with such structures elsewhere. If a well-heeled congregation in Illinois sends visitors to Central America to locate pastors who merit its assistance because they have a sufficiently entrepreneurial vision of the kind valued in Illinois, that is an example of such influence.

The claim that globalization draws people into beneficent markets that enhance their productivity and raise them from poverty is neither as true as so-called neoliberal supporters of free trade suggest nor as false as antiglobalists believe. The evidence certainly does not support the view that globalization benefits everyone. This argument nevertheless highlights the fact that integration into the global economy does provide new opportunities for some segments of the population in many parts of the developing world. In the process, whole communities are sometimes elevated marginally from abject poverty into jobs that provide meager wages sufficient to purchase basic consumer goods. The globalization of U.S. Christianity involves responding to these new opportunities by partnering with indigenous churches, inviting pastors to conferences, sending short-term mission teams, and selling religious videos and films. Where the beneficent-markets perspective falters is in failing to recognize that globalization spreads information more rapidly and to much larger numbers than it spreads wealth. Thus, the most likely consequences of globalization include rising awareness of goods and opportunities that are enjoyed elsewhere but are probably out of reach. It is not surprising that religious organizations respond to these rising but frustrated expectations by emphasizing economic success, moral discipline, and possibilities of divinely provided prosperity. In addition, global economic integration involves ties that combine religion with business, as in the case of business leaders serving on church boards, pastors making money from international tourism, and faith-based humanitarian organizations starting micro enterprises.

The argument about dislocation and immiseration emphasizes the other side of the coin. While globalization increases opportunities for employment in the tourist industry or opens markets for cheap goods produced by minimum-wage workers in developing countries, these opportunities are always limited. Others are left behind, and yet they too are affected by globalization through heavily filtered information about prosperity elsewhere or through free trade agreements that weaken local governments or discourage them from providing social services. The Urapmin example in Papua New Guinea illustrates the fact that globalization has religious implications well beyond those populations that are incorporated directly into international trading networks. In communities unaffected by the global economy there may be vivid awareness of having been passed by, with the imagined benefits of globalization being even greater than those realized elsewhere.[116] Christianity is easily associated with these imagined benefits and sometimes spreads easily, with no direct intervention from Western churches or missionaries, fueling hopes that something like the prosperity of the West will come with Christ's return, if not sooner. Similarly, the growth of healing ministries and of churches emphasizing deliverance from evil in the shantytowns of Rio de Janeiro, Cape Town, and Accra cannot be understood apart from these wider social and economic consequences of globalization. Just as possibilities for market growth encourage religious organizations to support lending programs to micro businesses, the realities of continuing—and in many instances, deepening—poverty influence the planning of missionaries and faith-based relief organizations.

At the local level where people live and worship, globalization is thus experienced less as some abstract agglomeration of dense international networks and more as the gradual and perhaps accelerating awareness of a rich world outside their own that is at once appealing and alarmingly alien. The identity of that foreign world may be the affluent village in the next valley or the rising middle class in the capital city of one's country. It may be symbolized by a Dutch missionary or an evangelist from England. It is even more likely to be the United States. In example after example, anthropologists (including ones from other countries) find evidence of the global reach of U.S. culture and religion. The missionaries bring American radios and Bibles, the television stations broadcast American films, and the visiting evangelist from the United States helps raise money to build the new church. It becomes hard to disentangle the Christian message from images of U.S. wealth and power.

Considering the globalization of religion in the larger context as I have done here underscores the importance of not viewing the future of global Christianity simply as a function of demography. Although the demographic center of gravity is shifting to the global South, the organizational and material resources of global Christianity remain heavily concentrated in the more affluent countries of North America and Europe. The one cannot be disconnected from the other. The spread of English is again an instructive parallel example. Although approximately four times as many people in the world speak Chinese as English, economists and ethnolinguists argue that the global power of English is far greater than the global power of Chinese. For instance, one estimate of so-called Gross Language Product (which values languages according to their economic role) places English ahead of Chinese by approximately eight times, with Japanese being the second-most powerful language, followed by German and then Spanish.[117] Like language, religions also depend on the resources of the countries in which they are located.

Bernice Martin provides a useful observation that underscores the central argument I have tried to make here. "Global capitalism," she says, "mediated through high level political and economic choices made by the big players in the geopolitico-economic game, has set the structural limits but does not minutely determine the range of responses to them."[118] The structural limits to which she refers can be conceived of as pathways of influence governed by guiding expectations and serving as conduits through which resources flow that provide opportunities as well as constraints. The influences along these pathways travel in both directions. At one end, it is true, as Martin suggests, that "persons with real power of agency" choose creatively among the opportunities and constraints with which they are faced. At the other end, it is equally true that organizational leaders make decisions about how to deploy their resources in hopes of assisting their counterparts. When these leaders are the heads of religious organizations in the United States, their actions explicitly and implicitly take account of the influences that accompany globalization. These are the global contexts in which U.S. Christianity is linked to the wider world.

CHAPTER 4

The Evolution of Transnational Ties

Changing Patterns of Social Organization

The fact that churches in the United States are increasingly linking themselves with people and programs in other countries is not surprising, given the nation's prominence in world trade and communication, as well as the teachings of Christianity itself, which from the start encouraged the religion to span borders. Yet the American efforts are recent enough that their history can be traced and the mechanisms through which they were established can be examined. It took ingenuity in the nineteenth century to connect local churches in Connecticut, New York, Tennessee, and Kentucky with programs on the opposite side of the globe. Organizations had to be invented and, as conditions changed, reinvented. If we are to understand the current global outreach of American Christianity, we must pay particular attention to how these organizational mechanisms have evolved.

All transnational endeavors—multinational business organizations, overseas military campaigns, diplomacy, missionary and humanitarian programs—share two central challenges: distance and difference. Distance increases costs and makes coordination more difficult. Difference is marked especially by the cultural and language barriers that have to be overcome or circumvented for relationships to be established. The literature on globalization emphasizes distance and difference, holding that both are less important now than in the past and that their reduction is the main reason for increased trade and communication. In this view, globalization can best be understood as a result of air travel replacing steamships and satellite communications replacing the slower transmission of telegraph and telephone messages through transoceanic cables. The world has literally shrunk to the point that business can be conducted instantly across great distances and without concern for cultural barriers.

But distance and difference pose obstacles that require more than technological solutions. Dissolving distance and difference also necessitates social organization. An army deployed to the other side of the world can stay in contact with its central command through computers and satellite phones, but it still has to be deployed, and deployment involves organization. So it is with transcultural evangelistic and humanitarian efforts. They are affected—but not determined—by technologies of travel and communication. It makes a difference that a missionary can fly to Johannesburg in less than a day instead of spending a month going by ship. The fact that a relief worker can e-mail her home office in a few seconds, rather than sending a letter and waiting for a reply to come several months later, is surely significant. Yet the increasing speed of travel and communication also implies changes in how a mission board or relief agency is organized and in how a local congregation decides to administer an overseas ministry.

Were it simply a matter of conquering distance and difference through technological innovation, we would have to say that globalization may have quickened the pace of change but is otherwise a process that has been taking place for a long time. When Britain's William Carey drafted his *Enquiry* in 1792, he was keenly aware of the impediments that distance and difference presented in carrying the gospel "among the heathen." He noted "their distance from us" and "their barbarous and savage manner of living." Carey nevertheless considered these impediments increasingly surmountable by new technology. "Whatever objections might have been made on that account before the invention of the mariner's compass," he wrote, "nothing can be alleged for it with any colour of plausibility in the present age."[1] For him, the mariner's compass was as much of a breakthrough as aviation and e-mail were for later generations of missionaries.

When the first American missionaries actually set forth to work in foreign lands, it was not so much technology as it was social arrangements that became the critical issue. Two decades elapsed between Carey's *Enquiry* and missionaries going abroad from the United States. Adoniram Judson and Ann Haseltine Judson arrived in Burma in July 1813. The journey began in the summer of 1810, when the Judsons and several others decided they wanted to go abroad as missionaries. The first leg of the journey involved a trip to England to request support from the London Missionary Society. The ship was captured by a French privateer and Adoniram Judson was taken prisoner. He arrived back in the States four months later, still with no support. It took until February 1812 to raise money for the next trip. This was a four-month voyage to India. When he and his new wife arrived, the British East India Company denied them permanent residency. They found another ship and, after surviving a monsoon in the Bay of Bengal, made their way to Burma, where Judson devoted himself to learning the language and translating the Bible. He made his first convert six years later.[2] Social organization was involved at every step—from the group that first inspired Judson to think about becoming a missionary, to his failed efforts to solicit support, to the agency that eventually sponsored him, to the political constraints that forced him from India to Burma.

The principal challenge that the first wave of American church leaders faced in launching international ministries was establishing a program that could function effectively on a strictly voluntary basis. Prior to this time, Christian missionaries had usually been on the government dole. To send them without such support required a new breed of organization. A mechanism was needed that would, on the one hand, have sufficient legitimacy with ordinary churchgoers to secure their financial support and their assistance in recruiting personnel and, on the other hand, be capable of getting their money's worth from a frontline worker thousands of miles away. Building and fine-tuning this mechanism occupied much of the nineteenth century. It relied heavily on the authority and organizational structures of major Protestant denominations. By the early decades of the twentieth century, these structures had become, in East Asia scholar John K. Fairbank's memorable words, "the first large-scale transnational corporations."[3] Still, there was room for additional overseas religious activity, and a second wave of innovation responded to this challenge, still grounded in principles of voluntary organization but making use of entrepreneurial leadership and closer ties between donors at home and workers abroad. World War II ushered in a new era that added another layer of innovation involving a combination of voluntary and government-funded relief and development activity. Yet another innovation took place after the war as television broadcasting, air travel, and trade made it increasingly possible for entrepreneurial preachers and congregations to have closer ties than ever before with communities in other countries. The recent globalization of American Christianity has been effected by utilizing all these organizational models. Tracing these changes will reveal how the present international ministries have drawn on lessons from the past and what is truly distinctive about the current patterns of organization.

THE RISE OF DENOMINATIONAL BOARDS

Alexis de Tocqueville's famous observation about Americans' proclivity for voluntary associations is the best starting place for considering the organizational basis from which American Christianity began to diffuse in the nineteenth century. "The Americans," Tocqueville wrote, "make associations to give entertainments, to found seminaries, to build inns, to construct churches, to diffuse books, to send missionaries to the antipodes; in this manner they found hospitals, prisons, and schools. If it is proposed to inculcate some truth or to foster some feeling by the encouragement of a great example, they form a society."[4] The first overseas Christian workers from the United States were in fact volunteers who were voluntarily financed and sponsored by a voluntary association. The body that sent them—the American Board of Commissioners for Foreign Missions (ABCFM)—was in many ways the quintessential voluntary organization. Founded in 1810, it became enormously successful at mobilizing and supporting evangelistic and benevolent endeavors. By the time Tocqueville visited the United States in the 1830s, the ABCFM had become one of the largest—if not the largest—of the many voluntary organizations he observed. By 1835 it had raised more than $1.4 million, not counting in-kind donations of clothing and bedding; printed and distributed some ninety million pages of tracts and other religious material; opened sixty-three overseas mission stations with 311 staff members; and initiated 474 schools for upwards of 80,000 pupils.[5] This was an achievement on a much larger scale than even its most optimistic founders had imagined possible a quarter century earlier.

The ABCFM set a pattern for U.S. religious activities that was not only distinctive but also differed from the features Tocqueville considered most characteristic of American voluntarism. Churches, prisons, hospitals, and schools generally arose in local communities, served those communities, and capitalized on their affinities. They reflected patterns of association rooted in kinship and proximity and on a scale only somewhat larger than barn raisings and social clubs. In contrast, the ABCFM drew support from scattered locations in numerous states and served quite dissimilar communities all over the world. It is thus instructive to regard it not simply as an example of American voluntarism but to examine more closely why it developed the organizational structure it did and why this structure has continued to play a significant part in the global reach of U.S. Christianity.

As its name implied, the American Board of Commissioners for Foreign Missions was a formal organization, an authorized and authorizing board that commissioned U.S. Christians to engage in overseas ministries. It was officially constituted, held regular meetings, had an appointed corresponding secretary and an elected president and vice president, and was governed by a five-member executive group of prominent clergy and educators known as the Prudential Committee. The board itself consisted of corporate members who were elected and held voting rights; corresponding members who generally lived at a distance and did not attend meetings; and dues-paying honorary members. By 1835, there were eighty-four corporate members from seventeen states, twenty-two corresponding members from sixteen countries, and 1,453 honorary members.[6] The board was the central decision-making body through which all matters of financing and coordinating the activities of its workers abroad were channeled.

By the end of the nineteenth century, boards of this kind had become so common that it was difficult to imagine transnational religious work being organized in any other way. Yet the twentieth century was to demonstrate that there were other possibilities. Even at the start of the nineteenth century other means were being tried and still others could in retrospect have been reasonable options. For instance, a Christian minister wishing to serve abroad could have signed on with one of the growing number of trading companies to receive support as an overseas chaplain—a practice that had been in use for more than a century by England's East India Company. An aspiring missionary could have sought support from a wealthy donor, as the ABCFM itself did and as was to become increasingly true in the twentieth century. Because the first missionaries were recent graduates, their support might have been raised by a college or seminary, which were well schooled in soliciting donations and at the end of the century did become an important source of missionaries. Although congregations were small and poorly financed, a few of the wealthiest in Boston and New York could have supported a missionary single-handedly, judging from the size of their donations to the ABCFM a few years later. All of these were conceivable alternatives.

The question these possibilities suggest is not why just any organization became the means of sending out missionaries but why the particular pattern represented by the ABCFM emerged and especially why it developed on the scale it did. That scale stood squarely between two equally likely alternatives, one smaller and one larger. The smaller option would have involved individual congregations, colleges, seminaries, citywide associations of the kind that already existed in Boston and a few other cities, or statewide organizations that were also in existence. For numerous reasons, including the sheer abundance of these associations, the widespread precedents for organizing associations on this scale, and the greater difficulties involved in travel and communication on a large scale, smaller and more localized organizations would have been the likely option. Alternatively, the ABCFM might have emerged on a larger scale. Indeed, its leaders sometimes described it as a "national" organization, worked to make it such, and likened it to the London Missionary Society, which they understood to be a national society. In Europe, there were in fact national missionary societies in the Netherlands, Denmark, and several other countries, and in the United States there was certainly an awareness following the American Revolution of the value of conducting activities on a national scale. That it was possible to organize voluntary associations that could reasonably claim to be national became evident with the American Bible Society and the American Tract Society. Yet the ABCFM remained largely a regional organization.

Why an organization with even the regional scope of the ABCFM was necessary to promote overseas religious activities is not as obvious as might be imagined. At first glance, the most likely explanation would seem to be its ability to mobilize resources. As social scientists have been at great pains to argue, social movements arise not simply from need or passion but because of "resource mobilization." In this view, it may have been the need to raise funds on a large scale that most clearly dictated the necessity of forming a strong coordinating agency. After all, sending missionaries to the antipodes was not cheap. In a related view, it may also have been the need for publicity on which the first wave of truly transnational religious activity depended. Without publicity, how would missionaries have been recruited or support for them raised? Yet neither of these arguments provides an adequate interpretation of the historical facts.

The question of financing was certainly on the minds of the ABCFM's founders. In the frequently repeated accounts of its origins, five students at Williams College came together in 1806, calling themselves the Brethren, and pledged to go abroad as missionaries upon graduation if they could secure the necessary funds.[7] When the ABCFM originated

four years later, funds remained the obstacle to sending anyone overseas (which is what prompted Judson's trip to seek financing in England).
In 1811, the widow of a wealthy merchant died and left the ABCFM
$30,000, but the money was tied up in court because heirs challenged her
will. As Judson and his wife and four other prospective missionaries, two
with wives, made final preparations for their trip to India, a mere $1,200
of the estimated $8,000 to $10,000 needed for their travel and support
had been raised.[8] The shortfall was so severe that several of the board
members argued against sending missionaries at all and others proposed
that only two of the men and none of the wives be sent.

Funding of this magnitude was, in the context of the early nineteenth
century, a significant undertaking. A sum of $10,000 in 1810 would
equal approximately $120,000 today.[9] The average wage earner in New
England in the early 1800s made only $16 a week or about $800 a year,
meaning that spending $10,000 to send missionaries to India would very
likely have seemed an outrageous sum. Church coffers were sufficiently
strapped that the need to pool resources was one of the reasons Congregationalists had signed a Plan of Union with the Presbyterian church
in 1792 and renewed it in 1801. With the U.S. population moving westward, leaders of both denominations saw greater value in building
churches on the frontier than in sending missionaries abroad. Congregational and Presbyterian church buildings at the time usually cost between $1,500 and $2,000, with the most lavish seldom costing more
than $4,000, and many on the expanding frontier were being con-
structed for less than $1,000.[10] If significant in absolute terms, the cost
of overseas missions was even larger, therefore, in relative terms.

Yet the need for financing should not be exaggerated or considered the
only reason the early missionary activities took the form they did. The
amount needed proved neither as high nor as difficult to raise as initially
assumed. Within three weeks of their announced intention to sail, Judson
and his party of seven other India-bound missionaries received $6,000,
which proved sufficient for their journey.[11] The ABCFM notwithstanding, a large infrastructure for raising funds was already in place. By 1810,
there were nearly 1,000 Congregational churches in New England and
an even larger number of Presbyterian churches in the mid-Atlantic
states. A mere three dollars per congregation would have supported the
India trip. Moreover, dozens of benevolent organizations and missionary societies were already in existence as potential sources of funds. The
largest of these included the New York Missionary Society, organized in
1796; Northern [New York] Missionary Society, 1797; Missionary So-

ciety of Connecticut, 1798; Massachusetts Missionary Society, 1799; Standing Committee on Missions of the Presbyterian Church, 1802; Missionary Society of Rhode Island, 1803; Western Missionary Society, 1803; and Standing Committee on Missions of the Dutch Reformed Church, 1806. Many of these were flourishing organizations (for instance, the Missionary Society of Connecticut collected more than $2,500 in 1809 and ended the year with a balance in excess of $30,000), and, despite the fact that none sponsored missionaries abroad, all included foreign as well as domestic missions among their stated goals.[12] If the ABCFM was needed to raise money, therefore, it was not because other means were unavailable.

The same was true of the ABCFM's role as a publicity machine. It might be imagined that the early nineteenth century required interest in supporting missionaries to spread by word of mouth in the absence of other means, in which case a coordinating body sending speakers from church to church would have made a considerable difference. That possibility was one reason for the state associations that began to appear at the end of the 1700s and, indeed, had been anticipated in England by William Carey. The Baptist denomination of which he was a part provided a vehicle for disseminating his ideas. "If there is any reason for me to hope that I shall have any influence upon any of my brethren," he wrote, "it may be more especially amongst them of my own denomination. I would therefore propose that such a society and committee should be formed amongst the Particular Baptist denomination."[13] It was not the case, however, that information could be diffused only by a central agency within a denomination.

The early nineteenth century was literally awash in newspapers, journals, and periodicals of all kinds.[14] Two of these, the *New York Missionary Magazine* and the *Connecticut Evangelical Magazine*, were founded by their respective missionary associations in 1800 and, along with the New Hampshire *Piscataqua Evangelical Magazine* (1805), had already popularized the idea of missionary activities among thousands of readers by the time the ABCFM came into existence. The *Panoplist*, founded at Harvard in 1805, played a more direct role in the origins of the ABCFM itself by promoting the orthodox theology in which the emerging missionary movement was grounded and creating a network among its eventual leaders. When the ABCFM wanted a journal of its own, it simply took over the *Panoplist*, later renaming it the *Missionary Herald* in 1821. The role of publications in spreading information about missionary activities was well illustrated in 1812 when Harriet Atwood

Newell, one of the three wives who departed for India with Judson's party that year, died of consumption on the island of Mauritius at the age of nineteen. Word of her death spread at first from church to church, but soon her diary and sermons about her were being published in Boston, New York, and Philadelphia, and eventually in Maryland, Kentucky, Britain, and France. "For half a century after her death," writes historian Charles A. Maxfield III, "the leaders of the missionary movement praised her as a model, and the supporters of missions devotedly loved her."[15] The ABCFM became a powerhouse in religious publishing during the 1820s and 1830s, along with the American Tract Society and the American Bible Society, but its success in doing so reflected the foundations that had already been laid and on which it was able to build.

An argument that comes closer to making sense of the ABCFM's organizational structure—and yet falters on closer inspection—is that it succeeded by imitating the federated structure of American politics. "The structure of government served as an organizational model," writes political scientist Theda Skocpol, noting the division of sovereignty among national, state, and local units and arguing that "from early national times, American civil associations began to imitate this structure."[16] The ABCFM was a central body figuratively atop various state associations and linked to local ones. Yet there is no evidence that its leaders sought to imitate government in this respect or that the three-tiered division of labor was anything more than mere resemblance. State and local associations were not subjurisdictions of something larger, nor was the ABCFM either nationally inclusive or sovereign in the way the federal government was. The relationships among these various organizations was more the result of congregations establishing statewide but also municipal and regional organizations, and the ABCFM sometimes complementing and other times displacing these organizations and often bypassing them entirely in working directly with local congregations and auxiliaries.

More than anything else, it was legitimacy that the fledgling overseas missionary movement required, and it was in this role that the ABCFM served most ably. Although there were ample theological arguments for local congregations and denominations to be interested in evangelization, the need for specific reasons to initiate a major undertaking abroad was evident at every turn. In pledging to become foreign missionaries, the five students at Williams College who formed the Brethren declared it a secret society for fear they would be dismissed as zealots or fanatics. Secrecy, not publicity, was what they desired until some respected organization could give them credibility. Nor was this an idle concern. New England's religious divisions necessitated walking a fine line between those, on the one hand, who disputed the very idea of a distinctive trinitarian message and those, on the other hand, who favored emotional fervor over theological credentials. Even after the ABCFM was formed, prominent national leaders remained critical. "Would it not be better to apply these pious subscriptions to purify Christendom from the corruptions of Christianity," John Adams wrote to Thomas Jefferson in 1816, "than to propagate these corruptions in Europe, Asia, Africa, and America!" "These Incendiaries, finding that the days of fire and faggot are over in the Atlantic hemisphere," Jefferson replied, "are now preparing to put the torch to the Asiatic regions."[17]

The financial barriers that had to be overcome consisted less in sheer scarcity than in the fact that new activities necessarily required justification in relation to the more pressing needs of the day. When little more than 20 percent of the population was churched, spending money to support preachers in neighboring communities was typically more appealing than sending missionaries abroad. As settlers ventured westward into newly acquired territory, evangelizing Indians seemed more important than going to India. As one critic of the ABCFM observed, it seemed "designed to afford the means of exporting religion, whereas there was none to spare among ourselves."[18] By whatever means a new organization was to raise money, therefore, it had to legitimate its activities in ways that did not threaten these other priorities.

The voluntarism that impressed Tocqueville was actually a well-established network of vested interests that could deter new activities deemed lacking in legitimacy just as easily as it could initiate them. This was especially true in New England, where mutual aid societies had been flourishing for more than a century. One of the first—the Massachusetts Charitable Society—had been founded in 1672 to assist the select families who formed it. In 1724 a mutual aid society restricted to members of the Episcopal Church was founded and a few years later a charitable society for Irish immigrants followed suit. The principle on which these voluntary organizations were based was exclusion. Charity was restricted to members in good standing who paid their dues, did their share of the work, and in turn received help if their business failed or if they died and left a widow and children in need of support. Participation was face to face and reciprocity was the grounds for trust. Fire societies, Freemason lodges, merchants' clubs, mariners guilds, and craft associations all functioned on the same basis.[19] Religious congregations were no exception.

Pew rents and doctrinal tests kept churches in the hands of the faithful few. Missions expenditures were always small and went mostly to new congregations with strong ties to existing ones. It was much harder to imagine how mutual aid could include someone on the other side of the world.

Legitimation is typically in the details as much as it is in grand arguments or ideals. The ABCFM justified its fund-raising activities by showing that they were separate from and therefore not in competition with the regular tithes and offerings of congregations. William Carey had urged his readers in England to demonstrate this fact by contributing small amounts saved by tightening household budgets. "If congregations were to open subscriptions of *one penny*, or more per week, according to their circumstances, and deposit it as a fund for the propagation of the gospel," he wrote, "much might be raised in this way."[20] In New England the female cent societies that began in 1802 under the auspices of the Boston Female Society for Propagating the Diffusion of Christian Knowledge were used increasingly by the ABCFM to raise money. Within eight years of its founding, an estimated 250 local associations were soliciting contributions on its behalf. By 1830, there were more than 1,600. In addition, the ABCFM raised money by selling subscriptions to its magazine, encouraged local congregations to take up an annual special collection, sent traveling agents to canvass churches and sell its work to pastors, and published commendations in its magazine for women's auxiliaries that raised money by holding auctions and selling handmade bags, necklaces, pincushions, and belts. Fund-raising even included encouraging local groups to sponsor a "heathen child," much like the adopt-a-child programs that were to gain popularity among relief agencies a century and a half later. Apart from these specific activities, ABCFM leaders simply argued that their enterprise would succeed without harming other ministries. As evidence, they pointed to the London Missionary Society, modeled themselves after it, referred often to themselves as its American counterpart, and cited its growth and apparent benefits for its sponsoring congregations. The same, they argued, would be true in America. Church members would be moved by the missionaries' example not only to provide a few pennies for an ABCFM auxiliary but also to "support the Christian minister who is exhausting his strength and expending his resources to advance *my* religious interests."[21]

Had it been free of all legal or governmental constraints, the ABCFM might have had less reason to evolve as a centralized formal organization, but its structure was in part determined by the fact that even voluntary associations exist within a political environment. As owners of property, cash, and other assets, churches were subject to state laws and judicial decisions and in some instances still received a portion of their support from taxes. Congregationalist leaders who formed the ABCFM frequently witnessed the courts' siding against them in disputes with Unitarians and stripping "exile congregations" of their assets. Initially, the ABCFM was merely a Congregational agency, but when the $30,000 bequest it hoped to receive was challenged in the courts, the board was forced to seek legal incorporation and thus became a freestanding and self-perpetuating organization with the right to govern itself and appoint its own members.[22] Henceforth, it was able to hold and invest the cash reserves it accumulated. As a legal entity, it was also able to hold property in some of the countries in which it established mission stations.

The ABCFM structure and the legitimacy of this structure were also a product of what might be called their institutional environment. Unlike mutual aid societies based entirely on locale, religious denominations provided one of the few structures through which larger networks of contact and obligation could be established. These networks were the means through which larger causes could be promoted. They were in fact an important contributor to the Great Awakening of the 1740s and 1750s and were reinforced both by that experience and by the American Revolution. The ABCFM was a product of these networks. Although Congregationalism favored local autonomy over denominational unity, the struggle of its orthodox evangelical leaders against Unitarianism led to greater recognition of the need for internal cooperation and to more vigorous efforts to institutionalize that cooperation. These efforts included initiating the *Panoplist* to disseminate orthodox trinitarian ideas, creating the General Association of Massachusetts in 1803 as a loose denominational structure among orthodox congregations, and founding Andover Theological Seminary in 1808 as a training center for evangelical clergy. The ABCFM used the *Panoplist* to publicize arguments for foreign missions and was officially constituted by the General Association of Massachusetts prior to becoming an independent organization; its leaders and first recruits had extensive ties to Andover. More than simply organizational tools, these institutions conferred legitimacy on the ABCFM and established it among the elites of New England society. At a time when only one out of every 1,500 people was college educated, nearly all of the ABCFM board and its missionaries were college graduates and most held advanced degrees. Its members soon reflected the same broad constituency involved in Andover, including leaders from Harvard, Yale, and Williams, and with experience in several of the largest statewide missionary societies. As an official representative of the Congregationalists' General Association, the ABCFM was positioned to negotiate as an equal with the London Missionary Society, enter into agreements with the Presbyterian General Assembly, and subsume the activities of state-level mission organizations.

Although the ABCFM was legally independent, both its legitimacy and its actual work was largely among Congregationalists. It aspired to be a national association but in practice was a denominational agency. Its strongest institutional relationships were with the General Association, with Congregationalist churches and auxiliaries within these churches, and with Congregationalist clergy and college administrators. Despite its fund-raising arrangements with Presbyterian and Reformed congregations, monthly lists of donors published in the *Panoplist* overwhelmingly suggest Congregationalist rather than Presbyterian or Reformed sources. Doctrinal differences certainly were important and became an increasing source of tension between Congregationalists and these other denominations. Perhaps to an even greater extent questions of ownership mattered, as became evident in disputes between the ABCFM and Presbyterian leaders about investments in mission stations in the United States.[23] In this respect, missions were like congregations, with buildings and assets to which legal claims could be made. Unlike the national associations that emerged to distribute Bibles and tracts or to promote temperance and combat slavery, therefore, missionary associations stayed more clearly within denominational lines and derived legitimacy from denominational leaders.

Once it had legitimated the idea of overseas missionary work, the ABCFM was then in a position to provide the other essential feature of such activity: coordination, which became the solution to distance and difference. At home, coordination consisted of channeling money from congregations, individuals, cent societies, and auxiliaries into a single account for use in supporting overseas missionaries and publicizing their work. Centralization reduced the likelihood of local or statewide organizations competing with one another or falling into disputes about priorities. The board's legitimacy defused concerns that monies were being spent unwisely. Above all, the board coordinated the commissioning of missionaries from start to finish: sending out speakers and publicizing missionary accomplishments to motivate potential recruits, using its ties with theological schools to ensure that the proper training had been undertaken, questioning prospects about their aims and theological views, formally licensing them, and holding them accountable once they were in the field. The board's overseas coordinating activities were equally important. Earlier efforts to sponsor overseas missionaries from Scotland, Germany, Sweden, and especially England were widely regarded as dismal failures. These early efforts resulted in few converts, included missionaries who failed to learn the appropriate languages, faced difficulties in recruiting qualified missionaries, ran into conflicts with trading companies, and were generally received with indifference by government officials from whom support was sought.[24] The London Missionary Society set a precedent for centralized voluntary coordination by an elected board. The ABCFM played a similar role in New England. It determined where a mission station should be opened and how it would be staffed, received regular reports from missionaries, maintained correspondence, authorized the extension or termination of each worker's support, and used its domestic network to generate this support.[25]

The pattern established by the ABCFM was widely imitated during the nineteenth century by overseas and domestic missionary organizations alike as well as by voluntary associations of all kinds. Within a few years of its founding, ABCFM leaders assisted in forming the American Bible Society and the American Education Society and lent their expertise to the American Tract Society and various Sunday school societies.[26] All of these organizations were governed by central coordinating boards who worked closely with local congregations and were even more successful than the ABCFM had been in transcending denominational barriers. By 1835, the American Sunday School Union was raising nearly as much money annually as the ABCFM, the American Bible Society's annual receipts had reached $100,000, and the American Tract Society, American Home Missionary Society, and American Education Society were each raising more than $80,000 annually.[27] By subsuming or expanding the work of local organizations, other centralized missionary societies emerged with structures similar to that of the ABCFM. In 1817 the United Foreign Missionary Society was commissioned by the General Assembly of the Presbyterian Church. This society was absorbed into the ABCFM in 1825 under somewhat strained circumstances and against considerable opposition, which led to the 1837 emergence of an independent Presbyterian Board of Foreign Missions. Other missionary organizations included the Baptist General Convention for Foreign Missions, founded in 1814; the Missionary Society of the Methodist Episcopal Church, 1819; the Missionary Society of the Protestant Episcopal Church,

1820; and the Foreign Missionary Society of the Evangelical Lutheran Church, 1837. These and similar organizations were able to draw on the expanding finances and membership rolls of their respective denominations. Presbyterians numbered approximately 220,000 in 1830 and grew to 250,000 by 1860. Baptists grew from 250,000 to one million in the same period and Methodists increased from 500,000 to two million.[28] Much of these organizations' work was confined to continental North America rather than being conducted overseas. The first Methodist foreign missionary, Melville Cox, departed for Liberia in 1832; during the next three decades missionaries were sent to Brazil, China, and India, with most of the Methodists' foreign missionary work coming after the 1880s. Baptist missionaries began work in China in 1836 and, through separately organized Northern and Southern societies, initiated work in Africa in 1846 and in Brazil in 1879.[29]

The appeal of a centralized coordinating board lay partly in the simple fact that it resembled the ABCFM structure and thus was more familiar and seemingly appropriate than something untried and untested. The board model in this distinctive form also resolved several of the key problems that any voluntary transnational organization would have faced. One of the most important was the need to have regular financial support for overseas workers. Although the various coordinating boards received occasional bequests from wealthy donors, it was essential that they be able to predict well in advance what their revenues would be. Typically, estimates of expenditures were approved a year or year and a half before the expenses were actually incurred. Advance planning of this kind made it possible to inform and commission new missionaries or tell existing ones what their budgets for schools and ministry would be. It was impossible to plan this far ahead, though, without knowing that contributions would arrive in a predictable flow. The key was having well-institutionalized relationships with hundreds of local groups, each of which encouraged its members to give habitually rather than on impulse and to meet whatever goals its leaders had pledged. Working with congregation-based auxiliaries gave the mission boards a significant infrastructure from which to solicit revenue in these ways. The related challenge was to staff a sufficient centralized organization to ensure that the work of fund-raising, recruitment, and administration was not left to chance. Although the finances needed to send a few missionaries abroad were negligible, the resources required to staff mission stations, open schools, and send out agents to canvass churches and seminaries for money and recruits were considerable. The larger the denominational base, the more it became possible to secure these resources without taxing the capacities of particular congregations. Having a well-oiled institutional mechanism for raising funds in a predictable fashion also dovetailed neatly with the idea that a missionary, once commissioned, should remain in the field for a long time. This idea was predicated on the fact that it had probably taken between five and ten years of education to train a desirable recruit and might take that long again for this emissary to learn the language and establish a successful mission station.

By the end of the nineteenth century, the number of U.S. Protestant missionaries in foreign fields had risen to 4,110 and approximately $5.4 million was being spent annually on their support. A list compiled on the eve of World War I showed that 128 Protestant missionary societies were engaged in overseas activities.[30] Nearly all of these societies were pyramidal structures with a single governing board at the top, well-orchestrated mechanisms for raising funds and recruiting personnel from local congregations, and a formal process for commissioning and supporting workers abroad and receiving reports from them. The number of societies had risen with the expansion and multiplication of their sponsoring denominations and with a greater emphasis on centralized national governance in many of these bodies.[31] The racial, ethnic, regional, and doctrinal divisions that H. Richard Niebuhr associated with denominationalism in general was evident in the proliferation of missionary societies as well. Examples include the foreign missionary-sending agencies of the African Methodist Episcopal churches in 1844, Reformed churches in 1857, Adventist churches in 1865, National Baptist churches in 1880, Christian and Missionary Alliance churches in 1887, Christian Reformed churches in 1888, Brethren churches in 1892, Nazarene churches in 1895, and Assemblies of God churches in 1914. "Denominations after 1850 were operating with new vigor in sponsoring mission personnel, managing mission stations and institutions, and organizing native churches," writes historian William R. Hutchison.[32] They sponsored missionaries willing to serve under ecclesiastical control and who could initiate congregations abroad that resembled those in the United States in liturgy and governance.

When American Catholics made plans to send missionaries abroad, they also formed an organization similar to the Protestant boards. The Catholic Foreign Missionary Society of America, headquartered at Maryknoll, New York, came into being in 1911; in 1918 the first Maryknoll priests left for China. Two years later, the Foreign Mission Sisters of St. Dominic formed and a year later its first missionaries went abroad.[33]

Although Catholic missionaries had been deployed from other countries for centuries, the American pattern was distinct. Father James Anthony Walsh, who with Father Thomas Frederick Price played the pivotal role in initiating the Catholic Foreign Missionary Society, had worked extensively with sodalities and organizations for young men and women in Massachusetts and had served as diocesan director of the Society for the Propagation of the Faith. He was instrumental in securing independent legal incorporation for the Catholic Foreign Missionary Society and organized it under a centralized board composed of prominent Catholic clergy, professionals, and business leaders. Like his Protestant counterparts, which he considered his rivals, Walsh also initiated a magazine about foreign missions (with 100,000 paid subscriptions by 1923), raised money through special offerings and mission circles, took out loans, purchased property, and traveled widely in the United States and abroad to promote recruitment and coordination.[34] After a decade there were 240 Maryknoll missioners in China and by 1946 this number had grown to 562.[35]

Despite the proliferation of centralized boards, many of which were sponsored by larger denominations, it is notable that the ABCFM remained an influential voice throughout the nineteenth century and represented the continuing power of Congregationalism in the United States and overseas. "American Board officials were regarded—and regarded themselves," writes historian James Eldin Reed, "as the spokesmen for five hundred thousand Congregationalists. The potential political significance of this constituency was seldom lost on government officials." The board's leaders included the commercial and professional elite of Boston and were connected formally and informally with centers of power in New York and Washington. These leaders included Senator George Frisbie Hoar from Massachusetts, Secretary of State John W. Foster, and New York merchant William E. Dodge Jr. The board's foreign secretaries were in constant correspondence with the State Department and frequently offered their advice on foreign policy. In these respects, therefore, legitimacy was not simply an abstract notion or merely a matter of gaining cultural acceptance. Legitimacy meant that the missionary movement enjoyed tangible power.[36]

THE EMERGENCE OF INDEPENDENT AGENCIES

Denominational boards worked well as mechanisms for soliciting money and recruits from member congregations and for sponsoring overseas ministries on behalf of their denominations. Their strength lay in having the legitimate authority to monopolize recruitment and solicitation for the transnational work of their denominations. However, this strength was also their limitation. To clergy and lay leaders who thought their denominations were progressing too slowly with transnational work, the denominational boards represented more of an obstacle than a resource. As new ways of mobilizing and coordinating funds and personnel became available, religious leaders realized that these mechanisms could be harnessed. By the end of the nineteenth century, entrepreneurial leaders were already experimenting with setting up nondenominational and interdenominational mission programs. These independent agencies would flourish during the twentieth century and become an increasingly significant part of the global outreach of American Christianity after World War II. Although they typically operated under the supervision of a governing board that administered funds and commissioned overseas workers, they did so without depending on the institutionalized frameworks that linked congregations into denominational networks. The earliest of these included the China Inland Mission, founded in England in 1865 and recruiting its first missionaries from the United States in 1888; the Student Volunteer Movement, launched in 1886 and officially organized as a foreign missionary society in 1888; the Africa Inland Mission, which emerged in 1895; and the Sudan Interior Mission, organized as an independent board in 1898.

Historical accounts of these independent agencies emphasize their spiritual and cultural origins. These factors include the possible influence of disillusionment with liberalism in established denominations or with bureaucratic structures in general and the evangelistic fervor resulting from premillennial eschatology. Some treatments credit a sudden impulse in the churchgoing public to become missionaries, thus generating more recruits than could presumably be supported by the same exuberant church members. Great emphasis has also been given to the sheer magnetism of the charismatic leaders who founded these new organizations. As useful as these arguments are, they fail to illuminate the social arrangements that made it possible for belief, fervor, and charisma to take concrete shape in new patterns of transnational religious practice.

By the last third of the nineteenth century social conditions were quite different from the ones the first missionary planners had faced at the start of the century. The first wave of mission boards had successfully legitimated the idea that Christian workers could be sent abroad without damaging the domestic programs of American churches. Legitimacy was less of a critical factor for the second wave than finding effective mechanisms for further expansion. Four characteristics of the wider society made it possible to organize transnational programs in new ways. The first was a series of diplomatic treaties and trade agreements between the imperial powers of western Europe and governments in other parts of the world. These treaties and agreements opened vast areas with large populations among whom Christian works could be initiated. Although the relationships between missionaries and imperialism were seldom harmonious, these arrangements played an important role in overcoming the political barriers that previously inhibited such endeavors. A second factor was private philanthropy and the close personal relationships that religious leaders were able to cultivate with wealthy donors, especially in the increasingly populous and affluent cities. These sources made it possible to raise money through direct solicitations that did not depend to as great an extent on the small regular offerings provided by congregations within denominations. Third, the new independent agencies' leaders were able to harness more technologically advanced communication strategies and to travel more easily both at home and abroad. Finally, the founders of these agencies were institution builders who set up colleges, revival meetings, conferences, and especially Bible institutes as ways of recruiting and training missionaries at a fraction of the cost expended by the established denominational boards.

The role of changing political treaties and commercial alliances is evident in the fact that the term "inland" came increasingly to be included in the names of the new agencies. These organizations were able to work inland because diplomatic agreements now included more than the port cities that had formerly been central in mercantilist approaches to international trade. The influence of these agreements is well illustrated in the evolution of the China Inland Mission (CIM). As a result of the Anglo-Chinese War that ended in 1842, five port cities were opened to foreigners by the Chinese, and by the mid-1850s the Chinese Evangelization Society had begun sending missionaries from England to these cities. A second Anglo-Chinese War from 1856 to 1860 curtailed missionary activity but also resulted in missionaries coming under closer protection from the British government. When Hudson Taylor founded the China Inland Mission in 1865, its first missionaries were commissioned to the provincial capitals in hopes of using these cities as bases for work in surrounding areas. Eventually the signing of the Chefoo Convention of 1876 gave foreigners in all parts of China official protection under the emperor. After this date, CIM missionaries traveled more extensively and in larger numbers and opened new stations in four additional provinces.[37] By the time the first missionaries from the United States joined in 1888, CIM had approximately three hundred missionaries from Great Britain at work in all eighteen of China's provinces. By 1947, the North American branch had supplied over six hundred more.

Private philanthropy played an important role in nearly all the independent agencies that began in the last decades of the nineteenth century. That the China Inland Mission formed a North American branch at all was partly attributable to Hudson Taylor's initial reluctance to start one being overcome by generous donations during his trip to the United States in 1888. Dwight L. Moody's evangelistic meetings depended on such influential donors as J. Pierpont Morgan and Cornelius Vanderbilt in New York and John Wanamaker and Anthony Drexel in Philadelphia. The Student Volunteer Movement succeeded in part because of its leaders' ability to attract funding from John D. Rockefeller, Mrs. Cyrus McCormick, and other wealthy contributors.[38] In later years, the Laymen's Missionary Movement pioneered new ways of raising money, and after World War I the so-called great drives continued to move the hearts and pocketbooks of prominent benefactors.[39]

Being able to tap private philanthropy was a function both of the increasing concentrations of wealth that characterized industrial America and of urban networks linking prominent church leaders with potential donors. However, philanthropists' connections with the new wave of missionary activity are easily misunderstood. Research among the wealthiest donors of the Gilded Age has shown that less than a quarter of their giving went to religious causes of any kind and that congregations and church-related colleges received most of this beneficence. "Virtually all giving was directed toward the local community," write historians Merle Curti, Judith Green, and Roderick Nash.[40] Philanthropy's role in restructuring overseas ministries consisted less of wealthy donors bankrolling new programs, although they sometimes did, than of encouraging religious leaders to be more aggressive in soliciting funds, just as business leaders were in forging new markets.

Arthur Tappan Pierson's success in promoting independent nondenominational organizations to carry Christianity from the United States to other parts of the world provides one the best illustrations of the new resources that were becoming available for these purposes after the Civil War. Pierson was named after his father's employer, Arthur Tappan, the New York philanthropist and backer of revivalist Charles G. Finney. Tappan, whose pioneering credit-rating agency (precursor of Dun &

Bradstreet) put him in regular contact with leading business owners and public officials, was a prodigious networker and institution builder who played important roles in founding the American Tract Society, financing Oberlin and Kenyon colleges, launching the *New York Journal of Commerce,* and promoting the antislavery movement. Pierson's boyhood home was an apartment above Finney's Second Free Presbyterian Church in what was formerly the Chatham Garden Theater. Pierson imitated Finney, traveling widely and speaking to large audiences, and undoubtedly recognized Tappan's role in Finney's ministry. Pierson's first pastorates were in Connecticut, upstate New York, Detroit, and Indianapolis, where he tried with only modest success to develop evangelistic outreach and social ministries to the poor. He nevertheless established himself as a gifted preacher and teacher. In 1883 he moved to Bethany Presbyterian Church, a south Philadelphia congregation founded by retailer and philanthropist John Wanamaker, who shared Pierson's premillennial views and aspirations for an innovative urban ministry. Within a few years, Pierson had built the church's membership to nearly 1,500 and its Sunday school program to more than 2,500. He had also paid off the congregation's debt, launched a college, and earned fame for the congregation's work with children and the poor. Wanamaker's contributions and assistance in financing Christian publications helped, but Pierson also abolished pew rents, canvassed rich and poor alike for donations, persuaded people to give by initiating new programs, defined their giving as a badge of faith, and promoted projects that transcended denominational boundaries. As his interest in foreign missions grew, he appealed to the presbytery of his denomination to allow uneducated people to become missionaries. His request denied, he launched his own efforts, never reporting to a denominational committee again.[41] Pierson soon became a well-known international figure and frequent speaker at large evangelistic conferences. It was from one of these meetings that the Student Volunteer Movement emerged, sending out five thousand student volunteers as foreign missionaries from the United States by 1911 to "evangelize the world in this generation." Pierson also played roles in linking American and British missionary efforts, publicizing missionary work, and demonstrating that overseas efforts could be organized in ways other than through denominational boards.

Communication and travel increased the opportunities to organize transnational ministries in new ways, just as philanthropy and fundraising techniques did. The earlier denominational boards depended on corresponding secretaries to stay in contact with missionaries and on the relative proximity of congregations and regular contacts among clergy to solicit money and new recruits. By the end of the nineteenth century, leaders like Pierson and Moody were able to cross the Atlantic on steamers in relative comfort and travel by train to Chicago or California for conventions and revivals. Urban density and public transportation may have been even more important to the success of ministries that transcended denominations. Whereas the revivals of the 1830s had typically been held in small towns and open fields, Moody's took place in New York, London, Chicago, and other large cities. At the Chicago World's Exhibition in 1893, more than 130,000 people heard him speak in a single day.[42] The smaller evangelistic conferences to which Pierson and others spoke about foreign missions were themselves an innovative mode of communication. Students whose families sent them to elite colleges could also afford to spend part of their summers and holidays mingling with students from other campuses. The month-long conference that resulted in the Student Volunteer Movement was attended by 251 students from 89 colleges, including many from Princeton, Cornell, Dartmouth, Harvard, and other elite institutions. Its leaders drew on YMCA networks and local student fellowships to spread the word. After the conference, two Princeton students, Robert Wilder and John Forman, spent the year traveling to 162 colleges to promote the idea of volunteering for foreign missions. Over the next three years, 6,200 did volunteer and more than three hundred actually began serving abroad.[43] The Student Volunteer Movement continued hosting annual conferences until 1936, when the organization disbanded, but its influence continued after World War II, when the Inter-Varsity Fellowship commenced campus ministries in 1946 and began holding national missionary conventions in 1948.[44]

Although philanthropy and communication technology played important roles in denominational mission efforts, just as they did for the newer independent agencies, the two differed dramatically in methods of recruitment and training. The first denominational boards earned legitimacy for overseas programs by choosing exceptionally well-educated young men who could be emissaries on a par with the most highly trained clergy of their denominations. The student conferences that drew young men from Ivy League colleges continued this tradition, but such recruits were sometimes difficult to attract to the mission field and in any event, at a time when even high school graduation rates were low, their numbers were small. The newer independent agencies circumvented these problems by recruiting workers from all walks of life. Training was still necessary, both to provide the requisite biblical knowledge and as a means of screening potential applicants. However, the training provided was relatively short-term, inexpensive, and open to all. It was offered through Bible institutes. These organizational inventions were closely associated with foreign missions from the start. One of the first was the East London Institute for Home and Foreign Missions in 1872, founded by Irish revivalist H. Grattan Guinness at the encouragement of Hudson Taylor to train missionaries for China. By 1915 the school had processed 1,500 young men and women, including many who initiated ministries in China, Africa, India, and Latin America. An 1873 visit to the school by Dwight L. Moody is said to have been the inspiration for Moody's own institute in 1886. Meanwhile, leaders in New York City organized the Missionary Training College for Home and Foreign Missionaries and Evangelists in rented space at a theater in 1882; in 1889 the Boston Missionary Training School opened. By 1915, thirty-two of these institutes had been founded, and by 1929 twenty-eight more were established, with another forty-eight in existence by 1947.[45] The goal of these schools was not to duplicate the work of established seminaries but to produce "gap men," as Moody called them, or lay workers who could fill the space between clergy and the common people.

The typical Bible institute student paid about three dollars a week for room and board, received free tuition in return for cooking and cleaning, took morning classes taught by the founding pastor or his wife and perhaps a retired missionary, and did evangelistic work in the afternoons and on weekends.[46] Although many of the Bible schools offered certificates at the end of two years of training, few students stayed longer than a year. The schools were thus an efficient instrument for recruiting, training, screening, and sending missionaries into the field.[47] Their imprint was especially evident in the changing composition of the missionary force. In 1868 approximately half of all missionaries from the United States and Europe were ordained men. By 1910, about 30 percent were ordained men, 55 percent were lay women, and the remainder were lay men.[48]

During the first half of the twentieth century, independent missionary agencies grew and multiplied, although they remained relatively small compared to the still thriving denominational boards. New ministries included the Gospel Mission of South America, founded in 1923 as a nondenominational sending agency for independent Baptist and fundamentalist congregations; the Unevangelized Fields Mission in 1931 with missionaries in the Congo and Brazil; and the New Tribes Mission in 1942 for evangelicals serving previously "unreached" peoples. By 1936,

the China Inland Mission was sponsoring more than three hundred missionaries, the Sudan Interior Mission was supporting nearly two hundred, and the Africa Inland Mission had more than a hundred workers
in the field.[49] These organizations functioned much like denominational
boards in providing centralized mechanisms for administering and coordinating the work of missionaries abroad. However, they transcended
denominational lines by recruiting through student networks, summer
institutes, Bible schools, conferences, and revival meetings that attracted
participants from a broad spectrum of denominations. With relatively
little training, these recruits then drew on family members and friends in
their home communities for financial support. "Stepping out on faith"
in this way relieved the agencies of long-term financial obligations to their
missionaries and gave the overseas workers themselves a strong incentive
to demonstrate their worth to family and friends.

THE ERA OF FAITH-BASED NGOS

Nongovernmental organizations (NGOs)—another distinct mechanism
for spanning the distances and differences involved in international
programs—are largely a twentieth-century invention, although they
have roots in the nineteenth century. The first usage of the phrase "nongovernmental organization" appears to have been in 1945, when the
United Nations Charter acknowledged a consultative role for organizations that were neither governments nor member states. This recognition
came in response to lobbying by the leaders of prominent U.S. private
voluntary organizations, many of which were associated with one another through the Union of International Associations, formed in 1910.
Thus, by definition, NGOs are independent of government; yet, and perhaps ironically, the very reason for calling them NGOs is that they typically work closely with government agencies and receive legitimacy
from government charters. NGOs usually adopt an administrative structure that resembles government bureaus and often play a role in distributing government funds. Governments, for their part, sometimes initiate
NGOs or bring influence to bear on established NGOs to promote government policies.[50]

Many of the organizations that came to be known as NGOs were initiated by religious groups and have continued to articulate a religious
vision among their goals. Examples include such well-known organizations as Catholic Relief Services, Church World Service, and World Vision International. These faith-based NGOs resemble denominational

boards and independent missionary agencies in being specialized, centrally administered, and separately incorporated. Just as did denominational boards and mission agencies, faith-based organizations often work with congregations, other local chapters, or individual benefactors and thus are sometimes called membership organizations. They differ from the majority of nineteenth-century transnational religious organizations in focusing more of their attention on hunger, poverty, and emergency relief than on evangelization alone. Another important difference is that many faith-based NGOs draw a significant share of operating revenue not from private donors but from government grants and subsidies. They reflect the fact, on the one hand, that government has become an increasing source of funding for international relief and development activities and, on the other hand, that faith-based organizations have become increasingly involved in such activities. Although the lion's share of faith-based NGO funding continues to be from private sources, their relationships with government play an important role in shaping what they do and how they do it.

The origins of U.S. government funding of voluntary organizations are often traced to the Civil War, although missionary societies providing schools for Native Americans through support of the Office of Indian Affairs are an earlier example. From 1816 to 1830, for instance, the American Board of Commissioners for Foreign Missions received regular subsidies from the federal government in support of approximately three hundred ABCFM teachers in Native American territories.[51] During the Civil War, secular voluntary organizations such as the Women's Central Association of Relief and the U.S. Sanitary Commission sent clothing and medical supplies and provided nursing care for wounded soldiers under the supervision of the War Department. Through the efforts of hundreds of local chapters, the Sanitary Commission raised nearly $5 million in cash and collected another $15 million in supplies. Government support for the Sanitary Commission's work was relatively small but included shipping supplies to battlefield hospitals and constructing buildings for volunteers to care for wounded soldiers.[52] At the end of the war, leaders of the relief effort encouraged the U.S. government to become a member of the emerging Red Cross movement, and in 1882 the American Red Cross came into existence—a secular voluntary organization that would nevertheless provide a model for many religious organizations. During the Spanish-American War, the Red Cross received funds from the U.S. government, which at the end of the war mandated that the organization be radically restructured. Government funding was withdrawn, but the organization was required to report annually to the War Department and a fraction of its trustees were appointed by the U.S. president.[53] The organization's funding from government was thus short-lived, but the Red Cross movement did bring government and voluntary relief efforts into a closer relationship. This relationship, especially with the War Department, deepened as the country prepared for World War I. In 1917 a public official in Wisconsin who criticized the Red Cross and refused its request for a voluntary contribution was charged with espionage on grounds that doing so interfered with the success of the American military itself.[54]

This incident notwithstanding, relationships between the Red Cross and public officials prior to World War II mostly illustrated the continuing conviction that voluntary associations and government should remain clearly in their separate realms. In 1930 and 1931, President Herbert Hoover reluctantly supported legislation to make loans available to drought-stricken farmers, insisting that the "American Way" of handling problems was through such voluntary associations as the Red Cross. For their part, Red Cross leaders worried that Hoover's expectations would bankrupt local chapters and refused to be drawn into partnerships with government agencies.[55] Well before, Christian groups had also held divided opinions about providing humanitarian aid and cooperating with government to do so. By the 1850s, ABCFM leaders were taking different positions on whether the board's missionaries should attempt to ameliorate the conditions of indigenous people or simply preach to them. When the Sanitary Commission enlisted the support of countless church-based ladies' auxiliaries in its relief efforts in the 1860s, the United States Christian Commission favored a more evangelistic approach and repeatedly clashed with Sanitary Commission leaders.[56] In the 1890s, independent mission agency leaders debated whether to seek protection in China and elsewhere through appeals to U.S. officials or simply to steer clear of government help. Thus, it is not surprising that a new pattern of cooperation between government and faith-based international organizations was slow in developing and that it took unusual circumstances—namely, war—to bring this relationship into being.

Prior to World War II, humanitarian organizations seldom received government funding, and especially during the 1930s the Great Depression severely restricted even their ability to raise private donations. Nevertheless, a few relief and development organizations did initiate overseas activities. One of the organizations that worked internationally in these years and that would become increasingly active after World War II was the American Friends Service Committee, founded in 1917. Focusing on helping Quakers and other conscientious objectors perform alternative service during World War I, the American Friends Service Committee provided relief assistance in Russia and eastern Europe after that war and in the 1930s helped refugees escape from Hitler's Germany. The Mennonite Central Committee emerged formally in 1920 and served in similar ways, as did Adventist relief and disaster programs, which emerged in 1918 to assist church workers, missionaries, and members in need as a result of World War I.[57] With these exceptions, the international activities of U.S. humanitarian organizations focused almost exclusively on helping refugees and indigent immigrants resettle in the United States. During and after the war, these efforts expanded and the United States became increasingly involved in helping displaced persons in other countries as well. Many of the faith-based humanitarian organizations that would become major players in the wider world in subsequent decades came into being during this period.

Catholic Relief Services began in 1943 under the name of War Relief Services of the National Catholic Welfare Conference, a name it retained until 1955. Although Catholic organizations had provided relief to displaced persons and refugees during the Civil War and World War I and had originated collections for overseas aid in local parishes in 1941, the immediate impetus for Catholic Relief Services was President Franklin Roosevelt's plan to incorporate religious voluntary agencies into relief and recovery efforts in cooperation with the War Relief Control Board.[58] With Lutheran World Relief, Church World Service, the American Jewish Joint Distribution, and the American Friends Service Committee, Catholic Relief Services was part of a loose confederation called the American Council of Voluntary Agencies in Foreign Services.[59] As a participant in the National War Fund, Catholic Relief Services received $2.4 million to assist Polish refugees in Mexico and Palestine and other Catholic refugees and prisoners of war in Europe.[60] In 1945 the agency gained attention when a U.S. Army Air Corps B-25 bomber crashed into the Empire State Building, killing eleven women at the Catholic Relief Services offices on the 79th floor.[61] As the war ended, the agency helped nearly 100,000 displaced persons settle in the United States, distributed food to people affected by the partition of India and Pakistan, and in subsequent years worked in Albania, South Korea, and the Philippines. Relief aid continued during the Korean War, and following the 1954 partition of Vietnam Catholic Relief Services provided relief aid to nearly a million refugees.[62]

The Protestant relief agencies that emerged during and immediately following World War II engaged in similar activities. By 1944, the major Protestant organizations, along with the National Catholic Welfare Conference, had collected more than fifteen million pounds of clothing in cooperation with the recently established United Nations Relief and Rehabilitation Administration and were poised to play a major role in postwar redevelopment efforts. When President Harry Truman licensed private charities to distribute relief in occupied Germany in 1946, eight of the eleven organizations selected were religious, including the American Friends Service Committee, the Brethren Service Committee, the Christian Science War Relief Committee, the Church Committee on Overseas Relief and Reconstruction, Federal Council of Churches of Christ, Lutheran World Relief, the Mennonite Central Committee, and War Relief Services of the National Catholic Welfare Conference. These organizations were authorized to accept contributions for purchase and distribution of such items as powdered milk, sugar, soap, clothing, shoes, and medical supplies. Lutheran World Relief had been founded in 1945 to coordinate assistance for the approximately 20 percent of Lutherans worldwide who had been left homeless by the war. Church World Service began in 1946 through consolidation of the Church Committee on Overseas Relief and Reconstruction, the Commission for World Council Service, and the Church Committee for Relief in Asia. The new agency included representatives from the Federal Council of Churches of Christ, the Foreign Missions Conference of North America, the American Committee for the World Council of Churches, the United Council of Church Women, and approximately fifty Protestant denominations. As a counterpart to these largely mainline Protestant organizations, the more conservative National Association of Evangelicals, which had been founded in 1942, formed a War Relief Commission in 1944 to assist evangelical congregations in Europe. In 1950 this organization's name was changed to World Relief. Other agencies of similar vintage included the Episcopal Church Presiding Bishop's Fund for World Relief and the United Methodist Committee on Relief, both founded in 1940.[63]

These faith-based relief organizations made use of organizational patterns established by the earlier missionary agencies but added several important innovations. The pattern of utilizing local congregations as a network for collecting donations continued. Besides money, clothing increasingly became a significant part of the collection process. For instance, Catholic Relief Services initiated an annual Thanksgiving Clothing Appeal in 1950 through which it collected millions of pounds of clothing for emergencies. The more significant innovation was working cooperatively with government as recipients of government grants and contracts. Legitimated by the need for unity in wartime, cooperation with government consisted of not only operating under War Department regulations and licensing but also receiving government funds and relying on government bureaus to arrange for shipping and military protection. The other major innovation involved developing partnerships with congregations and parishes overseas. These partnerships were both possible and necessary because, unlike with missionary efforts, the recipients of their relief aid were often Christians in largely Christian countries or regions who had been displaced by war.

The most successful of the new 1940s-era organizations in terms of eventual revenue and programming was World Vision International, a ministry that combined evangelistic with humanitarian activity and at the start relied entirely on voluntary donations. The inspiration for World Vision began in 1947 when Bob Pierce, a young staff worker with Youth for Christ, traveled to China to hold evangelistic rallies. Pierce became burdened by the plight of destitute children, took photos and home movies of them, and sent the pictures home to churches in the United States, encouraging members to "adopt" one of the children. Contributions flowed in, leading Pierce to incorporate World Vision in 1950.[64] During and after the Korean War, World Vision continued its highly successful orphan-adoption program, using photos in Christian magazines, direct mail, and television advertisements to raise money. As the organization grew, Pierce's idiosyncratic leadership style came increasingly into conflict with the need for a more orderly administrative structure.[65] In 1963 Pierce suffered a nervous breakdown and in 1967 he resigned from World Vision.

The late 1960s and early 1970s were a time of retrenchment for the World Vision organization. Pierce's experiences in China and Korea had not only developed the organization's capacity to work in war zones but also given it a strong anticommunist orientation. During the Vietnam War, World Vision International and Catholic Relief Services focused a large share of their resources in South Vietnam, and, as public sentiment in the United States turned against the war, both organizations experienced difficulty raising funds. When the South Vietnamese and Cambodian regimes fell, the two organizations also suffered casualties and lost assets. Yet both organizations soon recovered. World Vision's efforts to search for and support Vietnamese boat people became a new focus for fund-raising. It increasingly decentralized its efforts, working through partnerships with semiautonomous World Vision offices in developing countries, and its activities shifted increasingly from evangelism and relief toward economic development and self-sufficiency.[66] World Vision International applied for its first government grant in 1975—over opposition from a few of its leaders, but this marked the start of the organization's increasing reliance on revenue from government grants.[67]

Data for 1981 show that Catholic Relief Services and World Vision International were among the largest of all nonprofit humanitarian organizations in the United States. With overseas aid expenditures of $319 million, Catholic Relief Services was the largest of all such organizations and was rivaled only by CARE, with comparable expenditures of $257 million. World Vision's 1981 overseas aid totaled $60 million, which placed it slightly ahead of the American Jewish Joint Distribution Committee's budget of $49 million and well ahead of Church World Service's overseas expenditures of $35 million and the Christian Children's Fund's figure of $32 million. Several other faith-based organizations also ranked high among all agencies concerned with international relief, development, and technical assistance. The Summer Institute of Linguistics had a budget of nearly $25 million. The Adventist Development and Relief Agency expended $15 million and Lutheran World Relief reported expenditures of $9 million.[68]

The same study documented the extent to which these organizations had become partners with the U.S. government. Seventy-two percent of Catholic Relief Services' overseas expenditures came from government sources—a proportion nearly as high as that for CARE (78 percent). Other faith-based organizations with high shares of government revenue included the Adventist Development and Relief Agency, 78 percent; World Relief, 55 percent; and Lutheran World Relief, 35 percent. In contrast, several of the faith-based organizations remained largely independent of government funding: for instance, World Vision International, 6 percent; the Summer Institute of Linguistics, 3 percent; and the Christian Children's Fund, none.[69]

The U.S. government's relationships with NGOs grew significantly during the 1960s and 1970s as part of the nation's broader effort to stabilize poor countries against communism. One of the main sources of this growth was Public Law 480, which was passed in 1954 during the Eisenhower administration as a Food for Peace program. PL-480 evolved from a means of distributing U.S. agricultural surplus to help victims of war and natural disasters into a program that purchased commodities and encouraged larger development projects, such as road building, school construction, and health improvement for mothers and children. World Vision International, Catholic Relief Services, Church World Service, and other faith-based NGOs became trusted allies for distributing food and administering other government-sponsored relief and development programs. Another important development was a series of legislative acts, beginning in the 1960s, to encourage closer relationships between the U.S. Agency for International Development (USAID) and private voluntary organizations (or PVOs), as nongovernmental relief and development agencies were called. As a result of these acts, government funding increased from approximately 10 percent of total PVO income between 1946 and 1953 to 20 percent in 1964 and 27 percent in 1973.[70]

RECENT PATTERNS OF TRANSNATIONAL ORGANIZATION

The major organizational forms established during the nineteenth and early twentieth centuries all remained active at the start of the twenty-first century. Indeed, the last two decades of the twentieth century witnessed significant growth in the activities of many of the earlier denominational boards, an increase in the number and variety of independent agencies, and dramatic expansion in the work of international faith-based NGOs. This growth was furthered by globalization, especially through increases in communication and economic integration, but it was also in large measure attributable to the organizational patterns that had been devised for managing the complex tasks of soliciting funds, recruiting personnel, and coordinating efforts spanning long distances and cultural differences.

Denominational boards continued to draw revenue from regular and special offerings and through mandated appropriations from local congregations. Mergers of smaller ethnic and regional denominations into larger national bodies facilitated the centralized tasks of these boards, but denominational activities were sometimes hampered by declining memberships and finances and in other instances by schisms and proclivities for greater congregational autonomy. In consequence, and because of different views about overseas priorities, the international work of denominational boards diverged, with some maintaining a strong emphasis on traditional missionary programs and others dividing their energies into more specialized activities, such as evangelism, relief, and advocacy.

The International Mission Board of the Southern Baptist Convention provides one of the clearest examples of a denominational board continuing and expanding the work it had initiated before World War II. The board's start was concurrent with the Southern Baptist Convention's founding in 1845; it was known as the Foreign Mission Board until the mid-1990s. In broadest terms, its goal is to take the Christian gospel to every part of the world. It pursues this goal primarily by helping start congregations in other countries, and it allocates some support for other ministries, including education, health, and relief. After decades of providing only general oversight of its missionaries, the board has also begun to coordinate these activities more closely to ensure that they do in fact result in church planting. In 2005 the board's annual operating budget was $283 million. Unlike faith missions that require workers to raise their own support, the board follows the traditional model of soliciting contributions from the denomination's 45,000 congregations and paying for missionaries' salaries and expenses from a centralized fund. Approximately half of the board's budget comes from a cooperative program, established in 1925, through which congregations send a specified portion of their proceeds to the central office, and the remaining half is received through a special collection in congregations known as the Lottie Moon Christmas offering. The board itself is similar to the ones mission agencies used in the nineteenth century, with an appointed board of trustees that meets six times a year and a full-time staff. The most important difference from earlier agencies is that managing more than 5,000 full-time foreign missionaries—a fivefold increase since 1955—requires multiple layers of executives and a staff of nearly five hundred in the home office. The board is also responsible for training and deploying approximately 30,000 short-term volunteers. Through its missionaries and volunteers, the board claims approximately 600,000 baptisms annually worldwide and assists in the work of nearly 100,000 overseas churches.[71]

Second in size only to the Southern Baptist program, the Assemblies of God World Missions, which began in 1914, maintains a similarly centralized structure that focuses on evangelism and church planting. With an annual budget of $181 million in 2004, the World Missions board supported more than 2,500 full-time missionaries—a fourfold increase since 1955—who served in two hundred countries assisting in the work of the denomination's 270,000 churches. Although the Assemblies of God emphasize the authority of individual congregations, the mission board served from the start as a coordinating agency for recruiting and raising support for the denomination's missionaries. As these efforts expanded, the board has added staff and placed increasing emphasis on financial accountability. Money is received through offerings at the denomination's 13,000 churches in the United States, and, although a small amount comes from corporations and endowments, the denomination has a strict policy against government grants. The board itself functions as an executive committee, composed of thirteen full-time directors who meet weekly and share responsibility for six regional departments, one multiregional department, and special offices for personnel, missionary services, relations with U.S. churches, and media advancement. Approximately 120 staff work in these various offices. At each of its weekly meetings, the executive committee makes approximately two hundred decisions, which range from major financial commitments to details involving the more than 1,300 children of missionaries. Although the board has approved service projects initiated by its frontline workers, its emphasis has remained on supporting missionaries who preach, evangelize, teach Bible classes, and assist in starting new congregations.[72]

A contrasting case is the Presbyterian Church (USA) whose international work is organized under its Worldwide Ministries division, which reports to the denomination's general assembly and spends approximately $40 million annually on overseas programs. This division, located at the denomination's headquarters in Louisville, Kentucky, employs a staff of approximately a hundred people whose primary responsibilities include sending people and resources to other countries and building relationships with partner churches. Overseas missions, though on a smaller scale than at their height in the 1950s, remain an important part of the denomination's work, with four hundred long-term and seventy-five short-term missionaries in the field as well as partnerships with approximately 165 overseas congregations and numerous international mission trips and study seminars. However, Worldwide Ministries also includes international programs for health, hunger, economic development, and disaster assistance. With an annual budget of approximately $6 million, disaster assistance is one of the most active of these programs. It works in thirty-two countries and ministers to refugees and asylum seekers in the United States as well. The other programs provide staff assistance and small grants to various medical and development projects, such as a mushroom production project in Cameroon and a women's poultry business in Uganda. The Worldwide Ministries division also engages in advocacy, which includes meeting with policy makers and providing action alerts and educational materials to the denomination's membership. Support for these ministries comes entirely from member contributions, about half through offerings received in congregations and about half through designated giving from individuals.[73]

The Division of Overseas Ministries of the Disciples of Christ supports multiple ministries similar to those of the Presbyterian board. The Division of Overseas Ministries was created in 1973, subsuming the work of the Foreign Christian Missionary Society, which had been formed in 1874, and the United Christian Missionary Society, which had emerged through a reorganization in 1920. In 1996, the division formally merged with the United Church of Christ's Board for World Ministries under the name Common Global Ministries Board, following a series of joint programs beginning in 1965.[74] Through the United Church of Christ's Congregationalist lineage, the Common Global Ministries Board is a successor of the American Board of Commissioners for Foreign Missions. The early work of that board continues in the Common Global Ministries' emphasis on appointing missionaries, coordinating missionary efforts, and providing them with financial support. Women's groups in congregations continue to play an important role in these efforts, just as the first ladies' auxiliaries did. As of 2005, the board sponsored approximately a hundred overseas missionaries. About half of the board's $10 million annual budget comes from annual Easter offerings in congregations and the remainder is from designated gifts and investments. Besides its missionaries, the board also sponsors an intern program, short-term people-to-people pilgrimages for volunteers, and a number of service projects. Like its Presbyterian counterpart, it has devoted major resources to disaster relief. The board has also invested heavily in HIV/AIDS treatment programs, refugee and immigrant resettlement, and economic development.[75]

A study of U.S. mission agencies showed that the overall number of denominational boards increased from 46 in 1900 to 87 in 1950, and then from 105 in 1970 to 115 in 2001. Although this growth was overshadowed by a larger increase in the number of independent agencies, denominational boards still accounted for 28 percent of all revenue spent on overseas missions in 2001 and 36 percent of all long-term missionaries from the United States.[76] Denominational officials also emphasize that new structures are being added to, and are sometimes replacing, older patterns. A Southern Baptist leader observes that his denomination's Women's Missionary Union is no longer as vital as it once was. The Women's Missionary Union worked well, he says, when Baptist women lived in small towns and rural areas where they attended small congregations with few ties to the wider world. The organization provided a study guide that women could read at meetings to learn about and pray for missionaries in some remote part of the world. "That was fine," he says, "until the culture changed and you could hop on a plane and be in another part of the world in eight hours." Women's Missionary Union membership, he says, is becoming "old and gray," and as a result the denomination is having to invent new ways of exploiting the links its members have or want with Christians in other countries. A Presbyterian leader speaks of similar changes. "Everybody wants to get on a plane and go overseas and solve people's problems," she says, adding: "Gosh, what a headache!" The reason she feels this way is that people in the United States think they can fly to Africa or Latin America and show them how corn is grown in Iowa or a clinic is run in New Jersey. She says their ideas usually show little understanding of people's needs or of programs that actually work. As she sees it, the challenge is harnessing this volunteer energy without letting it interfere with the board's professional efforts.

Denominations have responded to changing conditions and opportunities by encouraging innovation, forming partnerships, and decentralizing the missionary and humanitarian activities that fall under their auspices. Lutheran Church–Missouri Synod leaders formed the Association of Lutheran Mission Agencies in the mid-1990s to assist congregations or clusters of congregations in setting up new overseas programs. Each program is an autonomous 501(c)3 nonprofit organization that is recognized, but not controlled, by the denomination and thus permitted to solicit funds from Lutheran congregations, receive start-up advice, and participate in the denomination's health and pension plans. By 2005, seventy-five new programs had been started under this initiative. Similar endeavors launched by other denominations include the Mission Society of the United Methodist Church, the Presbyterian Order for World Evangelization, and Episcopal Global Teams.[77] Other innovations include forming partnerships with NGOs in the United States and abroad. For instance, Presbyterian disaster-response teams have begun working more closely with small NGOs in other countries in order to employ local workers more efficiently and cut costly administrative overhead in the United States.

Besides denominational boards, the independent agencies, or "faith missions," that emerged at the end of the nineteenth century have continued to be active and indeed have proliferated in recent years. The total number of such agencies jumped from 28 in 1900 to 178 in 1950, rose to 351 in 1970 and reached 575 by 2001. At that date, these agencies accounted for 72 percent of all revenue for overseas missions, 61 percent of U.S. foreign missionaries, and 96 percent of foreign nationals supported by U.S. agencies.[78] Unlike denominational boards, these agencies were autonomous, drew contributions from church members affiliated with many different denominations and from nondenominational congregations, and generally required staff to raise support through personal networks. The largest of these organizations were New Tribes Mission and Campus Crusade for Christ, with approximately 1,500 and 1,100 U.S. workers serving abroad, respectively. Other independent agencies with at least five hundred U.S. staff overseas included Mercy Ships, TEAM (The Evangelical Alliance Mission), and SIM (formerly Sudan Interior Mission).

Entrepreneurial leadership and informal ties continue to be the key to faith missions' success and are the principal reasons for the dramatic rise of numerous small agencies and the growth of a few large organizations. Campus Crusade for Christ, founded in 1951 by business leader Bill Bright, focused on cultivating relationships with supporters in business and finance and recruiting college students during the 1950s, 1960s, and 1970s, and then used this base to launch its growing international ministries. By the end of the twentieth century, it had workers in 191 countries and was especially active in the former Soviet Union.[79] In 2005, Campus Crusade's revenue had reached $454 million, approximately a third of which was spent on overseas ministries.[80] Although the majority of its funding came from small donations, the organization received more than $54 million between 1999 and 2004 in grants from foundations, such as the Doudera Family Foundation in Virginia, the Corman Foundation in Alabama, and the Arthur S. DeMoss Foundation in Florida. DeMoss grants were targeted especially toward ministries in the former Soviet Union.[81] Besides sponsoring traditional missionary-style evangelism, Campus Crusade also developed a number of innovative techniques for engaging in international ministry. The most visible of these was the Jesus Project, a film about the life of Jesus. From the project's inception in 1979 through 2005, the organization estimated that 42 million videocassettes and 13 million audiocassettes were distributed, reaching an estimated 6 billion people in 105 countries and believed by the organization to have resulted in approximately 200 million "decisions for Christ."[82] Other Campus Crusade programs include semiautonomous spin-off organizations, such as the Global Aid Network for relief and development projects, Embassy/Executive Ministries International for embassy staff and international business leaders, and the International Leadership Academy to train indigenous pastors.

More typical of independent agencies were the numerous organizations that emerged to fill gaps left by larger programs or to capitalize on opportunities made possible by education, the professions, travel, and communication. Artists in Christian Testimony emerged in 1973 to deploy arts-trained missionaries and as of 2003 was sponsoring four such artists at a cost of approximately $240,000. Audio Scripture Ministries, founded in 1989, was spending about $380,000 annually distributing audiotapes of the Bible. The Bible Training Centre for Pastors in Tucker, Georgia, established in 1990, was devoting $1.8 million annually to assist pastors in other countries. Blessings International, founded in 1981, had a budget of more than $16 million to provide pharmaceuticals and medical supplies to mission teams. Kids Around the World, with an annual budget of about $400,000, started in 1994 to provide Christian Sunday school materials to churches overseas. New agencies also emerged to take advantage of ties between the United States and particular countries. African Mission Evangelism, founded in 1968, worked exclusively with congregations in Ghana. Amazon Focus, founded in 1995, sponsored four missionaries in Belize, Bolivia, and Peru. The Japanese Evangelical Missionary Society was sponsoring one missionary in that country and organizing short-term visits for lay volunteers. Many of these organizations were initiated by a single pastor, lay leader, or nondenominational congregation and sought legal incorporation in order to receive and dispense funds.

Most of the independent agencies that emerged a century earlier also continued to be active in international ministry and found ways to adapt to new conditions. The Africa Inland Mission (AIM), founded in 1895, fielded more than four hundred overseas missionaries in 2004—nearly four times as many as it had a half century earlier—at a cost of nearly $20 million. SIM's operating budget climbed to more than $33 million from U.S. contributions, with an equivalent amount from other countries, and included not only the cost of its overseas missionaries but Bible schools and seminaries in which some 15,000 church leaders were reported to have studied. These organizations also underwent change. AIM's U.S. branch became one of five "sending councils," including South Africa, Britain, Canada, and Australia. Hampered by restrictive laws and the civil war in Sudan, AIM work shifted largely to other countries with better U.S. relations, including Kenya, Tanzania, and Uganda. SIM came to stand for "Serving in Mission," having absorbed the International

Christian Fellowship and Andes Evangelical Mission in the 1980s and the African Evangelical Fellowship in 1998. SIM's activities focused increasingly on partnering with churches in other countries and engaging in famine relief and agricultural development as well as evangelism. SIM was also part of a larger alliance, the Evangel Fellowship International Missions Association, which coordinated strategy and planning among a number of organizations.[83]

During the 1980s and 1990s, faith-based NGOs continued to grow significantly, marking another and perhaps the most notable aspect of American Christianity's expanding global reach. By 2003, World Vision's overseas aid expenditures had grown to $513 million, an inflation-adjusted increase since 1981 of 326 percent. The Catholic Medical Mission Board's overseas budget jumped from only $9 million to more than $136 million, an after-inflation increase of 680 percent. On average, inflation-adjusted budgets of the top twenty-five faith-based NGOs grew by 134 percent during this period. A few organizations' budgets remained relatively stable or increased slightly, which meant an actual decline when inflation was taken into account. Catholic Relief Services spent $479 million overseas in 2003, making it still one of the largest of all faith-based agencies, yet this figure represented a decline of approximately 25 percent when adjusted for inflation. World Relief registered an after-inflation decline of 18 percent and Church World Service, 52 percent. These, however, were the exceptions rather than the rule. Lutheran World Relief's overseas budget increased by an inflation-adjusted 41 percent to $26 million. The Adventist Development and Relief Agency's budget increased 110 percent to $64 million. And overseas expenditures of the Summer Institute of Linguistics grew 144 percent to $121 million. Other faith-based organizations with inflation-adjusted increases included the Evangelical Alliance Mission and the American Friends Service Committee. A handful of humanitarian organizations that were too small or nonexistent for inclusion in the earlier figures also emerged as important faith-based agencies during the closing years of the twentieth century. These included Samaritan's Purse, with overseas expenditures in 2003 of $170 million; Mercy Corps, $106 million; and Habitat for Humanity International, $47 million.[84]

With combined overseas expenditures totaling more than $2.3 billion, the major U.S. faith-based NGOs were active in nearly every corner of the globe. The Adventist Development and Relief Agency was present in 120 countries, World Vision International in 100, Catholic Relief Services in 90, Feed the Children in 51, Lutheran World Relief in 50, Mercy Corps in 30, World Relief in 28, and Food for the Hungry in 25. Central and South America, South and Southeast Asia, the Middle East, Eastern Europe, and Africa were all included. The largest organizations focused on disaster relief and hunger but also include medical assistance, technical training, digging wells, lending funds to micro businesses, and a variety of other economic development projects. Smaller organizations often offered multiple programs but sometimes concentrated their efforts regionally or focused on specialized activities. Enterprise Development International, for instance, worked primarily with small businesses in India, the Philippines, and a few other locations. The International Justice Mission concentrated on human trafficking issues. World Concern (formerly Medicines for Missions) devoted special attention to helping tribal peoples and marginalized farmers.

The earlier pattern of high variation in levels of government support for international faith-based organizations continued. Catholic Relief Services received 74 percent of its 2003 support from government sources. Government's share of Church World Service expenditures was 64 percent. World Relief's overseas budget included 50 percent from government. The Adventist Development and Relief Agency received almost the same share (46 percent). And whereas World Vision's earlier government share was only 6 percent, this proportion now represented 37 percent of its overseas budget. At the other extreme, the Catholic Medical Mission Board and Summer Institute of Linguistics received nearly nothing from government sources.[85]

Besides funding from the U.S. government, the largest faith-based NGOs frequently received grants from the United Nations, especially through its World Food Program, and from other governments through separately incorporated NGO offices. World Vision International in Canada, for example, supplemented its annual budget of private donations with grants from the Canadian International Development Agency for relief, development, HIV/AIDS treatment, and peacebuilding efforts, including one in 2000 for $730,000 to fight HIV/AIDS in Cambodia, one in 2004 for $600,000 to support the organization's efforts in Southeast Asia, and a $500,000 grant in 2005 to assist earthquake victims in Pakistan. Other recipients of Canadian International Development Agency grants included the Adventist Development and Relief Agency, Africa Inland Mission, Canadian Council of Churches, Canadian Lutheran World Relief, the Evangelical Medical Aid Society, Mission Aviation Fellowship, and Wycliffe Bible Translators. Similar relationships existed between faith-based NGOs and government aid programs in Australia and the United Kingdom.

The most obvious consequence of government funding for faith-based NGOs is that the resources available for these organizations' overseas work have significantly increased. For agency officials, seeking government grants has become an important way of expanding programs deemed useful. Besides the sheer increase in activity, government funding has also resulted in two associated developments. One is that faith-based NGOs are no longer segmented within particular denominations or confessional traditions in the way that earlier transnational religious organizations often were. Catholic Relief Services, World Vision International, and the Adventist Development and Relief Agency all compete for the same government dollars and sometimes cooperate in administering programs. This means that the largest organizations with the best track records and experience in grant writing enjoy an advantage over smaller and newer organizations. A second consequence, which agency staff often lament, is an increase in formal reporting requirements. Agencies receiving government grants must provide the usual audited financial information required of any nonprofit organization, but in addition must submit periodic reports about the effectiveness of their programs and undergo independent evaluation studies. Unlike the denominational bureaus and independent agencies of the nineteenth century, faith-based NGOs are also dependent to a much greater degree on being integrated into networks of Washington officials.

The overarching consequence of these developments is that faith-based agencies must engage more intensely in a wider variety of coordinating activities than any of the earlier transnational religious organizations did. They cannot rely on seminary training to keep missionaries in line the way the early nineteenth-century mission boards did or on severing missionaries' financial support the way late nineteenth-century independent agencies did. The practice of corresponding secretaries and itinerant religious leaders who kept in touch with frontline workers in those eras clearly is no longer sufficient. Faith-based agencies must not only raise money from local congregations and channel it to staff in distant locations but also work increasingly with indigenous clergy and community leaders in other countries and with the staff of other faith-based and nonsectarian NGOs in those locations. In addition, NGO officials in the United States coordinate their efforts increasingly with the budgets and program priorities of government agencies. Unlike the single-issue focus of traditional missionary organizations, NGO officials also coordinate an increasingly diverse portfolio of specialized projects, ranging from emergency relief to health care to economic development. The more complex, multilateral coordination required of contemporary faith-based agencies is in part possible because of electronic communication and more efficient travel. Staff can more effectively stay in contact with a wider variety of relevant people and organizations through these means. Coordination also depends on several other features of contemporary agencies. One is the increasingly specialized expertise present among the professional staff of these organizations. Training typically includes a graduate degree in some relevant field, such as finance or public health, fluency in a language besides English, and at least three years in service work abroad. Second, coordination is facilitated by the fact that international humanitarian, relief, and development work is administered largely through formal organizations. Thus, communication is concentrated among representatives of these various NGOs and government agencies. And third, coordination is further enhanced by the fact that the largest faith-based agencies also have significant resources in other countries. These resources include local offices of their own, relationships with government officials and indigenous NGOs, and extensive ties with local churches. The fact that these resources are so abundant is not only testimony to the considerable budgets and experience of the U.S. faith-based agencies but is also an outgrowth of the work of earlier mission organizations and of the more recent expansion of Christianity in many parts of the world.

As the need for more extensive coordination has increased, the ways in which transnational religious organizations legitimate their activities have also changed. Faith-based organizations must balance and reconcile the appeals that justify their activities to several key constituencies. Insofar as faith-based agencies continue to rely heavily on private donations from congregations and individual church members, their legitimacy depends on articulating a distinctive Christian rationale for their activities. Increasingly, this rationale emphasizes that souls cannot be saved without prior attention being paid to people's physical needs. Humanitarianism does not so much replace evangelism as evangelism becomes redefined as showing Christian love through humanitarian work. For purposes of securing government grants, faith-based NGOs must demonstrate that they are nonsectarian, nonpartisan, effective, and willing to abide by such procedural norms as regularly audited financial reporting. Humanitarianism fits well with these criteria. In addition, faith-based NGOs must also be especially concerned about maintaining their credibility among the people they seek to serve in other countries. They do this by describing themselves as partners with local leaders, by sometimes de-emphasizing overt evangelistic activities, and by demonstrating their commitment to cultural and even religious diversity.

Although government grants and contracts have been a source of the recent expansion of international ministries, most organizations continue to rely heavily on private contributions. Leaders of international religious organizations credit new communication technologies and media expertise with playing an important role in their growing ability to solicit private donations. While television and direct mail have remained important, computerized information and financial management systems have been particularly significant. These systems have made it possible to target potential donors with specialized appeals, receive small and large donations for highly specific projects, credit those donations to accounts associated with hundreds of different projects, keep the donors informed of relevant progress and needs, and track individual donors' histories.

Samaritan's Purse is an example of an international relief organization that grew dramatically within a relatively short period, in significant part because of media exposure and information technology. Its 2003 overseas expenditures of $170 million made it one of the largest faith-based relief and development agencies in the United States. It was also one of the more recent of these endeavors, having been founded in 1970 by World Vision's Bob Pierce three years after his resignation from that organization. After Pierce's death in 1978, Franklin Graham, son of evangelist Billy Graham, assumed leadership of the agency, which still saw itself as a "purse" or fund to which other relief organizations could apply rather than as a frontline service agency. Through his father's evangelistic association, Graham had access to churches and donor lists and knew the value of mass publicity. Samaritan's Purse's most successful media campaign was Operation Christmas Child, which provides gift-filled shoeboxes to needy children in nearly a hundred countries. The program was widely advertised, used the same emphasis on needy children that had been instrumental in World Vision's early success, and provided a relatively simple way to establish contact with thousands of churches and individual donors.[86] In addition, Samaritan's Purse contracted with one of the most successful Christian-oriented media firms to publicize Operation Christmas Child as well as the agency's increasing involvement in relief efforts in such highly visible conflict zones as Kosovo and the Sudan. This media firm, the DeMoss Group (headed by Mark

DeMoss, son of philanthropist Arthur D. DeMoss), included among its communications and public relations clients such prominent organizations as the Billy Graham Evangelistic Association, Campus Crusade for Christ International, and Habitat for Humanity.[87] Besides the innovations employed by denominational boards, faith missions, and faith-based NGOs, a new organizational form also appeared during the closing decades of the twentieth century. This form, adopting a business model, could appropriately be termed for-profit ministries. Throughout most of American history, religious leaders with international concerns had to cultivate captains of industry to secure philanthropy over and above what ordinary church members could provide. Religion itself was not a way to become wealthy. All that changed during the last half of the twentieth century as a few U.S. preachers began to amass large fortunes by running successful television businesses. These earnings permitted them to expand operations overseas without relying on wealthy donors or being beholden to denominational boards to the extent that previous missionary and humanitarian organizations had been. Although these for-profit ministries by no means replaced or threatened to replace the earlier models, they have played an important role in the global diffusion of American Christianity.

Televangelist Pat Robertson's Christian Broadcasting Network (CBN) is one of the most prominent examples of a for-profit ministry. Founded in 1961, CBN grew into the world's largest supplier of round-the-clock cable programming, reaching as many as sixty-six countries by the 1980s. Robertson's popular *The 700 Club* offered millions of viewers daily exposure to biblical commentary, testimonials, prayers, stories about miraculous healings, and interpretations of news and political events. In 1985, some 600,000 people donated $139 million to *The 700 Club*. By 1988, the year that Robertson ran for president, CBN was also earning between $60 million and $70 million from its Family Channel and other for-profit subsidiaries.[88] In 1997, Robertson sold International Family Entertainment, the parent company of the Family Channel, to media mogul Rupert Murdoch for $1.9 billion. As part of the sale, CBN received $136 million and another $109 was held in trust for CBN to receive in 2010. In addition, Robertson's Regent University received $147 million.[89] In 2005, CBN reported total assets of $252 million, contributions of $457, and expenses of $424 million. Among the international activities supported by CBN was Operation Blessing, a relief and development ministry, which receives approximately $10 million annually from CBN and provides an estimated $180 million in goods, medicine, and other relief supplies through gifts-in-kind.[90] The laws governing U.S. nonprofit organizations are sufficiently flexible that religious television ministries were able to generate large revenues that provided ample opportunities for their leaders to expand overseas operations and in some instances enjoy lavish lifestyles as well. Trinity Broadcasting Network (TBN), the only television ministry on a scale matching CBN, was founded by Paul and Jan Crouch in 1973 and grew into an enterprise supplying programming to more than 3,000 television stations with twenty-one satellites and cable systems around the world. English- and foreign-language broadcasts cover much of Central and South America, Europe, the Middle East, India, Africa, and Southeast Asia. The network has been the largest international outlet for American televangelists Kenneth Copeland and T. D. Jakes, faith healer Benny Hinn, and exorcist Bob Larson, as well as Christian music produced at its state-of-the art Trinity Music City in Nashville and International Production Center in Irving, Texas. In 2004, TBN reported assets of $749 million, revenue of $188 million, and expenses of $119 million. Paul Crouch's salary was $403,700 and his wife's salary was $361,000. Besides their private jet, the couple owned thirty homes, including two mansions in Newport Beach and a ranch in Texas.[91]

Like the nation's role in the world more generally, U.S. Christianity's recent expansion in global affairs is rooted in a long history of transnational involvement. The period leading up to World War I was in many ways the great century of missionary innovation, as Kenneth Scott Latourette describes it, and yet the half century after World II could equally be described as a time of major expansion and innovation.[92] It is less important to compare the relative magnitude of overseas efforts in various periods, however, than to understand the organizational structures that underlie the recent globalization of American Christianity. The denominational boards that appeared at the start of the nineteenth century continue to be an important means of harnessing the generosity of church members, of regularly soliciting contributions, and of channeling them to the support of missionaries, schools, hospitals, relief efforts, and indigenous churches abroad. The independent agencies that emerged at the end of the nineteenth century have become a vast network of transdenominational parachurch organizations that sponsor specialized ministries, work on college campuses, host conferences, supply Bibles and transportation, and organize short-term mission trips. The large faith-based NGOs of the World War II era raise money through direct solicitations and government contracts and work with community organizations and public officials around the world on relief, economic development, and health care. For-profit ministries use satellite telecasts to beam U.S. preaching and healing services into homes and churches around the world. Congregations and individual church members participate in the activities of these intermediaries but increasingly engage directly in transnational activities as well. Direct ties between congregations in different countries, as well as short-term mission trips and visits by international teams, have in fact increased to the point that leaders of centralized agencies sometimes find themselves overwhelmed with requests for help in coordinating these efforts.

Were the face of American religion to be considered only in terms of the worship services, choirs, Sunday school classes, and the community projects of local congregations, the extensive organizational ties that link the United States with other parts of the world could be missed. The same is true of abstract discussions of globalization that feature generalizations about the world as a whole but fail to take adequate account of the grassroots mechanisms through which global ties occur. The connections between people of faith in the United States and the rest of the world are organized ties that draw on patterns of coordination and control that leaders have devised and improved upon over the past two centuries. These organized structures conquer distance and difference by informing people about events and opportunities in the wider world and, even more important, by creating channels through which money and personnel and ideas flow. The voluntary spirit that Tocqueville identified in the 1830s has continued—and has also increased, resulting in a thickening of international networks and including a role for government that Tocqueville could hardly have imagined.

CHAPTER 5

The Global Role of Congregations

Bridging Borders through
Direct Engagement

When the tsunami of 2004 killed an estimated 273,000 people in Southeast Asia and left millions homeless, thousands of congregations across the United States responded in small—and sometimes large—ways to help the victims. The response of a quiet middle-class Southern Baptist church in suburban Little Rock was typical. After praying about what they should do, the deacons took up a special offering on four consecutive Sundays and sent the proceeds to the denomination's international mission board. This agency in turn distributed the funds through Baptist workers who were on the scene in the affected region.

During the same month, a small Nazarene church in Lakeland, Missouri, collected $1,000 in a special offering for a program similar to the Southern Baptists'. At a Church of Christ in upstate New York, the pastor distributed in the church newsletter the address of a relief organization he trusted. An independent church in Frederick, Maryland, posted information on its Web site about relief organizations and sent money to Southeast Asia through an international disaster emergency services program sponsored by a fellowship of like-minded independent congregations.

By January 2005, a national poll found that 36 percent of the public had donated money to their churches for tsunami victims.[1] The Southern Baptist Convention collected $16 million, United Methodists took in more than $6 million, the United Church of Christ contributed more than $3 million, and the Evangelical Lutheran Church in America raised $2.5 million. Catholic Relief Services alone accounted for $114 million.[2]

Tsunami relief efforts were widely publicized in newspapers and on television so it comes as little surprise that congregations were a conduit for fund-raising. However, relatively little has been known about churches' efforts to assist disaster victims more generally and to alleviate such problems as hunger and malnutrition through organized programs. For instance, hardly anything has been reported on whether churches regularly collect money for relief chests or wait until a disaster happens to appeal for money. Nor has much attention been paid to the kinds of programs that congregations support. Do church leaders favor ministries that respond to emergency needs or do they prefer programs that focus on long-term solutions to endemic problems? Are churches mainly interested in humanitarian efforts, in assisting Christian congregations in other countries, or in converting people to Christianity?

The global role of U.S. congregations extends well beyond the occasional offering for disaster relief. These efforts are important, but for a growing number of congregations they are but one aspect of a highly coordinated global outreach program involving humanitarian assistance, partnering with international agencies and local congregations in other countries, working with refugees, sponsoring missionaries, and on occasion becoming involved in peacemaking and human rights issues. All of these are being facilitated and shaped by globalization.

INTERNATIONAL HUNGER AND RELIEF EFFORTS

Nationally, 76 percent of church members report that an offering has been taken at their congregation within the past year to "raise money for an overseas hunger or relief program" (76 percent also say they personally gave money in the last year for international relief or hunger projects). Catholics are the most likely to say their congregation has done this (86 percent say so), followed by mainline Protestants (84 percent), with evangelical Protestants and members of black Protestant denominations (68 and 62 percent, respectively) being somewhat less likely to say so. The larger the congregation, the more likely it is to have been involved in overseas relief in this way. In congregations averaging two thousand members or more, 86 percent of members say their church has raised money for overseas hunger or relief, whereas among congregations averaging one hundred members or less, this proportion drops to 53 percent. Whether the congregation is Catholic, mainline Protestant, evangelical Protestant, or black Protestant, larger churches are more likely to be involved in such efforts than smaller ones.[3]

Congregations typically receive offerings for international hunger or relief between four and six times a year, although local practices vary considerably. Methodists, Episcopalians, and other mainline Protestant churches usually participate in the national One Great Hour of Sharing program that raises money for overseas relief at least once a year, and many congregations sponsor additional offerings. In Catholic parishes, the annual schedule may include monthly collections for such purposes as aid to churches in Latin America or eastern Europe, the American Bishops' Overseas Appeal, and World Mission Sunday. Among all church members whose congregations have any offerings for international relief, 30 percent say there is an offering every two or three months. Twenty percent say their church has an offering of this kind once a month and 8 percent indicate one is taken every week. At the other extreme, 11 percent say the overseas hunger and relief offering at their church is taken only once a year and 23 percent say it is taken twice a year (8 percent are unsure how often the offering occurs). This pattern holds for evangelicals, mainline Protestants, historically black churches, and Catholics, although regular offerings are somewhat more customary in Catholic parishes than in Protestant churches. For instance, four Catholics in ten say their congregation has an offering for overseas hunger or relief at least once a month, compared with about a quarter of Protestants.

Generally, the money congregations raise for hunger and relief goes to trusted denominational or independent agencies that administer and distribute the funds. For instance, a Pennsylvania congregation of the Presbyterian Church of America that recently raised $22,000 as part of its annual Thanksgiving offering sent the money to World Relief to be used for famine victims in sub-Saharan Africa. A mainline Presbyterian church in Evanston, Illinois, raised $10,000 for its denomination's famine relief effort in Malawi. A Catholic leader in San Antonio, Texas, says her parish is helping with water projects in Brazil primarily through the Bishops' Relief Fund. A United Methodist church in Syracuse, New York, like most other Methodist congregations, channels the proceeds of its annual Thanksgiving offering through the United Methodist Committee on Relief; the committee also supplies inserts for church bulletins, informing members about special needs following a tornado, flood, or other disaster. Working with independent and denominational agencies in this way saves congregations from having to make on-the-spot decisions about where to send donations or how to justify particular programs. The process becomes routine, as one Baptist leader illustrates in saying that the reason her church contributes to World Relief is "because our denomination does."[4]

Increasingly, though, congregations are channeling monies to specific programs with which they have direct connections. These programs vary in size and function but permit churchgoers in one location to have a personal impact on individuals' lives in a distant setting. After the members of a large Presbyterian church in Atlanta became dissatisfied with sending money only to large-scale disaster relief agencies, for example, the congregation is now working with an organization in India called Friends of the Poor that links American churches with people in particular villages in rural India. The program is geared toward elevating people from the lowest income strata by teaching them how to initiate and operate small businesses. The church's Global Outreach director says the connection has generated keen interest among businesspeople in the congregation, some of whom have gone to India to help personally with the training program.

A large independent congregation in Springfield, Illinois, illustrates the growing importance churches attach to selecting, approving, and monitoring their own projects. The pastor in charge of international ministries says disaster relief is a lower priority than identifying programs that "deal with the structural issues of poverty." Describing himself as a "big believer in micro-enterprise activities," he says his committee works mainly through eight hand-picked congregations in Central America to facilitate job training. His congregation recently sponsored a "gift in kind" drive that sent computers and sewing machines to these churches for use in their training programs. Working with these congregations gives his committee the assurance it wants that the church's money is put to good use.

International relief organizations are responding to congregations' demands for a more personalized approach. When a Southern Baptist congregation in Raleigh, North Carolina, signaled interest in pursuing humanitarian work in Africa, staff at World Vision International designed a special program for it in Zambia. The project consisted of helping people in a community that had been particularly devastated by AIDS. Church members took responsibility for the care of about five hundred orphans in the community. The congregation also raised money for education, health care, water, and micro-economic development projects.

Each year several teams from the church make trips to the community to supervise these projects.

Some congregations favor working directly with congregations abroad because humanitarian assistance then contributes to evangelization. For instance, the pastor of a Pentecostal church in Birmingham, Alabama, explains that her congregation engages in humanitarian efforts overseas by providing food and that this assistance is devoted to feeding people who come to Pentecostal leadership conferences. As an example, she describes a recent leadership conference in the Philippines that brought 250 Pentecostal pastors together from remote villages, many of whom traveled for several days by bus to attend the conference. Her church provided them with food and lodging. These "foot soldiers," as she calls them, then return to their villages better equipped to preach. "Through the people that these pastors influence," she says, "my [church's] influence is exponential."

The international humanitarian assistance a Methodist church in Irving, Texas, provides consists mainly of raising money to build houses for indigent families in Mexico and sending teams across the border to help construct these dwellings. The congregation further personalizes these relationships by participating in worship services at the church that many of these families attend. Evangelization is not an issue because the people are already Christians. The goal is rather to cultivate trust. "I've always believed that works of mission are really about building relationships," the pastor says. Her theology boils down to the simple proposition that "peace will reign on earth when we really, truly get down to understanding one another as brothers and sisters."

Other churches initiate direct programs in particular locations because an immigrant from that country becomes a member of their congregation. An African immigrant who came to Philadelphia as a graduate student, for instance, inspired the congregation he was attending to become involved in an irrigation project in his homeland. At one point, the pastor himself visited the area and was appalled by its poverty. He says the church is uninvolved with any of the big relief organizations but is proud just to be doing "our own little thing." A water tank high on one of the hills in Africa exists because of his church's contributions.

Church leaders say there are several reasons to give directly rather than through an intermediary. One is that direct giving seems more personal and voluntary and thus less like "a tax," as one pastor put it. Another is that leaders regard direct giving as a way to save money and channel relief into the right hands more quickly than by working through a middleman. Yet another reason is that church members acquire a personal stake in the outcomes as they see immediate results and establish long-term relationships. "This is what Jesus would have us do," one leader explains. "It causes people to feel in touch with God's love." The larger relief organizations have also been finding ways to personalize their relationships with congregations. For instance, a Congregational pastor in Stanton, Connecticut, whose church supports a medical clinic initiated by World Relief in Sudan, reports being pleased with videos provided by World Relief and the sense of being able to assist with a specific project.

It is evident in these examples that congregations' relief efforts are becoming more diverse. Although many of the programs churches support provide temporary food, shelter, and clothing to victims of natural disasters, a growing number of faith-based ministries are seeking to effect longer-term, self-sustaining improvements in living conditions. Medical clinics and micro-business leadership programs are two examples. Another is setting up water purification systems, such as the ones a Presbyterian church in Texas is helping with in Darfur and an independent church in California is sponsoring in Peru. Yet another is combating environmental devastation that destroys land and jobs. For instance, a Methodist church in Pennsylvania has gotten excited about a project in Haiti that plants trees in deforested areas to curb further erosion of topsoil and protect small-scale farming. Besides sending money, the congregation has also sent a youth team to help plant trees. The pastor thinks this is a better investment of the church's time and money than simply putting a twenty-dollar bill in the offering plate in response to some special appeal. That may salve one's conscience, he says, but it is better to be part of a planned program.

In addition to sponsoring such programs abroad, many churches are involved in humanitarian efforts that assist in resettling refugees who come to the United States. Data compiled by the United Nations between 1980 and 2005 showed an annual average of approximately ten million refugees worldwide, with figures ranging as high as seventeen million in the early 1990s. At least double this number were listed as being of concern to the United Nations for reasons of temporary displacement, seeking asylum, or needing ongoing assistance. The "of concern" category includes approximately one million people in North America, of whom more than 600,000 had come as refugees.[5]

Twenty-nine percent of U.S. church members say their congregation has helped support a refugee or refugee family within the previous twelve months. Among Catholics and mainline Protestants, this proportion rises to 35 and 31 percent, respectively, and falls to 25 and 22 percent among evangelicals and black Protestants, respectively. Like other specialized ministries, large churches are more likely than smaller ones to help refugees. For instance, 39 percent of members in congregations of two thousand or more say their church has helped refugees in the past year, compared with 24 percent of those in churches of fewer than one hundred members.

Because refugees have been forced from their homes by such major events as war or natural disaster, congregations usually receive requests to assist these displaced persons from the large international organizations that have helped them relocate. For instance, Catholic parishes often respond to referrals from Catholic Charities, which cares for refugees for a period of six months, after which volunteers are needed to help with transportation and tutoring. Protestant leaders describe similar referrals from nondenominational agencies, such as World Relief and World Vision International, or from an interdenominational organization, such as Church World Service. One pastor, for example, whose church has worked with the immigration and refugee division of Church World Service, notes how easy it is for congregations to tap into this program. "The family is picked up and approved by the State Department. They arrive at the airport and then it is your job to get them hooked up with appropriate government services and move them from dependence to independence." In these instances, a congregation may take responsibility for the family's overall needs, but it is also common for congregations to specialize by setting up, say, a fund for emergency assistance or a language class.

Pastors whose churches have been involved in sponsoring refugees report that government agencies in their communities are increasingly backlogged, underfunded, and unable to keep up with the demand for refugee assistance. Congregation-based committees seek to fill the gap, providing personalized and enduring support. For instance, a church in southern Indiana adopted a Croatian family with two children who had fled the war in the former Yugoslavia. Their effort lasted for more than five years and involved separate committees for job placement, housing and furniture, life skills (such as handling money and learning to use public transportation), medical needs, and governmental issues such as obtaining food stamps and negotiating the naturalization process. A congregation in Riverside, California, found it necessary to obtain a grant and hire a caseworker to handle the increasing flood of refugees in its community. "The sponsoring agencies tend to drop them within a few weeks," the pastor says. The church has now established a refugee network through which it supplies a wide range of services, including emergency food, workshops on health issues, legal advice, and simply a place for worship and fellowship—"lots of big African gatherings with African food and singing and dancing."

As these examples show, helping refugees is often a long-term commitment. Besides the work that takes place locally, this kind of humanitarian relief also involves congregations in additional efforts outside the United States. For instance, a Baptist church in Pennsylvania offered itself as a sanctuary for refugees during the civil war in El Salvador and through those connections became well acquainted with several Salvadoran families. When the war ended, church members went to Honduras and accompanied refugees on their trek back to El Salvador to protect them from being attacked by government soldiers. The congregation has continued to support several sister congregations in El Salvador whose members are working for social and economic justice in the face of opposition from the ruling political party.

Congregations are also providing relief in response to the devastation resulting from HIV/AIDS, especially in Africa, usually by working more closely with international organizations. At the Baptist church that is sponsoring AIDS orphans in Zambia, the pastor says that "you'd have to be dead in the soul not to be moved by what's happening there." However, he also acknowledges that Bono and other celebrities "shamed the church into action." Other leaders report that initial resistance to helping victims of a sexually transmitted or drug-related disease is gradually being overcome. The pastor of a nondenominational church relates a typical story. Long active in disaster relief, his congregation decided it wanted to become more involved in HIV/AIDS education and prevention. It sent a six-member team from the congregation on a ten-day trip to Southeast Asia to examine various programs dealing with these issues as well as others concerned with child wellness and micro enterprise. Its goal is to establish a long-term partnership with one or more of these ministries and to make a $50,000 annual commitment to their support. Although the proportion of congregations that have initiated ministries like this is probably small, compared with those that raise money for more general humanitarian and relief programs, there appears to be widespread interest among church members in doing more. Nationally, 93 percent of church members think their congregation should emphasize "the suffering in

Africa caused by hunger, AIDS, and other illnesses" (41 percent think this should be emphasized "a lot").

With such serious needs, church leaders are often haunted by concerns that they are not doing enough. As one observes, "A million dollars sounds like a lot, but in the immensity of need, it feels like a drop in the bucket." Yet clergy also sense that interest in alleviating suffering in other countries is increasing. Through television, travel, and other means of communicating, people in their churches are becoming more aware of global needs. "The world is right there on your TV screen," says a missions director in California. It becomes harder to escape into one's island of comfort when needy people are brought to mind in this way. "I'm not saying we've corrected everything," she explains, "but at least there's a feeling that maybe I could wait another year before I buy a new car or help by contributing the money I was going to spend on a vacation."

SPONSORING MISSIONARIES

Although it is believed that approximately 118,000 full- and part-time missionaries from the United States currently serve in other countries, it has not been clear except for a few denominations whether these missionaries are being supported by a large cross-section of American congregations or whether the support is coming from a relatively small fraction of local churches.[6] The issue is not so much about finances as it is about interest and involvement. A thousand dollars is the same whether it comes from one individual or a hundred. Traditionally, though, church leaders have taught the importance of all believers being involved in spreading the gospel, including outreach beyond one's immediate community.

The evidence indicates that supporting missionaries continues to be an activity that engages a large majority of American congregations. Nearly three-quarters (74 percent) of U.S. church members say their congregation has supported a missionary working in another country during the past year. The auspices under which this support is given divides about equally between helping particular missionaries and helping through a missionary organization. Thirty-eight percent of those whose congregations provide any support say their church directly helps a particular missionary, 31 percent say the support goes to a missionary organization, and 22 percent say their congregation does both.

If most churches are involved at least minimally in supporting missionary efforts abroad, congregations nevertheless vary in how much they emphasize this kind of ministry. For instance, some congregations merely send monetary support while others feature letters from missionaries in newsletters, post photos of missionary families on bulletin boards, and highlight mission allocations prominently in their budgets. An evangelical church in Pennsylvania provides an interesting example. The hallway in the children's Sunday school wing includes a wall-sized map of the world with photos of the congregation's missionaries. For the adults, large photos of missionaries and descriptions of their work fill bulletin boards outside the main auditorium and a table provides copies of prayer letters and decks of prayer cards. A poster nearby shows pictures of missionaries in the past who became martyrs, including one from the congregation. In all, 61 percent of U.S. church members say their congregations emphasize "supporting missionaries" a lot and another 26 percent say "some." Eight percent say "only a little," 3 percent say "none," and 2 percent are unsure.

Conversations with church leaders show how visible missionaries are in many congregations. Consider a large Lutheran church that has more than a thousand members and a weekly schedule packed with everything from prayer meetings to soup pantries. When asked about missionaries the pastor states the first and last names of a missionary couple the church sponsors in Tanzania without skipping a beat and goes on to describe their work, the gender and ages of their children, and what hobbies they enjoy. The congregation is thoroughly familiar with these missionaries. The family has spent sabbatical time at the church and sends regular letters that are posted on the congregation's Web site.

Popular reports about missionaries in the field give the impression that missions work is no longer of interest except in evangelical churches. The picture from church members themselves is quite different. It is true that evangelicals are more likely than anyone else to say their congregation supports missionaries abroad (84 percent say so)—and even the smallest of these congregations are typically involved.[7] However, a large majority of mainline Protestants and Catholics also say their congregations support international missionary work (73 and 69 percent, respectively). Perceptions of emphasis on missions show a similar pattern. Seventy-five percent of evangelicals say their congregation emphasizes supporting missionaries a lot, but 51 percent of mainline Protestants and 50 percent of Catholics give the same response. Black Protestants are also involved but probably focus more on domestic than on foreign missions, compared with the other groups.[8] The other notable difference is that Protestants (evangelical, mainline, and black) are more likely to say their congregation directly helps a particular missionary, whereas Catholics say their parish supplies support through a missionary organization.[9]

Small congregations usually have meager resources and thus support a single missionary family or send money to a mission agency as part of their regular budget. Larger congregations are able to do considerably more, meaning that an effective administrative apparatus becomes crucial. For instance, in congregations of two thousand members or more nearly half have a missions or overseas outreach committee, whereas in congregations of fewer than a hundred members only a quarter do. In the largest congregations at least five full-time staff members is the norm, and about half of these large multi-staff churches have a leader specifically for overseas missions and other global ministries.

A nondenominational church in California with a membership of twelve thousand and weekly attendance of seven thousand illustrates how large-scale missions programs are organized. The congregation provides partial support for twenty-seven or twenty-eight missionary families in twenty countries. One of the pastors is in charge of recruiting, training, and supervising the congregation's missionaries and overseeing their support. He sometimes identifies a young person he thinks has potential through a short-term mission trip, works with that person for a year or more, and then sends him or her into the field. He also visits some of the missionaries each year in their various locations. The job is too big for one person, though, so volunteers become important. The congregation is organized into small cell groups that meet regularly for Bible study, prayer, and fellowship. Each cell group adopts a missionary family, supplies some of its monthly support, stays in regular contact with it by e-mail or letter, and sometimes visits it. The missionaries largely make their own decisions about such specific activities as evangelism, helping at a medical clinic, teaching, or constructing churches, but they stay in close touch with the church in California so people there understand their needs and stay interested in their work.

Another way of assessing congregations' involvement with the international work of the church is to ask whether missionaries, indigenous clergy from other countries, or other foreign visitors are invited to speak at churches in the United States. Missiologists interested in Christianity's Southern shift and the possibility of reverse influences in Europe and the United States emphasize this kind of involvement. About half (48 percent) of U.S. church members say their congregation has hosted a guest speaker from another country within the past year and 43 percent say they personally attended such a meeting. This activity reveals a some-

what different pattern from the one shown by questions about supporting missionaries. For instance, Catholics are the most likely to say their
parish has hosted a speaker from another country (55 percent), compared
with 51 percent of evangelicals, 43 percent of mainline Protestants, and
33 percent of black Protestants. Within each tradition, the chances of
having heard a speaker from abroad are much greater in larger congregations than in smaller ones. A large Catholic parish in Michigan illustrates the kinds of speakers that congregations sponsor. During one recent summer, a bishop from India visited, spoke at several of the masses,
and took up an offering for his diocese. A priest who works with orphans
in Russia was scheduled to pay a similar visit the following summer. Oc-
casionally a missionary working with the Society for the Propagation
of the Faith or the Christian Foundation for Children and Aging visits
as well.

Churches with active missions programs often host foreign visitors
regularly, but even the occasional speaker from another country can
have a significant impact on the congregation, according to pastors. "It
charges people up, brings a fresh voice, and makes justice and mission
more tangible," observes an Episcopal rector whose parish hosted a
prominent church leader from Africa. World AIDS Day at his church
has had a very different meaning since this visitor spoke. In many
churches foreign speakers are easy to invite because they are already
part of the congregation or live in the community. For instance, a post-
doctoral fellow from Ghana gave a presentation about his research on
malaria at the Methodist church he was attending while studying in the
United States. After he returned to Ghana, the congregation helped
support his research.

However their congregations choose to do it, church members overwhelmingly believe that solidarity with Christians abroad should be an
important priority of churches in the United States. Five church members in six (84 percent) think their own congregation should emphasize
"the work of Christians and Christian organizations in other countries," with 45 percent saying a lot of emphasis should be placed on this
work. Only 4 percent say this work should receive no emphasis at all in
their congregation. Evangelical Protestants are particularly likely to
stress the importance of being connected with Christians abroad: 56
percent say their congregation should emphasize the work of Christians
and Christian organizations in other countries a lot (37, 43, and 36 percent of mainline Protestants, black Protestants, and Catholics, respectively, give the same response).

The traditional pattern of supplying money for mission projects in some distant part of the world through an official agency or mission board is still practiced in many congregations. A typical example is a mainline Protestant congregation in Illinois that decided it wanted to be more active in supporting overseas ministries. Through the denomination's national office for such projects the congregation opted to help finance the cost of constructing a church building in the Republic of Congo. Nobody from the congregation went to Africa, but one of the members erected a model of the proposed church and other members purchased mock bricks. The effort raised about $5,000. Another example is an Orthodox church where one of the leaders says the congregation contributes "not to a specific mission family with a name but through the mission program of our church." Congregations sometimes provide in-kind donations through such programs as well. For instance, a small African Methodist Episcopal church periodically collects used clothing, which it then sends via the bishop's office to sister congregations in Africa.

Projects like this work well for smaller congregations and for churches that prefer to channel resources through their denominational offices. However, congregations are also experimenting with a remarkable variety of new transcultural mission endeavors. An evangelical church in southern California provides an interesting illustration of one such endeavor. With much of northern Mexico reachable by car or truck in less than a day, the church has worked extensively to plant new congregations there and to supply material assistance. Its most popular project has been to construct prefabricated loft-style houses in the church parking lot, which are then shipped with a team of volunteers to Mexico for final assembly. Besides the church's own members, people from the wider community pitch in to help. In a recent twelve-month period, the church enlisted more than fifteen hundred volunteers. Being able to help families they deem worthy through this program has proven attractive to indigenous pastors in Mexico. The church in California has set up a 501(c)3 nonprofit organization to administer the project, purchased a training camp in Mexico, and begun recruiting other congregations to join in the venture.

Another example that highlights the growing influence of globalization as well as an innovative organizational style is a Bible church of about a thousand members in Michigan with an astonishing annual budget of $14 million, $2.5 million of which goes to overseas missions. At first blush, the church's mission program is conventional. Although it provides partial support to a large number of missionaries (about a hundred), the missionaries are mostly supervised by well-established independent mission agencies. Believing strongly that Christianity is a global movement, though, the congregation has been working to build a thoroughly multinational network of relationships by sponsoring missionaries from countries other than just the United States. For instance, it has helped send a team from Belfast to work in Africa and one from Africa to work in Latin America. It also pays for pastors from Africa, Latin America, Asia, and Europe to come together for periodic meetings and conferences. The idea is that each culture has something to learn from the others.

In congregation after congregation, we found U.S. churches heavily involved in overseas ministries but in innovative ways that reflect the changing dynamics of global Christianity. A nondenominational church in Massachusetts with a membership of about three thousand and an annual missions budget of about $1 million illustrates the range of these adaptive programs. Of the sixty missionaries it supports, twenty are from the congregation itself, twenty are from elsewhere in the United States, and twenty are indigenous to the countries in which they are serving. The church raises about 50 percent of this support from members and secures the remainder from partner agencies within the United States. Because it is committed to nurturing churches in other countries, the congregation recently endowed a professorship in mission studies at a seminary in Latin America. It has adopted a sister congregation in eastern Europe to which it sends short-term visitors. It sends educational materials, funds, and a medical team to Africa where local clinics work through local congregations to assist families affected by HIV/AIDS. In the Massachusetts congregation about a third of the members are foreign-born, drawn to the area from India, South Korea, Taiwan, Mexico, and elsewhere by high-tech jobs. Dozens of the members serve on boards of faith-based nonprofit organizations that oversee international humanitarian and relief efforts.

Whether they follow a traditional or more novel pattern, congregations increasingly rely on personal contacts as they initiate transcultural missionary activities. A Presbyterian church in Georgia supports a community health clinic in Guatemala. The project came about because a member of the church is the child of former missionaries in Guatemala. She and several other members of the church make periodic visits to the clinic. The pastor of a Presbyterian church in Texas relates a similar story. The outreach program his church supports in Kenya resulted from a couple at his church spending vacations in Kenya, eventually retiring there, and now helping congregations construct new buildings. A Pentecostal church in Alabama built a home for abandoned children in Tanzania where the congregation's pastor formerly served as a missionary. Her church also sends sewing machines to churches that set up little factories right in the church building to give local women an income. A Methodist church in Kansas recently bought a van and sent it to a sister congregation in Poland. The pastor in Poland and his family have visited the church in Kansas and some of its members have visited the church in Poland.

A question that has long preoccupied church leaders is whether missionary efforts should go hand in hand with hunger relief and other humanitarian efforts or whether the two should be regarded as competing priorities. Most of the examples church leaders describe suggest that missions and humanitarian work are complementary. The survey responses shed additional light on this question. Overall, 78 percent of church members whose congregations support missionaries abroad say their churches take up offerings for overseas hunger and relief work, and 80 percent of those whose congregations receive such offerings say their churches support missionaries. This statistical relationship is true among evangelicals, mainline Protestants, black Protestants, and Catholics. It also holds when members of medium-sized and large congregations are compared.[10] The exception is among members of smaller congregations where the relationship is weaker or nonexistent, suggesting that tradeoffs may be necessary when resources are scarce. It is also worth noting that about one member in four belongs to a congregation that supports only one or the other of these ministries. Usually, though, congregations support both.

This blending of evangelistic and humanitarian activity makes it increasingly difficult to attach a specific dollar value to the transcultural ministries of American congregations. The estimated $3.7 billion that U.S. churches devote to overseas missions does not include the materials and volunteer labor that go into the loft-style houses the California church ships to Mexico. It does not include the money the Georgia congregation sends to the community health clinic in Guatemala or the Alabama church's sponsorship of the children's home and sewing factories in Tanzania. It does not include the time members of the church in Massachusetts donate to boards of international organizations or the money they raised for the professorship in Latin America. Yet all of these, like thousands of other programs, contribute directly to the ministries of indigenous churches in the global South.

PEACEMAKING AND CONCERNS ABOUT WAR

It is difficult to consider transcultural ministries apart from questions about war. The twentieth century gave church leaders many opportunities to formulate statements about just and unjust wars and to engage in peacemaking efforts. The twenty-first century has presented leaders with continuing responsibilities to support, oppose, or attempt to reduce the likelihood of international conflicts and mitigate their consequences. From the United Nations to the Vatican to the World Council of Churches and other organizations, officials have repeatedly called on congregations to be involved in this important aspect of international ministry.

Although war and peacemaking are of major concern to high-level leaders, they appear to be topics in which far fewer congregations are involved than in such ministries as overseas missions and humanitarian relief. Only 23 percent of U.S. church members say their congregation has "held a meeting at which questions about war and peacemaking were the main topic" within the past year and only 18 percent say they personally participated in a meeting of this kind. During this period the United States was at war in Iraq and continued to be involved in pacifying Afghanistan, yet only 10 percent of those surveyed had taken part in meetings at their church concerned with U.S. military involvement in countries such as Iraq or Afghanistan. This was also a time when violence between Israelis and Palestinians made daily headlines, as did recurrent struggles in Sudan, Somalia, Korea, and many other parts of the world. Members of Catholic parishes and black Protestant churches are more likely to say their congregations had hosted such meetings (28 and 29 percent did so, respectively) than are members of mainline and evangelical Protestants (21 and 19 percent, respectively). Unlike most other ministries dealing with particular needs or issues, these meetings are apparently no more common in large congregations than in smaller ones. The central questions, therefore, are why so few congregations engage in this kind of transcultural ministry and how those that are engaged manage to mobilize this activity.

The key factor in congregations' avoidance of issues involving war and peace appears to be the language or frame of reference in which these issues are categorized. Whereas evangelism and humanitarian assistance are generally described in terms of need, war and peace are defined as political concerns. Thus, it makes sense to church leaders and their members to support a missionary or relief worker because people are hungry, without shelter, or in need of salvation. In contrast, war and peace are seen as issues that governments decide. As one pastor remarks, her congregation would not deal with concerns about international peace and conflicts in other countries politically but would consider it appropriate to pray for peace and for government leaders. Or, in another pastor's words, "No, that really gets into the political situation. We think the best way to peace internationally is the Gospel of Jesus Christ."

To engage in peacemaking is often to leave the church's familiar turf and enter into what is perceived as alien territory. Leaders speak with confidence about preaching, witnessing, supporting missionaries, and helping individuals who need housing or medical assistance. The images are personal and warm. The ground shifts when they talk about peacemaking. There are now frightening forces to be confronted. Leaders imagine having to "march against" some ill-defined foe. Persons in need become abstract concepts, such as "inequities." Instead of helping widows and orphans, the task becomes some hideous confrontation with "city hall," "principalities," "corporations," "political groups." We do not feel "very equipped" to do that, one pastor admits. Another says there would be "cultural things" and "historical factors" that "we really can't understand." Global reality ceases to be a secure place in which people around the world are fellow Christians and instead presents a picture of chaos and confusion.

Of course church leaders know that Jesus encouraged his followers to be peacemakers, just as he taught them to feed the hungry and clothe the naked. Yet when confronted with this point, a common response is to interpret peace to mean something emotional or spiritual, such as being calm or serene or having peace of mind. "I believe there is a false peace," one pastor explains, adding that Jesus's definition meant "peace with God" and "not as the world gives." The distinction between false and true peace coincides with another difference. False peace of the kind that involves politics is complicated, whereas true peace is simple. To imagine a program specifically concerned with peacemaking is thus to feel burdened, heavy, and puzzled compared with advocating a simple message of spiritual peace, which is uplifting, light, and straightforward.

Another objection to peacemaking is that it deviates from leaders' interest in planting or helping to plant churches. Sending a missionary is a direct way to further this cause. Supplying food, shelter, or medical assistance helps the people who belong to new churches or gives local pastors a way to attract people. Peacemaking suggests diverting time and resources from these important activities. "Our focus is on raising up churches and bringing the message that we have to people," explains one pastor. Peacemaking connotes something the World Council of Churches might try to do, but it does not resonate with his philosophy of the church or spark a burning desire. His goal is to "change individual hearts" with the expectation that peace of that kind "will somehow filter through any violent situation or oppressive environment."

Church leaders also want their efforts to be successful. In describing humanitarian and missionary programs, they point to a medical clinic that was established, a church built, a conference funded, a water system installed. They do not talk about millions starving, homeless, or living in abject poverty. When they consider peacemaking, they have no ready success stories to tell. They think about Rwanda or the Middle East. With these examples in mind, they ponder peacemaking and say, as one pastor observes, "I question the ultimate effectiveness of it." With no hope of success, as they see it, the best course is thus to minister after the fact to the displaced persons and casualties of war.

At churches where concerns about war and peace are emphasized leaders generally use categories that render the topics understandable in terms other than politics, personal serenity, or spiritual calm. For instance, one pastor says his church tends to "take more of a holistic view," explaining that people are "part of the whole" and that this understanding of peacemaking "is much healthier and much less likely to make it simply a political thing." His church has been able to assist with ministries involving reconciliation between Jews and Muslims, for instance, and among Christians in non-Christian countries. Another leader admits that his congregation lacks resources to do much with peacemaking but says he wants to do more. When asked why, he explains, "We are all concerned about justice issues" and illustrates the point by talking about labor relations and fair trade, which he regards as similar to war and peace. A Catholic priest makes a similar argument, asserting the need to be a "moral" voice on issues that are too often narrowly defined by politicians. Other leaders note the connection between peacemaking and humanitarianism, arguing that one is a way of achieving the other. Yet another way of reframing the topic is the language of reconciliation. To be a peacemaker means being involved interpersonally in difficult situations, such as in a country where Muslims and Christians have been at odds with each other. In this sense, activities such as listening and being a good neighbor can qualify. However, these understandings are the exceptions more than the rule.

Peacemaking is thus a transcultural issue that most congregations are happy to delegate to larger and more specialized entities such as governments or nongovernmental organizations. Pastors who have thought about peacemaking point to the State Department, the United Nations, and such organizations as African Enterprise, the International Justice Mission, Witness for Peace, and Amnesty International. Because peacemaking, as they perceive it, involves political issues that are difficult to understand, church leaders are content to let somebody else deal with them. Pastors say, in effect, we know our limits. If they become involved, they do so by serving on a board or committee external to the congregation. They figure church members will do the same rather than involving the congregation in something that might well be a failure.

RELIGIOUS FREEDOM

Another international issue that congregations are gingerly becoming involved in is religious freedom and human rights. This issue sometimes suffers from the same lack of attention as war and peacekeeping because clergy and lay members define it as a political concern rather than as a matter of faith. Questions about religious freedom and human rights have in fact been addressed by policy makers. In 1996 the Clinton administration created a State Department Advisory Committee on Religious Freedom. A year later the first congressionally mandated State Department report on human rights violations associated with religion appeared, and in 1998 the International Religious Freedom Act became an official part of U.S. foreign policy. Political scientist Allen D. Hertzke writes that the movement behind this act is "the major force in pressing for U.S. leadership against global religious persecution" in such places as China, Sudan, and Saudi Arabia. Hertzke suggests that these efforts have pumped energy into a broader array of human rights issues, "from gulags in North Korea to human trafficking" in prostitution.[11]

As a policy initiative, the effort to promote religious freedom appears to have resulted from a convergence of two powerful forces: a broad coalition of specialized nongovernmental organizations and a cluster of influential lawmakers interested in promoting democracy abroad. The NGOs that became involved read like a *Who's Who* of the international community: American Civil Liberties Union, Amnesty International, Catholic World Relief, Human Rights Watch, International League for

Human Rights, Safe Harbor International, and the World Council of Churches, among others. Besides Presidents Bill Clinton and George W. Bush, other public officials who played a pivotal role in supporting the effort include congressional leaders Dick Armey, Frank Wolf, and Arlen Specter and such executive branch figures as John Bolton, Paul Wolfowitz, and James Woolsey.

The foreign policy perspective on religious freedom, though, begs the question of whether this is an issue that draws the hearts and minds of grassroots churchgoers and enlists the energies of the ordinary congregation. On the one hand, both the history and the continuing prevalence of religious persecution in the world suggest that rank-and-file church members should be keenly interested in this issue. According to one source, more than thirteen million Christians worldwide died between 1950 and 2000 under conditions that could be described as "martyrdom," with approximately 160,000 dying each year at the start of the twenty-first century and foreign missionaries constituting one of the categories at greatest risk of premature or violent death.[12] On the other hand, the International Religious Freedom Act appears to have animated leaders inside the Beltway more than in the nation's heartland. The news media certainly publicized it less than policy debates about abortion and gay marriage.

It is difficult to obtain an accurate picture of what congregations are doing about religious freedom and international human rights because these issues are framed in varying language and often dealt with by specialized agencies that receive support from individuals rather than directly from congregations. Most church members believe their congregations should be concerned with these issues. For instance, 40 percent say their congregation should emphasize the "problem of religious persecution in other countries" a lot and another 38 percent say this problem should be emphasized some. Fewer than one in five think this is a problem that their congregation should emphasize only a little (11 percent) or not at all (8 percent).

Our interviews with church leaders suggest that the proportion of congregations currently involved in religious freedom and human rights issues is probably no greater than 25 to 30 percent. Some of the factors that deter congregations from being involved in peacemaking activities pertain here as well. These include the perception that human rights are technical or legal matters and are thus too complicated to understand and deal with effectively. There is, however, a line of argument that draws pastors into the issue. This is the idea that Christians everywhere are part of the same body and thus should stand together with those who are being persecuted. In fact, pastors usually respond to broader questions about religious freedom and human rights by focusing on instances where Christians are being persecuted. In so doing, they often mention activities such as prayer vigils and awareness days that grew out of concerns about persecution in communist countries during the Cold War era. They also emphasize current examples, including persecution of Christians in China and conflicts between Christians and Muslims or Christians and Hindus.

One pastor expresses the typical view in stating that "we are all one. We are all part of the Body of Christ. If you stub your toe, the whole body hurts. There are whole portions of the Body of Christ in the world today that are being heartily persecuted. We need to be concerned for them. We need to be praying for them. We need to be advocating on their behalf." Other leaders speak of the need for Christians in the United States to overcome their cultural isolation and to understand the difficulties fellow believers face in other parts of the world. The rationale for being involved is, in this respect, quite similar to the reasons leaders give for humanitarian work. The Christian obligation when people are hurting is to help them. The same holds when people are oppressed.

Increasingly, the language of rights is also part of the argument for being concerned about religious freedom. Church leaders insist that rights are God-given and apply to everyone on earth. Rights language thus extends beyond the claim that Christians should be concerned about fellow Christians. Global humanity replaces global Christianity, leveling the playing field for people of all faiths. One's concern about persecuted Christians becomes an instance of a wider principle, not just of solidarity, even though a church member may be especially vexed by injustices toward Christians. The pastor of a nondenominational church with extensive ties to religious organizations in other countries and a history of protesting at embassies in Washington, D.C., expresses the idea particularly well. "We believe that freedom of worship and religion is a right," he explains. "Just like Muslims who want to worship God, Christians love to worship God. So every human being should be given that freedom to choose who to worship and how to worship without any human interference."

Because they are receptive to doing something about religious persecution, congregations sometimes sponsor activities on a modest scale that aim to raise awareness of the problem. At a small Presbyterian church in Michigan a prayer circle prays twice a month for the "persecuted church around the world." For the International Day of Prayer held each November the pastor reminds members to include persecuted Christians in their prayers. At an Assembly of God church in Ohio the pastor asks people twice a year to pray for persecuted Christians. The prayers sometimes become more urgent when a missionary sends a letter about persecution. The missions director at a California church describes praying for a missionary in an Asian country who recently fled across the border on foot after hearing he was going to be arrested. Some of the leaders speak from general knowledge about instances of persecution that have been in the popular media, but most refer to stories they hear from acquaintances involved in outreach programs. They speak often of Christians being oppressed in China, the Sudan, Cuba, Indonesia, Libya, and Iraq. They try at least to mention these places during Sunday worship services.

When fueled by personal knowledge of persecution, these small reminders sometimes blossom into larger events. The pastor who said the whole body hurts when a toe is stubbed found there was growing concern in his congregation about religious freedom. One member had contacts in Washington. Others were hearing about persecution from missionaries in Africa. An annual awareness day during which the congregation was supposed to remember persecuted Christians in their prayers turned into a weekend conference. A keynote speaker who had served as a missionary in Africa told about violence that he had personally witnessed toward Christians. Another speaker, a Masai, spoke about persecution of his people. In all, the conference focused on ten countries in which Christians were being persecuted.

When they do not sponsor such activities, church leaders usually attribute their inattention to a lack of resources. Unlike war and peacemaking, which more often strike pastors as being alien to their central purpose, religious persecution is clearly relevant but simply a lower priority than other missions and humanitarian programs. Although their denomination's central office may be involved, the clergy view the issue as remote. "I think it is seen as an issue that is so far away that they can't do anything about it," one denominational official remarks. Pastors echo this sentiment. "There are lots of places in the world where we could be involved," says one, "but we're a small congregation with lots of commitments so it's important for us to focus where we can."

The issue of religious freedom is similar to peacemaking, though, in how church leaders think it should be addressed. Other than the occasional meeting or awareness Sunday, religious freedom is best handled by specialized organizations, pastors say. Denominational agencies, such as the Washington offices of major denominations, are one example. A "level of sophistication" is required, one pastor explains, "that might better be done on the denominational level." Other examples include Amnesty International, which a number of pastors say they support, at least personally, and the International Justice Mission, with which a number of congregations have worked by hosting fund-raisers and sponsoring human rights attorneys to investigate instances of discrimination against Christians in such diverse contexts as Uganda, India, and Turkey. Church leaders also perceive government to be an effective way to address questions of religious freedom and thus encourage church members to sign petitions or support legislation. "We sent mailings to our congressional delegations in support of the administration's efforts," recalls a Catholic lay leader. At another church the pastor mobilized the youth group to write letters to officials concerning an amnesty issue that had arisen in Guatemala. At yet another church a network of members regularly sends e-mails to officials in Washington.

THE MARKS OF A TRANSCULTURAL CONGREGATION

Most church members in the United States are involved at least to some degree with congregations that do something to support transcultural ministries, but some congregations are much more involved with these activities than others are. These differences are evident in leaders' descriptions of their programs. Congregations also vary in the number of transcultural ministries they sponsor. For instance, 89 percent of church members say their congregations have been involved during the past year in at least one of the activities we have just considered, but only 24 percent have been involved in more than two of them.[13]

The fact that some congregations are more transculturally engaged than others is also apparent in members' perceptions. When asked, "Overall—through preaching, programs, and other activities—how much does your congregation focus on people living outside of the United States?" 12 percent of members say a great deal, another 41 percent say a fair amount, 32 percent say only a little, 12 percent say hardly any, and 4 percent are unsure. These response indicate that relatively few members think their congregations are primarily concerned with people in other countries. However, an alternative question gives a somewhat different impression: 37 percent think their congregation emphasizes "international ministries" a lot (another 32 percent say "some"). And even more—46 percent—say their congregation emphasizes "helping people who live in other countries" a lot (with 35 percent more saying "some").[14]

What then are the distinguishing marks of a transcultural congregation? When church leaders reflect on this question, they naturally emphasize theological reasons to be involved in ministries to the wider world. Mark's Great Commission teaching of taking the gospel to all people is alive and heeded in transcultural churches. To be a Christian means sharing the gospel, and this responsibility entails a global as well as a local commitment. Being witnesses in Judea and Samaria implies serving one's community and nation; going to the ends of the earth is not only commanded but also possible. A missional emphasis is another theological mark of the transcultural church. An emphasis on missions encompasses and extends beyond specific international programs. It defines the central purpose of the congregation, providing the rationale for all its activities, whether these are the children's ministry, a men's fellowship group, or the choir. As the pastor of an African American congregation in Illinois explains, "We don't look at it as the work of the missions department but as the basic mission of our church to go out to the nations and make disciples. This is what God commanded us to do." It is thus unnecessary to make special appeals to enlist members in overseas activities. A seamless connection exists between these activities and everything else the congregation does.

There is scarcely any disagreement about these theological arguments, although they surface more often and with greater emphasis among leaders who are involved in international ministries than among leaders who are not. Besides theology, though, organizational factors are critical. Some of these factors have become well established over the years, while others have emerged more recently as global ties become more common. As an example of the former, nearly all congregations that are heavily invested in transcultural activities take up special offerings to help needy people outside the United States. However, about half of other congregations do too. The sheer fact of having special offerings, therefore, is not a distinguishing mark of a transcultural congregation.[15] Another factor that at first blush would seem to set apart transcultural congregations is having a designated staff member who specializes in international work, such as a missions pastor or global outreach director. Among church members nationally, 18 percent say their congregation's full-time staff includes someone with special responsibility for overseas missions and other global ministries. More of the congregations that are most involved in transcultural work do have such staff. However, the data show that having a missions or global outreach director is more a function of being a large congregation than anything else. What matters more is having a missions committee—currently a feature of about four in ten congregations.[16] Smaller and larger congregations alike can organize one, if they are committed to transcultural work, and when they do, an effective committee can go a long way toward generating interest throughout the congregation. From the statistical evidence, it also appears that being involved with missionaries—supporting them, inviting them to speak, and sending people on trips to help them—are still the most distinguishing feature of a church truly committed to transcultural ministry. This is not to say that other activities, such as meetings about war and peace or prayers for persecuted Christians, are unimportant. It does mean that those concerns—or others involving relief efforts and refugees—do not signal a congregation's dedication to international ministry among its members in the same measure that missionary efforts do.

The marks of a transcultural church include leadership strategies as well. One that comes up frequently is the importance of concentrating energy rather than dissipating it. If even a few members express interest in a particular program, it will succeed more than if the congregation seeks to be involved in too many activities. One pastor puts it clearly: "We don't think that a need in itself constitutes a reason to start a ministry. We think that there also has to be a point person. If there's not a point person, we're just not going to take it on." A related strategy is to do one thing well. "I always think of KFC," a pastor in Missouri says. "You know, 'We do chicken right.'" Yet another strategy is to build enduring relationships spanning geographic boundaries. Transcultural ministries may be global, but they are also local in this respect. Pick a spot, keep going back, become well acquainted, and grow from there. Those are the best practices, leaders say.

SENDING PEOPLE ABROAD

For many churches "doing chicken right" means enlisting members to work abroad, often for no more than a few days. These programs have become increasingly attractive. They make use of the fact that members have vacations from school or work, can afford to pay for their own trips, and are looking for adventure. Placing a team of high school students in Guatemala for a week or taking a medical team to the Sudan for a month can significantly expand the efforts of full-time missionaries and relief workers. The church committees that organize these excursions anticipate larger gains as well. Seeing a mission station, school, or orphanage firsthand, they hope, will encourage church members to give more generously of their time and money in the future.

A man I will call John Ridley illustrates the potential impact of congregations' sending people abroad. He says the most significant event in his life was going to Mexico the summer he turned eighteen. Mr. Ridley is a life-long member of a conservative nondenominational church in central Ohio that has grown over the years to nearly four thousand members. With his two brothers he runs a tractor repair shop his father started in the 1950s. He and his wife enjoy living in a small town away from the bustle of urban life, which they see enough of when they visit their grown son and his family in Chicago.[17]

The trip to Mexico was arranged by Teen Missions International, an organization that specializes in short-term missionary trips. Mr. Ridley learned about it from a high school classmate who had gone to South America the summer before. The moment he heard about it, he knew it was his big chance to get out and see the world. As one of eight children, he had gone to a Christian school through ninth grade and been heavily involved in the youth group at his church. Leaving that environment for a public high school was difficult and he was glad to see it coming to an end. While his fellow students made plans for summer vacations and college in the fall, he worked at his dad's shop. Not only did he lack the money for adventures like his classmates, but his Christian values told him he should be doing something more meaningful with his life. Going to Mexico was the perfect option. He could afford it because the church helped cover the cost, and his father was willing to give him the time off because it involved missionary service.

"It was just a fantastic time," Mr. Ridley recalls. "God met me in a very special way. There is a book in the Bible called Jonah. God asked him to do something, but Jonah said no and ran in the opposite direction until he understood that he'd made the wrong decision. That was my experience. I wasn't walking with God the way I should have been. It wasn't anything more than bad thoughts in my head, but there was no meaning to my life as far as my relationship with God was concerned. God used that trip to wake me up."

God's wake-up call came to Mr. Ridley that summer as he hammered nails to construct a Bible institute in which indigenous pastors were to be trained. He remembers thinking that "this is what the world is really like. We live in a bubble in the United States and don't know the intensity and the struggles of life almost everywhere else in the world." This realization left him feeling vulnerable. "I experienced the fact that I wasn't in control. I suddenly realized that I needed God in a personal way more than I had thought. For the first time in my life, I understood that God was close to me and was interested in me. That was exciting." The next summer Mr. Ridley went back to Mexico and the following summer, now married, he and his wife "honeymooned" in Bolivia as the adult sponsors of a mission trip with two dozen teenagers. Financial constraints and raising children prevented the Ridleys from being directly involved in international missionary work for more than a decade, but they continued supporting Teen Missions through prayer and small donations, and one summer Mr. Ridley did volunteer work for three weeks at the organization's training center in Florida. When their children were in grade school and high school, the Ridleys once again became more active. One summer the whole family helped build an airstrip in the middle of a tropical rain forest in New Guinea. They worked with bush knives and handsaws for five weeks. As parents, they wanted their children to understand that "American life wasn't really the real world." The next summer their oldest daughter went back and worked as a nurse's assistant at a clinic. The experience convinced her she wanted to be a nurse, and after high school she went to nursing school and later worked for several years abroad.

More recently, the Ridleys have spent a few weeks doing mission work in other countries nearly every summer. One year they went back to Mexico to do maintenance at the Bible institute Mr. Ridley helped build on his first trip. Another year they assisted in starting a Bible training center in Ecuador. The next year they did volunteer work at an AIDS orphanage in Malawi. The following year they helped build a church in Ethiopia for refugees from Sudan and the year after that they led a short-term mission team from their church on a trip to the Philippines.

The Ridleys are but one example of the many American churchgoers who currently participate in transcultural religious and humanitarian programs by spending a few days or weeks abroad. Like the Ridleys, some get hooked and return again and again to participate in short-term missions, while others go once or twice and a much larger number stay at home but contribute financially, pray, provide logistic support, host fund-raisers, send their teenagers, serve on committees, attend dinners, and hear reports.

By all indications, short-term mission trips have become quite popular. Nobody knows exactly when amateur volunteers started thinking of themselves as short-term missionaries, but studies of the phenomenon generally locate its origins in the 1950s and 1960s and suggest that it experienced a dramatic increase in popularity during the 1980s and 1990s.[18] One of the pioneers in this effort is an organization called Youth With a Mission, founded in 1960 by a young man inspired by a church trip to Mexico, which encouraged him to think about organizing trips for other students, some 30,000 or more of whom were being sent annually by the late 1990s. Teen Missions International followed a few years later and since 1971 claims to have sent more than 40,000 youth to 200 locations in more than 110 countries. Campus Crusade for Christ, Operation Mobilization, and Bethany College of Missions began sponsoring such programs about the same time.[19] Christian colleges, denominations, and individual congregations are also turning increasingly to short-term mission volunteers. For instance, the Southern Baptist Convention reportedly sends more than 150,000 of its members abroad annually as short-term team members or volunteers, and the United Methodist Church sends more than 100,000. Saddleback Church in Lake Forest, California, claims to send about 4,500 of its members on such trips each year.[20] Another indication of the growing popularity of short-term missions is that 12 percent of active churchgoers who were in high school youth groups since 2000 have gone overseas on a mission trip, and that figure is up from only 5 percent among churchgoers who were teens in the 1990s, 4 percent of those who were teens in the 1980s, and only 2 percent before that.[21]

In addition to their numeric growth, short-term mission trips have attracted increasing attention in the mass media. During the U.S. invasion of Afghanistan in 2001, two American women who were captured by the Taliban and then rescued by U.S. troops were short-term missionaries.[22] In 2004 an American Airlines pilot made major headlines and was eventually suspended for asking his passengers to raise their hands if they were Christians. He had just returned from a mission trip to Costa Rica, he explained to reporters, and "felt that God was telling me to say something."[23]

The growing popularity of short-term mission trips has generated considerable debate among church leaders themselves. On the one hand, proponents argue that short-term volunteers greatly expand the work of Christianity in other countries by bringing extra hands to teach Bible classes and repair buildings or supplying technical advice to indigenous micro businesses and medical assistance at health clinics. Proponents also envision these trips as ways to motivate long-term giving to mission programs and to recruit full-time missionaries. On the other hand, critics contend that short-term volunteers are often poorly trained or organized and are essentially a drain on the busy schedules of full-time workers and on the scarce resources of those who provide hospitality. Gospel tourism, the pejorative term some critics use, can be a substitute for more serious engagement.[24] As one leader observes, "I'm not sure that going to Cancun to witness on the beach for a few days is what our church should be supporting." Whichever view is correct, short-term missions are an increasingly important transcultural bridge between churches in the United States and communities in other countries. They bring Americans into contact with other cultures and expose people elsewhere to American customs and values.

The most comprehensive guide to these programs is *Maximum Impact Short-Term Mission: The God-Commanded, Repetitive Deployment of Swift, Temporary, Non-Professional Missionaries,* by Roger Peterson, Gordon Aeschliman, and R. Wayne Sneed.[25] These authors argue that short-term mission trips can significantly amplify the global outreach of Christians in the United States by making use of lay people who are neither called nor trained to be career missionaries but whose time and interests encourage them to spend a few days or weeks serving abroad.[26]

The authors of *Maximum Impact Short-Term Mission* guess that about 10 percent of U.S. congregations are or have been involved in sponsoring short-term mission trips.[27] In reality, the actual number is probably much higher. Forty-four percent of church members nationally report that their congregation sent a group to another country to do short-term missions or relief work during the past twelve months. If we correct for the over-representation of large churches and count all congregations, large or small, equally, an estimated 32 percent of all congregations sponsor short-term mission trips annually. In raw numbers, this is closer to 100,000 congregations, rather than the 35,000 suggested by *Maximum Impact* or the 40,000 reported by *Christianity Today.*[28]

Maximum Impact's authors guess that the average mission trip consists of twelve people. But again this estimate appears to be low. Most of these trips do involve small numbers, according to church members who claim to know. For instance, 34 percent say the group at their congregation included fewer than ten people, and 28 percent say between ten and twenty people participated, whereas only 4 percent say it involved more than fifty people. However, the mean number is about eighteen instead of twelve.

Large U.S. congregations are particularly likely to sponsor short-term mission trips. For instance, 57 percent of the members at churches of a thousand or more report that their congregation sponsored a short-term mission trip in the past year, compared with only 27 percent of members in churches of fewer than two hundred. The groups from large congregations are also composed of more people. For instance, a majority of the groups at large churches include more than ten people, whereas at smaller churches only a third do. Evangelical churches are the most likely to sponsor mission trips, but nearly half of mainline Protestants say their congregations do as well, compared with about a third of Catholics and members of historically black denominations.[29]

Maximum Impact says short-term missions reflect a new paradigm that is replacing old-style missionary programs and overcoming the "well-intentioned efforts [that] birthed structures *limiting* involvement rather than facilitating involvement."[30] In this spirit, some leaders speculate that interest in short-term programs may be growing because of declining strength in traditional approaches. However, the evidence suggests that short-term missions are less a replacement than a complement to more conventional outreach programs. Not only is it untrue, as we have seen, that full-time missionary and relief efforts have declined (they have in fact grown), but churches that sponsor short-term mission trips are also significantly more likely than other congregations to sponsor a wide variety of transcultural ministries. For instance, 88 percent of congregations with short-term mission trips also support missionaries abroad, according to members, compared with 62 percent of congregations without mission trips, and 62 percent have hosted a guest speaker from another country, compared with 38 percent of those lacking mission trips. Thirty-six percent of the former but only 24 percent of the latter have helped support a refugee family.

When churches sponsor short-term mission trips, members are also significantly more likely to perceive their congregation as part of a global community. For instance, 61 percent of members at these churches say their congregation emphasizes helping people who live in other countries a lot, whereas only 35 percent of members at other churches say this, and 68 percent of the former say their congregation's overall programs focus a great deal or a fair amount on people living outside the United States, compared with 41 percent of the latter.

The reason mission trips and perceptions of the congregation's commitment to international programs go hand in hand is that these trips are typically well-publicized and require the congregation's prayers and financial support. "Any time a team goes out," the pastor of a Baptist church in Kentucky observes, "we put up a picture of the team and somebody will speak at the worship service about where the team is going." A member of the missions committee at an Episcopal church in Connecticut says there is a big display board with pictures from recent trips and sometimes a banquet to help raise money.

Besides size and confessional tradition, several factors influence the likelihood of congregations sponsoring short-term mission trips. Larger congregations are generally better financed than small congregations and this, in turn, gives them the opportunity to hire more staff. Thus, among churches with one full-time pastor, only 29 percent sponsor mission trips, but this proportion rises to 46 percent among churches with two or three full-time clergy and to 70 percent among churches with more than ten. Seventy-six percent of congregations with a staff person specializing in global ministries sponsor short-term mission trips. Lay committees are also important. Sixty-four percent of congregations that have an overseas missions committee sponsor short-term mission trips, compared with only 28 percent of those without a missions committee.

Whether a congregation is located in a city, suburb, or small town bears little relationship to its likelihood of sponsoring short-term mission trips, nor does it matter much if the church is in a religiously diverse community; however, churches on the West Coast are somewhat more likely than congregations in the Midwest or South to sponsor these trips, while ones on the East Coast are somewhat less likely to do so. Having a large number of immigrants in one's congregation would presumably motivate it to engage in mission trips abroad, but the only notable fact associated with immigrants is that congregations with no immigrants are less likely to sponsor mission trips than those with even a few immigrants (28 percent versus 50 percent).

By contacting church leaders and mission agencies, the authors of *Maximum Impact* estimate that about one million, or about 1 percent of U.S. church members, personally participate in a short-term mission trip to another country during any given twelve-month period.[31] Like their guess about the number of congregations that sponsor such trips, this estimate is probably low. Nationally, 2.1 percent of active church members say they have gone to another country on a religious mission trip during the past year. If there are (conservatively) 80 million active church members in the United States, this means that approximately 1.6 million are involved in short-term mission trips annually. Although sampling error must be considered, an estimate of 1.6 million is reasonable in view of the fact that the one million described in *Maximum Impact* is limited largely to evangelical Protestants and to those who participate through national agencies and other formal programs. Members' estimates of the number participating from their congregations yield similar overall figures of between 1.5 million and 1.8 million.[32] Most of this number are indeed short-term participants. The median is eight days abroad, not counting travel, the mode is seven days, and 83 percent spend two weeks or less abroad. In total, then, short-term volunteers contribute approximately 30,000 person-years to U.S. mission efforts abroad—about a fourth the amount provided by professional missionaries. The dollar value of this effort, using rates established by the Washington-based research organization Independent Sector, is approximately $1.1 billion (not counting preparation time and travel days).[33]

If about 2 percent of church members go abroad on a mission trip each year, the probability of someone participating at least once in his or her lifetime is close to 100 percent, since there is about a fifty-year span between the ages when most people go on a mission: in their late teens and seventies. If that were true, 100 percent of American churchgoers might participate in a short-term mission trip sometime in the next fifty years. Anecdotal evidence, though, indicates that the actual lifetime probability for any given person is considerably lower because some who participate one year are the same who take part in another year. Nevertheless, the lifetime probability of a particular church member going abroad on a short-term mission trip could reasonably be 20 to 25 percent, assuming that few participate more than four or five times, and meaning that a fifth to a quarter of all U.S. church members could be involved at some point in their lives.

Youth With a Mission, Teen Missions International, and the programs of local congregations encourage teenagers to go abroad on mission trips, like Mr. Ridley did. The idea is that young people typically have summers and school holidays free, may be looking for a transcultural experience, and could become inspired at an opportune moment to think about full-time mission work in the future. Among adults who are currently active church members, about five-sixths were involved in church activities during high school (38 percent were very or extremely active), and of those who were involved at all, 16 percent went on a mission trip of some kind at least once (meaning that among all church members, 13 percent did so). Nearly three-quarters went on mission trips within the United States, while about a quarter participated in an activity in another country. Thus, among all currently active church members about 3.6 percent went abroad on a short-term mission trip during high school.[34]

Published accounts and conversations with church leaders give the impression that short-term mission trips are usually composed of young people who have the time and energy or retirees with flexible schedules or church women serving on missions committees. Although people of all ages, locations, occupations, and church traditions go on mission trips, the typical participant is a white, married, college-educated male in his forties or fifties whose children are grown and who lives in a relatively homogeneous suburb in the South or Midwest. Religiously, he is affiliated with an evangelical church where he has been a member for at least three years, attends every Sunday, and holds a lay leadership position, such as chairing a committee or teaching Sunday school.[35] The short-term mission participant is thus similar to the person who is simply a faithful churchgoer, period, with the significant exception that active churchgoers are more likely to be women. It may be that men are more likely than women to go abroad on mission trips because congregations discourage women from assuming leadership roles, but this possibility seems doubtful as a blanket explanation.[36] A more likely reason is that men in general are more likely than women to travel overseas because of military service or business. For instance, in one national study 66 percent of men, compared with 52 percent of women, said they had traveled or lived outside the United States, and among those who had traveled, men were also more likely than women to have gone significant distances, such as to the Middle East, China, Japan, or India.[37] Men's freedom to travel may also be less constrained than women's by family obligations, such as caring for children or aging parents.[38] Having served in the armed forces definitely increases the likelihood of going on a short-term mission trip, as does having lived abroad for at least a year.

If the typical participant in a mission trip is in many ways indistinguishable from the active churchgoer, some characteristics are nevertheless distinctive among the former. For instance, mission participants tend to be in their thirties to fifties because congregations on the whole have more of this age group, but younger adults are actually about twice as likely to go on a mission trip in a given year as middle-aged adults are.[39] This is partly because younger adults have fewer family responsibilities. Having a college education is not only a characteristic of the typical participant in mission trips but also one that doubles the chances of being a participant.[40] Those with college educations may be better able to afford an international trip or have a more flexible work schedule. They may simply have been taught that broadening one's horizons through travel is desirable. The typical participant does not live in a religiously diverse community, but those who do are more likely to become participants than those who do not. It is not the case, however, that belonging to a congregation with a large number of immigrants increases the likelihood of being part of an overseas mission trip. Frequent attendees at church services are naturally more likely to go on mission trips than infrequent churchgoers. Members of small congregations are less likely to participate in these trips, but contrary to some views, the chances of participating are just as great among members of medium-sized congregations as among those of megachurches.

The processes through which short-term mission participants are recruited and their motivations for going are quite varied but reflect the growing impact of international networks and awareness. Mr. Ridley's desire to see the world and having an idea of how to fulfill this desire in an acceptable way is an example. He says he "just needed to experience something new and exciting" and "faraway places are new and exciting." Going to Mexico was a way to escape the "normal routine." Yet it was truly a temporary escape. After a few weeks, he returned to the tractor repair shop where he resumed the familiar routine. He did not have to join the military or become an airline pilot to see the world. Teen Missions provided a relatively painless alternative. Yet he would likely have stayed at home had it not been for his classmate who, in a sense, paved the way. He also had an older brother who was interested in missionary work and eventually became one. Personal networks always matter, but now they are more likely to involve friends and relatives who have traveled or lived in other countries.

The networks through which Mr. Ridley became involved in short-term missions included a church and a well-established international organization. For many people, these are the key ingredients. Although it may be a happenstance that a friend encourages someone to participate, the likelihood of this occurring increases significantly when congregations join forces with specialized agencies. In these instances, church members frequently go on mission trips because they have already been heavily involved in the international programs of their congregation.

At a nondenominational community church in northern Virginia, Mark Linder illustrates the process by which the combined effort of a congregation and an international agency leads churchgoers to become personally involved in an overseas program. Founded in the 1980s by a small group of adults in their twenties from various Catholic and Protestant backgrounds, the congregation initially struggled to gain a foothold in its busy suburban neighborhood, but by the mid-1990s was well on its way to being an established church and now has about five hundred members, a full-time pastor, and a leadership team of five elected lay people. Unlike large congregations, it was unable to organize a significant global outreach program of its own, but some of its members worked for international companies and the congregation generally agreed that it was important for Christians to be concerned about humanitarian needs in other countries. To this end, they invited a representative from World Relief to make a presentation about its work in Africa, launched a series of studies and meetings, organized a prayer group, met with some other international relief agencies, tentatively decided to participate in a five-church consortium to support World Relief's efforts, and sent a group from the church to Sierra Leone to view the situation there firsthand. Mr. Linder was one of those who went.

He says he felt like God had been working in his life for a long time to prepare him for this moment. Although he had joined the church only three years earlier, he had been involved in missions and relief programs at other churches for twenty years. At one, he had made friends with a man from Sierra Leone who often spoke of the civil war in that country. Mr. Linder was especially moved by the attack on the Pentagon on September 11, 2001. His interest in Sierra Leone increased because it is largely a Muslim country and he felt the urgency of building bridges with the Muslim world.

On their first trip to Sierra Leone, Mr. Linder and the others visited villages in which World Relief was rebuilding about twelve hundred homes of mud brick for returning refugees. They provided some contributions, participated in several of the projects, met with local pastors, and made connections with some of the churches in the area that were cooperating with World Relief. U.S. State Department helicopters helped the group move from place to place more easily. They were particularly affected by the plight of children in the area, a third of whom die before the age of five. Their report when they returned home persuaded the congregation to focus its efforts on a nutrition and educational program for the children. A year or so later, Mr. Linder and three others from the congregation went back to Sierra Leone to see how the program was going and to gain additional cross-cultural training. They brought with them a large number of wheelchairs and assisted with several health-related projects but mainly focused on building relationships and providing encouragement. Since then, Mr. Linder has been organizing activities to further the congregation's involvement. Some have been fund-raisers, such as hosting a benefit concert by a jazz band and encouraging church members and their families to purchase gifts for the people in Sierra Leone instead of for themselves. They have also developed personal connections with a Sierra Leone congregation in their local community.

As this example shows, short-term mission trips can no longer be understood simply as Americans doing volunteer work abroad. They include informational "site visits," much like a prospective donor to a university campus might make before deciding to make a financial contribution, and they are meant to build trust, assess needs, and ascertain whether funds are being put to good use. Typically, they involve a direct link between a local congregation in the United States and the growing number of Christian organizations that are present in other countries. In Sierra Leone, for instance, the number of Christians grew more than tenfold during the twentieth century and their proportion more than doubled, from 4.6 percent to 11.5 percent.[41] Thus, despite being a religious minority, Christians are a significant enough presence that an organization like World Relief and a church in northern Virginia can work directly with local congregations.

PARTICIPATING AT HOME

Besides the short-term volunteers who actually spend time abroad, millions of American churchgoers assist in their own congregations and communities by providing logistical support for these and other international efforts. A survey of major Protestant mission agencies identified approximately 22,000 full-time staff serving in the United States, an increase of about 50 percent in the past decade, and more than 600,000 volunteers, a more than tenfold increase.[42] The number assisting as volunteers for international programs in congregations is of course significantly larger, including between 700,000 and one million who serve on missions committees, and as many as sixteen million—20 percent of active church members—who do volunteer work that they perceive to be of international benefit.[43] Beyond this, at least thirty million church members hear missionaries or other religious workers from abroad speak each year and sixty million give money to international relief and hunger projects.

Min Chu, a Stanford graduate who is the daughter of Chinese immigrants and has lived and studied abroad, provides insight into the behind-the-scenes activities involved with international programs by people whose work is mainly within the United States. She attends a 2,500-member Presbyterian church in Los Angeles where she serves on its missions committee. Her primary interest is the International Justice Mission, which she became involved with almost from the time it began in 1997. Although she has made trips to India and Thailand on behalf of International Justice Mission, her responsibilities as a mother have made it easier to support the organization through her church and by speaking at other churches and Christian groups. Ms. Chu's conviction about the importance of working for justice in the world preceded her involvement in the International Justice Mission but was reinforced by seeing the plight of young prostitutes firsthand. She remembers one she met in India who had been rescued twice and resold by her father and stepmother. A couple of months later the girl, only seventeen, died of AIDS.

Ms. Chu says none of the trips people from her church have taken on behalf of the International Justice Mission would have been as likely had it not been for the missions committee. The group is a leadership team under the supervision of a staff member in charge of global outreach. It administers an annual budget of more than $1 million, which supports programs in ten countries, and functions like the board of directors of a large organization, voting on policies, approving budgets, and monitoring results. Besides the International Justice Mission, the team maintains contact with about fifty missionaries, sends out about three hundred short-term volunteers each year, works with partner churches in Africa, and holds meetings to enlist the involvement of local business leaders who may have international ties. The team also oversees a number of subcommittees with specialized responsibilities, such as training short-term volunteers, organizing informational events, maintaining a Web site, and coordinating prayer requests. She says it is an awesome infrastructure that handles an amazing number of details, from arranging plane tickets to scheduling guest speakers.

Ms. Chu's activities range from attending committee meetings once or twice a month, to co-teaching a course on global Christianity sponsored by several congregations in the area, to brainstorming plans for future projects. One of the ideas that has been particularly successful is to identify members of the congregation who take a special interest in a particular country even though they have never lived there. At some point the person may have an opportunity to visit; meanwhile, he or she learns about its culture, reads about programs the church is sponsoring there, communicates with missionaries and indigenous leaders by e-mail or letter, and prays for them. In this way, the church member is able to personalize what might otherwise seem remote or abstract.

Like many volunteers, Ms. Chu believes that the more one becomes involved the more one learns how to be effective. One thing she learned about international justice work is that young people, who are more idealistic, are easier to mobilize than older people. She has been working more with the congregation's youth for this reason. Another lesson is to get in and get out, meaning that local churches in other countries ultimately bear the responsibility for promoting justice in their own communities.

Ms. Chu also reports that serving on a committee greatly increases the chances of being asked to do things one never imagined. For instance, she has learned a lot about starting small businesses in developing countries and she recently hosted a refugee family in her home for a week to help them learn simple things such as going up and down a staircase and using a gas stove. "It's really a high privilege to be part of this work," she says. "We get first class seats to see what God is doing around the world and it is an amazing thing. It is very exciting."

Volunteers who become involved with helping people in other countries share some of the traits of those who embark on short-term mission trips, but are a larger and more diverse segment of the churchgoing population and are thus harder to characterize. They are most likely to be in their forties or fifties, live in the South or Midwest, and attend services every Sunday. Unlike those who go abroad, they are more likely to be women than men and are less likely to be college graduates or from an evangelical church.[44]

Compared with church members who do not volunteer for international ministries, these people are clearly more involved in their congregations and more interested in the variety of ways in which churches serve people abroad. Nearly all of them have given money in the past year for international hunger or relief projects, and they are about three times more likely than the average church member to have gone to another country on a religious mission trip in the past year or to have done so when they were in high school. On average, they give more money to religious causes and a larger percentage of their giving goes to international ministries. A majority have attended a meeting where a missionary or religious worker from another country spoke and about a quarter have signed a petition or written to a political official in the past year about an international issue such as poverty or human rights. They attend church services more often than nonvolunteers do, are more likely to hold leadership positions in their congregations, and have more church friends.

All of these factors, especially being actively involved in their congregations and sharing an interest in the plight of others, are conducive to becoming a volunteer but do not describe the actual process. The best way to motivate someone to become involved in international ministries, leaders say, is to demonstrate a need and then give the person a job that makes use of his or her talents. A large proportion of Americans do volunteer work of one kind or another, studies show. Among active church members, about four in ten do volunteer work in any given year. An even larger proportion value being helpful and try to express this ideal through their work, caring for their families, and being good neighbors. In one national study, 98 percent of Americans said "helping people in need" was at least fairly important to them personally, and 73 percent said it was very important or absolutely essential.[45] Among active church members, 67 percent say it is important for Christians to share their faith with non-Christians (and most of the remainder say this is fairly important), by which they generally mean showing love by helping others rather than simply seeking converts, and nearly everyone (92 percent) agrees that "people of faith have a moral responsibility to learn about problems in other parts of the world and do what they can to help." Thus, the motivation to help is usually present; it takes leadership, though, to translate this vague desire into concrete action.

The role of leadership is nicely illustrated in the experience of Frank Burke, a financial analyst in his forties who attends a 3,000-member Baptist church in Atlanta. Having grown up in a large family with a meager income and seeing his mother cry because there was not enough money to buy groceries, Mr. Burke vowed to make as much money as he could and then later in life help others. "The grand plan was to become stinking rich like Bill Gates and then at some point do philanthropy," he says. "The first part wasn't working out so well so I kept waiting. Meanwhile, we were actually living in a nice house, owned a boat, and were enjoying life pretty well." At work, he rubbed shoulders with upper-middle-class people, presented an image of success, and learned how to win in the marketplace. Always, though, there was "this tapping at my heart." Eventually he realized he was reaching middle age and decided it was "insane" to keep postponing his desire to be of greater service to people in need. "I thought there had to be something I could do and I started reading about things but never felt anything really connect."

By this time Mr. Burke and his wife had been attending their church for about ten years. She had served on committees, but he had never been more than marginally involved. One day the senior pastor invited him to a meeting for "business guys." About a dozen showed up. The pastor described several programs he was thinking about initiating and asked the group to do some brainstorming. One idea was to help widows and orphans of the AIDS crisis in Africa. Mr. Burke was intrigued. "For one thing, poverty was something I'd always been curious about. Why are some countries so poor? What keeps them that way?" Secondly, this was an opportunity to help children, and, as a parent, Mr. Burke was close to his own children and felt his heartstrings being pulled as he thought about orphans. He was also fascinated by the AIDS crisis itself, especially its relationship to sexual orientations and the devastation it has brought to Africa.

Had it not been for the pastor inviting him to this meeting, Mr. Burke might have continued thinking about ways to serve without actually becoming involved. The pastor was also wise to lay out several ideas (some of the other men were less interested in Africa than in local ministries). As plans to help orphans and vulnerable children in Africa unfolded, Mr. Burke found a niche for his own abilities. "I'm a very good manager and a pretty good people leader," he says. "But I know my weaknesses. I thought this might be a chance to grow and to develop some additional leadership skills."

He needed those skills as the work progressed. Some of the tasks, such as setting up a Web site and e-mail address, were relatively simple, but the personnel aspects were complex. Several people blasted him with e-mails saying the project was off target because preaching Jesus is the only way to help people in Africa. One wanted to drop everything and go help build a church in Africa. Another volunteered for an important task but failed to follow through. Gradually, Mr. Burke built a team of fellow businesspeople, mostly women, who shared his concerns about the AIDS crisis.

Like Ms. Chu, Mr. Burke says it is essential to partner with a specialized international agency (in this case, World Vision), and then with the help of that organization learn more about the needs in a specific location. His committee is now supporting World Vision's work in one county composed of seventy-five little villages with about five huts in each. Among other things, the committee sponsors an annual churchwide fund-raising drive that has provided enough money to sponsor more than 250 orphans.

RETURN ON INVESTMENT?

There is little controversy about serving on humanitarian committees, the way Ms. Chu and Mr. Burke do. The wisdom of sending people abroad has sparked more debate. The cost is high, critics charge, relative to the alternatives for which the same funds might be used. Although many Americans can afford it, participating in short-term mission programs is not cheap and thus questions about its real and perceived benefits inevitably arise. Judging from interviews with participants and from information on the Web sites of churches and sponsoring agencies, the average trip costs at least $1,000 per person and many total much more. Thus, in a given year Americans spend an estimated $1.6 billion—at minimum—on short-term mission trips, equaling nearly half the amount spent on all other U.S. mission programs combined. More than four million of the world's poorest people could live on that amount for a full year.

Mission trips do contribute to the programs of churches in other countries. Mr. Ridley's assistance with construction projects and airstrips is one example; the people in Sierra Leone are probably receiving more help because of Mr. Linder's trip than if he had not visited. The same is true of Ms. Chu's and Mr. Burke's activities. Although most of their effort has been inside the United States, both have made visits to the people their churches are helping and are in a better position to engage in effective planning. Others who have gone on mission trips argue that the money was well spent, compared with having sent a check somewhere and being unsure how it would be used. Although their contribution could easily have been channeled through a responsible humanitarian agency, they feel their presence abroad has also built lasting relationships of caring and trust that will continue to assist those in need.

Yet the proponents of mission trips concede that these programs often benefit those who go from the United States more than those being assisted in other countries. Rubbing shoulders with Christians in other countries, leaders say, is worth the time and effort because it encourages deeper and longer-lasting commitment to transcultural ministries. A woman who went to Peru with her Presbyterian high school youth group about ten years ago speaks for many when she says the trip made her "more sensitive to missions" by showing her the suffering people experience in other parts of the world. One evening in Peru she felt that God was speaking to her, calling her to dedicate her life to something worthwhile.

Comparisons of mission trip participants with other church members suggest that these experiences may encourage greater commitment to transcultural ministries. Participants are more likely than nonparticipants to say their congregation should emphasize such topics as the problem of religious persecution in other countries, the responsibilities of the United States toward poor countries of the world, and the work of Christians and Christian organizations in other countries. They are more likely to have participated in church meetings about war, peace, refugees, or some other international issue and to have attended a church meeting at which a missionary or religious worker from another country was the main speaker. Although financial giving is difficult to measure, it too seems to differ. Participants' overall giving is substantially higher than nonparticipants' and the former report that about 5 percent more of their giving is devoted to international ministries than the latter do.[46] Participants also perceive their experience to have been personally transformative. Sixty-two percent say it had a major impact on their life and 92 percent say it made them more hopeful.

We must exercise caution in interpreting these differences, though. Participants in mission trips are simply more active in their congregations than the average church member is, so differ from nonparticipants for this reason. However, statistically controlling for differences in frequency of church attendance, holding a leadership position, size of congregation, religious tradition, and level of education does not explain away the differences between participants in mission trips and nonparticipants. Those who go abroad are still more likely than those who stay home to believe their congregation should emphasize the problem of religious persecution, be interested in U.S. responsibilities to poor countries, and support the work of Christians in other countries, and they are more likely to have participated in church meetings about international issues. Nor do these factors eliminate the difference in total giving, even when family income is taken into account (only the difference in perceived percentage of giving to international ministries becomes statistically insignificant).[47] Still, the fact that things correlate with participating in mission trips does not mean that mission trips cause them. It would be just as reasonable, for instance, to argue that valuing congregational emphases on international ministries and attending meetings about them happen first and are thus the source rather than a consequence of going on mission trips.

Comparing people who went on mission trips when they were teenagers with those who did not comes a bit closer to addressing the question of causality. If an experience during one's youth is associated with differences in outlook and activity some years later, that is an indication of a possible effect. The statistics suggest that having gone on a mission trip as a teenager is in fact associated with the various measures of transcultural commitment we have just been considering, even controlling for current levels of involvement in one's congregation. However, having gone abroad on a mission trip as a teenager is itself not a significant factor. What matters is simply having gone on any kind of mission trip.[48]

Like other kinds of voluntary service, mission trips seem to have the strongest effects when they are accompanied by adequate preparation and subsequent time for discussion and reflection. A woman who decided after several mission trips to enter full-time ministry remembers feeling a "mission high" as she helped people and saw smiles on their faces. That emotion provided motivation temporarily, but when she returned home she felt depressed because of the suffering she had seen and because her job in software sales seemed completely meaningless. A man who went on a mission trip to India had a similar experience, describing himself after his return as burdened with a kind of "heaviness." For both, the natural impulse was to deny their feelings and get back into their familiar routine as quickly as possible. Having a church group to talk with helped. Eventually the momentary call they had felt to serve others became a permanent part of their identity.[49] To heighten the chances of such beneficial effects, congregations and sponsoring agencies are increasingly adopting uniform standards, encouraging prospective participants to enroll in cross-cultural classes, offering debriefing sessions, and forming oversight committees.[50]

The potential weaknesses of short-term mission trips include not only the actual cost but also the time and energy they require. Although a growing number of international agencies appear to be encouraging these trips, some leaders worry that efforts are being devoted to ameliorative projects at the expense of mobilizing around government policies that could also make a difference. Pastors worry that the trips sometimes become ends in themselves instead of springboards for wider service. "The assumption," one pastor says, "is that people go overseas, fall in love with a project, and become cheerleaders for it, but often there is a breakdown and what they become cheerleaders for is raising the support to go on their next short-term trip." He thinks there is real danger in people getting addicted to the adventure and missing sight of the larger picture.

Scholars and church leaders will undoubtedly continue to debate whether mission trips provide an adequate return on investment. Most of the studies are inconclusive because they are done by mission agencies themselves or in limited contexts without adequate statistical controls. From the national data, we are at least able to draw some systematic comparisons—albeit limited by the relatively small percentages of the churchgoing public who participate in these trips. The evidence shows no harm in participating and supports the view that those who go abroad are usually more involved in other aspects of congregational and missions activities. As we saw earlier, those who currently serve as volunteers for international programs are more likely to have been on short-term mission trips both within the past year and as teenagers. Several other studies come to similar conclusions. The immediate "high" short-termers experience probably does not have the lasting effects they think it will, at least not for the specific program in which they have been involved, but may have modest benefits of other kinds, especially when structures are in place to sustain motivation.[51] The aggregate cost of these trips is huge, but church leaders are probably right in arguing that this is money that people would be unlikely to have contributed to other offerings or programs. Still, a focus only on the economics of international service is always too narrow.

TRANSCULTURAL PERSPECTIVE

The critical role that personal involvement in international ministries is playing in the global outreach of American Christianity is less its contribution toward the financing and staffing of these programs and more its larger influence on hearts and minds. To a person, those who are directly involved in projects abroad say that their outlook has been altered. Those who have spent significant time in other countries are especially likely to report that they see the world and their own faith differently.

Mr. Linder says the most important result of his time in Sierra Leone is realizing that "God will provide the strength to do whatever is called of you in that situation, no matter how extreme it gets." Moving out of his mental comfort zone has meant that God's presence is more vivid. Mr. Burke says his faith and his appreciation of prayer have deepened, but he is still struggling to be patient because the needs in Africa and other parts of the world are so great and the resources of his own congregation are so small. A man who went overseas with the International Justice Mission says he never realized the power of evil until he saw the plight of child prostitutes, and this realization has strengthened his resolve to do whatever he can to "take a swing at Satan." A woman who has helped at an orphanage in Africa says she feels sad about the cultural decay she sees in the United States and is just thankful for the blessings God showed her in Africa.

The fact that people who have served in other countries view the world and themselves differently is in itself not surprising (people who travel as tourists often say the same thing). What is interesting is how the world now seems to those who have seen it at its worst. For some, it does become flat, homogeneous, as one man notes in remarking about the common bond he has come to feel with people in vastly different circumstances. For most, it is rather the distinctiveness and meaning of America that comes into focus in a new way.

Mr. Ridley's remark about the United States not being the real world illustrates one of the most common ways in which perspectives shift as American Christians become engaged in ministries abroad. He means not only that the privileges Americans enjoy are not common to much of humanity but also that life in the United States is in many ways superficial. Television and consumerism give us a false sense of reality. "All the commercialism and materialism," sighs a woman who recently spent seven weeks in Mozambique, "the screaming message from every advertisement and all the commercials on TV—I just look at all that and it becomes very frustrating." Being in another part of the world provides a measure of critical distance. Mr. Linder puts it this way: "When you come back into our culture, you just don't identify with it totally."

There is little sense, though, that those who serve abroad come home racked with guilt about the comforts they enjoy relative to the rest of the world. Their response is governed more by a theology of stewardship. Of those to whom much has been given, much is required. Ms. Chu expresses this view clearly when she explains her motivation for being involved in international ministries. "The reason God blesses us is so that we can be a blessing to others." She wishes she could do more and is sometimes depressed thinking about the immensity of the world's problems. Yet she realizes "as humans we can only do so much. This is God's work, not mine. I have only a small part to play, but I can do that part faithfully." Mr. Linder articulates much the same view. "In the United States we have so many benefits economically and politically," he says. "I think a lot of responsibility goes along with that." Enacting that responsibility entails exercising one's role as a Christian, moving "beyond our own comfort," as he observes, and becoming more engaged as a citizen as well. For instance, he believes Christians should write to public officials, encouraging them to focus more attention on AIDS, debt relief, and economic development in poor countries.

Being transcultural, then, is not so much to have lived in two places or even of having realized that one's home is not as secure as it once seemed. Nor does transcultural Christianity mean that a person from the United States incorporates an African interpretation of the trinity into his or her theology or a Latin American appreciation of the Holy Spirit. For those most directly involved, the globalization of American Christianity is relativizing how they think about America. With privilege comes responsibility. Living in the United States is not a right that somehow has been earned, either by oneself or by the nation's heroes and good practices, but a divine gift. As gift, it incurs not only gratitude but also obligation. It reinforces the sense that whatever one does must have purpose, even if the accomplishments that derive from that purpose are small.

THE IMPACT OF GLOBALIZATION

The evidence we have considered demonstrates clearly that the global Christianity paradigm is wrong in two important respects. Churches in the United States are not just moribund organizations that have abandoned missions work to the point that whatever vitality Christianity is experiencing in the rest of the world must be understood strictly as an indigenous development. The vast majority of U.S. congregations are still intensely interested in transcultural ministries ranging from missions to humanitarian efforts to refugee assistance and peacemaking. In addition, many congregations have responded specifically to globalization not by sitting back and saying, well, the global South is on its own, thank God, but by developing innovative ways of partnering with Southern Hemisphere churches and learning from them even as the congregations also supply resources. The congregation in California that sends prefabricated loft-style houses to Mexico is a vivid example. Its leaders do not assume, as many of the global-shift writers do, that the United States is so secular that all it can do is host missionaries from Mexico. Instead, it supports pastors in Mexican shantytowns by making low-cost housing available to needy families. Similarly, the congregation in Michigan that sponsors teams from Africa working in Latin America and from Latin America working in Asia is doing its part to strengthen the emerging fact of global Christianity. As its pastor observes, "The church globally has changed dramatically to where 60 percent of world Christians are outside of North America. Yet we have the predominant amount of financial resources." In his view, the proper response is to listen and learn but also to serve by being responsibly involved in transcultural ministries.

Globalization does not mean that U.S. congregations are fundamentally altering their outlook on the world, but it does provide new opportunities. American churches can afford to make pastoral visits to missionaries in other parts of the world; porous borders make for more frequent interaction. Church members are likely to have traveled abroad or to have met immigrants living in their own communities. The personal connections that result can be more easily maintained through electronic communications than was ever true in the past. In most instances, churches in the United States do not send missionaries to places where no Christian has gone before; missionaries instead work with indigenous churches and help their ministries grow by supplying humanitarian assistance, in-kind donations, and Bibles, or by creating opportunities for local pastors to gain additional training. Globalization also presents challenges, such as stripping families of traditional networks or forcing them into refugee camps or subsistence jobs. Congregations are tailoring their programs to respond in small ways to these challenges, and even though the efforts seldom produce large-scale results, the firsthand relationships that churches cultivate protect against the fraud and misuse of funds that worry critics of large government-funded aid programs.

Innovations in transcultural ministry reflect the reality that U.S. congregations with a vision for the wider world have abundant resources and the fact of literally hundreds of thousands of congregations abroad with which to partner. A congregation in Michigan or Ohio that wishes to train pastors in Kenya does not have to send money to a denominational office to be combined with funds from other churches and sent to a seminary in New York or Nairobi. It simply flies these pastors to Detroit or Cleveland for an extended stay in the United States. Yet its ability to initiate a program like this depends on the fact that clergy and churches already exist in Kenya. The same is true of a church in Atlanta or Charlotte that wants to build an orphanage in Managua or a worship center in Cape Town. Chances are good that a direct link can be established.

Transcultural programs are in many ways producing a flat earth among Christians, to borrow Friedman's image again, just as global markets do in business. In the view of church leaders the more a congregation in Duluth or Tucson interacts with Christians in Abuja or Singapore the more its members feel indistinguishable from believers everywhere. Beyond feeling the same, ties across borders also produce similar structures by channeling resources to indigenous congregations that conform to a certain model of entrepreneurialism or holistic ministry. At the same time, cultural differences remain and perhaps become more vivid than ever before. Serving abroad becomes a way of learning about these differences, gaining a new perspective, and, if leaders' hopes are realized, building bridges of understanding and acceptance.

Faith and Foreign Policy

Does Religious Advocacy Matter?

Besides altering the programs of local congregations, globalization has posed new challenges and created new opportunities for religious groups interested in influencing U.S. foreign policy. Leaders of faith communities as well as those in broader policy arenas point out that religious organizations can have an impact on the wider world not only—or even primarily—by sending dollars and volunteers but also by voicing their opinions to policy makers on critical issues such as foreign aid, free trade treaties, human rights, and the use of military force. Whereas congregations engage in international ministries by taking up offerings and sending out short- and long-term missionaries, the voice of faith communities is also expressed through the pressure that large faith-based agencies bring to bear on government. In short, religious organizations can and should be advocates in international relations. But does this happen? Do religious convictions influence how Americans view these issues? Are religious organizations effective in initiating, supporting, or opposing policy agendas? Or are the churches inconsequential in relating to the challenges of globalization in these ways?

Many observers of American policy argue that the Christian community—or at least part of it—became an increasingly influential voice in policy decisions during the first few years of the twenty-first century. According to journalist Esther Kaplan, President George W. Bush "happily ceded huge swaths of his domestic and international policy" to Christian fundamentalists, even using "his global AIDS initiative, his foreign aid policy, and his war on terror to please religious radicals."[1] Kaplan's view, though markedly polemical, is echoed by other writers. "The influence of Christian evangelicals now extends to many essential matters of foreign policy," wrote former under-secretary-general of the United Nations Brian Urquhart in a 2005 essay, describing this influence as "dogmatic, unilateralist, and radically nationalistic."[2] Writers sympathetic to Christians' shaping policy decisions also perceived a growing influence. Journalist Susan Page wrote appreciatively of Christian activists' increasing willingness to form alliances with such unusual partners as Planned Parenthood and the American Civil Liberties Union to champion international religious freedom and to combat AIDS in Africa.[3] "The President's faith-based foreign policy," declared *Christianity Today*'s Tony Carnes, "brings to fruition a decade-long effort to link [Christians'] vision for international human rights, religious freedom, democracy, free trade, and public health directly with the executive branch of the federal government."[4] Similarly, *Wall Street Journal* writer Peter Waldman suggested that "interest in global issues" had "galvanized" evangelical Christians and led to greater involvement in efforts to curb international sex trafficking and promote peace in southern Sudan.[5]

Not everyone agreed with these assessments, of course. However, an alternative view differed only in seeing greater continuity between Christians' recent role in foreign policy and the past. Historian Edith Blumhofer observed that Christian publications in the nineteenth century frequently commented on issues in other countries, but that travel and prosperity have made it easier for twenty-first-century Christians to engage directly in foreign policy. Paul Marshall, a senior fellow at Freedom House, said he did not "know if religion's influence is increasing" but was certain its role was becoming more visible.[6] Richard Cizik, vice president of government affairs for the National Association of Evangelicals, also noted continuities with earlier missionary and humanitarian efforts but argued that evangelical Protestants play a larger role in shaping public policy than in the past. "We are the new internationalists in our capacity to affect congressional legislation," he said.[7]

But broad assertions about the role of faith in U.S. foreign policy must be treated with caution. Neither religion nor public policy is monolithic. On domestic issues such as abortion, homosexuality, the death penalty, and welfare spending, the Christian community has been deeply divided between evangelical or conservative Protestants and those with moderate or progressive theological leanings. It is conceivable that the same is true on international issues where considerations about sexuality, morality, and government spending also arise. These international issues cover a vast range of topics, from trade and armed conflict to questions about human rights and economic development and for this reason are unlikely to elicit uniform reactions even from the same religious constituencies. What it means to say that religious groups influence policy makers must also be questioned. Does evidence of influence lie in the rhetoric used to justify policy proposals? Does it reside in successful lobbying, public declarations, and resolutions? Are religious groups influential because they act effectively alone or when they participate in coalitions with other powerful interest groups? And at what levels is influence to be gauged? Does it take place primarily at the highest levels of government? Or does it also involve the typical congregation and rank-and-file church members?

Scholarly interest in the relationships between religion and international policy has risen sharply since September 11, 2001. Much of this interest has focused on Islam and thus has been more concerned with how U.S. policy might be obliged to take account of religion in other countries than with American religion itself. There has nevertheless been increasing recognition that religion is of wider relevance to foreign policy discussions than previously assumed. Historian R. Scott Appleby argues that religious "fundamentalisms" are a pervasive feature of world politics and that the peacemaking potential of religious organizations must also be recognized. Indeed, he suggests that the best antidote to religious extremism is to give other religious values a greater voice in public life.[8] Daniel Philpott asserts that September 11 fundamentally challenged the secularist assumptions on which Western understandings of international relations have been based for the past three centuries. His argument rests not only on the claim that Muslims view the world differently but also on the fact that Western perspectives stem from the Westphalian synthesis that ended the religious wars by radically separating public policy from private convictions. In this view, international relations scholars must at least rediscover the religious roots of their own perspectives in order to understand the current situation.[9] From firsthand experience in international diplomacy, Douglas Johnston argues that religious groups, along with other nongovernmental organizations, play an increasing role in international politics because the end of the Cold War greatly reduced possibilities for foreign affairs to be conducted simply among the leaders of the most powerful nation-states. As evidence, Johnston points to such examples as religious groups mediating conflicts in the Philippines and South Africa and religiously motivated liberation movements in eastern Europe and Central America.[10] Political scientist Eric O. Hansen also encourages foreign policy analysts to move past the Westphalian and Cold War perspectives and take greater account of the complexities that arise when religious communities participate more actively in global politics. He argues that religion cannot be dismissed from policy discussions, but neither can it be understood as part of a single integrating theory of political influence.[11] Other scholars have initiated wide-ranging discussions about the rediscovery of religion for theoretical and normative approaches to the study of foreign policy.[12] Yet dominant perspectives on international relations suggest that considerations about power, national security, law, and economic interest are more important determinants of public policy than religious convictions.[13] These perspectives may underestimate the role of religion, but they do need to be taken seriously. Doing so means that the influence of religion cannot be assumed simply on the basis of presidential rhetoric or the claims of religious activists themselves. Instead, the ways in which religious groups seek to shape decisions about particular issues must be understood empirically.

This chapter examines the role of Christianity in U.S. policies toward current international issues. My argument has five parts. First, I show that there are at least four reasons to believe that Christian groups have exercised increasing influence on U.S. foreign policies in recent years. Second, I argue that there are also good reasons to question each of these views. Third, I outline an argument suggesting that policy makers and religious leaders do, on occasion, have reason to give an appearance of listening to one another. Fourth, I examine the evidence in four specific policy arenas—free trade, human rights, militarism, and foreign assistance—and show that tangible influence on governmental policy by the Christian community has been quite limited, though not insignificant. Finally, I suggest that the role of American Christianity in foreign affairs is largely nongovernmental but that there are particular circumstances under which this role directly influences public policy. Considering these arguments will also provide an empirical basis from which to address the broader question, What does *influence* mean?

WHY THE POLICY INFLUENCE OF CHRISTIANS
MAY BE INCREASING

Observers who believe that Christian groups have exercised increasing influence over U.S. foreign policy in recent years emphasize the prominence of religious conviction and rhetoric in the presidency of George W. Bush, especially after the September 11, 2001, attacks and in the person and words of Bush himself and his inner circle of advisors. "There are some code words," Bush told Doug Wead, a friend and former aide to Mr. Bush's father, in 1998: "I am going to say that I've accepted Christ into my life. And that's a true statement."[14] Bush's most trusted foreign policy advisor was former Stanford provost Condoleezza Rice, who served first in the George W. Bush administration as national security advisor and then as secretary of state. The daughter of a Presbyterian minister, Rice has been described by friends and family as a person "very close to the Lord." Like Bush, she is said to have "a deeply religious foundation that seems to infiltrate nonreligious issues."[15] Others close to the president included speechwriter Michael Gerson, an evangelical Christian and former employee of Prison Fellowship, and Karen Hughes, an evangelical who taught Sunday school and spoke often to Christian audiences.[16]

Beyond the White House, Christian leaders were thought to have gained access to power through secretive informal networks. One such network was the Council for National Policy, a pro–free enterprise group of business and political leaders that hosted closed-door meetings with the president as well as Vice President Dick Cheney and Defense Secretary Donald H. Rumsfeld around the time of the invasion of Iraq in 2003. Members of the Council for National Policy included the Reverend Tim LaHaye, author of the popular *Left Behind* novels about an apocalyptic Second Coming of Christ, Dr. James Dobson of Focus on the Family, Moral Majority founder the Reverend Jerry Falwell, and former Christian Coalition director Ralph E. Reed Jr.[17] Another network in which Christians were prominent was the so-called Fellowship, organizer of the annual National Prayer Breakfast attended by congressional leaders and representatives from around the world. "We can be confident in America's cause in the world," Bush told the gathering in 2003. "We can also be confident in the ways of Providence."[18]

A second cluster of arguments focuses less on the president and his inner circle and more on the wider influence of Christian organizations that might have a special interest in foreign policy. An example of such influence arose in conjunction with U.S. policies concerning abortion. As one of his first acts in public office, President Bush reinstated the so-called Mexico City Policy, originally passed in 1984 under the Reagan administration, that prohibited U.S. taxpayer money from supporting foreign nongovernmental organizations that perform or lobby for abortion in their respective countries.[19] The global gag rule, as it was termed by critics, was firmly supported by a number of religious groups, including the Catholic Family and Human Rights Institute, the Secretariat for Pro-Life Activities of the National Conference of Catholic Bishops, and the Family Research Council. The possibility that international faith-based relief and development organizations were influencing foreign policy is also suggested by the fact that many of these agencies had close ties with the U.S. Agency for International Development (USAID) and depended on it for grants and contracts. USAID director Andrew Natsios, whose term began in 2001, had previously served as vice president of World Vision International. Kent R. Hill, USAID's administrator for global health, was a former president of the Institute on Religion and Democracy. In 2004, faith-based agencies holding USAID grants included World Vision International, Catholic Relief Services, World Relief, Lutheran World Relief, Adventist Development and Relief, Feed the Children, Samaritan's Purse, MAP International, Mercy Corps, and Catholic Medical Mission. Catholic Relief Services alone received government grants of $145.2 million, up from only $46.7 million in 1998. Staff from the largest of these organizations, including Catholic Relief Services and World Vision International, routinely met with legislators in charge of foreign appropriations and testified at congressional hearings.

A third reason for thinking that Christians have increased their role in U.S. foreign policy is the broader and more active posture of certain segments of the Christian population. Political advisor Karl Rove told an American Enterprise Institute seminar in 2001 that stay-at-home Christians had nearly cost George W. Bush the election in 2000; Rove pledged to increase evangelical turnout by four million in 2004.[20] A national survey conducted during the 2004 campaign found that 86 percent of Christian evangelicals planned to vote for Bush.[21] On election day, exit polls showed that 70 percent of weekly-churchgoing Protestants had voted for Bush.[22] If churchgoers played a special role in re-electing the president, the possibility that they might be influencing foreign policy is suggested by polls about particular issues. For instance, a 2004 survey showed that 60 percent of evangelical Protestants felt "the U.S. has a special role to play in world affairs and should behave differently than other nations" (only 45 percent of the religiously unaffiliated agreed). In the same poll, 72 percent of evangelical Protestants agreed that the United States "must be able to take preemptive military action against other countries" (57 percent of the unaffiliated held the same view).[23]

A final argument in support of the view that Christians have played an important role in U.S. foreign policy in recent years is that historical examples can be found when similar influence was evident. A favorite example is William McKinley's 1903 assertion that after praying to "Almighty God for light and guidance," he authorized the U.S. invasion of the Philippines "to educate the Filipinos, and uplift and civilize and Christianize them, and by God's grace do the very best we could by them, as our fellow-men for whom Christ also died."[24] Essayist Saul Landau, citing this example, adds, "President William McKinley's words should echo with President Bush and his Evangelical zealots."[25] Sociologist William Martin, who also mentions McKinley, discusses numerous other instances in which religious arguments infused U.S. statecraft, including John Foster Dulles's famous and perhaps apocryphal meeting with a Jewish leader and an Arab leader at which Dulles began by saying, "Why can't we all sit down together and work this thing out like Christian gentlemen." Martin emphasizes that Christian conservatives' efforts during the past quarter century to fund anticommunist forces in Central America, defend apartheid in South Africa, attack the United Nations, and weigh in on numerous other foreign policy issues are simply the latest example of religion's continuing prominence in American life and religious activists' willingness to breach the wall separating church and state.[26]

A CLOSER LOOK AT THE ARGUMENTS

With a popular base, well-financed organizations, and friends in high office, it would be surprising if Christians did not exercise influence in U.S. foreign policy. Yet the connections drawn in journalistic accounts clearly require closer scrutiny. For instance, does the fact that George W. Bush identified himself as a born-again Christian, spoke often of America's "calling" and "Almighty God's gift" to humanity, and included Christians in his inner circle mean that the 2003 invasion of Iraq was attributable to Christian influence? If so, the president had a stronger voice in major foreign policy decisions than allies and critics believed or was extraordinarily beholden to Christian conservatives. However, Bush confidants and journalists close to the White House believed that the president had little interest in foreign policy and that plans to invade Iraq were formulated by others in the Bush administration, especially Vice President Cheney, Defense Secretary Donald Rumsfeld, and Deputy Secretary of Defense Paul Wolfowitz.[27] The president's rhetoric may have aimed to garner support for the war from Christian supporters, yet the war was embraced only marginally by more evangelicals than in the public at large, and, for that matter, the president's re-election depended as much on Catholics, whose leaders argued for continuing negotiations, as on evangelical Protestants.[28] The Council for National Policy may have given religious leaders an inside track, but if so, this role was shared by hundreds of other council members who represented secular organizations. The Fellowship offered a better platform for specifically religious interests. Yet sociologist D. Michael Lindsay's study of Fellowship members, based on personal interviews with numerous public officials and religious leaders, found no evidence that this group played a significant role in foreign policy discussions. The Fellowship was able to serve a convening function, for instance, by arranging for foreign diplomats to meet with White House staff out of view of the press. But being able to arrange such meetings, Lindsay concluded, served more to confer prestige on the Fellowship than to shape policy outcomes.[29]

The second argument—that faith-based agencies increasingly shaped foreign policy as they drew funds from government coffers—will deserve further scrutiny after examining these agencies' role on specific issues. It is worth noting, though, that the largest of these agencies had been receiving substantial support from USAID well before the administration of George W. Bush. Moreover, these agencies were quite diverse theologically and included ones that vehemently opposed Bush administration policies. What is evident about faith-based agencies is that they have not been alone in seeking to influence foreign policy. The large number of nongovernmental organizations with interests in international affairs means that rivalries alone are sufficient to ramp up the claims and counterclaims about who is influencing what. Responding to the global-gag-rule debate, for instance, Concerned Women for America's Janice Crouse argued that her group was simply having to work harder to combat the influence of groups with opposing views. "One of the things that has been a problem for us is that the radical nongovernmental organizations are so well funded," she said. "They know how to get grant money, they know the political structures, and they are unified in their purpose."[30]

The global-gag-rule debate illustrates another difficulty in taking arguments about increasing Christian influence at face value. Pro-choice and pro-life critics alike observed that Bush's order to reinstate the Mexico City Policy was not all that it seemed. On the one hand, it did not prevent funds from being used for programs that might encourage abortions but for reasons other than family planning or by U.S. nongovernmental agencies themselves. On the other hand, it did little to change actual practices since no government funds had been spent directly on abortion programs for more than a quarter century.[31] These criticisms suggested that the president's order was perhaps window dressing and yet implied that the rhetorical gesture itself was a means of signaling affinity with certain constituencies.

Yet another cautionary note comes from research about the role of government funding for domestic faith-based service agencies. Evidence indicates that less was spent on domestic faith-based programs than the White House claimed. Even if faith-based initiatives had been central to the Bush administration's efforts to reward its Christian base, it is surprising that so little planning went into these initiatives and that more attention was not paid to supporting them.[32]

The argument about conservative Christians shaping U.S. foreign policy as a result of their being a larger and more active segment of the general electorate is compelling only if it is assumed that conservative Christians held distinctive views on major foreign policy issues. We will look at these views in subsequent sections, drawing on evidence from the Global Issues Survey. What we know from previous surveys, though, casts doubt on the idea that major policy decisions were driven simply by popular demand. The survey I mentioned earlier, about attitudes toward America taking preemptive military action, illustrates how closely the sentiments of evangelical Protestants resembled those of the public at large. In that 2004 survey, 65 percent of evangelical Protestants favored cooperating with international organizations instead of going it alone, and among evangelicals, only those who further defined themselves as traditionalists were significantly less likely than the general public to give this response.[33]

Finally, the idea that Christians must be shaping foreign policy now because they have done so in the past, such as during the Spanish-American War, is difficult to accept at face value for two reasons. One is that if the historical precedents are as frequent as some observers suggest, then the recent period should not be regarded as a time of unusual influence. The other is that the historical examples point as often to religious groups opposing government policy as supporting it or to religious leaders making statements without those statements necessarily influencing actual decisions. For instance, William Martin cites examples of religious groups opposing the Vietnam War, resisting the Reagan administration's policies in Central America, and arguing against U.S. environmental policies.[34]

The point of these considerations is not to conclude that Christians have had no influence on American foreign policy in recent years. It is rather to suggest that pundits' arguments about policies being the handiwork of certain religious constituencies can seldom be taken at face value. Policy makers and religious leaders may invoke religious rhetoric in public speeches, but rhetoric alone is no indication of the considerations that actually shape foreign policy. Although metaphors and rhetorical framing devices have power, these tools are typically more complex than observers who never talk to real people assume. Similarly, public opinion may appear to support particular policies, but there is seldom a direct line between popular sentiments and governmental decisions.

HOW RELIGION MAY MATTER

The fact that there appears to be both more and less than meets the eye in popular arguments about religion's influence in foreign policy suggests the need to come at the matter from a different perspective. Religious communities in the United States are not part of the government, but they are one of many kinds of nongovernmental organizations that have a stake in trying to influence government policy. Secular voluntary organizations and foundations, businesses, labor unions, ethnic associations, and religious groups all compete to shape policies that their members care about. In all of these cases, the leaders of nongovernmental organizations try to influence policy makers' decisions by deploying lobbyists and other professionals with specialized expertise on particular issues and by soliciting money and votes from their members. Churches and church leaders sometimes do this by sending resolutions from their members to denominational officials in the nation's capital or by sponsoring delegations to meet with members of Congress and by making statements to the media about political issues they support or oppose.

But what is often missed in discussions of religious groups' efforts to influence government policies is the fact that religious leaders and policy makers both have reasons, on occasion, to claim that influence has indeed been exercised—whether it has been or not. A religious leader who claims to have the ear of the president is a big shot, to put it crudely. That leader's constituents feel good, just knowing that their leader is so powerful. They say to themselves, well, sending money makes good sense because this leader can tell the president what we would like the president to hear. Donations increase, more direct mailings go out, the leader is sought after by television talk shows, and the leader's empire grows. In the process, the religious leader actually may gain clout in the political process. At some point, the White House does worry about keeping this powerful leader happy. That is one of the reasons policy makers, for their part, may want to claim that a religious constituency has exercised influence. What has actually shaped foreign policy on, say, assistance to HIV/AIDS victims in Africa may be quite complex, but public officials may want to signal to certain religious groups that their voice has been heard. They do this by inviting representatives of those groups to a meeting at the White House or on Capitol Hill. Ironically, public officials sometimes find it in their interest to blame religious groups as well. For instance, suppose there are sticky diplomatic negotiations that make it awkward for the United States to give aid to a particular country. A good excuse for not doing so could be that religious groups were against it.

These ways of describing the relations between religious groups and policy makers are not as cynical as they may seem at first glance. It is the case that political decisions are often made for self-interested reasons. But the larger point is that signaling matters. Appearances become realities. Religious groups that can make credible claims of having influence in the public arena do in fact gain greater capacity to exercise influence. Policy makers also have reasons to signal that they have been influenced. And of course critics of particular policies often have a stake in suggesting that one of their enemies—perhaps a religious group—was to blame and that money should be raised to quash this enemy.

The implication of this perspective is to take claims about faith and foreign policy seriously—but strictly as claims. They are part of the rhetoric that religious leaders, policy makers, and critics use to justify what they do. They are not necessarily the real reasons or the main reasons why foreign policy takes the form it does. To take these claims at face value is usually to exaggerate them. For example, to believe that U.S. military and economic support of Israel is primarily driven by Pat Robertson's and other evangelical Christians' belief that Jesus will someday return to the Holy Land is simply naive. At the same time, the fact that religious leaders and public officials make this claim does help to justify those policies to certain constituents. It is also important to recognize that other groups may be working quietly behind the scenes to influence foreign policy in ways that are less visible to the media. Christian groups seeking justice for Palestinians would be an example.

The other implication of this emphasis on claims is that care must be taken to understand the different meanings that the same words convey in policy discussions and within a faith community. For instance, a president who includes the phrase "wonder-working power" in a political speech may intend to signal an affinity with Christians who know the phrase is part of a familiar hymn. It is a leap of logic, though, to conclude that these constituents necessarily understand the signal in the way it may have been intended. The reason is that the speech says this wonder-working power is "in the goodness and idealism and faith of the American people," whereas the hymn says it is "in the precious blood of the Lamb." Instead of sensing an affinity with the president, a thoughtful Christian could just as well view the speech as bad theology.[35]

I turn next to an examination of how American Christians have responded to—and on occasion sought to influence—U.S. policy in recent years in four areas: free trade, human rights, militarism, and foreign assistance. In each of these areas, it is essential to examine what church members think about the issues and what organized religious groups, including denominations and faith-based agencies, have said and done. The lines connecting these opinions and efforts with actual policy outcomes, I argue, are usually tenuous. In tracing these lines, it is nevertheless possible to see more clearly how Christians have tried to influence policies and, on occasion, how they have succeeded. Perceptions and the management of identities have played a key role in these efforts.

FREEDOM AND FREE TRADE

The rhetorical uses of the term "freedom" in American politics provide a useful entry point into the relationships between Christianity and U.S. foreign policy. In a discussion of speeches at the 2004 Republican National Convention, linguist George Lakoff argued that freedom was a dominant motif. President Bush asserted that a "compassionate conservative philosophy" meant "greater opportunity, more freedom, and more control over your own life," being "truly free—to make your own choices and pursue your own dreams." Freedom was thus personalized and connected with individual aspirations and a moral imperative to be strong and self-sufficient. As he addressed international issues, the president repeated "freedom," "free," and "liberty" more than thirty times.

"Freedom will bring a future of hope." "Free societies in the Middle East will be hopeful societies." Elaborating on a theme he had expressed many times after the 9/11 attacks, the president argued that terrorists had attacked not the World Trade Center or the Pentagon—but freedom. "The terrorists are fighting freedom with all their cunning and cruelty because freedom is their greatest fear and they should be afraid, because freedom is on the march." The advance of freedom was America's mandate: "America is called to lead the cause of freedom in a new century." Moreover, the calling (as callings tend to be) was from God: "Freedom is not America's gift to the world, it is the Almighty God's gift to every man and woman in this world."[36]

Although the president's speech left implicit the connection between freedom and free enterprise, the war on terror connoted an expansion of the same principle in business as in military affairs and in personal life. Freedom to control one's life tangibly meant "restraining federal spending" and "reducing regulation." "America must be the best place in the world to do business." Being truly free meant being able to "compete in a global market that provides new buyers for our goods." To be a free society was thus to encourage the entrepreneurial spirit. To advance freedom, "we will expand trade and level the playing field to sell American goods and services across the globe." "Our deepest commitment," the president asserted, can be expressed simply: "In our world, and here at home, we will extend the frontiers of freedom."[37]

Freedom provides a powerful language with which to draw the disparate elements of personal, national, and international life under one umbrella and thus to legitimate the pursuit of policies that advance these basic priorities. The idea that freedom is "God's gift" implies a strong connection with religion and thus raises the possibility that a political speech in which freedom figures so prominently plays especially well in religious circles. This connection further raises the possibility that freedom in Christian usage readily blends with arguments about freedom as a national goal and with free enterprise as a mode of economic organization. As globalization contributes to the worldwide expansion of U.S. Christianity, the inevitable question is what this expansion may imply about freedom. Do American Christians believe that freedom is God's gift for the world? And, if so, are they tacitly giving assent to policies and organizations deemed to be promoting U.S.-style freedom abroad?

The emphasis on freedom in American Christianity derives from the gospel's assertion that following Christ makes one spiritually free. A redeemed person is a liberated person. Redemption means being lifted from sin and despair into a fulfilling relationship with God. A person who has been redeemed has a changed heart, is a new person who can make a clean start, and is free to obey God and live a productive and happy life. To have been redeemed literally implies that something or somebody has been bought back or freed from debt or a lien. Redemption implies deliverance from bondage or suffering or pain and thus the ability to make choices unencumbered by the past. Metaphorically, redemption is characteristically associated with rising up, bouncing back, making a comeback, and experiencing discovery, newness, goodness, progress, strength, and growth.[38] This emphasis, while present in all of Christianity and indeed in much of American culture, is especially evident in conservative Protestantism and is particularly significant in arguments about evangelism. An important task of overseas ministries is thus to show individuals by word and deed how to experience personal redemption.

But does this emphasis on personal redemption reinforce a mentality favorable to the spread of American business methods that involve free trade, participation in markets, and aspirations for individual success? "Christian fundamentalism," write social scientists Steve Brouwer, Paul Gifford, and Susan D. Rose, "is intertwined with the homogenizing influences of consumerism, mass communication, and production in ways that are compatible with the creation of an international market culture by global capitalist institutions."[39] They point not only to fundamentalist leaders encouraging a gospel of prosperity but also to conservative Protestantism's emphasis on personal renewal and reluctance to challenge unjust social arrangements. Philanthropist George Soros describes the United States as a culture in which "religious fundamentalism comes together with market fundamentalism to form the ideology of American supremacy."[40] Remarks by prominent evangelical Protestant leaders lend credence to these views. Jerry Falwell liked to argue that "God is in favor of freedom, property, ownership, competition, diligence, work and acquisition. All of this is taught in the Word of God, in both the Old and New Testaments."[41] Similarly, former National Association of Evangelicals president Ted Haggard is widely known as an avid proponent of free markets. "Free markets," he says, "have done more to help poor people than any benevolent organization ever has."[42]

Observers of American religion make the related point that conservative Protestantism itself is a cultural hybrid that reflects distinctive American values as much as it does authentic biblical teaching. Historian Randall Balmer describes an affinity between the American ethos of upward mobility through individual achievement and the conservative Protestant offer of "spiritual upward mobility, a chance to improve your lot in the next world and also (according to the promises of some preachers) in this world as well."[43] Balmer notes a tendency to conflate the freedom to pursue one's material aims with the freedom to express oneself religiously and to view individual success as evidence of moral worth. Christian ethicist Wyndy Corbin extends Balmer's observation, arguing that evangelical Protestants accept "laissez-faire capitalism as not just a neutral, value-free economic system, but one that is morally good" and view social problems as "mere extensions of personal problems that are moral or spiritual in nature."[44]

The American Dream of achieving upward mobility through hard work is certainly not limited to conservative Protestants.[45] Yet the connection between the two is evident in research results. In a national study of American evangelicals, sociologist Christian Smith identified a "personal influence strategy" for solving social problems that renders evangelicals "blind to the supraindividual social structures, aggregate effects, power dynamics, and institutional systems which profoundly shape human consciousness, experience and life-chances."[46] In a national study that included a survey of the U.S. labor force and hundreds of qualitative interviews with clergy and lay members, I documented a form of "Christian individualism" that encourages "charity to individuals rather than large-scale social reforms." Theologically conservative pastors and members favored individual charity because it helped ensure that the recipients would become Christians and live morally, while they regarded social reforms as ineffective or unnecessary.[47]

In scattered locations around the globe research gives additional support to the possibility that conservative Protestantism is promoting ideas that are conducive to the kind of open markets, work ethic, and personal morality that Americans value. Pentecostalism in its myriad manifestations, resembling Baptist and Presbyterian congregations in some contexts and organized into truly independent congregations in others, is routinely described in these terms. It is a religion that "belongs by nature to open markets," writes sociologist David Martin.[48] He means that people whose lives have been disrupted by globalization are attracted to the personal discipline and biblical authority of conservative Protestantism. He argues, too, that these rules and the churches that enforce them help people to be better workers in the emerging global economy.

Yet an affinity between spiritual freedom and eagerness for free markets should not be assumed too readily. We need to look more closely at how exactly religious people talk about spiritual freedom and how, perhaps paradoxically, this emphasis on freedom results in the moral asceticism that Martin and others associate with Pentecostalism and with upward social mobility. It is important, too, to recall Birgit Meyer's observation about the ambivalence that conservative Christians in Africa register toward material goods. The same ambivalence can be seen among U.S. Christians toward the materialism they associate with American culture. Thus, delicate cultural work is required for American Christians to embrace freedom while distancing themselves from raw Americanism. To anticipate my argument, this ambivalence is reflected in survey responses to questions about free trade and in what might be described as a Christian counterdiscourse against free trade. The net result is that the Christian emphasis on freedom has been difficult to mobilize for or against free trade policies, even though certain ideological affinities remain.

In Christian discourse, the language of freedom emerges most clearly in statements that knowing Jesus results in freedom. "Christianity is the basis of choice," says a Methodist minister in Florida. "It's the most intense type of freedom there is." A Presbyterian lay woman in West Virginia says that true freedom in Christ "sets you free from worry" and "gives you freedom to not live in the past." For her, the most important result is "joy." A Catholic priest in Kansas argues that "knowing Jesus allows us to be who we are." "Jesus offered his life in sacrifice to the Father," he explains, "buying us back from our sins and then setting us free from all the guilt that our sins might impose upon us." A missionary in Kenya writes of her work among the Samburu: "They believe that [God] lives in or near big things such as mountains, trees, rock formations, and rivers. They believe that his blessings are evident in the rain and in the health of their animals. They do not know the one true God or His Son Jesus. Through the Bible stories that they are learning, they are discovering who N'kai truly is. They are finding freedom in Christ."[49]

The words American Christians use to describe their freedom in Christ emphasize emotions more than anything else. To be spiritually free is to experience an emotional uplift, a feeling of self-fulfillment, confidence, and hope. Physical realities, such as health and wealth, generally do not change, although self-confidence and freedom from worry can sometimes make it easier to achieve good health and material comforts. Nevertheless, freedom does have its limits. A responsible person must be disciplined and avoid abusing his or her freedom. The relationship between freedom and moral discipline occurs through the argument that freedom in Christ means choosing not just anything, but to obey Christ.

Obedience to Christ means following biblical rules, such as the Ten Commandments, living responsibly, being a good worker and a good family member, and behaving in a way that will offer a positive witness to others. The missionary in Kenya hoped that converts would have "courage and direction" to do God's will and be "faithful," "obedient," and "discerning to live godly lives." Focusing too much on the rules themselves can become "a ball and chain," as one woman remarked, but obedience inspired by gratitude for divine love is freeing.

Coupled with the value it places on moral discipline, the Christian idea of freedom can thus produce the kind of ascetic lifestyle that Max Weber and a host of subsequent scholars have associated with upward economic mobility. Once a person has been redeemed, the key is to exercise responsibility for one's behavior. The person is free to participate in the marketplace as a responsible worker and consumer. In Papua New Guinea, for instance, Joel Robbins says that "what is most striking about the way the Urapmin talk about rebaibal [revival] is their assertion that through that movement they have largely taken responsibility for changing their own lives and constituting themselves as subjects suitable to participate in the global culture." The Holy Spirit, whom the Urapmin characterize in almost the same terms as they do white foreigners, Robbins believes, guides the Urapmin in taking on this responsibility. Old fertility and nature rituals are replaced by the long church services in which people learn how to interact with the Holy Spirit and deal with the challenges of hunting, gardening, and overcoming illness in new ways. "In embracing the movement and in being embraced by the Holy Spirit," Robbins says, "the Urapmin entered a relationship with the white world and its God from which they could not turn back." No longer able to rely on the ancestral help they have rejected and yet far from actually benefiting from the global economy, they nevertheless "live in a very globalized world, where they understand themselves as creating a modern society in accord with the dictates of a worldwide religion."[50] In this respect, freedom in Christ produces responsible individuals who become exactly the kind of employees and consumers on which free trade policies depend.

Yet American Christians seldom see it this way. In the prevailing view, encouraging people in other countries to experience freedom in Christ is quite different from promoting an economically convenient ideology. The ability to distinguish spiritual freedom from the brand of freedom that American culture extols (and perhaps exports) depends on two arguments: first, that American society, while giving lip service to freedom, does not promote true freedom the way belief in Christ does, and second, that a person who becomes a Christian in another national context does not have to give up his or her cultural traditions in order to be free. Dissociating spiritual freedom from American values typically includes conceding that the United States is not the only good place to live and arguing that spirituality is emotional, intangible, and personal enough to be experienced (or not experienced) in any context. A Presbyterian woman in West Virginia explains that she is deeply patriotic and values the American way of life, but she thinks it is "very dangerous" to confuse freedom in Christ with patriotism. A priest in Kansas says the "freedom that we value in the United States is a different kind of freedom" that can "be misused" to "amass power or wealth or to control other people." Freedom in Christ, he says, is not freedom from pain, suffering, illiteracy, or hunger, but "freedom to not be controlled by evil." A Baptist pastor expands on the same idea, arguing that freedom in America too easily means something we have earned or aspire to, such as "making another dollar" or "buying another car," while forgetting that spiritual freedom is a gift. If spiritual freedom is culturally neutral, it follows that Christians in other countries do not have to abandon their traditions to be free. They need not give up tribal and familial ties the way Robbins observes the Urapmin doing. As Americans see it, spirituality is sufficiently inward—sufficiently concerned with overcoming worry or guilt and being joyful—that it can easily be distinguished from culture. Indeed, the greater the cultural variety that exists among Christians, the clearer this distinction becomes and the more one realizes how freeing Christianity is. For instance, a Methodist minister in Florida recalls attending a global gathering of Methodists and regarding it as "the most freeing time in my life" because people spoke in their own languages and worshipped in their own ways, even though they all believed in Jesus. "God created the diversity we have," echoes a woman who attends a nondenominational church in Washington. "When I go to the Philippines or Latin America or Africa, I love the culture. You have people there who love Jesus and they are not into the American way. They don't need to be because being American is not synonymous with being a Christian."

If clergy and church members in the United States value freedom because of their faith, the distinctions they draw among kinds of freedom, therefore, reduce the chances of Christian beliefs providing straightforward reinforcement for American policies that encourage free markets, free enterprise, and free trade. Thoughtful Christians are at best conflicted about these issues. A woman in Washington State illustrates clearly how complex the considerations can be. Having lived and traveled in other countries, she has thought a lot about international relations. Part of her favors free trade and part of her does not. She thinks free trade is good "provided the trade helps the people it should be helping." Citing the large population of the world living in poverty, she says people should be empowered and given the chance to become self-sufficient. Trade could help. But she immediately backtracks: "I'm always guarded because my idea of what is a good deal isn't how it is. I'm amazed at the sleazy stuff that occurs." So much of trade, she adds, is "self-serving." Still, she is reluctant to dismiss the possibility that trade might help people in other countries. She toys momentarily with the idea that trade relationships are like personal relationships—encouraging greater understanding and cooperation. Having brought personal considerations into the picture, though, she ventures that perhaps motivation is what matters most. "If your motivation is right with God, you can accomplish just about anything if you just hang in there and keep working." Free trade would be good if people's motives were good. And yet she knows this is not always the case. "Many times it ends up being fraught with crime and all kinds of illegal activities." "I don't know," she concludes, "I just don't know."

Not everyone is as thoughtful or as conflicted as this woman. But the views clergy and lay people express about free trade point mostly to complexities that cannot be easily resolved. A Presbyterian minister in West Virginia says she "absolutely" agrees that the United States should promote free trade agreements and that Christians should support these agreements. But she also believes trade is sometimes "empowering and freeing" and at other times is "like putting the ball and chain on the ankle of someone." A member of an Assemblies of God church in Illinois says "it depends on what kind of trade." She thinks opening markets for handmade goods is probably beneficial but points to the danger of sweatshops and exploitation. A Catholic woman in the same community says, "The U.S. always has to make out the best and get something out of it. It can't just be equal fair trade. It always has to be someone is profiting and the little person in the Third World country is not." A Baptist pastor in Georgia thinks the "church should definitely support the government" and if that includes free trade agreements, then so be it. He says poor villagers in Central America who sell coffee to Starbucks benefit. In this sense, free trade is a form of "deliverance." But he also thinks the church should be helping the poor in other ways.

Surveys are ill suited for eliciting complex thoughts; yet it is evident even in survey responses that American Christians are conflicted about free trade. On the one hand, some responses suggest that church members overwhelmingly believe trade is good for the world. For instance, in the Global Issues Survey 76 percent agreed that "promoting trade throughout the world helps to reduce hunger among people in poor countries" (34 percent agreed strongly), while only 16 percent disagreed. Another question found that 39 percent of church members thought the rationale "It is better to solve these problems by promoting international trade" was a good reason for not doing more to help poor people in other countries (41 percent thought it was not a very good reason). On the other hand, 81 percent thought "protecting the jobs of American workers" should be a very important foreign policy goal of the United States. And when posed with the possibility that "a large American company decided to move its operations to another country," 53 percent said this would bother them a lot and another 30 percent said it would bother them some. In short, American church members seem to think that promoting trade is beneficial for the world but are less supportive if it hurts the American worker. On all of these questions, the responses of evangelical Protestants, mainline Protestants, Catholics, and members of historically black denominations are nearly identical.[51] Nor are the responses of those who attend religious services every week significantly different from those who attend less often. What does matter are differences in levels of education and income. Those with high school educations are more favorable toward trade as well as more concerned about American jobs than those with college or advanced degrees. Those with lower incomes are more favorable toward trade than those with higher incomes, but concern about protecting American jobs does not vary significantly across income categories.

There are at least three reasons, then, to suspect that faith does not matter much to U.S. Christians' thinking about foreign policies concerned with free trade. The first is that believers draw distinctions among kinds of freedom. They value freedom as God's gift but distinguish this spiritual freedom from the cultural values they associate with America and with the traditions of Christians in other countries. The second is that their thinking about free trade is complicated by such considerations as who benefits and what motives are involved. And third, survey responses also suggest complex considerations and point to factors other than religion as having the most bearing on attitudes. How then might religious organizations be relevant to policies about free trade?

Christian lobbying groups and other faith-based organizations have been outspoken about free trade despite the fact that rank-and-file Christians seem an unlikely constituency for such involvement. Opposition to free trade agreements has been expressed by such organizations as Church World Service, the U.S. Conference of Catholic Bishops, the General Assembly of the Presbyterian Church USA, the General Synod of the United Church of Christ, and the World Alliance of Reformed Churches and has generally been more visible than support for free trade. For these opponents, what trumps the language of freedom are concerns about injustice. In the abstract, free trade might be compatible with freedom in Christ, but the moral imperative that follows from spiritual freedom includes an obligation to uphold fairness. A missionary headed for work in Africa puts it this way: "From a justice point of view, it's very important for the U.S. to seek to alleviate poverty because it's responsible for a lot of it." However, he feels that free trade simply aggravates the problem. "Free trade favors the rich nations and the heads of corporations. It increases stratification. It's helping multinational corporations make a lot of money, but really is not helping out the poorest of the poor."

In a 2004 policy statement, Church World Service articulated an alternative to free trade called "just trade," based on principles of respect for the dignity of the human person and concern for "our common humanity."[52] A resolution passed in 2003 by the General Assembly of the Presbyterian Church (USA) opposing the proposed Free Trade Area of the Americas agreement asserted that justice requires the "inclusion of all members of the human family in obtaining and enjoying the Creator's gifts for sustenance" as well as "equitable sharing and organized efforts to achieve that end."[53] A Presbyterian leader from the United States who had spent considerable time in Latin America explained the rationale for the church's opposition to free trade. "Countries across Latin America are lining up to sign free trade agreements with the empire, eliminating trade barriers to foreign corporations," he observed. But opening markets creates "the cruelest of ironies; even as a country's macroeconomic stability grows . . . more and more people end up living in poverty."[54]

Christian groups opposing free trade have worked in partnership with other organizations. Although these partnerships usually bring together religious organizations, they sometimes include other nongovernmental organizations. For example, the New York State Labor-Religion Coalition, which formed in 1997, is an alliance of unions, religious institutions, youth groups, and individuals engaged in advocacy on behalf of the state's low-wage workers. The alliance has sought to increase awareness of the "global consequences of corporate control" by publicizing the struggles of maquiladoras and *colonias* (workers' neighborhoods) in Mexico along the Texas border. It has also opposed trade agreements deemed harmful to workers on both sides of the border.[55] Another example is the Trade for People Campaign organized by a coalition of nongovernmental organizations including the World Council of Churches, the Third World Network, Oxfam International, Public Services International, the World Wildlife Fund, and the Institute for Agriculture and Trade Policy.

Coalitions like these illustrate two of the ways in which nongovernmental organizations play a role in foreign policy. They broaden the constituency in hopes of achieving greater impact. In the case of Christian groups, the fact that Christians are divided about free trade means that these coalitions can mobilize selectively from the Christian population, and combine aspects of faith with other motivating factors. By participating in these coalitions, Christian organizations also enhance their own position symbolically. If, for instance, the coalition experiences success, then the Christian organization can claim to have played a role, even though this role may have been small.

On balance, it is difficult to see that Christians and Christian organizations have been a strong or distinct force in recent years either in promoting or opposing free trade policies. Proponents and opponents apparently gain some stature by weighing in on free trade policies. Having a position on these policies is a way of demonstrating to these organizations' constituencies that they are concerned about larger governmental policies. Some tangible benefits to Christian organizations may also accrue when free trade policies are implemented. For instance, free trade agreements between the United States and Ghana have made it easier for U.S. televangelists to purchase airtime on Ghanaian radio stations and to sell videos and tapes of sermons and religious music. Similarly, free trade with Mexico has facilitated U.S. church programs that ship relief supplies across the border or work with Mexican citizens who have ties to the United States. Yet U.S. Christian organizations have little to gain from identifying themselves closely with free trade policies. Those policies can be viewed as harming American workers or being too much in the interest of big business. With strong backing from business itself, free trade policy is in sparse need of legitimation from churches.

HUMAN RIGHTS ISSUES

Where the language of freedom has forged a considerably stronger bond between American Christians and U.S. foreign policy has been on issues of human rights. Beliefs about freedom in Christ lead seamlessly to arguments about freedom to worship and freedom from religious persecution, especially when those persecuted are fellow Christians. As a pastor in Michigan who directed overseas missions efforts for his denomination observes, "There is no better way to show someone the freedom of Christ than to liberate them from unjust systems." On the policy front, the move during the 1990s to include greater emphasis on international religious freedom in relations with other countries drew widespread interest from Christians and Jews. Support for legislation came from such diverse groups as the Southern Baptist Convention, Concerned Women for America, and the U.S. Catholic Conference and from such prominent individual leaders as Charles Colson of Prison Fellowship, Reform rabbi David Saperstein, Senator Joseph Lieberman, and Congressman Frank Wolf. Although differences were often evident in opinions about specific measures, the combined efforts of these organizations and individuals resulted in legislation that established the U.S. Commission on International Religious Freedom to monitor the status of freedom of thought, conscience, and religion and to combat religious persecution in other countries. With an annual budget of approximately $3 million, the agency's commissioners were sent to visit countries where human rights violations were suspected, issued reports, and provided background information that resulted in various House and Senate resolutions about religious freedom.[56] Countries of particular concern to the commission included Myanmar (Burma), China, North Korea, Iran, Saudi Arabia, Sudan, and Vietnam.

Championing human rights for persecuted religious minorities does take concerted action and political maneuvering, but it is hardly a difficult cause for religious groups to embrace. As early as 1978, 79 percent of the public believed that "promoting and defending human rights in other countries" was a very important or somewhat important foreign policy goal for the United States, while only 14 percent said it was not important (and 7 percent were unsure). In subsequent years, tacit support for international human rights never fell below 80 percent. The proportion who regarded promoting and defending human rights in other countries as at least somewhat important stood at 95 percent in 1982; 87 percent in 1986; 91 percent in 1991; 83 percent in 1995; 86 percent in 1998; 87 percent in 2001; and 86 percent in 2002, 2003, and 2005. In four of the surveys, more than 50 percent of the public felt that promoting and defending human rights was "very important," and in all the surveys this proportion averaged 44 percent.[57] Being in favor of international human rights, moreover, entails very little in tangible costs to the American public. If U.S. officials criticize China or Somalia for violating religious freedom, their remarks do not imply that American jobs would be lost or that the military budget would increase. "These are all-win issues for the [Bush] administration," one spokesperson observed in 2003. "They're not issues that will alienate large segments of the center in America."[58]

Human rights is thus quite different from free trade in its implications for religious advocacy groups. Whereas free trade has been controversial enough that many groups said nothing and the ones who did spoke in opposition, human rights is the kind of issue that religious groups could eagerly embrace as they scramble to present themselves as its most vocal supporters. The winners in this contest clearly have been evangelical Protestants. They could lay legitimate claim to having played a significant role in bringing religion more visibly into human rights discussions. Such key advocates as Richard Land of the Southern Baptist Convention, Charles Colson of Prison Fellowship, Senator Sam Brownback of Kansas, and Congressman Frank Wolf of Virginia are all self-identified born-again Christians. In his account of the interfaith alliance that promoted the international religious freedom legislation, Allen D. Hertzke writes that evangelicals provided the grassroots muscle behind the alliance, bringing their theological intensity, entrepreneurial leadership, and vast social networks to bear when the movement most needed them.[59] Columnist Nicholas D. Kristof of the *New York Times* went further, suggesting that Colson and company might deserve "sainthood" for their humanitarian efforts.[60]

Evangelical leaders themselves argued that the triumphs in human rights legislation were largely due to their efforts. After interviewing a number of their leaders, a reporter for the *Wall Street Journal* described evangelicals as "organized, motivated, and self-confident" in their campaign for human rights.[61] "They call us," Richard Land asserted, describing his access to the White House. "They say, you know, 'What do you think about this?' "[62] "We represent organizations which led efforts to enact . . . ground-breaking human rights initiatives," Ted Haggard of the National Association of Evangelicals argued in a 2004 letter to President Bush that carried signatures from the leaders of fifty evangelical organizations.[63] Other conservative leaders emphasized their successes in human rights advocacy by criticizing religious organizations they deemed to have taken alternative positions. The conservative Institute for Religion and Democracy, for instance, commissioned a report that accused mainline Protestant leaders of "old prejudices," "anti-Semitism," and an "eagerness to make peace with America's enemies."[64]

Yet it is unclear that evangelical Protestants were actually the earliest or the most ardent proponents of international human rights. Hertzke's account emphasizes the roles of Michael Horowitz, David Saperstein, Joseph Lieberman, and other Jewish leaders and notes that some evangelical Protestant leaders expressed doubts about impending human rights legislation even as others supported it. Of mainline Protestants, Hertzke credits Episcopal lobbyist Thomas Hart with outspoken support for religious freedom.[65] Hertzke's severest criticism of mainline leaders is directed toward National Council of Churches lobbyist Albert Pennybacker, who testified against religious freedom legislation in 1998.[66] However, closer inspection of the record of the National Council of Churches shows that the organization has consistently supported the protection of religious liberty since 1955 and as recently as 1996 joined with the National Association of Evangelicals in condemning all forms of religious persecution and affirming a commitment to religious freedom. Where the National Council of Churches urged caution was in taking at face value the word of American Christians that people in other countries were being persecuted, rather than incorporating indigenous testimony. The National Council of Churches also urged greater attention to religious persecution of all kinds in addition to specifically anti-Christian persecution.[67]

Other religious bodies that have long supported human rights and religious freedom, including efforts in the mid-1990s within the U.S. State Department to monitor religious persecution, counseled against passage of new legislation on narrow grounds as well. One such, the U.S. Catholic Conference, has strongly supported the State Department's efforts to promote religious freedom, viewing them simply as an extension of the Universal Declaration of Human Rights, which the church worked to promote a half century earlier, along with the teachings of Pope John XXIII in *Pacem in Terris*.[68] However, the Catholic Conference nevertheless urged revisions in the 1998 legislation in hopes of limiting harm to ordinary people if presidential sanctions were imposed for human rights violations. Likewise, the Presbyterian Church (USA) argued that the establishment of a White House office for religious freedom was a step toward greater presidential authority and U.S. unilateralism—concerns that became increasingly prominent a half decade later during the war in Iraq.[69] Exceptional support for human rights among evangelicals is even less apparent at the grassroots than among leaders. In the Global Issues Survey, 56 percent of evangelical Protestants thought promoting and defending human rights in other countries should be a very important U.S. foreign policy goal, but so did 52 percent of mainline Protestants, 55 percent of the members of historically black denominations, and 60 percent of Catholics. Only when religious persecution was mentioned specifically in the survey did evangelical Protestants express greater concern than other Protestants or Catholics. For instance, when confronted with the possibility that "a foreign government decided that nobody in that country was allowed to practice Christianity," nearly all evangelical Protestants (88 percent) said this would bother them a lot, whereas the proportions giving the same response among other groups were somewhat lower: 74 percent among mainline Protestants, 80 percent among black Protestants, and 74 percent among Catholics. Members of evangelical churches were also somewhat more likely to say their congregation should be concerned about religious persecution in other countries.[70] Still, evangelical Protestants were no more likely than other members to say they favored the U.S. government "requiring other countries to protect the religious freedom of their citizens." Support for this idea ranged from 73 percent among black Protestants to 79 percent among Catholics, with 78 percent of both evangelical and mainline Protestants giving the same response.

The role of religious organizations as advocates for human rights is poorly understood if it is regarded chiefly as a means of passing specific legislative initiatives or as an expression of popular support from American churchgoers. This role is both significantly broader and often less directly aimed at influencing foreign policy than at providing information. It includes serving as a vehicle through which information from indigenous church groups about violations against human rights in their countries is channeled to U.S. officials and to the American public at large. For instance, an agency director (who spoke anonymously because of the sensitivity of what he was saying) acknowledged that his organization frequently reports instances of religious persecution that field staff observe, not directly to the U.S. embassy but to the embassy of another Western country and that embassy in turn passes the information to an

American official. Another agency learned through its relief efforts about ethnic Baptists being persecuted in Southeast Asia and, by working with the U.S. State Department, assisted a thousand of these refugees to gain asylum in the United States. In these ways, U.S. religious organizations with ties to missionaries, congregations, and relief workers in other countries become the eyes and ears of the American government. Bringing these violations to the attention of policy makers is a way to exert pressure on the policy community.

Information about human rights violations feeds into foreign policy decisions, but that is often not its primary purpose. Pastors and leaders of international agencies frequently argue that they can do little to shape public policy, either in Washington or in other countries. Thus, they aim to combat religious persecution by "standing with" churches in countries lacking religious freedom. "Standing with" means learning about hardship, telling these stories to American church members, and using these messages to raise donations to help the overseas congregations. "Standing with" also means visibly connecting indigenous congregations with the United States in hopes that this visibility will discourage local authorities from suppressing worship in those countries. For instance, a Catholic sister who works with churches in Indonesia says she prefers to work with persecuted Christians because "they are willing to go out on a limb for their faith." She mentions a Christian woman who was arrested and in danger of being stoned to death before being released. She says her organization would not get involved in official negotiations in a case like this for fear of causing an international incident. Instead, her organization visits local Christians and supplies other support. As a result, she believes, the local authorities "realize that these people are not just individual Indonesian Christians, they are connected to a larger family of faith." The officials know that stories about persecution would filter out to the wider world, she says.

Besides supplying information about persecution, religious organizations promote human rights by working with immigration officials to keep U.S. doors open to refugees fleeing persecution. An alliance of a rather different kind than the one resulting in the 1998 religious freedom legislation in the United States is called InterAction. This is a coalition of more than 160 of the largest international relief and development nongovernmental organizations in the United States. It includes most of the well-established Christian agencies, such as the American Friends Service Committee, Bread for the World, Catholic Relief Services, Church World Service, the United Methodist Committee on Relief, World Relief, and

World Vision International. It also includes such organizations as B'nai B'rith International, the Islamic American Relief Agency, Latter-Day Saint Charities, the Unitarian Universalist Service Committee, and United Jewish Communities. InterAction works closely with the United Nations High Commission on Refugees (UNHCR) to protect, feed, and resettle victims of war, persecution, and national disasters. The 2006 UNHCR budget for regular and supplementary programs was $1.15 billion.[71]

Presbyterian Disaster Assistance is one of the member organizations of the InterAction coalition. Although its primary focus is relief for victims of natural disasters, Presbyterian Disaster Assistance also works with public officials and nongovernmental agencies to provide assistance for refugees. Religious persecution is one of the leading reasons that people come to the United States seeking asylum. The agency's role in the larger effort to promote religious freedom is thus to help refugees directly and to advocate for U.S. policies that facilitate refugee resettlement. Advocacy takes place in a variety of venues. For instance, the head of the agency's refugee ministry is a member of the humanitarian protection committee of InterAction. This committee works with the UNHCR to identify the human rights needs of internally displaced persons and to encourage laws aimed at guaranteeing these rights. Presbyterian Disaster Assistance also brings religious freedom issues to the attention of the U.S. State Department and participates in UNHCR executive committee and standing committee meetings in Geneva. In addition, most of the agency's work is concerned with meeting the immediate needs of refugees themselves. Examples range from helping a congregation of Pakistani Presbyterians in New Hampshire deal with the special registration requirements instituted by the Department of Homeland Security to assisting Church World Service in resettling thousands of refugees annually through local congregations. The agency also provides funding for the pastoral care of refugees through the World Council of Churches' Global Ecumenical Network for the Uprooted and, in cooperation with Lutheran Immigration and Refugee Services, supports more than two dozen legal assistance agencies for those seeking asylum in the United States.[72]

The work of Presbyterian Disaster Assistance illustrates a different nongovernmental strategy for influencing human rights policies from the one that led to the creation of the Commission on International Religious Freedom. Presbyterian Disaster Assistance's relatively small budget of $600,000 for refugee work comes entirely from members of local Presbyterian congregations through the denomination's One Great Hour of Sharing program.[73] Thus it is imperative for this agency to work in cooperation with other agencies, both to be effective and symbolically to communicate its effectiveness to donors. Working closely with Church World Service and Lutheran Immigration and Refugee Services is the most immediate way in which Presbyterian Disaster Assistance expands its activities. Participating in the InterAction coalition, working with the World Council of Churches, serving on United Nations committees, and meeting with State Department officials further increases its role. Playing a relatively small role in the much larger efforts of organizations like the UNHCR means that no single religious agency can take credit for swaying particular policies in most cases. However, these agencies do have a voice and their influence is more credible because of the actual work the agencies do to protect against religious persecution. As one agency director explained, "We bump into government through our service activities and we have points of view about how things ought to be changed to make our country more welcoming toward people who are fleeing to our country. Then if our advocacy is successful, that gives us more opportunity for service."

Another significant area in which religious organizations have become increasingly involved is aimed at combating the international human-trafficking industry. The U.S. government defines trafficking as any act involved in the "transport, harboring or sales of persons within national or across international borders through coercion, force, kidnapping, deception or fraud, for purposes of placing persons in situations of forced labor or services, such as forced prostitution, domestic servitude, debt bondage or other slavery-like practices."[74] Trafficking represents the underside of globalization. As trade and transportation have increased and as the power of nation-states to control their borders has decreased, human trafficking is promoted by criminal organizations, which earn huge profits from this traffic. An estimated 800,000 to 900,000 people, mostly women and children, are trafficked annually.[75] Rising concern about trafficking resulted in the Trafficking Victims Protection Act of 2000, which requires the U.S. Department of Justice to monitor and combat trafficking domestically and encourages the State Department to reduce aid to countries involved in trafficking. Governmental initiatives against trafficking have included the establishment of an interagency task force to coordinate activities among the major executive branch agencies and a State Department trafficking office to prepare reports and promote international cooperation. The State Department office has sought to obtain input from and supply ideas and assistance to nongovernmental organizations in this effort.

Although trafficking had received some attention earlier, it was not until the 1990s that there emerged activist organizations focusing specifically on trafficking. The first was Equality Now, founded in 1992 by Amnesty International activist Jessica Neuwirth. The second was the Protection Project, founded in 1996 by feminist leader Laura Lederer. The third was the International Justice Mission, founded in 1997 by former Justice Department lawyer Gary Haugen. Each of the three organizations was small and depended largely on the energy and expertise of its founder. This knowledge and motivation and the relative newness of the issue made it possible for the three to be mutually supportive and to draw in different constituencies. Haugen was the only one with strong connections with churches. These ties helped him recruit volunteers and collect stories. Despite the enthusiasm of these activists, the Trafficking Victims Protection Act would likely not have succeeded had it not been for the network that had formed around the International Religious Freedom Act. Michael Horowitz, the key figure in that effort, drew on his connections with Richard Land, Charles Colson, Frank Wolf, and others. Implementation of the legislation in 2000, nevertheless, proved disappointing to those who had promoted it. Thus, the additional effort that resulted in a more aggressive antitrafficking policy required advocacy with the White House to place a person in charge of the program who would assume a stronger leadership role. After that took place in 2003, policies against trafficking became more effective.

With broad public support for human rights, at least in principle, the policy effectiveness of religious groups lies largely in their capacity to command resources relevant to specific human rights issues. As these examples illustrate, effectiveness in passing new legislation depends both on personal ties and on gaining wider visibility, whereas other programs are more highly institutionalized and thus rely more on formal participation in committees and coalitions. In the case of the 1998 international religious freedom legislation, religious leaders with close personal connections to Washington officials were able to facilitate passage of the legislation and thus to bring questions about religious freedom more clearly into discussions about human rights. In cases where specific human rights violations are at issue, the relevant networks reside more in working relationships with churches and nongovernmental organizations in other countries. The fact that international religious agencies have become highly specialized means that some organizations can do more than simply promote legislation or supply information. Relief agencies with long histories of resettling refugees contribute to the promotion of religious freedom through that means. Combating international trafficking requires new expertise and has resulted in new organizations such as the International Justice Mission. Human rights are thus an issue that illustrates the range of ways in which the religious community can be involved.

AMERICAN MILITARY ACTION

The attitudes of American Christians about war—and especially the U.S. invasion of Iraq in 2003—have been considerably more divided than their attitudes about human rights and even about free trade. The extent of this division is evident in responses to the Global Issues Survey, where 45 percent of those whose congregations had discussed the war said members held divided opinions. Divided opinions in congregations may also have been a factor in 2003 Pew Research Center poll results showing that 57 percent of pastors (according to attendees) had spoken about the war, but only 21 percent had taken a position on the issue.[76] Other polls, too, showed that the public at large held mixed opinions about the desirability of war in the months preceding the invasion. A Gallup poll in December 2002 showed that 40 percent favored invading Iraq, depending on "events over the next few weeks," and 27 percent opposed the invasion with similar reservations, while only 15 percent favored invasion without qualifications and 12 percent flatly opposed invasion.[77]

Evangelical Protestants were more likely to support U.S. military intervention in Iraq than were liberal Protestants and Catholics. In the Pew survey, 15 percent of evangelicals said their pastor had spoken in favor of the war, whereas only 1 percent of mainline Protestants, 5 percent of black Protestants, and none of the Catholics said this. The survey also showed that 77 percent of evangelicals favored the United States taking military action to end Saddam Hussein's rule, compared with 62 percent of mainline Protestants and Catholics, and only 36 percent of black Protestants. Evangelicals were more divided in their views about how military action should be taken, but 48 percent favored the use of force even if U.S. allies did not participate, compared with 43 percent of mainline Protestants and 37 percent of Catholics who held the same view. In the Gallup poll, 68 percent of evangelicals favored invading Iraq, compared with 57 percent of mainline Protestants, 43 percent of black Protestants, and 58 percent of Catholics.

The relatively high level of support among evangelicals for invading Iraq was one of the reasons commentators came to believe that evangelicals were exercising an increasing influence on U.S. foreign policy. No serious observers of the discussions leading up to the invasion of Iraq believed that Jerry Falwell or Ralph Reed was pulling strings the way Paul Wolfowitz, Richard Perle, and Vice President Dick Cheney were. Yet it was tempting to view the presumed powerbrokers of the 2000 election as a force behind the growing unilateralism of U.S. military planning as well. It was imaginable that evangelicals' messianic views of Israel were now somehow being exploited by Wolfowitz and company.[78] And if evangelicals were somehow eager to invade Iraq, the possibility that they might help tilt the administration toward further preemptive engagements was also interesting.

Although some of evangelicals' support for the war may have stemmed from their earlier and more general enthusiasm for President George W. Bush, the larger question raised by this support was whether evangelicals were simply more militaristic than other Americans. A 2002 poll conducted for the Council on Foreign Relations suggested that this might be the case, but if so, not by much. When asked if they thought "maintaining superior military power worldwide" should be a "very important" policy goal of the United States, 74 percent of evangelical Protestants said yes, but so did 68 percent of mainline Protestants, 61 percent of black Protestants, and 71 percent of Catholics. Only among respondents with no religious affiliation was the figure—51 percent—significantly lower.[79] Responses to the same question in the Global Issues Survey showed less overall support for maintaining military superiority but again revealed that evangelical Protestants were only somewhat more likely than several other groups to hold this view. Fifty-nine percent said military superiority was very important, compared with 47 percent of mainline Protestants, 54 percent of black Protestants, and 57 percent of Catholics.[80]

If these denominational categories showed few differences, how people identified themselves mattered more. For instance, among Protestants who thought of themselves as "fundamentalists," 65 percent thought military superiority was very important, compared with only 33 percent of Protestants who identified themselves as religious "liberals." Among Catholics, 66 percent of those self-identified as "traditional" Catholics held the same view, compared with only 46 percent of "liberal" Catholics. And on views of the Bible, 61 percent of biblical literalists said military superiority was very important, compared with

50 percent of nonliteralists who nevertheless believed the Bible was divinely inspired, and only 35 percent of those who regarded the Bible as a book of fables and legends.

These patterns suggest two important implications. One is that there is probably a mutual influence between religious identities and policy positions. For instance, if a fundamentalist leader endorses war, as Jerry Falwell did the invasion of Iraq, then people who consider themselves fundamentalists may be more inclined to agree, and by the same token, a person who favored the war and who was merely a theologically conservative Christian might be more likely to embrace the label "fundamentalist." Similarly, the label "traditional Catholic" might mean that a person identifies with the policies of a conservative president as well as holding conservative theological views. The other implication, though, is that labels of this kind, which are convenient in surveys and bandied about by news commentators, do not adequately express what people actually think.

A 2005 article in *Foreign Affairs* by pollster Daniel Yankelovich provides an example of how categorical conclusions drawn from limited information can be misleading. "In the minds of white evangelical Protestants, the nation is faced with an apocalyptic threat," Yankelovich observed. They regard President Bush as a "God-fearing" leader who "inoculates them against weakness, faltering, and realpolitik." In their eyes, the president is "on the side of good" and "what he does is right." Evangelicals' sentiments "echo the traditional theme of American exceptionalism: Americans are a people chosen for a special mission in the world and especially blessed by God."[81] Yankelovich's conclusions were based on a poll that provided no explicit comparisons of evangelicals with other Americans or evidence about any of these particular beliefs.

Among Christian conservatives, attitudes toward war are considerably more nuanced than pundits who know little about religion assume. A good example of Christian conservatives' ambivalence is the observation provided by the director of an influential Pentecostal agency. Like many Christian conservatives, he believes that evil is a palpable presence in the world and that it cannot be thwarted by goodwill alone. There are "thugs" in the world and the United States' power gives it the responsibility of serving as the "world's policeman." However, that responsibility should not be exercised injudiciously. He says power should not be "flaunted" around the world or used to "pick fights" and that we should "never occupy a country." He thinks the U.S. invasion of Afghanistan was justified but is less sure about the war with Iraq. Having lost friends in Vietnam, he knows that "war is hell" and says we need to remember that in order not to pursue it too readily. It is not appropriate for him to criticize the president, he feels, but he worries when presidents use theological justifications for war. In his view, theology and eschatology should not determine foreign policy.

With nuances like these to be taken into consideration, religious organizations have more often tried to adopt a neutral position toward particular wars than to endorse or oppose them. The neutral position is most readily defended on grounds that church and state should be separate. For instance, a Southern Baptist official says his organization adopts a "very apolitical stance" toward war, which is in keeping with Baptists' historical emphasis on separation of church and state. Adopting a neutral position is also consistent with viewing the church's primary mission during war as one of providing humanitarian relief ("working to relieve suffering among peoples on both sides of the conflict," he says).

If neutrality is the default option, there are nevertheless instances in which religious leaders do vocally endorse or oppose war. In these situations, support or opposition is usually expressed in one of two ways. It comes in the form of an official pronouncement or resolution endorsed by a religious body or as a statement uttered by a particular religious leader. For example, in 2002 the National Council of Churches issued a statement under the signature of its general secretary and the heads of fifty Protestant and Catholic organizations expressing opposition "on moral grounds [to] the United States taking further military action against Iraq now" and asking the government "to reflect the morals and values we hold dear—pursuing peace, not war; working with the community of nations, not overthrowing governments by force; respecting international law and treaties while holding in high regard all human life."[82] As an example of a statement uttered by an individual religious leader, Southern Baptist Richard Land stated in September 2002 that "the U.S. would be doing the world a favor and acting in the best interest of future citizens of the U.S. by removing Saddam from power." Land was also quoted as saying that "an act of war" had been committed against the United States, so if critics are "looking for just cause, we have already passed that threshold."[83] Resolutions appear to express opposition or counsel caution more often than they specifically endorse war, whereas statements by individual leaders appear to endorse war with greater frequency. Thus, one of the reasons that religious conservatives appear to have given more vocal support to recent wars may be the greater autonomy that many of their leaders enjoy. As heads of large independent churches, televangelists, and media personalities, these leaders are less constrained by the deliberative processes traditionally involved in denominational resolutions.

Unlike entrepreneurial religious leaders or traditional denominations, faith-based nongovernmental organizations typically do not address issues of war and peace by expressing individual opinions or passing resolutions. It might be supposed that the globalization of American Christianity through the work of these nongovernmental organizations would be a force in favor of an increased U.S. military presence in the world. A military presence could be favorable for protecting missionaries and relief workers, military intervention might be regarded as a way of bringing the downfall of oppressive regimes, and even failed military actions might give relief organizations a greater role on the international stage. An organization might refrain from openly condoning war but quietly regard it as an opportunity, as an American missionary in Baghdad appeared to do in 2004 when he told a *Los Angeles Times* reporter that "God and the president have given us an opportunity to bring Jesus Christ to the Middle East."[84] However, none of these suppositions appears to be correct. The most powerful faith-based nongovernmental organizations have nearly all been strong proponents of multilateralism, and many of them have encouraged the use of cooperative arrangements to promote diplomacy and maintain peace.

At a meeting attended by representatives from forty of the largest faith-based nongovernmental organizations in June 2001, a range of peacebuilding strategies that had been employed in the past and that could be implemented in the future were examined. These strategies included working cooperatively with secular nongovernmental organizations, playing a role in mediation, and incorporating peacebuilding activities into more traditional relief and development efforts. In pursuing these strategies, faith-based organizations often bring valuable experience to bear on international conflicts because of their relationships with local communities. At the same time, conflict-ridden situations require faith-based organizations to work cooperatively with agencies from other countries and representing different religions.[85]

Examples of faith-based organizations engaging in peacebuilding efforts range from training efforts and conflict prevention to interfaith dialogue and mediation. Training is most likely to be conducted by organizations that specialize in peacebuilding. For instance, the Plowshares Institute trained more than a thousand grassroots leaders in South Africa during its transition from apartheid rule. Conflict prevention is emphasized by relief and development organizations, such as Catholic Relief Services and World Vision International. World Vision leaders consider their emphasis on partnerships with local organizations as an indirect way of drawing diverse groups together and establishing trust. Some organizations, such as the International Center for Religion and Diplomacy, and agencies within larger bodies, such as the World Council of Churches, engage in high-level mediation processes, especially in contexts where religious divisions are at issue, such as in Sudan, Nigeria, and Sri Lanka. Such work has also been promoted through grassroots dialogue. For instance, the Center for Strategic and International Studies has conducted conflict resolution seminars among religious groups in the former Yugoslavia at which participants use storytelling to personalize their faith.[86]

Although many of these activities happen outside the United States and are invisible to the American public, U.S. congregations are an important base of support. For instance, the Plowshares Institute draws recruits and financial contributions from Mennonites and other congregations with pacifist teachings, while World Vision's peacebuilding efforts are part of the support it receives for relief and development projects. Faith-based organizations also include advocacy activities that alert supporters to pending legislation or comment on major policy decisions. For instance, during the months preceding the U.S. invasion of Iraq, Catholic Relief Services provided numerous bulletins and action alerts urging supporters to "ask the President to work with other nations and the United Nations to address Iraq's threats by pursuing effective alternatives to war."[87] When armed conflict is undertaken, faith-based agencies become involved as well through relief and resettlement efforts. For instance, a list compiled in 2005 by Catholic Relief Services of major international nongovernmental organizations active in Iraq included the American Friends Service Committee, Catholic Relief Services, Church World Service, Lutheran World Relief, Mercy Corps, and World Vision International.[88]

The multilateralist approaches taken by religious relief and development organizations do not ensure that policy makers will follow their lead. The tensions frequently evident in U.S. military policies between the Department of Defense and the State Department are symptomatic of how faith-based agencies intervene in policy discussions. Faith-based agencies are more closely aligned, both in practice and on principle, with State than with Defense. This alliance favors multilateralism, even as it supports American interests abroad. Faith-based nongovernmental organizations gain influence through this alliance, but the influence acquired is easily overshadowed by that of other governmental units. To the extent that faith-based intervention is effective, though, an important reason for its success is the ability of faith-based organizations to secure the material and symbolic support of government. This support ranges from small events, such as the June 2001 meeting of forty nongovernmental agencies, which was hosted by the United States Institute of Peace (established and funded by Congress) to the substantial role played by USAID in the work of Catholic Relief Services and World Vision International.

FOREIGN ASSISTANCE

The aspect of U.S. foreign policy in which religious organizations have arguably had the greatest influence in recent years is foreign aid. This influence has not been as controversial as the supposed role of religious groups in promoting unilateral military action and for this reason has less often caught the attention of the mass media. However, there were some notable instances in which religious groups played a role in advocating for policies aimed at facilitating economic development, poverty reduction, and medical assistance. One of these issues was international debt relief, an effort spearheaded by Catholic and mainline Protestant advocacy groups under the banner of Jubilee 2000. This effort was joined by Christian groups in other countries and by the World Bank and was popularized by a papal call and such celebrities as Bono and the rock group U2. Catholic Relief Services, with offices in twenty-six of the forty-five countries identified by the World Bank as "heavily indebted poor countries," worked with the World Bank and partners in Bolivia, Honduras, Cameroon, and elsewhere to develop and implement poverty reduction strategies. Staff at the Washington offices of the Presbyterian and Episcopal churches helped draft bipartisan legislation for debt relief, and staff at the Lutherans' office organized and coordinated one of the main rallies in the nation's capital on behalf of Jubilee 2000.[89] Bread for the World generated approximately 250,000 letters from church members to Congress in support of the initiative.[90] The campaign was instrumental in obtaining forgiveness of approximately $34 billion of the $207 billion owed by the world's poorest countries.[91] "It wasn't as much as we wanted," one of the religious leaders recalled, "but it was certainly more than was on the radar screen of Washington when we began." The effort's success was testimony to the leverage available through advocacy networks and coalitions.

The largest faith-based relief and development agencies have consistently written position papers and testified repeatedly about legislation affecting U.S. foreign aid. In 2001 a proposed increase in foreign assistance by Senate Foreign Relations committee chair Jesse Helms that included a plan to abolish USAID was roundly opposed by faith-based agencies even though the measure would have channeled funds directly to nongovernmental organizations.[92] In 2004, faith-based agencies joined other members of the InterAction coalition in urging Congress to add significantly to the administration's proposed budget for children's health and HIV/AIDS programs and to maintain and enhance traditional humanitarian and development assistance levels in the face of new expenditures for post-conflict reconstruction in Afghanistan and Iraq.[93] In 2005, faith-based agencies supported closer coordination of aid programs that had become scattered among federal agencies, and in 2006 when Secretary of State Condoleezza Rice restructured USAID and other programs under a single director of foreign assistance, many of these agencies' directors wrote in support of the change.[94]

Religious groups were also advocates for a number of specific programs funded through Foreign Operations and the State Department or coordinated through the United Nations. Bread for the World and other faith-based organizations facilitated congressional approval in 2001 for a bipartisan proposal calling for increased levels of development assistance to sub-Saharan Africa. Faith-based organizations played a key role in strengthening provisions of the 2003 Clean Diamonds Act that aimed to reduce the illegal mining and sale of diamonds in countries such as Sierra Leone, Angola, and Liberia. Faith-based organizations were instrumental in formulating the United Nations' Humanitarian Charter and Minimum Standards in Disaster Response, a protocol specifying minimum nutritional needs for disaster victims. These standards were implemented through a coalition of churches in Burundi, through Catholic Relief Services in the Democratic Republic of Congo, with the assistance of Lutheran World Relief and World Vision International in El Salvador, and with the participation of Christian Aid, Catholic Relief Services, and World Vision International in Honduras.[95] On a smaller scale, agency staff were frequently engaged in advocacy efforts involving personal and other informal contacts with policy makers. These included informing congressional staff about economic conditions in Cuba or Guatemala, meeting with USAID and other State Department officials, and providing background information to legislators about the potential impact of foreign appropriations bills.

The major faith-based organizations that received government funds for overseas programs typically employed staff who served as policy liaisons for specific programs. Catholic Relief Services' Washington staff included approximately a dozen full-time employees whose responsibilities covered such programs as debt relief, counternarcotics, family planning, HIV/AIDS, Iraq reconstruction, refugee aid, and terrorism. World Vision International, the Salvation Army, Lutheran World Relief, and Church World Service were among the other faith-based agencies that employed staff in advocacy roles. These staff were sometimes called on to testify at congressional hearings but more often worked quietly behind the scenes through personal contacts with staff at USAID or legislative aides on Capitol Hill. "We are very well respected," one agency staff member explained, "because they know that they can call us and we sometimes know more about what is happening on the ground" than they do. At another agency, the director described this approach as "experience-based advocacy." In his view, advocacy was most effective when "the evidence of our programs" could be used "to influence government and donor policies and practices."

Critics of U.S. foreign aid argue that it could be far more generous than it has been. Although the United States gives more in absolute dollar amounts to foreign aid than other countries, its foreign aid contributions amount to approximately 0.1 percent of Gross National Product, placing it last among the world's wealthiest countries in that comparison.[96] Another measure that scores nations' commitment to development by including trade and investment as well as aid put the United States in a more favorable light but still ranked it twelfth among the twenty-one richest countries.[97] Critics also question whether U.S. aid is sufficiently motivated by humanitarian aims or is driven by such strategic interests as deterring communism or stabilizing regions through support for authoritarian regimes.[98]

To the extent that these criticisms are warranted, it is puzzling that religious groups have not been able to bring more pressure on officials to expand foreign aid. Among grassroots Christians, there would seem to be strong support for government efforts to help the needy in other countries. Since the early 1970s, national polls have consistently shown that reducing world hunger is a foreign policy goal supported by a majority of the American public.[99] In the Global Issues Survey, 60 percent of active churchgoers thought "combating world hunger should be a very im-

portant foreign policy goal of the United States" (and nearly everyone
else thought it should be at least somewhat important). This view was
shared among all the major denominational traditions, with the highest
support from black Protestants (74 percent) and Catholics (64 percent),
followed by evangelical and mainline Protestants (each 56 percent).
Other questions elicited even more support for U.S. engagement. Eighty-
seven percent (with no significant variation among the denominational
traditions) said they favored the U.S. government "doing more to supply medical help to people in poor countries." More than three-quarters
(78 percent) agreed that "there should be major new efforts, led by charitable and religious groups, with some taxpayer support, to make sure
that fewer people in poor countries suffer from hunger and malnutrition." Black Protestants were the most likely to agree (89 percent), followed by evangelicals (79 percent), Catholics (78 percent), and mainline
Protestants (75 percent).

However, American Christians also hold mixed views toward poor
countries and thus have ambivalent feelings about how much the U.S.
government should be involved. On the one hand, various reasons for
helping people in other countries resonate with many American Christians. For instance, 48 percent say that "God does not want poor people
to suffer" is a very good argument for doing more to fight hunger in the
world. Thirty-five percent think "the United States has a moral responsibility to help the poor in other countries" is also a very good argument.
And at least a quarter think there are some other good arguments, such
as helping people being good for American business, consistent with U.S.
abundance, and conducive to national security. On the other hand,
nearly a third (31 percent) of American Christians think that looking out
for people in our own country is a very good reason not to help people
in other countries. And more than four in ten worry that the money
Americans spend helping people in other countries is wasted.

American Christians are also more ambivalent about economic development and about government programs in general than they are
about charity to alleviate specific problems such as hunger and disease.
Compared with the 60 percent who think combating world hunger
should be an important foreign policy goal, only 38 percent think this
about "helping to improve the standard of living of less developed nations." Whereas 27 percent express a great deal of confidence in faith-
based humanitarian organizations, 15 percent say the same about the
United Nations, and only 4 percent do so for the World Bank and International Monetary Fund.

Ambivalence can be a strong barrier against supporting specific initiatives. In July 2005, religious leaders joined other activists in calling for demonstrations at the Group of Eight economic summit in Edinburgh. However, other religious leaders urged congregations to ignore the call. "We are all concerned about feeding the hungry, relieving poverty, and serving the poor," a Southern Baptist leader wrote. He nevertheless counseled against advocacy of this kind on grounds that poverty in Islamic countries is "religio-cultural" and in other countries is due to socialism. In contrast, he pointed to economic growth in countries that "freed their economies of unnecessary state control and are trading their way out of poverty." Southern Baptists, he argued, should be wary of governmental waste and channel their charity through the denomination's International Mission Board.[100]

Given ambivalence and resistance of this kind, religious advocacy groups have emphasized efforts to educate church members and develop small cadres of supporters for specific policies rather than relying on the general goodwill of American Christians. The national office of the Presbyterian Church (USA) in Louisville, Kentucky, enlisted one of its staff to work full-time on behalf of Jubilee 2000. Her job included participating in monthly steering committee meetings, writing and disseminating educational materials, speaking at congregations, and developing an action alert network to link various hunger, peace, and women's advocacy groups.[101] The Center of Concern, established as a joint initiative of the United States Conference of Catholic Bishops and the Society of Jesus, has participated in events sponsored by the United Nations since the early 1970s and played an important role in the Jubilee 2000 planning. Lutheran World Relief developed a speaker's bureau consisting of approximately a hundred volunteers who visit projects in other countries and tell congregations in the United States about these projects. The Christian Reformed Church's Office of Social Justice and Hunger Action focuses less on educating the denomination's general membership than it used to and concentrates more on the 10 percent who are already interested in justice work and advocacy. The head of another denominational office explains that "advocacy" means primarily "convincing our own churches that these are the kinds of things they should be doing." Other agency directors note that they partner with Bread for the World because its experience in political advocacy is greater than their own.

In developing these networks, religious relief and development organizations have walked a fine line between focusing on advocacy and raising charitable donations for their programs. Besides the possibility of losing tax exemption, too much advocacy poses dangers for organizations that present themselves to individual contributors as nonpartisan service agencies. The delicacy of this balance is evident in the remarks of an agency director who reports that her organization has become increasingly convinced of the need "to influence the hearts and minds of people in Washington, predominately in Congress and the administration" but who hastens to add that advocacy is "not a huge part of our budget." Indeed, it is less than 2 percent of the agency's budget. It is important, she says, not because the agency depends on government for a significant share of its support but because suffering in other countries is sometimes caused by civil conflicts and other political conditions that only pressure from the U.S. government can address. Advocacy is not a substitute for nongovernmental relief efforts but a way of enlisting the organization's grassroots supporters to bring pressure on their elected representatives.

Public policy is always a matter of negotiation, which means that religion's role is seldom straightforward. One of the clearest illustrations of this complexity was the food aid debate of 2005 and 2006. The debate centered around the relative desirability of shipping surplus grain and other agricultural products from the United States to other countries or using U.S. funds to purchase these commodities within the recipient countries or from neighboring countries. The former position was favored by U.S. agricultural interests, while the latter was increasingly favored by administrators at USAID as a way of reducing costs and promoting agricultural development in other countries. The large faith-based relief and development agencies, such as World Vision International and Catholic Relief Services, were popularly regarded as being caught in the middle of the debate. U.S. agricultural products were an important source of these organizations' programs, not only as food itself but also as commodities that the agencies could sell to produce revenue for other activities. The faith-based agencies also had close ties with USAID, notably in top administrators moving back and forth between the agencies and USAID, and the agencies were committed in principle to overseas agricultural development. However, the faith-based agencies did not support the USAID position because they feared it would transfer too much control over food aid to the World Trade Organization and thus eliminate or drastically reduce in-kind food aid and possibilities for bilateral agreements between nations and nongovernmental organizations. When the USAID plan was defeated in Congress, analysts blamed the faith-based and other nongovernmental agencies and argued that they had been in league with the farm lobby.[102]

As this example suggests, faith-based relief agencies do not always see eye to eye with government officials, even those with whom they work closely. However, food aid also illustrates that religious advocacy for relief and development cuts across party lines and liberal-conservative divisions to a greater extent than many domestic policy debates, such as those in which abortion and homosexuality have been central. Liberal Christian organizations, such as the World Council of Churches, that long have argued for greater generosity in U.S. foreign aid, have been joined by evangelical organizations such as World Vision International and World Relief. In addition, evangelical organizations previously devoted to personal evangelization and Christian missions have also joined in supporting policy proposals concerned with economic development. For instance, an initiative called the Micah Challenge emerged in 2004 under sponsorship of the World Evangelical Alliance and an international network of 260 Christian-based community development agencies to raise awareness of and advocate for the United Nations' Millennium Development goal of cutting world poverty levels in half by 2015.[103]

The puzzle that faith-based advocacy for relief and development poses for the larger question of nongovernmental policy influence is why these agencies have done relatively little to advertise their close relationships with government. Both the financial support they receive from government and their role in advising government officials are arguably stronger than in any other area of U.S. foreign policy, including human rights, religious freedom, trade, and military action. Yet, unlike those issues, where some religious groups make highly publicized claims about influencing policy, relatively few such claims are evident in this arena. A possible explanation is that these claims become less common the longer religious groups actually do exercise influence. This possibility is consistent with the fact that the more vocal claims in recent years seem to have been made by evangelical groups relatively new to the policy process. However, another possibility is worth considering. Faith-based relief and development organizations do make claims, but they direct these claims not at the public at large but at policy makers, and these claims primarily emphasize the vast international work that the organizations are doing. The argument, in effect, is that policy makers should pay heed because of the agencies' experience, knowledge, and effectiveness. When policy makers do listen, the results contribute to the agencies' further effectiveness. The public is then encouraged to support these agencies voluntarily not because they have clout with government but because they are effective in delivering services. In addition, the relatively low-profile relationship of these agencies with government helps in relationships with overseas partners. The agencies can present themselves less as an arm of U.S. government policy and more as an expression of humanitarian goodwill.

POLICY INFLUENCE IN PERSPECTIVE

In the perspective on policy influence that I have outlined here, self-perceptions and public perceptions of religious organizations being able to influence government sometimes play an important role in these organizations' overall effectiveness. With publicity in recent years about the presumed rise in policy influence of Christian groups, it might be supposed that the leaders of these organizations would share that perception, especially when they do in fact have close ties with government officials. However, these leaders generally deny that they and other religious organizations have much influence. A Salvation Army leader expressed a typical view when he observed that the Bush administration had a more pronounced view about faith influencing foreign policies than in previous administrations, but, he hastened to add, "It's one view. It's not representative of how all Christians would think or react." He added that "government policies are much more driven by what's best for the U.S. economically than anything else. It may be phrased differently by who's in office, but the bottom line is self-preservation." A Methodist leader offered a similar view. There is a lot of "lip service" given to religion in foreign policy of late, she said, but this lip service has more to do with "Western culture" and "civic religion" than with a deeper understanding of Christianity or Judaism. She thinks the church "has not done a very good job of connecting faith and action."

Denials of this kind might be regarded simply as accurate appraisals of how foreign policy is shaped. However, it is also interesting that religious leaders think their influence should be limited. They want the values embodied in religious teachings to be part of the discussion, but they do not think policies should be based only on religious arguments or that policy makers should justify initiatives by crediting themselves with divine insight. An executive at the Lutheran Immigration and Relief Agency expressed this view particularly well. "I would hesitate to suggest that religion should be the guiding force in our foreign policy," he observed, "because the question then is what religion and whose religion.

We are a diverse country with people from many different religious traditions." The same guarantees against the establishment of religion in domestic life should apply to foreign policy, he argued. "The debate about foreign policy, while being influenced by people of faith, needs to be conducted on the basis of the principles and values of our country." Religious leaders' desire to be a voice in foreign policy while abiding by the constitutional principles of American democracy means that influence is generally attempted through the same mechanisms used by nongovernmental civic organizations to bring pressure on domestic policy debates. These mechanisms, and the language used to describe them, are evident in the advocacy activities we have considered concerning free trade, human rights, military action, and foreign aid. With few exceptions, religious leaders' statements about these activities do not claim to have resulted directly in specific legislative or policy successes. Instead, they emphasize having made statements, having been at the table, and having been heard. Influence consists less of being instrumental in shaping public policy than in being able to present one's perspective. This means that when outcomes are favorable, an agency can claim to have represented its constituency but not to have bullied its way. When outcomes are not favorable, the agency can still claim to have represented its constituency and can also limit its responsibility. These are important ways of maintaining a presence in the policy arena. By demonstrating that the religious organization is close to power, its leader facilitates what the organization actually does in programmatic terms. These programmatic activities can best be summarized as mobilization, implementation, education, and legitimation.

The most active way of influencing foreign policy is to mobilize resources that shape how policy makers think and behave. Mobilization is what journalists have in mind when they imagine powerful religious leaders and their constituents being the reason behind the United States providing aid to Israel or invading Iraq. As we have seen, these journalistic claims are usually overblown. However, religious organizations do attempt to be a presence in Washington. They speak up at foreign policy briefings, provide testimony at congressional hearings, meet with elected officials, accept positions at USAID and other agencies, raise funds, and solicit petitions and letters from church members. Bread for the World is probably the best example of a faith-based organization concerned primarily with advocacy. Its lobbying staff on Capitol Hill keeps Bread members informed of pending legislation in addition to meeting personally with representatives. These 57,000 members are scattered in congregations throughout the nation. These members solicit others in their congregations to write letters to Congress about legislation involving policies that will affect hunger in other countries. Through these networks, the organization generates between 100,000 and 200,000 letters each time an issue of major importance arises. The National Association of Evangelicals and the National Council of Churches include similar advocacy functions that seek to connect grassroots members with policies in Washington. In most of the other examples we have considered, mobilization takes place largely at an elite level, for instance, in meetings between Catholic Relief Services staff and USAID staff or between World Vision leaders and legislators. The critical aspect in these various styles of mobilization, however, is the capacity to forge a symbolic link between a policy or policy maker and a constituency. When this connection is present, policy makers can signal that they have listened to a particular constituency and it in turn can feel represented.

To implement a foreign policy program is to carry it out, accepting its basic principles and doing the work to make it as effective as possible. The leaders of international faith-based agencies are much more likely to view their job as implementation than as mobilization. "Faith has an influence," says the head of one of these organizations, "not so much from the leadership side as from the implementing side, from organizations like Salvation Army, World Vision International, and others who are implementing programs." As evident especially in the human trafficking example, legislation can be relatively ineffective unless an aggressive administrator decides to take action. In other instances, where foreign aid is simply wasted by being spent unwisely or by self-interested regimes, faith-based organizations with experience in running effective service programs can help ensure that foreign aid dollars go further. Being able to administer government programs has given large faith-based organizations an opportunity to shape how policies are actually put into practice. For instance, most agency directors insist that their involvement has made it possible for U.S. programs to be carried out through partnerships with local communities in other countries and thus to be more responsive to cultural and contextual differences.

Besides mobilizing influence and implementing programs, religious organizations often seek to educate their members about foreign policies and related international issues. They do this by passing resolutions that encourage members to think about and pray about major topics of international importance, by producing study materials for Sunday school classes, by sending speakers to congregations, and by generating newsletters. Increasingly, the Internet has become the means through which these materials are communicated to interested clergy and lay members. E-mails are another important educational tool. Examples of influence through education include the National Council of Churches' research about the effects of NAFTA, the Presbyterian General Assembly's resolutions about trade agreements, the International Justice Mission's reporting of stories about sex trafficking, training sessions provided by Witness for Peace, and the Center of Concern's seminars for United Nations personnel. Education is sometimes oriented toward promoting a specific policy, as when an organization called Church Folks for a Better America forms to encourage church members to speak out against torture. Education is more broadly conceived of as a contribution to the democratic process. If democracy functions best with an informed citizenry, then the educational role of nongovernmental organizations contributes to this process by encouraging citizens to learn, reflect, and discuss.

The other way in which religious organizations influence foreign policy is by providing endorsements. Formal resolutions passed by religious bodies sometimes endorse a policy that has already been passed or that is under consideration. The more common form of endorsement comes from individual religious leaders who have enough public visibility to be of interest to the mass media. Examples range from Richard Cizik endorsing George W. Bush's interest in programs to combat HIV/AIDS in Africa, to Jerry Falwell's favorable comments about free trade or military intervention in Iraq, to Catholic Relief Services' support for the State Department's reorganization of USAID. It seems doubtful that endorsements from religious leaders matter very much to the policy process, other than perhaps to reinforce the likelihood of certain religious constituencies voting for a particular candidate or party in a subsequent election. The role of endorsements is probably more aptly understood as a means for religious leaders to gain legitimacy for themselves. By associating themselves with a president, policy, or program, they demonstrate to their own constituents that they have a voice and are on the side of goodness, decency, and moral principle. It is, after all, the elected official who has the primary power to confer legitimacy. As Ronald Reagan observed to an enthusiastic audience of religious broadcasters in 1980, "I know you can't endorse me, but . . . I want you to know that I endorse you."[104]

CHAPTER 7

The Challenges Ahead

Good for America, Good for the World?

The evidence I have presented in previous chapters casts serious doubt on three widely held assumptions about American Christianity. The first assumption is that American Christianity has withdrawn from the wider world, leaving global Christianity to flourish largely on its own. That assumption is simply untrue. American Christianity is more engaged in the wider world than ever before. There are more American missionaries, more faith-based humanitarian and relief workers, and more short-term volunteers serving abroad now than in the past. Budgets for these activities have expanded significantly in recent years. Trade, travel, communication, and affluence have all contributed to this growth. The second assumption is that local congregations have imploded, serving as self-help societies for their own members, and doing little to help people outside their communities, let alone outside the United States. That assumption is also patently false. Nearly all U.S. congregations are involved in some kind of international ministry, whether it be collecting money for global hunger programs, sponsoring missionaries, or working directly with international nongovernmental agencies. Congregations are increasingly finding ways to partner with ministries in other countries, and larger congregations are taking the lead in cultivating these ties. The third assumption is that American Christianity is primarily an evangelical voice in U.S. foreign policy that encourages the nation's leaders in imperialistic adventures involving free trade and unilateral military action. This assumption also flies in the face of empirical evidence. The evangelical voice may give tacit assent to such policies by keeping silent, but the organized activities of America's faith communities focus much more on criticizing administration policies than supporting them. Religious advocacy networks have been outspoken critics of free trade agreements and U.S. military action, and they have been among the most engaged proponents of human rights, peacebuilding efforts, and foreign assistance.

I have identified four social factors that have contributed to the increasing global engagement of American Christianity. One is the shrinkage of distances between the United States and other parts of the world that has come about through transportation and communication technology, economic integration, and international migration. Religious organizations find it easier to send people, goods, and information across national boundaries, just as businesses do. A second factor is the cultural flattening of the world that has occurred with the spread of English, with television and popular music, and with the disruption of local community traditions that is often associated with international trade. Globalization has not produced anything like a single world culture, but it has infused common elements into previously isolated contexts. For American Christianity, the fact that there are many more Christians in other parts of the world than a century ago is a significant reason for easier and more frequent interaction. This is the truly notable aspect of the so-called Southern shift in global Christianity. The third factor is the organizational muscle in international faith-based humanitarian and relief agencies. The strength of these organizations reflects not only a history that is nearly two centuries old but also new alliances, hybrid structures, coalitions with secular agencies, and, perhaps most important, greatly enlarged support from government. World Vision International, Catholic Relief Services, and dozens of smaller agencies have become indispensable to U.S. foreign assistance programs. The final factor is the grassroots energizing activity of congregations themselves. This activity consists of preaching and teaching about Americans' common bond with and responsibility to be engaged with the rest of the world. It also includes thousands upon thousands of hours devoted to learning about the needs of people in other countries, hosting speakers, raising money, and organizing ways of getting people involved.

Globalization is a continuing and constantly changing process. Christianity in the United States will continue to be affected by it, and religious leaders will surely do what they can to engage responsibly with the opportunities and challenges globalization presents. The specific forms these international efforts take will depend on such conditions as whether the nation is at peace or at war and whether the global economy is flourishing or declining. If the experience of recent years is any indication, the expansion of international markets will help in some instances but also produce disparities of wealth and leave many people behind. Religious congregations are often little more than bit players in these larger economic and political dynamics. Congregations nevertheless have opportunities to be engaged and to encourage their members to be thoughtful about the deeper values that unite them with the rest of humanity.

It is always an act of hubris to posit what may be the challenges ahead for religious leaders and the nation, or even the questions that ordinary citizens may need to consider. Having examined the recent relationship between globalization and American Christianity, I am nevertheless persuaded that some of the tensions currently evident are likely to continue and will pose important considerations about the future role of the United States in the world. I focus on five of these.

CONNECTING LOCAL AND GLOBAL

The strength of American congregations lies clearly in the fact that they are local. They draw people who live close enough to one another that they can participate regularly in activities of mutual interest. Although congregations are not as integrated into local neighborhoods as they once were, they continue to attract people who know one another, care for one another, send their children to the same schools, and shop at the same stores. Even the largest congregations create a kind of quasi-local community among participants by drawing people into fellowship groups, catering to sports interests and other hobbies, and sometimes forging networks among neighbors. At the same time, congregations are always stronger if they have connections beyond the local community. In the past, these connections resided in denominational and diocesan affiliations, in circuit riders, in immigrants' ties to their countries of origin, and in missionaries. At present, the possibilities for links to other parts of the world exist in opportunities for travel, congregation-to-congregation partnerships, international advocacy networks, and of course the mass media. Translocal connections give congregations a sense of being involved in some larger and more powerful ministry. These connections also provide ballast against the idiosyncrasies of local needs and personalities, and they promote better understanding of the world's diverse needs.

As desirable as it may seem for congregations to be both local and global, achieving a workable balance between the two is seldom easy. The reason is that congregational dynamics are strongly tilted toward a nearly exclusive emphasis on local activities. Pastors function in a competitive market that rewards them for congregational growth. Participants are attracted to programs that serve the needs of their family, such as a day care program, children's Sunday school, youth choir, or fellowship group for parents. Church growth is thus dependent on fulfilling these local interests. The typical congregation is also quite strapped for resources. Its budget is likely to be expended mostly on building maintenance and salaries. If more money can be raised, the most attractive commitment for donors is likely to be a new building or renovation. The typical pastor already puts in the longest workweek of anyone in the congregation. He or she is unlikely to have energy to take on new projects. If the congregation is committed to serving the needy, more than likely these programs focus on the local community and are conducted in cooperation with local service organizations. Despite the fact that the congregation regards itself as being part of the larger body of Christ and perhaps takes up an offering for world hunger or sponsors a missionary, its center of gravity is clearly within itself.

The social arrangements that have been devised historically to bridge the distance between congregations and the wider world ensure that some international activities receive support, but these arrangements also limit that support. An apportionment from the regular budget to assist the denomination in its overseas work can be taken without the congregation ever knowing much about that work, just as the occasional special offering for world hunger can. The mission committee keeps tabs on the congregation's missionaries so that the rest of the congregation does not have to. The morning prayer dutifully includes petitions about national and international leaders and victims of the latest bombing or earthquake, but it is said ritualistically while the congregation's closed eyes allow their minds to wander or the members await hearing in the prayer who of their congregation is ill.

For these reasons, the link between local congregations and global programs has generally been indirect. The missions programs that flourished from the early nineteenth century depended on small contributions from a large number of congregations. The minimal investments involved were relatively painless for the coffers of local churches but collectively produced enough revenue to staff a small centralized office from which missionaries could be recruited, trained, and commissioned. The faith missions that began at the end of the nineteenth century turned the money question over to prospective missionaries themselves. If they could raise support on their own, they could go, and if the funding ran out, they had to return. The nongovernmental agencies of the past half century have supported themselves to a degree from congregations but to a greater degree from direct-mail solicitations, television appeals, and government grants. In the larger scheme of things, these arrangements have worked reasonably well. Sociologically, they have been masterful inventions, built as it were on the infrastructure of American congregations without extracting a serious cost to the local church. Theologically, they fit well with the teaching that the body of Christ is not local but universal and flourishes by developing specialized organs in the way a physical body does.

The weakness of these historical arrangements has been theological more than sociological. If the church universal was to be in Samaria and the uttermost parts of the world as well as in Judea, it was nevertheless to be one body, united in its prayers and concerns, and capable of bridging cultural barriers in personal interaction as well as through correspondence and the occasional apostolic visit. This dual mandate for unity and community was easier to accomplish locally than globally. In practical terms, the limits were also sociological. Congregations restricted in outlook to their local communities provided poor training grounds for truly cosmopolitan endeavors, as the parochialism of nineteenth-century mission efforts demonstrated again and again. As globalization overtook these patterns at the end of the twentieth century, congregations offered a safe haven in which to retreat from the complexities of the wider world. How one thought about global issues was likely to depend more on television than on faith-informed discussions in one's congregation.

What has partly overcome this institutional separation of the local and global is the fact that church members are increasingly exposed to international issues in other venues. Work, travel, migration, and mass communication all bring rank-and-file Americans into greater contact with people and events elsewhere in the world. It becomes increasingly difficult for congregations to escape these influences. Members take note of the perfunctory prayer about religious leaders in Myanmar because they have watched a television story the night before. The congregation includes a family in danger of being deported by Immigration and Naturalization Service officials. The pastor has recently completed a study leave abroad. If the congregation is responsive to these influences, it becomes more interested in how it can serve beyond its local community. A second development that is facilitating congregational interest in international activities is the growth of megachurches. By amassing resources in a single location, megachurches make possible the same division of labor that formerly occurred through denominations and dioceses. A single megachurch may have as many staff members as an entire denomination had within a statewide convention or presbytery. It thus becomes possible for the church's staff to include one or more staff members responsible for global outreach. It also becomes possible for the congregation to sponsor missionaries or contribute to relief organizations without imposing dramatically on the giving of any particular member.

The advantage of the megachurch model is that international activities remain connected with local interests. Although the global outreach director may not be known personally to many in the congregation, he or she is known to some and is familiar to all because of an occasional appearance in the pulpit. Whereas the typical member might pay little attention to the central activities of his or her denomination, he or she will be more likely to hear a speaker at the church or watch a video presentation during Sunday school. The other advantage is that the megachurch model has demography in its favor. With a projected increase in U.S. population of nearly 100 million by 2050, thousands of additional congregations will be required to keep pace. Many of these will be new and many will be large, attracting members because they are new and large and because they offer a full menu of programs. These congregations will be able to find members in abundance without taking members from smaller congregations, simply because of the enlarged population. They will have the capacity to sponsor international ministries.

The challenge for congregations large or small will nevertheless be one of striking an appropriate balance between the needs of the congregation itself and of people in other countries. Because of the tendency to emphasize local concerns, effort will be required to motivate involvement in global activities. What the leaders of congregations and of international agencies have learned thus far is likely to be of particular value. The suggestion given most often by these leaders is to bridge local to local. A congregation of three hundred or even three thousand people is more likely to find it manageable if their international focus is on a single congregation, community, or region. The connection becomes more personal, visits become possible, and projects can be started and finished.

A second suggestion is to build from current interests. If a member has lived in Honduras or the Ukraine, that experience may provide a foundation for establishing a longer-term commitment in that country. In another congregation, a member with experience in international law may be the springboard for involvement in a ministry to combat human trafficking. The other suggestion is that information is abundant but needs to be focused in ways that generate action. A film about torture in military prisons can be shown at a forum where a speaker from an advocacy group tells participants how to send a letter or attend a rally. The short-term mission team that returns from a week in Mexico tells about its experiences and also invites participation in the next trip. The advantage congregations have in these processes is being able to tap into the resources and networks that already exist among members.

BALANCING SERVICE AND SPIRITUALITY

The challenge that Christian organizations in particular face as they engage in international work is finding an appropriate balance between serving the needs of people who are poor, hungry, homeless, exploited, dying, in poor health, or lacking in education and jobs and doing work aimed at converting people to Christianity. To some, this is a false distinction because service is simply the best way to show Christian love and bring people to Christ. However, it is a tension not so easily reconciled. It raises the same concerns that Rufus Anderson and the American Board of Commissioners for Foreign Missions struggled with in the nineteenth century. With scarce resources, should a mission board focus on preaching or should it open schools and clinics? Today, the question would not be posed as one of "bringing civilization," but similar issues emerge, such as whether missionaries should try to discourage female circumcision, whether a Christian clinic should dispense condoms, and whether it matters if a micro-business loan is administered by an indigenous church or some other organization.

The leaders in my study clearly tried to identify ways in which they could uphold the value of evangelism as well as the value of service. On the one hand, they argued that sharing the Christian faith and encouraging others to become Christians was inherent to any basic understanding of Christianity. As one leader put it, "Evangelism is part of the Christian faith. It might be intrusive and it might step on the toes of some folks who don't think it's right, but it's there and we have to recognize that it's there." On the other hand, they believed it important to serve people's needs and to avoid making this service contingent on anything that might smack of evangelism. "Our programs are offered to people of all faiths or of no faith," the same leader observed. "We certainly don't condition one thing on another."

The social pressures to emphasize service rather than evangelism nevertheless are quite powerful. Given the prevailing ethos of tolerance in the United States, it seems quite wrong to confront a devout Muslim or Hindu about his or her need to believe in Jesus, whereas no questions would be raised about giving a starving Muslim or Hindu a meal. Beyond these cultural norms, more mundane matters also come into play. A missionary intent on evangelism probably has to raise small donations from friends and family, whereas a humanitarian relief worker is likely to be employed by a large international organization that takes in millions in private contributions and government contracts. In addition, the missionary may be prevented by local laws from making converts, while the humanitarian worker is likely to be welcomed with open arms by local officials. The question for Christian organizations, therefore, is how to follow the path of least resistance and yet preserve something distinctly Christian.

Not surprisingly, a popular solution to this dilemma is to redefine service as evangelism. The leader quoted previously expressed this view. "Christian aid is an expression of God's love for a person and that expression of Christian love is going to draw someone or have the potential to draw someone to Christ," he said. What this means in practice, though, is more difficult to decide. One view is that it does not matter if the people being served associate what they receive with Christianity; the link is still there, perhaps mystically or mysteriously, in God's mind, and that is what counts. In short, the essence of Christianity is love and thus can be manifested equally well by Christians, Buddhists, atheists, and communists. An alternative view is that the experience of giving and receiving service is enriched if people do associate it specifically with Christianity. It becomes more powerful because people can then learn about love from the life of Christ or better understand and experience God's grace. Evangelism as such may not be necessary, in this view, but it is a good idea if the service organization includes something about Christianity in its mission statement.

Including Christianity in an organization's mission statement, though, is seldom quite as simple as it sounds. Large service organizations such as World Vision International, Catholic Relief Services, and Church World Service include language in their materials that explicitly identifies the work as Christian. Yet conditions arise that constrain the extent to which the organization can function in ways that are distinctly Christian. One of these conditions is the constraint imposed by receiving government funds. Such funds may entail restrictions against being used for proselytization or conducting worship services, against favoring clients from a particular faith, against hiring staff from a particular faith, or withholding services (such as birth control or abortions) that conflict with the organization's faith. Although these restrictions can often be minimally intrusive in the services provided, a more subtle form of constraint may also be present. This is the need to behave professionally, to hire skilled professionals, and to conform to the expectations of foundations and government organizations that provide revenue. A faith-based organization that makes decisions in keeping with sound accounting practices, rewards employees on the basis of job performance, monitors the effectiveness of its programs, and essentially acts like any other nongovernmental organization is likely to flourish. In contrast, an organization led by a charismatic leader who claims to be inspired by the Holy Spirit is likely to experience greater difficulty.

Given these considerations, it is probably not surprising that Christian organizations that want to pursue a more distinctly Christian approach to ministry have focused increasingly on church planting and what they call "enabling." This approach avoids the problem of becoming a service entity with very little about it that is explicitly Christian but also circumvents some of the cultural concerns associated with overt evangelization. In the simplest case, a congregation in the United States sends money to a church in another country rather than sending a missionary or evangelist. It is then up to the indigenous church to decide how to spend the money. Its pastor may use it to boost his salary, construct a building that attracts members, help the needy, or hire an evangelist. In this way, the local Christian community receives additional resources and is thus enabled. However, this approach can also be criticized because it concentrates resources in communities that are already Christian and perhaps does not serve the neediest in these communities.

The other solution that in effect wishes away the tension between service and evangelism is to argue that this distinction is only found in the United States and thus should be transcended. There is some truth in this assertion, at least in terms of different views being taken historically by different religious organizations. However, it is not so easy to transcend such longstanding cultural assumptions. Nor is it clear that these distinctions are absent in other settings.

For these reasons, striving for balance between service and evangelism is likely to be a continuing challenge for Christian organizations engaged in international ministries. If this prediction is correct, the challenge may pose opportunities as well. The value of holding humanitarian service and Christianity in tension is that the faith component is a strong motivating factor. It inspires service when results are meager. The possibility of divine grace instills hope that small deeds are not without merit. At the same time, acts of service put people in harm's way of needing faith to sustain their efforts.

"DOING FOR" VERSUS "PARTNERING WITH"

A challenge that has confronted international religious organizations as long as the question of service and evangelism has is how to appropriately structure the relationships between parties that differ in resources and power. When a mission or relief agency works with people who are the recipients of its assistance, the agency has resources that it chooses to offer and thus has power that the recipients lack. The problems that arise are many. If the donor organization tells the recipients what to do, it runs the risk of being viewed as paternalistic and of imposing its values. Without sufficient input from the recipients, the assistance is unlikely to be effective. Yet few donor organizations consider it wise to offer assistance without some expectations being applied. In the worst scenarios, assistance of that kind results in waste.

For Christian organizations, the problem is sometimes compounded by the desire to convey the idea that God's love is unconditional. Leaders of Christian relief organizations sometimes argue that God's love is a free gift and for this reason their organization helps anybody who is in need, regardless of who that person is or what that person's religion may be. However, there are always conditions. The organization has limited resources so its leaders must decide who is most worthy. Leaders are also accountable to private contributors and often to government officials. Assistance is more likely to be given to recipient organizations with preexisting ties to the relief organization, to people who think the same way, and to recipients who will work hard to get back on their feet.

International nongovernmental organizations, like earlier missionary efforts, have been widely criticized for imposing Western models that may not be appropriate in non-Western situations. Critics argue that the strings attached to assistance programs sometimes undercut the very goals of these programs. Formal organizations that are used to dealing with other organizations cultivate those networks, rather than looking to village leaders or family networks. They communicate by inviting potential recipients to Western-style conferences and briefings and argue that certain medical practices or economic development strategies are better than others because they are "scientific."

Research on the relationships between caregivers and recipients suggests that these interactions are always fraught with potential for misunderstanding. For the caregiver, providing assistance may be a routine act that is inscribed in the organization's charter and in the caregiver's job description. For the recipient, the assistance may be perceived as an act of extreme generosity. The asymmetry of perceptions leads the recipient to experience more of a bond with the caregiver than the reverse. Indebtedness results, constituting an obligation on the part of the recipient to pay back that is not in fact expected by the caregiver. If there is no adequate way to reciprocate, the recipient's self-worth is likely to be diminished. The recipient feels subservient to the caregiver.

The professional training that helps full-time caregivers to understand these relational dynamics is often lacking for volunteers who participate in short-term mission trips. As reality tourists, their experience is likely to be profoundly moving for themselves but less meaningful for recipients, who have grown accustomed to hosting volunteers. In these situations, the question of who benefits becomes paramount. Volunteering of this kind may well be beneficial for Americans who bring back experiences that chasten their love of materialism or inspire them to embark on careers in human service or ministry. Whether as much good has been contributed to people in the host societies is less clear.

The solution to these problems that has come to be preferred by many U.S. religious organizations is partnering. The idea behind partnering is that it is better to "work with" people from other countries than to conceive of oneself as "doing for" them. Partnerships range in scale from small pairings of individual congregations to massive multinational structures encompassing the work of the largest relief and development organizations. Congregational partnerships work well when they involve long-term personal relationships and shared decisions about needs and programs. Large-scale partnerships involving relief and development are more likely to consist of national representatives who vote to approve and oversee projects. Symbolically and financially, these partnerships aim to demonstrate shared ownership and thus allay the criticism that American or Western models are being imposed.

Partnerships alone do not solve the problems involved in asymmetric relationships, however. Partnerships in businesses and in marriages are seldom without differences in power. Negotiation is required to build trust and to arrive at agreements about appropriate contributions and responsibilities. Cultivating understandings of this kind takes time. Religious organizations that have developed stable partnerships with groups in other countries have been able to cultivate such understandings. Maintaining long-term relationships is nevertheless a continuing challenge. Short-term volunteer programs and short-term government grant programs, as well as economic instability and political unrest, often work against such relationships.

THE HISTORICAL LEGACY

Religions, even ones like Christianity that claim to be universally true, are always situated within particular cultural contexts. American Christianity is American as much as it is Christian. With increasing globalization, the challenge is to maintain, understand, and benefit from this cultural legacy and at the same time move beyond it when movement seems necessary.

Americans like to think of themselves as a generous, compassionate nation. Public officials remind us that we have sacrificed lives in the cause of freedom and that we send humanitarian aid to victims of disasters. We are a good people, we tell ourselves, because we help those less fortunate than ourselves. The historical legacy that defines America is replete with these stories. The first settlers welcomed others who were fleeing from hunger and persecution, or so the stories go. Later, the nation shed blood to free its slaves and welcomed millions of immigrants to its shores. It sent soldiers to fight fascist oppression and stood tall against communism. It aroused freedom marchers to demonstrate for civil rights and initiated the Peace Corps. All of these narratives contribute to our national pride.

The stories about U.S. missionary history generate greater ambivalence. On the one hand, the heroes of missionary lore resonate deeply with some segments of the Christian community. Lottie Moon is a hero and the fictional tales of Danny Orlis motivate youngsters. The sacrifices of medical missionaries in Africa and of Christian teachers in China and Japan inspire pride. On the other hand, the missionary past is a source of embarrassment for many Americans. Mention of an Indian mission school conjures images of Native American children being robbed of their heritage and word of a mission hospital in Shanghai or Bangkok sparks questions about Western imperialism.

Stories of the past are always an important filter through which we interpret the present. The vast extent to which U.S. missionaries, churches, and faith-based agencies are currently involved in international activities is a story not everyone has been eager to think about. This reluctance is rooted in the ambivalence we feel about such involvement in the past. Ignoring the present endeavors, however, does not make them go away. At the same time, it helps little to imagine only the worst of these international activities by associating them with neoliberalist trade perspectives and American militarism, or to see only the best by disconnecting them completely from the past. It has been tempting for critics to assume that every mention of a U.S. missionary or relief worker was a signal that imperialism has returned. It is equally significant that so many of those involved in Christian activities abroad deny any continuity with the past, seeing themselves as an entirely new breed who never spread American values or proselytize and in the final analysis are really quite insignificant compared to what is happening through indigenous churches and missionaries from other countries to the United States.

The future of American Christianity's engagement with globalization depends on coming to a clearer understanding of its past. There is no reason to think that the mistakes of the past will inevitably be repeated, but there is also no doubt that new mistakes will be made. There are remarkable continuities between present efforts and earlier ones. Government funding of faith-based agencies is not new. Christians have long gone to other countries to teach English and fight disease. Resistance to these efforts on grounds that efforts should be focused at home has an equally long history. Missions programs did not simply stop with the end of colonialism or quietly shift to a different branch of American Christianity. The organizations and techniques involved in current international ministries were invented long ago. Stories about starving orphans have long been used to generate contributions. At the same time, it is also true that international programs have proliferated as a result of greater affluence, easier travel and communication, and more abundant government funding.

The challenge is to incorporate the historical legacy more fully into current discussions about international programs and to learn from this legacy. If our stories about America are too often half truths that inspire pride and make us feel good, then it is beneficial that there is ambivalence about American Christianity's international role in the past. For all its problems and amidst all the cultural changes it has experienced, Christianity is still the dominant religion—numerically and culturally—in the United States. It is internally diverse, but its overseas activities cannot be attributed only to evangelical Protestants. All of its major traditions are deeply involved in ministries that extend beyond national boundaries. At its best, Christianity is a religion that examines its stories, recognizes its mistakes, learns from the past, and embraces the future.

CONSCIENCE OF A NATION

Christian leaders sometimes describe themselves as the conscience of the nation. What they mean is that people of faith have a responsibility to think about and live in conformity to the deep values they hold to be true. However, there is danger in regarding oneself and one's fellow believers as the righteous remnant. To speak of a moral imperative that derives from one's faith can be a powerful incentive for supporting humanitarian efforts, but it can also lead to reckless unilateralism in military affairs. When this happens, moral perspectives become pitted against realpolitik, as they have been increasingly in discussions of foreign policy. What matters is no longer a sober inventory of global realities, but raw conviction.

Conscience is better understood as an institutionalized reality. It takes form in families, in school rooms, and in houses of worship. It has power not only because people feel strongly about their values but because of networks and organizations through which these values can be expressed. The challenge is not to pit people who presume to be guided by values against people who are not. It is rather to maintain spaces in which alternative values can be considered. If the prevailing international arrangements encourage cultivating profits, then opportunities must also be available for lifestyles governed by different values. When democracies work best, they encourage these alternative possibilities to be expressed. Markets are not inimical to similar opportunities being available. However, religious communities also have a special role to play. They can serve as the conscience of a nation by helping the needy in other countries when there is no economic incentive to do so and by posing hard questions about the social and moral costs of free trade or military intervention.

The conscience of America has been tested repeatedly. During the Cold War, religious leaders searched for an appropriate response to the threats posed by totalitarianism and nuclear weapons. Such prominent figures as Reinhold Niebuhr, Abraham Heschel, and John Courtney Murray struggled to identify realistic alternatives to appeasement on the one hand and aggression on the other. The post-9/11 world calls again for the voice of conscience to be heard. It beckons policy makers to argue about new threats to old values, such as the threat of terrorism to American freedom, and about the new dangers and opportunities presented by a resurgence of religious conviction. As religion has reentered the public arena, the possibilities for convictions to be exploited for political ends have increased. Conscience requires more than assuming that a person of faith can be guided silently by an internal compass. For people of faith, conscience is increasingly expressed in the very tangible social arrangements that connect the United States with the rest of humanity. It takes shape in church partnerships, mission trips, relief and development agencies, and foreign policy.

It is unlikely that the conscience of America will not be tested again in the near future. By all indications, terrorism, the threat of terrorism, and the global dispersion of weapons large and small will continue to pose dangers and evoke fears. Equally likely is the prospect of American decline as military expenditures take their toll on the national economy, as a political system that privileges short-term self-interest over long-term collective reason generates spiraling national debt and deteriorating national health care, and as the trade deficit puts U.S. interests increasingly in the hands of foreign creditors. When the familiar comforts of life erode, the natural inclination is to hunker down. The ease with which Americans have written checks for tsunami victims and sent their youth on mission trips to Guatemalan orphanages will diminish. It will be harder for legislators to approve spending bills that include appropriations for foreign assistance.

The needs of families displaced by natural disasters and of children whose parents have died of AIDS or been killed in bloody insurrections will not diminish, however. With declining resources, the national conscience will be tested. It will be tempting for Christian leaders to imagine that the indigenous churches planted in better times will pick up the slack, that relief efforts will no longer be needed by the United States because they are being carried out by missionaries from Korea, Mexico, the Philippines, and Ghana. The problem with this expectation is that worse conditions in the United States do not imply better conditions in other countries. Were the United States to end its faith-based humanitarian efforts, there is little reason to think that these efforts would be picked up by China, Japan, or the European Union.

There is wisdom in the adage that being faithful is sometimes better than being effective. The conscience of a nation does not require its efforts to produce economic miracles. Conscience does necessitate being steadfast. It involves the pursuit of that which is effective and the knowledge that failure will happen and successes will be small. It does not mean becoming involved in hopeless tasks, but it does imply recognizing the responsibility humans bear to their species wherever they may live.

Globalization has tempered American Christianity. It has exposed the most devout Christians to other religions and to other ways of being Christian. The cultural crucible in which Christianity is inevitably shaped remains. It cannot be escaped. In subtle ways, the spread of Christianity continues to include the spread of American practices, whether in music or styles of administration. Yet it is also the case that Christian organizations have had to rethink what it means to be followers of Christ and to be witnesses to love.

The skepticism one hears about American Christianity is often well-founded. There is good reason why Jews, Muslims, and people adhering to no faith are suspicious of the religious majority in a powerful nation that seems intent on launching crusades, securing government dollars for its enterprises, disbelieving in the counsels of science and of reason, and reproducing itself around the world. At the same time, it is important to recognize that this skepticism is sometimes one-sided. It fails to take account of the diversity within Christianity and the ways in which its humanitarian impulse has continued to be expressed through charitable giving that spans borders. It too easily assumes that people are driven by class interests or by superficial beliefs, instead of recognizing the intrinsic and energizing appeal of faith itself—a powerful, ambiguous, confusing, enduring, and seemingly boundless feature of social life.

Appendix

The Global Issues Survey was conducted between January 19 and June 22, 2005, and consisted of approximately two hundred fixed-response questions asked in thirty-five-minute telephone interviews to a total of 2,231 church members. The field component of the survey was conducted by Schulman, Ronca, and Bucuvalas, Inc., a highly respected firm in New York City that regularly subcontracts with major universities and research centers. Sampling was achieved through a random digit dial method, prescreened for business and nonworking telephone numbers. Prenotification letters on Princeton University letterhead were mailed out, and up to fifteen calls were made to eligible households. Follow-up letters, access to an 800 number, and a small monetary incentive were also offered to encourage participation among nonrespondents. Randomization among residents within households composed of more than one adult age eighteen or over was achieved by selecting the person with the most recent birthday. The calls were all conducted by experienced professional interviewers using state-of-the-art computer-assisted telephone interviewing equipment. Interviews were conducted in Spanish as well as in English. The screening process to identify church members for inclusion in the study involved explaining that this was a "national study of church members and people who go to church," asking how many adults age eighteen or older in the household were "church members or attend church services at least once a month," and, after selecting the designated person within the household, verifying that the respondent was in fact "a member of a church or attends religious services at least once a month." In all, 41 percent of the households contacted included an eligible church member by this criterion. The cooperation rate for the study was 68.4 percent and the response rate was 56.2 percent. The survey included questions about religious preference, attendance at religious services, religious identity, length of involvement in one's congregation, holding a leadership position in the congregation, congregation size and location, the congregation's emphasis on various domestic and international programs, specific congregational activities such as raising money for overseas hunger and relief or sponsoring missionaries, short-term mission trips involving members of the congregation, the respondent's own participation in these and other congregational activities, beliefs about the Bible and Jesus, views on a number of theological issues, arguments for and against programs concerned with world hunger and foreign aid, confidence in various international organizations, selected aspects of U.S. foreign policy, interest in international issues and news, sources of international information, and a battery of standard demographic questions. Copies of the questions and data are available from the author.

The denominational distribution of respondents in this Global Issues Survey is very similar to that found in the 2001 American Religious Identification Survey (summarized online at www.adherents.com). Twenty-six percent of the respondents to the Global Issues Survey were Catholics, as were 24 percent in the American Religious Identification study. Baptists made up 20 and 16 percent, respectively; Methodists were 7 percent in both studies; Lutherans were 6 and 5 percent, respectively; Presbyterians were 3 and 4 percent, respectively; and Pentecostals were 2 percent in both studies.

A useful way of comparing the characteristics of people included in the Global Issues Survey with those of respondents in other studies is to examine the distributions obtained in a national survey I conducted two years earlier, using the same firm and the same telephone interviewing methodology; the 2003 Religion and Diversity Survey, which examined 2,910 respondents, is described in my *America and the Challenges of Religious Diversity*. Questions about religious affiliation, attendance, and major demographic characteristics were identical in the two studies, although not asked in the same order. The Religion and Diversity Survey was based on a sample selected to be representative of all U.S. adults, not just church members. Thus, it permits a comparison of church members with characteristics of the overall adult population. In that survey, respondents who attended religious services at least a few times a year were asked if they were currently a member of their congregation, thereby making it possible to determine how the screening process for members in the Global Issues Survey may have affected the sample composition. The comparisons are shown in Table 1.

The religious-tradition variable is constructed from detailed questions asking about denominational preference (e.g., making it possible to distinguish among various kinds of Baptists, Presbyterians, Methodists, Lutherans, and so on). The Global Issues Survey naturally includes very few church members who say they have no denominational preference, compared with the Diversity study in which 17 percent fell into that category. When only church members in the two studies are compared, the proportions are markedly similar but with slightly more evangelical and mainline Protestants in the 2005 study. By screening at the outset for church members, the Global Issues Survey also made it easier for relatively inactive members simply to opt out. For instance, only 5 percent attend religious services less than once a month, compared with 15 percent of members in the Diversity study. In my view, it is thus preferable to describe the Global Issues

TABLE I

Comparison of church members in 2005 Global Issues
Survey with 2003 Religion and Diversity Survey (in percent)

	Global Issues	Diversity (members)	Diversity (all)
Religious tradition			
Evangelical Protestant	38	35	30
Mainline Protestant	19	16	13
Black Protestant	· 7	9	7
Roman Catholic	26	28	24
Other	8	9	9
Unaffiliated	2	4	17
Attendance			
More than once a week	25	24	14
Every week	43	34	22
Almost every week	9	10	6
Once or twice a month	19	17	16
Less often	5	15	40
Gender			
Male	36	38	42
Female	64	62	58
Race			
White	81	76	75
Black	10	15	12
Asian	1	1	2
Hispanic	10	9	11
Age			
18–30	14	20	27
31–64	65	63	58
65 and over	21	18	15
Education			
College graduate	40	38	22
Region			
Northeast	15	18	19
Midwest	26	26	25
South	42	41	38
West	17	15	19

Survey as a study of active church members, rather than saying that it accurately represents all church members. The Global Issues Survey appears to underrepresent African Americans but includes a sufficient number for comparisons with whites and does as good a job as the other study of representing Hispanics. Because of the self-selection into the study among active churchgoers, the Global Issues Survey includes fewer young adults than among members in the Diversity study. The proportion of college graduates is similar among respondents in the Global Issues Survey and church members in the Diversity study. The geographic distribution is also quite similar in the two studies.

A second comparison is possible by examining results from the General Social Survey, conducted in 1993–94. The strengths of the General Social Survey are that it was conducted within households rather than by telephone and achieved a higher response rate than most other surveys do. The weakness for present comparisons is that the General Social Survey did not include a question about membership in one's congregation. However, in the General Social Survey, respondents were asked if they were members of various organizations including a "church group." Analysis of the responses suggests that some interviewees who may have been church members said no because they did not belong to a specific group, such as a Bible study or prayer fellowship. Nevertheless, the question does provide a way to compare the relatively active church members who participated in the Global Issues Survey with a subset of a national survey who were also apparently involved in a congregation or religious group. The comparisons are shown in Table 2.

The religious-tradition variable is operationalized in almost the same way in the two studies, although the General Social Survey questions about denomination were sometimes not as specific. The distribution of religious tradition in the two studies is very similar, the main exceptions being that there are fewer mainline Protestants in the 2005 Global Issues study than in the earlier study (a result consistent with declining mainline memberships documented in other studies) and more Catholics. The greater proportion of Catholics in the Global Issues Survey is at least partly a function of the fact that General Social Survey interviews were not conducted in Spanish. Attendance is more frequent among the Global Issues respondents, again suggesting that they are not only members but active members. The gender, racial, age, and regional composition of the two studies are all quite similar.

A third point of comparison is the 1996 survey on which Christian Smith's valuable *American Evangelicalism: Embattled and Thriving* is based. Smith was mainly interested in churchgoing Protestants, so his sample differs from the Global Issues Survey, but otherwise the methodology is similar in that both studies involved random digit dialing and screened for a churched subset of the U.S. population. To qualify in Smith's study, interviewees had to define their religious preference as Protestant and say either that they attended religious services at least two or three times a year or that religion was extremely important to them. For purposes of comparison, 114 Catholics were also included in the study. The Protestants were divided into four categories—evangelical, fundamentalist, mainline, and liberal—by first asking respondents to say if each label described their religious identity and background and then, for those answering yes to

TABLE 2

Comparison of 2005 Global Issues Survey with 1993–94
General Social Survey (in percent)

	Global Issues	General Social
Religious tradition		
Evangelical Protestant	38	39
Mainline Protestant	19	23
Black Protestant	7	8
Roman Catholic	26	20
Other	8	8
Unaffiliated	2	1
Attendance		
More than once a week	25	21
Every week	43	39
Almost every week	9	10
Once or twice a month	19	18
Less often	5	12
Gender		
Male	36	35
Female	64	65
Race		
White	81	83
Other	19	17
Age		
18–30	14	15
31–64	65	62
65 and over	21	23
Region		
Northeast	15	16
Midwest	26	25
South	42	40
West	17	19

Note: The General Social Survey figures are for members of a "church group."

more than one label, asking two questions requiring respondents to select only one of the four labels. The Global Issues Survey included questions that made it possible to sort Protestants into these four categories as well, although the questions were not exactly the same as in Smith's study. Instead of using the categories of attending two or three times a year or saying that religion was extremely important, a subset of Protestants in the survey was selected on the basis of attending services at least "a few" times a year or saying that "growing in their spiritual life" as an adult was extremely important. Then, instead of three questions about religious identity, Smith's second and third questions were used to ask respondents to self-identify as evangelicals, fundamentalists, mainline Protestants, or liberal Protestants. The two procedures resulted in the same four categories of Protestants, plus Catholics, but the different wording of the questions yielded different distributions: specifically, 24 percent of Smith's Protestants self-classified as evangelicals compared with 35 percent in the Global Issues Survey; 21 and 24 percent, respectively, were fundamentalists; 31 and 20 percent, respectively, were mainline Protestants; and 24 and 21 percent, respectively, were liberal Protestants. Besides the different wording of the questions, social changes between 1996 and 2005 may also account for some of these differences, especially the apparent growth of evangelicals and decline of mainline Protestants.

The characteristics of respondents in the two studies are compared in Table 3. Overall, the similarities are far greater than the differences. Both studies include more women than men, and the pattern among the five subgroups is fairly similar. The percentages who were white, black, or Asian are similar within the five subgroups in the two studies. The percentage who were Hispanic is considerably larger in the Global Issues Survey, especially among Catholics and evangelical and mainline Protestants, probably because interviewing was conducted in Spanish but also because the Hispanic population has increased. Marital status shows some variation between the two studies among the Protestant groups but is almost identical for Catholics. College graduates are more common among mainline Protestants than among evangelicals or fundamentalists in both studies, and it appears that education levels may have risen between 1996 and 2005 among mainline and liberal Protestants and Catholics more than among self-identified evangelicals and fundamentalists. Finally, the two studies yielded very similar proportions of respondents in each subcategory who said they attended church services weekly.

IN-DEPTH QUALITATIVE INTERVIEWS

My research assistants and I conducted in-depth qualitative interviews with a total of 300 people. Of this total, 150 were clergy or lay leaders of congregations (such as missions and global outreach directors) who described the ministries of their congregations. For 108 of these interviews, we selected interviewees who were directly involved in international outreach and were able to serve as informants about those programs. As a comparison, the other 42 were clergy who described the overall activities of their congregations and gave us an opportunity to see how significant or insignificant the international ministries were in relation to other programs. An additional 40 clergy were interviewed, not to explore church activities, but to gain greater insight into the teachings and theological understandings involved in contemporary international outreach programs. Sixty interviews were conducted with rank-and-file church members. Fifteen of these were follow-up interviews with people who had participated in the national survey. All 60 had been involved at some point in their life in congregation-based

TABLE 3
Comparison of religious preference in 2005 Global Issues
Survey with Smith's 1996 survey (in percent)

	Evangelical Protestant	Fundamentalist Protestant	Mainline Protestant	Liberal Protestant	Roman Catholic
:male					
Global Issues 2005	65	55	59	72	65
Smith 1996	65	57	66	67	70
ʼhite					
Global Issues 2005	83	86	87	77	82
Smith 1996	87	81	92	73	84
ack					
Global Issues 2005	9	10	9	18	2
Smith 1996	9	14	7	22	2
ispanic					
Global Issues 2005	7	2	4	2	20
Smith 1996	3	1	0	2	9
sian					
Global Issues 2005	1	1	1	2	2
Smith 1996	0	1	1	1	3
arried					
Global Issues 2005	71	70	70	61	64
Smith 1996	78	69	74	57	64
ever married					
Global Issues 2005	11	12	9	15	15
Smith 1996	8	18	9	20	16
ivorced or separated					
Global Issues 2005	8	9	12	11	10
Smith 1996	7	8	9	16	12
ʃidowed					
Global Issues 2005	9	8	12	12	8
Smith 1996	8	5	9	7	8
ollege graduate					
Global Issues 2005	38	24	50	44	43
Smith 1996	36	26	40	29	34
ttend weekly					
Global Issues 2005	82	77	63	50	66
Smith 1996	80	67	63	47	65

activities concerned with people living in other countries or emigrated from other countries. We also conducted 50 interviews with agency directors and staff. These provided information about independent organizations such as World Vision International and the International Justice Mission and about ecumenical and denominational agencies such as Church World Service, Catholic Relief Services, and the United Methodist Committee on Relief.

We identified prospective interviewees in most cases through Web sites, denominational directories, and referrals from other respondents in this study and in previous studies. To maximize the likelihood of learning about distinctive programs and perspectives, we selected interviewees who were quite diverse geographically and religiously as well as on such demographic factors as gender, race, and age. For instance, the clergy and mission directors who told us about their congregations' ministries were located in twenty-nine states and the District of Columbia (Alabama, Arizona, California, Colorado, Connecticut, Florida, Georgia, Idaho, Illinois, Indiana, Iowa, Kansas, Maryland, Massachusetts, Michigan, Minnesota, Missouri, New Hampshire, New Jersey, New York, North Carolina, North Dakota, Oregon, Pennsylvania, Tennessee, Texas, Virginia, Washington, and Wisconsin) and their congregations were African Methodist Episcopal, American Baptist, Assemblies of God, Baptist General Conference, Bible Baptist, Bible Church, Calvary Church, Church of Christ, Christian, Community Church, Congregational, Disciples of Christ, Episcopal, Evangelical Free, Evangelical Lutheran Church of America, Friends, Holiness, Independent, Independent Baptist, Lutheran Church–Missouri Synod, nondenominational, Orthodox, Pentecostal, Presbyterian Church of America, Presbyterian Church (USA), Roman Catholic, Southern Baptist, Unitarian, United Church of Christ, United Methodist, Wesleyan Methodist, and the Willow Creek Association. Although our focus was on Christianity, we also conducted interviews with ten rabbis for purposes of comparison.

The in-depth interviews averaged about ninety minutes in length. All were tape-recorded and professionally transcribed. Interviewees who wished to do so were given the opportunity to review their transcription and make corrections. Following federal guidelines for interviewing human subjects as interpreted by the Princeton University Institutional Review Panel, all names of interviewees and congregations are kept confidential. The interviews incorporated a semistructured format involving standard open-response questions with follow-up questions tailored accordingly. Besides descriptive information about specific programs and activities, interviewees provided contextual information about their congregations and personal backgrounds, stories about particularly memorable or illustrative events, explanations about the reasons for various activities and their perceived consequences, and comments about beliefs and attitudes.

Notes

INTRODUCTION

1. Of particular relevance are the essays in Max L. Stackhouse and Peter J. Paris, eds., *God and Globalization*, vol. 1: *Religion and the Powers of the Common Life* (Philadelphia: Trinity Press International, 2000); Max L. Stackhouse, Don S. Browning, and Peter J. Paris, eds., *God and Globalization*, vol. 2: *The Spirit and the Modern Authorities* (Philadelphia: Trinity Press International, 2001); Max L. Stackhouse with Diane B. Obenchain, eds., *God and Globalization*, vol. 3: *Christ and the Dominions of Civilization* (Philadelphia: Trinity Press International, 2002); and Cynthia D. Moe-Lobeda, *Healing a Broken World: Globalization and God* (Minneapolis, Minn.: Augsburg Fortress, 2002).

2. World Council of Churches, Central Committee, "Major Features of Globalization Affecting the Church," *Ecumenical Review* 54 (October 2002): 483–94; quotation is on p. 483.

3. International Telecommunication Union Database, online at the International Networks Archive (www.princeton.edu/~ina); see also www.itu.int.

4. U.S. Department of Transportation (www.dot.gov).

5. Percentages among active church members in this and subsequent paragraphs are from the Global Issues Survey, conducted in 2005 among 2,231 nationally representative adult church members; see the appendix for details.

6. David B. Barrett, *World Christian Encyclopedia: A Comparative Survey of Churches and Religions in the Modern World A.D. 1900–2000* (Oxford: Oxford University Press, 1982), 801, and David B. Barrett, George T. Kurian, and Todd M. Johnson, *World Christian Encyclopedia: A Comparative Survey of Churches and Religions in the Modern World,* 2nd ed. (Oxford: Oxford University Press, 2001), 839.

7. John Boli, Thomas A. Loya, and Teresa Loftin, "National Participation in World-Polity Organization," in *Constructing World Culture: International Nongovernmental Organizations since 1975*, ed. John Boli and George M. Thomas (Stanford: Stanford University Press, 1999), 54; figures were not reported separately for Latin America.

8. World Vision, Inc., 2006 Consolidated Financial Statements.

9. U.S. Department of Commerce (www.commerce.gov).

10. *U.S. Statistical Abstract 2004–05*, table 563, online at www.census.gov.

11. For International Mission Board annual figures, see www.imb.org.

12. For an overview, see Scott Thumma and Dave Travis, *Beyond Megachurch Myths: What We Can Learn from America's Largest Churches* (San Francisco: Jossey-Bass, 2007).

13. The figures for the 1996–2003 period refer to full communicant or confirmed members as reported in Eileen W. Lindner, *Yearbook of American and Canadian Churches 1998* (Nashville: Abingdon Press, 1998) and Eileen W. Lindner, *Yearbook of American and Canadian Churches 2005* (Nashville: Abingdon Press, 2005); earlier figures are from Dean M. Kelley, *Why Conservative Churches Are Growing: A Study in Sociology of Religion*, rev. ed. (Macon, Ga.: Mercer University Press, 1986), 21–25. On Southern Baptists, see also Thom S. Rainer, "A Resurgence Not Yet Realized: Evangelistic Effectiveness in the Southern Baptist Convention since 1979" (unpublished paper, Southern Baptist Theological Seminary, 2005).

14. Kelley, *Why Conservative Churches Are Growing*, 21, cites a figure reported in *Christianity Today* of 2,494 Southern Baptist foreign missionaries in 1971; a comparable figure of 5,238 was recorded in June 2005 on the denomination's Web site (www.imb.org).

15. Cynthia Moe-Lobeda, "Journey between Worlds: Economic Globalization and Luther's God Indwelling Creation," *Word & World* 21 (2001): 413–23; quotation from p. 423.

16. Marietta Holley, *Josiah Allen's Wife as a P.A. and P.I.: Samantha at the Centennial* (Hartford, Conn.: American Publishing Co., 1893), 256.

17. Chapter 1 provides an overview of these constraints and influences.

18. I take up these issues in chapters 2 and 3.

19. See chapter 4.

20. These considerations are the focus of chapter 5.

21. See chapter 6.

1. AT HOME AND ABROAD

1. Norman Rockwell, *Walking to Church*, *Saturday Evening Post*, April 4, 1953, cover.

2. Mark Chaves, *Congregations in America* (Cambridge, Mass.: Harvard University Press, 2004), 232–33; based on reports by clergy or other congregational leaders in a national study of congregations, Chaves estimates that the median income in the year preceding the survey (weighted according to size of congregation) was $258,000 and that of this $12,350 was given to the denomination; unweighted results (all congregations counting equally regardless of size)

showed a median income of $60,000, with $1,671 being paid to the denomination.

3. Ibid., 225.

4. Robert Wuthnow, *Saving America? Faith-Based Services and the Future of Civil Society* (Princeton, N.J.: Princeton University Press, 2004), 81.

5. Ibid., 25–63.

6. Nancy Tatom Ammerman, *Bible Believers: Fundamentalists in the Modern World* (New Brunswick, N.J.: Rutgers University Press, 1987); R. Stephen Warner, *New Wine in Old Wineskins: Evangelicals and Liberals in a Small-Town Church* (Berkeley and Los Angeles: University of California Press, 1988).

7. Robert Wuthnow and John H. Evans, eds., *The Quiet Hand of God: Faith-Based Activism and the Public Role of Mainline Protestantism* (Berkeley and Los Angeles: University of California Press, 2002).

8. Wade Clark Roof, *Spiritual Marketplace: Baby Boomers and the Remaking of American Religion* (Princeton, N.J.: Princeton University Press, 1999).

9. Wade Clark Roof, *Community and Commitment: Religious Plausibility in a Liberal Protestant Church* (New York: Elsevier, 1978).

10. Bernard Lazerwitz, J. Alan Winter, and Arnold Dashefsky, "Localism, Religiosity, Orthodoxy, and Liberalism: The Case of Jews in the United States," *Social Forces* 67 (1988): 229–42.

11. Thomas P. Holland and William L. Sachs, *The Zacchaeus Project: Discerning Episcopal Identity at the Dawn of the New Millennium* (New York: Cornerstone, 1999), 13, 37.

12. Nancy Tatom Ammerman, *Pillars of Faith: American Congregations and Their Partners* (Berkeley and Los Angeles: University of California Press, 2005), 168.

13. Ibid., 190; emphasis added.

14. I of course have in mind the recent best seller by Robert D. Putnam, *Bowling Alone: The Collapse and Revival of American Community* (New York: Simon & Schuster, 2000).

15. Victor Turner, *The Ritual Process: Structure and Anti-Structure* (Ithaca, N.Y.: Cornell University Press, 1969).

16. For instance in the Religion and Diversity Survey, a nationally representative study I conducted in 2003, 48 percent said, "I mostly trust the Bible for spiritual guidance," and 47 percent said, "I mostly trust my own personal experience for spiritual guidance." Among respondents age eighteen through twenty-four, the proportion giving the second response rose to 60 percent. See Robert Wuthnow, *America and the Challenges of Religious Diversity* (Princeton, N.J.: Princeton University Press, 2005), for more details about this study.

17. Of the many sources on the strength of U.S. Christianity compared with religion in other countries with similar economic and political characteristics, a helpful recent book is Pippa Norris and Ronald Inglehart, *Sacred and Secular: Religion and Politics Worldwide* (Cambridge: Cambridge University Press, 2004).

18. The striking feature of such otherwise divergent histories of Christian missions as Stephen Neill's *A History of Christian Missions* (London: Penguin, 1964) and David J. Bosch's *Transforming Mission: Paradigm Shifts in Theology*

of Mission (Maryknoll, N.Y.: Orbis, 1991) is how little the story of Christianity's first millennium and a half involved anything resembling what is currently regarded as missionary activity, namely, the commissioning of individuals charged specifically with spreading the gospel in new venues.

19. Ann Douglas, *The Feminization of American Culture* (New York: Knopf, 1977).

20. Fred Field Goodsell, *You Shall Be My Witnesses* (Boston: American Board of Commissioners for Foreign Missions, 1959), 161–64.

21. United Nations, *Human Development Report: 2004* (New York: United Nations, 2004).

22. Ibid.

23. David B. Barrett, George T. Kurian, and Todd M. Johnson, *World Christian Encyclopedia: A Comparative Survey of Churches and Religions in the Modern World,* 2nd ed. (New York: Oxford University Press, 2001); see esp. vol. 1, table 1–1, p. 4.

24. Samuel P. Huntington, *The Clash of Civilizations and the Remaking of World Order* (New York: Simon & Schuster, 1998).

25. United Nations, *Human Development Report: 2004,* v.

26. Daniel Philpott, "The Challenge of September 11 to Secularism in International Relations," *World Politics* 55 (2002): 66–95; quotation is from p. 95.

27. Chaves, *Congregations in America;* the figure mentioned is from my own analysis of the National Congregations Survey data set. Eight percent refers to the self-weighting sample that takes account of congregation size; this figure drops to 3 percent when the weight variable to count all congregations equally regardless of size is applied.

28. John C. Green, "Evangelical Protestants and Civic Engagement: An Overview," in *A Public Faith: Evangelicals and Civic Engagement,* ed. Michael Cromartie (Lanham, Md.: Rowman & Littlefield, 2003), 11–30. The percentage contributing to international programs through religious venues was lower than the percentages contributing to traditional charities, youth programs, elderly programs, family programs, and rehabilitation programs, but higher than to environmental programs, education programs, and pregnancy programs. Mainline Protestants were significantly more likely to contribute to international programs through religious venues than evangelical Protestants, black Protestants, or Catholics.

29. Ram A. Cnaan and Stephanie C. Boddie, "Philadelphia Census of Congregations and Their Involvement in Social Service Delivery," *Social Service Review* (December 2001), 559–80.

30. Dotsey Welliver and Minnette Northcutt, *Mission Handbook, 2004–2006: U.S. and Canadian Protestant Ministries Overseas* (Wheaton, Ill.: Billy Graham Center, 2004), 12–13. Harlan Cleveland, *The Art of Overseasmanship* (Syracuse, N.Y.: Syracuse University Press, 1957) reports that in 1956 there were 28,000 U.S. missionaries serving abroad. This number apparently included both Protestants and Catholics. In 1957, there were 24,284 Protestant missionaries serving abroad from the United States; see Kenneth Scott Latourette, "Missionaries Abroad," *Annals of the American Academy of Political and Social Science* 368 (November 1966): 21–30.

31. Julia Berger, "Religious Nongovernmental Organizations: An Exploratory Analysis," *Voluntas: International Journal of Voluntary and Nonprofit Organizations* 14 (March 2003): 15–39.

32. Giving USA Foundation, *Giving USA 2006* (Glenview, Ill.: American Association of Fundraising Counsel, 2006).

33. Bryan T. Froehle and Mary L. Gautier, *Global Catholicism: Portrait of a World Church* (Maryknoll, N.Y.: Orbis, 2003), 172, 265; most, but not all, of the figures reported by Froehle and Gautier are from the year 2000.

34. David B. Barrett and Todd M. Johnson, *World Christian Trends, A.D. 30–A.D. 2200: Interpreting the Annual Christian Megacensus* (Pasadena, Calif.: William Carey Library, 2001), 408–17. I discuss questions about the validity of Barrett and Johnson's numbers and their uses in chapter 2.

35. Welliver and Northcutt, *Mission Handbook 2004–2006*, 362.

36. Robert Wuthnow, "Beyond Quiet Influence? Possibilities for the Protestant Mainline," in *The Quiet Hand of God: Faith-Based Activism and the Public Role of Mainline Protestantism*, ed. Robert Wuthnow and John H. Evans (Berkeley and Los Angeles: University of California Press, 2002), 381–404.

37. These results are from my analysis of a national survey conducted in 2002 by the Harris Poll (Chicago Council on Foreign Relations, *American Public Opinion and US Foreign Policy*, 2002); machine-readable data file available from the Roper Center for Public Opinion Research, Storrs, Connecticut.

38. Thomas L. Friedman, *The World Is Flat: A Brief History of the Twenty-First Century* (New York: Farrar, Straus, and Giroux, 2005).

39. Philip Jenkins, *The Next Christendom: The Coming of Global Christianity* (New York: Oxford University Press, 2002).

40. Darrell L. Guder, ed., *Missional Church: A Vision for the Sending of the Church in North America* (Grand Rapids, Mich.: Eerdmans, 1998), esp. 5–7, 267.

41. See Kristen Renwick Monroe, *The Heart of Altruism: Perceptions of a Common Humanity* (Princeton, N.J.: Princeton University Press, 1996).

42. Gauri Viswanathan, *Outside the Fold: Conversion, Modernity, and Belief* (Princeton, N.J.: Princeton University Press, 1998), esp. 5–6.

43. Among writers associated with the idea of Christians being an exile-like community, Stanley Hauerwas, *Resident Aliens: Life in the Christian Colony* (Nashville: Abingdon, 1989), is among the most prominent; the idea of an embattled community has been examined in Christian Smith, *American Evangelicalism: Embattled and Thriving* (Chicago: University of Chicago Press, 1998).

44. For an effort to conceptualize "transnational" in this restricted sense, see Alejandro Portes, Luis E. Guarnizo, and Patricia Landolt, "The Study of Transnationalism: Pitfalls and Promise of an Emergent Research Field," *Ethnic and Racial Studies* 22 (March 1999): 217–36; also useful is Peggy Levitt, *The Transnational Villagers* (Berkeley and Los Angeles: University of California Press, 2001). The perspective I take here is also summarized in Robert Wuthnow and Steve Offutt, "Transnational Religious Connections," *Sociology of Religion* 69 (2008): 110–21.

2. THE GLOBAL CHRISTIANITY PARADIGM

1. The idea that Christian missions have gone through a number of such paradigm shifts in the past and, during the last decades of the twentieth century, experienced a crisis that resulted in another paradigm shift is taken from David J. Bosch, *Transforming Mission: Paradigm Shifts in Theology of Mission* (Maryknoll, N.Y.: Orbis, 1991).

2. Thomas S. Kuhn, *The Structure of Scientific Revolutions* (Chicago: University of Chicago Press, 1962).

3. Tomoko Masuzawa, *The Invention of World Religions* (Chicago: University of Chicago Press, 2005).

4. Todd M. Johnson and Sandra S. Kim, "Describing the Worldwide Christian Phenomenon," *International Bulletin of Missionary Research* 29 (April 2005): 80–82. The sentence in which the phrase appears is "Fragmented they may be still, but these widely scattered individual believers, several thousand in number, have helped to produce a survey in which global Christianity emerges as a single whole, even as the Body of Christ"; David B. Barrett, *World Christian Encyclopedia: A Comparative Survey of Churches and Religions in the Modern World A.D. 1900–2000* (New York: Oxford University Press, 1982), vol. 1, p. v. The preface in which this sentence appears is dated 1981, although the publication date is 1982.

5. "Position of Church in Wartime to Be Discussed by Leaders," *Washington Post*, June 12, 1943.

6. Joann Stevens, "Clerics Differ in Reaction to Pope's Visit," *Washington Post*, October 11, 1979.

7. Martin E. Marty, "The True Believers," *New York Times*, May 8, 1994.

8. F. J. Verstraelen, *Missiology: An Ecumenical Introduction, Texts and Contexts of Global Christianity* (Grand Rapids, Mich.: Eerdmans, 1995).

9. Francis John McConnell, *Human Needs and World Christianity* (New York: Friendship Press, 1929). Johnson and Kim, "Describing the Worldwide Christian Phenomenon," say the first book title in which "world Christianity" appeared is Henry Smith Leiper's *World Chaos or World Christianity: A Popular Interpretation of Oxford and Edinburgh* (New York: Friendship Press, 1937); however, this book is predated two years by Leiper's *The Ghost of Caesar Walks: The Conflict of Nationalism and World Christianity* (New York: Friendship Press, 1935).

10. These figures are from my analysis of keywords in the online texts of these newspapers. I am mindful of the terminological debates among scholars about "global Christianity" and "world Christianity." See Johnson and Kim, "Describing the Worldwide Christian Phenomenon," for a brief summary.

11. Philip Jenkins, *The Next Christendom: The Coming of Global Christianity* (New York: Oxford University Press, 2002).

12. Ibid.; see the back cover of the paperback edition, which roughly paraphrases the assertion on p. 2 that "the center of gravity in the Christian world has shifted inexorably southward, to Africa, Asia, and Latin America." See also Philip Jenkins, "A New Christendom," *Chronicle Review*, March 29, 2002, and Mort Kondracke and Fred Barnes, "Interview with Philip Jenkins," *Fox News*,

December 21, 2002, online transcript. In a response to critics Jenkins affirmed as a fact that "is not open to serious controversy" that "the center of gravity of the Christian world has moved decisively to the global South, to the continents of Africa, Latin America, and Asia, and that trend is continuing apace"; Philip Jenkins, "After the Next Christendom," *International Bulletin of Missionary Research* 28 (January 1, 2004): 20–22; quotation is from p. 20.

13. R. Scott Appleby's review in the *New York Times* opened with this assertion: "Mark your calendar. By the year 2050 six nations—Brazil, Mexico, the Philippines, Nigeria, Congo and the United States—will each have 100 million Christians or more. Sub-Saharan Africa will have long displaced Europe as the leading center of Christianity, while Brazil will count 150 million Catholics and 40 million Protestants. And more than one billion Pentecostals, the poorest of the poor, will be spreading their distinctive brand of Christian supernaturalism" (Appleby, "Marching as to War," *New York Times*, May 12, 2002). Other reviews were similar; for instance, Philip Jenkins, "The Christian Future," *Wall Street Journal*, December 24, 2002; Dwight Longenecker, "Christianity Is Not on the Wane in the World, It's Just Reshaping and Relocating," *The Times (London)*, March 22, 2003; Uwe Siermon-Netto, "Surprise: Resilient Christianity," *World & I* 18 (July 2003): 29–31; Alex MacLeod, "A New Reformation Is Happening in Global Christianity," *Presbyterian Record* 128 (February 2004): 44–45; Thomas C. Langham, "Review of *The Next Christendom*," *Sociology of Religion* 65 (Spring 2004): 95–97; and Jeremy Lott, "The Faith of the Global South," *Touchstone* (2002), online at www.touchstonemag.com. In his *New York Times* editorial column, Nicholas D. Kristof echoed the same central observation: "One of the most important trends reshaping the world is the decline of Christianity in Europe, and its rise in Africa and other parts of the developing world, including Asia and Latin America" (Kristof, "Where Faith Thrives," *New York Times*, March 26, 2005).

14. Philip Jenkins, "The Next Christianity," *Atlantic Monthly* 290 (October 2002): 53–68.

15. An especially useful argument about the broader implications of Jenkins's book and the global Christianity paradigm is that of Joel A. Carpenter, "The Christian Scholar in an Age of Global Christianity" (unpublished paper presented at the conference on Christianity and the Soul of the University, Baylor University, March 25–27, 2004). See also Joel A. Carpenter's preface in Lamin Sanneh and Joel A. Carpenter, eds., *The Changing Face of Christianity: Africa, the West, and the World* (New York: Oxford University Press, 2005), vii–ix.

16. Andrew Walls, "Culture and Coherence in Christian History," *Evangelical Review of Theology* 9 (1984): 215; reprinted in Walls, *The Missionary Movement in Christian History: Studies in the Transmission of Faith* (Maryknoll, N.Y.: Orbis, 1996), 16–25; quotation is on p. 22. In a subsequent essay, Walls wrote specifically about the United States: "The position of the United States in the world Christian situation is . . . peculiar; it represents the West—indeed the West writ large—and the West will matter progressively less in Christianity as the South comes to mean more"; A. F. Walls, "World Christianity, the Missionary Movement and the Ugly American," in *World Order and Religion,*

ed. Wade Clark Roof (Albany: State University of New York, 1991), 147–72; quotation is from p. 152.

    17. Leslie Newbigin, *Foolishness to the Greeks* (Grand Rapids, Mich.: Eerdmans, 1986), 3.

    18. David B. Barrett, George T. Kurian, and Todd M. Johnson, *World Christian Encyclopedia: A Comparative Survey of Churches and Religions in the Modern World*, 2nd ed. (New York: Oxford University Press, 2001); the percentages are calculated from the raw figures shown in table 1–3, p. 12. The specific percentages of the total world Christian population in 2000 are Africa, 18; Asia, 16; Latin America, 25; Europe, 28; North America, 11; and Oceania, 2. For 2025, the respective estimates are Africa, 24; Asia, 18; Latin America, 26; Europe, 21; North America, 9; and Oceania, 2. A few of the statistics in the *World Christian Encyclopedia* can also be found in Eileen W. Lindner, ed., *Yearbook of American and Canadian Churches, 2005* (Nashville: Abingdon Press, 2005). Well before Jenkins's book, Barrett's statistics charting the shifting demographics of Christianity were being widely discussed; see for instance Kim A. Lawton, "Faith without Borders: How the Developing World Is Changing the Face of Christianity," *Christianity Today* 41 (May 19, 1997): 38–49.

    19. David Martin, *Tongues of Fire: The Explosion of Protestantism in Latin America* (Oxford: Blackwell, 1990); Kurt Bowen, *Evangelism and Apostasy: The Evolution and Impact of Evangelicals in Modern Mexico* (Montreal: McGill-Queen's University Press, 1996); Elizabeth Brusco, *The Reformation of Machismo: Evangelical Protestantism and Gender in Colombia* (Austin: University of Texas Press, 1995); Paul Gifford, *Ghana's New Christianity: Pentecostalism in a Globalizing African Economy* (Bloomington: Indiana University Press, 2004); David Maxwell, "'Delivered from the Spirit of Poverty?': Pentecostalism, Prosperity, and Modernity in Zimbabwe," *Journal of Religion in Africa* 28 (1998): 350–73; Birgit Meyer, "Christianity in Africa: From African Independent to Pentecostal-Charismatic Churches," *Annual Review of Anthropology* 33 (2004): 447–74; Birgit Meyer, "Powerful Pictures: Popular Christian Aesthetics in Southern Ghana," *Journal of the American Academy of Religion* 76 (2008): 82–110; and Julie Hearn, "The 'Invisible' NGO: US Evangelical Missions in Kenya," *Journal of Religion in Africa* 32 (2002): 32–60; see also the very useful literature review in Joel Robbins, "The Globalization of Pentecostal and Charismatic Christianity," *Annual Review of Anthropology* 33 (2004): 117–43, and the excellent firsthand accounts in Donald E. Miller and Tetsunao Yamamori, *Global Pentecostalism: The New Face of Christian Social Engagement* (Berkeley and Los Angeles: University of California Press, 2007).

    20. Kwame Bediako, *Jesus and the Gospel in Africa* (Maryknoll, N.Y.: Orbis, 2004), 3. Or as missions scholar Dana L. Robert put it, "a massive cultural and geographic shift away from Europeans and their descendants toward peoples of the Southern Hemisphere"; Dana L. Robert, "Shifting Southward: Global Christianity since 1945," *International Bulletin of Missionary Research* 24 (2004): 50–58; quotation is from p. 50.

    21. I largely follow the thinking about narrative here of Christian Smith, *Moral, Believing Animals: Human Personhood and Culture* (New York: Oxford University Press, 2003).

22. Walls, *The Missionary Movement in Christian History*, 22.

23. This emphasis on the *missio dei*, previously articulated by Karl Barth, is especially evident in Bosch, *Transforming Mission*, and in Darrell L. Guder, ed., *Missional Church: A Vision for the Sending of the Church in North America* (Grand Rapids, Mich.: Eerdmans, 1998). See also Philip L. Wickeri, "Mission from the Margins: The *Missio Dei* in the Crisis of World Christianity," *International Review of Mission* 93 (April 2004): 182–98.

24. For instance, see especially Samuel Escobar, *The New Global Mission: The Gospel from Everywhere to Everyone* (Downers Grove, Ill.: InterVarsity Press, 2003), and Lamin Sanneh, *Whose Religion Is Christianity? The Gospel beyond the West* (Grand Rapids, Mich.: Eerdmans, 2003). See also Viggo Mortensen, "What Is Happening to Global Christianity?" *Dialog: A Journal of Theology* 43 (Spring 2004): 20–27.

25. I have in mind especially the major collaborative project whose first volume is Dale T. Irvin and Scott W. Sunquist, eds., *History of the World Christian Movement: Earliest Christianity to 1453* (Maryknoll, N.Y.: Orbis, 2001); also of relevance is John W. Coakley and Andrea Sterk, eds., *Readings in World Christian History* (Maryknoll, N.Y.: Orbis, 2004). See also Richard A. Kauffman, "Scholars Uncovering Church's Hidden History," *Christianity Today*, July 13, 1998, 22–23.

26. This thesis was developed most clearly in Jenkins's "The Next Christianity" and was picked up repeatedly by subsequent writers.

27. These phrases are from Lamin Sanneh, "Global Christianity and the Reeducation of the West," *Christian Century*, July 16, 1995, 715–18. Sanneh draws liberally from Walls as well as offering his own views about the significance of the new paradigm. See also Alister E. McGrath, *The Future of Christianity* (Oxford: Blackwell, 2002), esp. 118.

28. For instance, Laurie Goodstein, "More Religion, but Not the Old-Time Kind," *New York Times*, January 9, 2005.

29. Academic institutions with professorships in world Christianity included Drew University, Emory University, Perkins School of Theology at Southern Methodist University, Yale University, New York Theological Seminary, Columbia Theological Seminary, Emmanuel School of Religion, United Theological Seminary, Boston Theological Institute, Princeton Theological Seminary, McCormick Theological Seminary, and Fuller Theological Seminary, among others. I do not mean to suggest that these and other professorships necessarily reflect the new global Christianity paradigm.

30. Bosch, *Transforming Mission*, 6.

31. William Carey, *An Enquiry into the Obligations of Christians to Use Means for the Conversion of the Heathens* (Leicester, U.K.: Ann Ireland, 1792), 62. On Carey's role, see Basil Miller, *William Carey: The Father of Modern Missions* (Minneapolis, Minn.: Bethany House, 1985).

32. Discussed in Todd M. Johnson, *Countdown to 1900: World Evangelization at the End of the 19th Century* (Hamilton, Mass.: Center for the Study of Global Christianity, 2002), chap. 2; online at www.globalchristianity.org/books.

33. Rufus Anderson, *Foreign Missions: Their Relations and Claims* (Boston: Congregational Publishing Society, 1874), 92–93.

34. James S. Dennis, *Centennial Survey of Foreign Missions* (New York: Fleming H. Revell, 1902).

35. James S. Dennis, *Christian Missions and Social Progress,* 3 vols. (New York: Fleming H. Revell, 1897–1906); discussed in William R. Hutchison, *Errand to the World: American Protestant Thought and Foreign Missions* (Chicago: University of Chicago Press, 1987), 107–11.

36. David B. Barrett and Todd M. Johnson, *World Christian Trends, A.D. 30–A.D. 2200: Interpreting the Annual Christian Megacensus* (Pasadena, Calif.: William Carey Library, 2001), ix–x; see also table 14–7, pp. 454–61, for a list of specific titles. See also the excellent short history in Robert T. Coote, "Finger on the Pulse: Fifty Years of Missionary Research," *International Bulletin of Missionary Research* 24 (July 2000): 98–105.

37. Jenkins, *The Next Christendom,* esp. 85–89, 223–24.

38. Gerald H. Anderson, "World Christianity by the Numbers: A Review of the *World Christian Encyclopedia,* Second Edition," *International Bulletin of Missionary Research* 26 (July 2002): 128–30; quotations are from p. 129.

39. Mark A. Noll, "Review of *World Christian Encyclopedia: A Comparative Survey of Churches and Religions in the Modern World,*" *Church History* 71 (2002): 448–54; quotation is from p. 453.

40. Becky Yang Hsu, Amy Reynolds, Conrad Hackett, and James Gibbon, "Estimating the Religious Composition of All Nations: An Empirical Assessment" (working paper, Princeton University, Center for the Study of Religion, 2005). The value of this study is that, unlike reviews that focus on a particular anomaly here and there to cast doubts on the accuracy of the World Christian Database, it used statistical methods to determine precisely how similar or different the database figures were to those of other cross-national sources. Correlations between World Christian Database estimates of the percentage Christian in more than two hundred countries and estimates from the U.S. State Department and CIA, for instance, were above .925. The World Christian Database provides estimates for more countries than most other sources and does a better job in most instances of estimating the nonreligious population. Unfortunately, similar validation procedures cannot be performed for many of the specific indicators the World Christian Database provides about numbers of worship centers, Christian workers, missionaries, funds, and the like.

41. Douglas John Hall, *The Cross in Our Context: Jesus and the Suffering World* (Minneapolis, Minn.: Fortress Press, 2003), 161. A similar point about Jenkins's "over-reliance" on statistics was made at a session about the book at the American Academy of Religion; see Gene TeSeele, "Scholars Look at Religion in Society," *Witherspoon on the Web,* November 26, 2003, online at www.witherspoonsociety.org. The point, though, is not whether the statistics may have flaws, as Jenkins acknowledged, but that the argument about a global shift to the South is rooted essentially in such statistics.

42. Barrett and Johnson, *World Christian Trends,* 406–31.

43. The exception of course is population growth or decline due to transnational migration, but the literature on Christianity's shift to the global South does not (rightly, in my view) regard migration as a major factor. This literature also treats conversion largely as if it were a function of local conditions.

44. Pippa Norris and Ronald Inglehart, *Sacred and Secular: Religion and Politics Worldwide* (New York: Cambridge University Press, 2004), 90.

45. Ibid., 87–88. See also Todd M. Johnson, "Demographic Futures for Christianity and the World Religions," *Dialog: A Journal of Theology* 43 (Spring 2004): 10–19, for a helpful short summary that distinguishes demographic shifts from other changes in global Christianity and that criticizes writers who exaggerate the decline of Christianity in the United States.

46. After the collapse of the Soviet Union, the term "Third World" (referring to poorer countries unaligned with either the United States or the Soviet Union) came to be replaced by "global South." The defining aspect of the global South is not geographic location but low incomes and vulnerabilities associated with subsistence living; United Nations, *Forging a Global South* (New York: United Nations Development Programme, 2004). Missions scholars have themselves expressed unease with the geographic categories; for instance, Robert, "Shifting Southward," 57n4.

47. Barrett, Kurian, and Johnson, *World Christian Encyclopedia,* 2nd ed., vol. 1, p. 307.

48. Todd M. Johnson and Sun Young Chung, "Tracking Global Christianity's Statistical Centre of Gravity, AD 33—AD 2100," *International Review of Mission* 93 (April 2004): 166–81.

49. A related discussion of neglected points is offered in Ralph D. Winter, "Review of Philip Jenkins, *The Next Christendom,*" *Mission Frontiers* (January–February 2003): 14–15.

50. Barrett and Johnson, *World Christian Trends,* esp. Barrett's preface and part 1. Samuel P. Huntington, *The Clash of Civilizations and the Remaking of World Order* (New York: Simon & Schuster, 1996), esp. 64–66, also emphasizes that Christians have remained nearly constant as a percentage of the world's population.

51. Escobar, *The New Global Mission,* 167.

52. Anderson, "World Christianity by the Numbers," 129.

53. The popularity of the new global Christianity paradigm among scholars in the United States is undoubtedly elevated by the fact that many of these scholars teach at Christian colleges and seminaries where a growing proportion of the student body comes from Africa, Asia, and Latin America. As they look out at the diverse composition of their classes, though, these professors should remember that they are still teaching in the United States at institutions largely supported by benefactors in the United States, and that their teaching and these resources are indications of the important and continuing role of the United States in global Christianity.

54. Recent books that illustrate naturalistic arguments aimed at debunking religion include such popular works as Richard Dawkins, *The God Delusion* (New York: Houghton Mifflin, 2006), and Daniel C. Dennett, *Breaking the Spell: Religion as a Natural Phenomenon* (New York: Penguin, 2006).

55. I refer readers especially to the valuable argument of Mark Chaves, "Secularization as Declining Religious Authority," *Social Forces* 72 (1994): 749–74, which also includes an extensive bibliography. Also of particular value are Christian Smith, ed., *The Secular Revolution: Power, Interests, and Conflict in the*

Secularization of American Public Life (Berkeley and Los Angeles: University of California Press, 2003), esp. Smith's introductory essay; and Steve Bruce, *God Is Dead: Secularization in the West* (Oxford: Blackwell, 2002). An initial sketch of how globalization may lead to rethinking of the secularization debate has been provided by Jose Casanova, "Religion, the New Millennium, and Globalization," *Sociology of Religion* 62 (2001): 415–41. For an argument parallel to my own about the role of secularization theory in shaping larger debates about religion, see David Nash, "Reconnecting Religion with Social and Cultural History: Secularization's Failure as a Master Narrative," *Cultural and Social History* 1 (2004): 302–25.

56. Guder, *Missional Church,* 80.

57. James F. Engel and William A. Dyrness, *Changing the Mind of Missions: Where Have We Gone Wrong?* (Downers Grove, Ill.: InterVarsity Press, 2000).

58. Guder, *Missional Church,* 78.

59. On the critique of secularization theory, see especially Rodney Stark and Roger Finke, *Acts of Faith: Explaining the Human Side of Religion* (Berkeley and Los Angeles: University of California Press, 2000).

60. Leigh Eric Schmidt, "Mixed Blessings: Christianization and Secularization," *Reviews in American History* 26 (1998): 637–43, argues that we should also be reminded of Alex de Tocqueville's skepticism about the "corrosions, duplicities, and fragilities" of American religion in view of "our new-found confidence in gauging religion's vigor through . . . seemingly ever-rising rates of churchly affiliation" (642).

61. Carpenter, "The Christian Scholar in an Age of Global Christianity," 7. See also David B. Barrett, Todd M. Johnson, and Peter F. Crossing, "Missiometrics 2005: A Global Survey of World Mission," *International Bulletin of Missionary Research* 29 (January 2005): 27–30, who declare that "the secularization myth has been soundly discredited." Of course their statement is based only on numeric trends and not on a sophisticated understanding of secularization theory itself.

62. Dale T. Irvin, "A Review of *The Next Christendom: The Coming of Global Christianity* by Philip Jenkins," *Journal of Pentecostal Studies* 13 (2005): 273–80; quotation is on p. 278. Interestingly, only one page of Jenkins's book draws on Troeltsch.

63. I am usually hesitant to inject Foucault into discussions of religion, but for the theoretically inclined, it may be worth revisiting his arguments and diachronic and synchronic analysis; see especially Michel Foucault, *The Archaeology of Knowledge and the Discourse on Language* (London: Tavistock, 1972), and Michel Foucault, *The Order of Things: An Archaeology of the Human Sciences* (New York: Random House, 1970).

64. Robert, "Shifting Southward," offers an excellent short summary of foreign mission organizations' ambivalent relationships with imperialism; see also Stephen Neill, *A History of Christian Missions,* rev. ed. (London: Penguin, 1986), and Catherine Keller, Michael Nausner, and Mayra Nivera, eds., *Postcolonial Theologies: Divinity and Empire* (New York: Chalice Press, 2004).

65. Anderson, *Foreign Missions,* 114.

66. Hutchison, *Errand to the World*, 77–84, provides further details about Anderson's views.

67. J. W. Bashford, *World Missionary Conference* (Cambridge: Henry Martyn Centre, 1910), vol. 9, p. 246.

68. Charles Clayton Morrison, "The World Missionary Conference," *Christian Century*, July 7, 1910, online at www.religion-online.org.

69. Wolfgang Gunther, "The History and Significance of World Mission Conferences in the 20th Century," *International Review of Mission* 92 (2003): 521–37; quotation is from p. 525.

70. Hugh McCullum, "Healing and Reconciliation Theme," *Conference on World Mission and Evangelism News* (2005), online at www.mission2005.org.

71. Lausanne Committee for World Evangelization, *The Lausanne Covenant* (1974), section 8 (online at www.lausanne.org); quoted in Escobar, *The New Global Mission*, 164.

72. Irvin, "Review of *The Next Christendom*," 279. See also Mrinalini Sebastian, "Mission without History? Some Ideas for Decolonizing Mission," *International Review of Mission* 93 (January 2004): 75–96.

73. Edward W. Said, *Culture and Imperialism* (New York: Vintage, 1993), 36.

74. Jenkins, *The Next Christendom*, 56.

75. Sanneh, *Whose Religion Is Christianity?* 37. See also Tom Marfo, "Churches as Healing Communities" (Church and Mission Society 12th Assembly, Trondheim, Norway, June 2003).

76. Escobar, *The New Global Mission*, 26.

77. Newbigin, *Foolishness to the Greeks*, 2–3.

78. Sanneh, *Whose Religion Is Christianity?* 35.

79. Jenkins, *The Next Christendom*, 202; see also this emphasis in the review by Ross Douthat, "The Christian Future," *Policy Review* 117 (February–March 2003): 89–94, and its further elaboration in Philip Jenkins, *The New Faces of Christianity: Believing the Bible in the Global South* (New York: Oxford University Press, 2006).

80. Escobar, *The New Global Mission*, 15.

81. Kwame Bediako, "Africa and Christianity on the Threshold of the Third Millennium: The Religious Dimension," *African Affairs* 99 (2000): 303–23; quotation is on p. 307.

82. Ibid., 313.

83. Michael Jaffarian, "The Statistical State of the Missionary Enterprise," *Missiology* 30 (January 2002): 15–32.

84. Jenkins, "The Next Christianity," 64. See also Mark Hanson, "The Ligaments and Landscapes of Ecumenism," *Dialog: A Journal of Theology* 42 (Winter 2003): 366–67.

85. Jenkins, *The Next Christendom*, 209.

86. Escobar, *The New Global Mission*, 17.

87. R. Stephen Warner, "The De-Europeanization of American Christianity," in *A Nation of Religions: The Politics of Pluralism in the United States*, ed. Stephen Prothero (Chapel Hill: University of North Carolina Press, 2005).

88. Grace Davie, "Pluralism, Tolerance and Democracy: Theory and Practice in Europe" (conference on the New Religious Pluralism and Democracy, Georgetown University, April 21–22, 2005).

89. Richard D. Alba and Victor Nee, *Remaking the American Mainstream: Assimilation and Contemporary Immigration* (Cambridge, Mass.: Harvard University Press, 2003). An alternative argument, known as "segmented assimilation," suggests that the melting pot model may not apply to large numbers of Latino immigrants but also suggests that Latino religion itself may remain segmented rather than profoundly infusing into the wider culture; see Alejandro Portes and Ruben G. Rumbaut, *Immigrant America: A Portrait*, 3rd ed. (Berkeley and Los Angeles: University of California Press, 2006), 299–341. For a useful overview of the literature, see Elaine Howard Ecklund and Wendy Cadge, "Immigration and Religion," *Annual Review of Sociology* 33 (2007): 17.1–17.21.

90. Rita Abrahamsen, "African Studies and the Postcolonial Challenge," *African Affairs* 102 (2003): 189–210; quotation is from p. 191.

91. Sanneh, *Whose Religion Is Christianity?* 3.

92. David Stoll, *Is Latin America Turning Protestant? The Politics of Evangelical Growth* (Berkeley and Los Angeles: University of California Press, 1990).

93. The emphasis on U.S. influence is taken to considerable lengths in Steve Brouwer, Paul Gifford, and Susan D. Rose, *Exporting the American Gospel: Global Christian Fundamentalism* (New York: Routledge, 1996), and new paradigm proponents have branded this approach "radical" and "imperialistic."

94. C. Rene Padilla, "The Future of Christianity in Latin America: Missiological Perspectives and Challenges," *International Bulletin of Missionary Research* 23 (July 1999): 105–11; quotation is from p. 108.

95. For example, see Pablo Richard, *Death of Christendoms, Birth of the Church: Historical Analysis and Theological Interpretation of the Church in Latin America* (Maryknoll, N.Y.: Orbis Books, 1987).

96. Said, *Culture and Imperialism*, 49, 19.

97. Examples of efforts to craft an alternative story of global Christianity along these lines are not hard to find. For instance, William J. Larkin, "The Contribution of Luke-Acts to Missionary Moves of the Christian Religion in 21st Century Post-Modern Global Context," *Global Missiology* (January 2004): 1–9, online at www.globalmissiology.net; and Cynthia D. Moe-Lobeda, *Healing a Broken World: Globalization and God* (Minneapolis, Minn.: Augsburg Fortress, 2002).

3. FOUR FACES OF GLOBALIZATION

1. Marleen De Witte, "Altar Media's *Living Word:* Televised Charismatic Christianity in Ghana," *Journal of Religion in Africa* 23 (2003): 172–202; quotation is on p. 195.

2. Of the many books that provide definitions and overviews of globalization, my favorite is Manfred B. Steger, *Globalization: A Very Short Introduction* (New York: Oxford University Press, 2003), which offers several brief definitions, including this one: "Globalization refers to a multidimensional set of so-

cial processes that create, multiply, stretch, and intensify worldwide social interdependencies and exchanges while at the same time fostering in people a growing awareness of deepening connections between the local and the distant" (13). The best coverage of economic aspects of globalization in my view is that provided by the essays in Michael M. Weinstein, ed., *Globalization: What's New?* (New York: Columbia University Press, 2005). Other books that provide helpful insight into the various economic, political, and ideological aspects of globalization include Leslie Sklair, *Globalization: Capitalism and Its Alternatives*, 3rd ed. (New York: Oxford University Press, 2002); Mark Rupert, *Ideologies of Globalization: Contending Visions of a New World Order* (New York: Routledge, 2000); John Urry, *Global Complexity* (Cambridge: Polity, 2003); David Held and Anthony McGrew, *Globalization and Anti-Globalization* (Cambridge: Polity, 2002); and David Held and Anthony McGrew, eds., *The Global Transformations Reader: An Introduction to the Globalization Debate*, 2nd ed. (Cambridge: Polity, 2003). Alfred E. Eckes Jr. and Thomas W. Zeiler, *Globalization and the American Century* (New York: Cambridge University Press, 2003), is useful for understanding the history of the changing role of the United States in the global economy. One of the few book-length attempts to theorize about the possible implications of globalization for religion is Peter Beyer, *Religion and Globalization* (Thousand Oaks, Calif.: Sage, 1994). Manuel A. Vasquez and Marie Friedmann Marquardt, *Globalizing the Sacred: Religion across the Americas* (New Brunswick, N.J.: Rutgers University Press, 2003), includes both a useful theoretical overview and several interesting empirical chapters.

3. *Tourism Highlights: 2006 Edition,* online at www.world-tourism.org.

4. David Dollar, "Globalization, Inequality, and Poverty since 1980" (World Bank Development Research Group Paper, November 2001); see also David Dollar, "Globalization, Poverty, and Inequality," in Weinstein, *Globalization: What's New?* 96–128; airfare statistics are on p. 99.

5. United Nations Conference on Trade and Development, *Development and Globalization: Facts and Figures 2004,* online at www.unctad.org.

6. United Nations Conference on Trade and Development, *Handbook of Statistics: 2006–07,* 26; online at www.unctad.org.

7. Afrobarometer Survey of 2,005 nationally representative Ghanaian adults, available from the International Consortium for Political and Social Research (www.icpsr.org).

8. United Nations Statistics Division, online at unstats.un.org.

9. Prior to the liquidation of Ghana Airways, its survival had been the subject of much prayer; J. Kwabena Asamoah-Gyadu, "'Christ Is the Answer: What Is the Question?' A Ghana Airways Prayer Vigil and Its Implications for Religion, Evil and Public Space," *Journal of Religion in Africa* 35, 1 (2005): 93–117.

10. *Tourism Highlights,* using available regional breakdowns for Europe and the Americas and for specific countries of destination.

11. United Nations Conference on Trade and Development, *Handbook of Statistics.*

12. United Nations, *Human Development Report 2004,* 99, online at www.undp.org.

13. *2003 World Development Indicators,* online at www.worldbank.org.

14. Dollar, "Globalization, Poverty, and Inequality," 99.

15. United Nations Conference on Trade and Development, *World Investment Report 2004,* online at www.unctad.org.

16. International Telecommunication Union, *ICT Statistics, 2004,* online at www.itu.int.

17. Eckes and Zeiler, *Globalization and the American Century,* 245.

18. *Global Telecom Indicators,* online at www.itu.int.

19. *Internet Usage Statistics,* online at www.internetworldstats.com.

20. United Nations Conference on Trade and Development, *Development and Globalization.*

21. International Monetary Fund data for 2002, when U.S. imports totaled $1.16 trillion, Germany's were $492.8 billion, Japan's were $301.8 billion, India's were $57.1 billion, and the forty countries with the fewest imports included Poland, Brazil, Norway, Indonesia, New Zealand, and Venezuela.

22. United Nations Conference on Trade and Development, *World Investment Report 2004;* transnational corporation figures and rankings are from 1990 and 2002.

23. Steger, *Globalization,* 48–49.

24. Ibid.

25. Ibid.

26. A. T. Kearney, "Measuring Globalization: The Global Top 20," *Foreign Policy* (May–June 2005): 52–60.

27. Miguel Centeno, Sara R. Curran, John Galloway, Paulette Lloyd, and Suresh Sood, "Visualizing Globalization: Observing Trade, 1980–2001" (presentation to the 37th World Congress of the International Institute of Sociology, Stockholm, Sweden, July 2005).

28. Institute of International Education, online at opendoors.iienetwork.org.

29. Erik Gruenwedel, "Dude, Surf's Up," *Brandweek,* November 13, 2000; online at www.findarticles.com.

30. Joseph E. Stiglitz, "The Overselling of Globalization," in Weinstein, *Globalization: What's New?* 228–61.

31. Centeno et al., "Visualizing Globalization," report that the number of scholarly articles about globalization rose from nearly zero in 1990 to more than six hundred in 2003.

32. The "four faces" discussed here are quite different from those outlined in Peter L. Berger, "Four Faces of Global Culture," *National Interest* 49 (1997): 23–29.

33. Marx's emphasis on bourgeois culture's erosion of traditional values is scattered through his work but is a prominent theme in Karl Marx and Frederick Engels, *The German Ideology* (New York: International Publishers, 1947). Max Weber, *The Protestant Ethic and the Spirit of Capitalism* (New York: Scribner, 1952), alludes similarly to the loss of meaning in reference to the emerging iron cage of rationality.

34. Theodor W. Adorno, *Culture Industry* (New York: Routledge, 1991), includes several of Adorno's most relevant essays written in the 1970s; Herbert

Marcuse, *One-Dimensional Man: Studies in the Ideology of Advanced Industrial Society,* 2nd ed. (Boston: Beacon Press, 1991).

35. See for instance John W. Meyer, John Boli-Bennett, and Christopher Chase-Dunn, "Convergence and Divergence in Development," *Annual Review of Sociology* 1 (1975): 223–46; George M. Thomas and John W. Meyer, "The Expansion of the State," *Annual Review of Sociology* 10 (1984): 461–82; John W. Meyer, John Boli, George M. Thomas, and Francisco O. Ramirez, "World Society and the Nation-State," *American Journal of Sociology* 103 (1997): 144–81; and John W. Meyer, "Globalization: Sources and Effects on National States and Societies," *International Sociology* 15 (2000): 233–48, who concludes that "globalization means the expanded flow of instrumental culture around the world" (233).

36. Sociologists will recognize that I am borrowing here from the widely cited article by Paul J. DiMaggio and Walter W. Powell, "The Iron Cage Revisited: Institutional Isomorphism and Collective Rationality in Organizational Fields," *American Sociological Review* 48 (1983): 147–60; these authors identify "coercive, mimetic, and normative" processes by which isomorphism emerges.

37. John Boli and George M. Thomas, eds., *Constructing World Culture: International Nongovernmental Organizations since 1875* (Stanford: Stanford University Press, 1999). See also Hartwig Hummel, "Global Pluralism? Merging IR and Comparative Politics Traditions in Developing a Theoretical Framework for Analyzing Private Actors in Global Governance" (paper presented at the annual meetings of the International Studies Association, New Orleans, March 2002).

38. See the essays in Walter W. Powell and Paul J. DiMaggio, eds., *The New Institutionalism in Organizational Analysis* (Chicago: University of Chicago Press, 1991).

39. "The World's Top Experts in Endangered Languages Meet at UNESCO," online at portal.unesco.org. See also Steger, *Globalization,* 85, which suggests that fewer than three thousand languages will remain within a few decades.

40. B. F. Grimes, *Ethnologue: Languages of the World* (Dallas, Tex.: Summer Institute of Linguistics, 1996).

41. Kenneth Keniston, "Cultural Diversity or Global Monoculture: The Impacts of the Information Age" (paper presented at the Conference on the Global Village, Bangalore, India, November 2, 1998).

42. Figures included in this paragraph are from David Graddol, *The Future of English? A Guide to Forecasting the Popularity of the English Language in the 21st Century* (London: The British Council, 1997); the quotation is on p. 14. An alternative argument that foresees a more robust future for African languages is presented in Isidore Ndaywel E Nziem, *Les Langues Africaines et Creoles Face a Leur Avenir* (Paris: L'Harmattan, 2003).

43. George Ritzer, *The McDonaldization of Society,* rev. ed. (Thousand Oaks, Calif.: Pine Forge Press, 2004).

44. Yasuki Hamano, "Building the Content Industry" (May 2004), online at www.jijigaho.or.jp.

45. United Nations, *Human Development Report 2004,* 97.

46. Manfred B. Steger, *Globalism: The New Market Ideology* (Lanham, Md.: Rowman and Littlefield, 2002), 36. On the uniformity of global consumer culture, see also Benjamin R. Barber, *Jihad vs. McWorld* (New York: Ballantine Books, 1996), and John Tomlinson, *Globalization and Culture* (Chicago: University of Chicago Press, 1999).

47. Steger, *Globalism*, 36.

48. Like its subject matter, the literature on global Pentecostalism is vast and rapidly expanding; overviews thus reflect the particular years in which they were written. Several that are of particular interest include David Martin, *Tongues of Fire: The Explosion of Protestantism in Latin America* (Oxford: Blackwell, 1990); David Martin, *Pentecostalism: The World Their Parish* (Oxford: Blackwell, 2002); and Andre Corten and Ruth Marshall-Fratani, eds., *Between Babel and Pentecost: Transnational Pentecostalism in Africa and Latin America* (Bloomington: Indiana University Press, 2001). See also Joel Robbins, "The Globalization of Pentecostal and Charismatic Christianity," *Annual Review of Anthropology* 33 (2004): 117–43.

49. David Lehmann, "Review of David Martin, *Pentecostalism: The World Their Parish*," *Journal of Religion in Africa* 3 (2003): 120–22; quotation is on p. 121. See also David Lehmann, *Struggle for the Spirit* (Cambridge: Polity, 1995). Although Lehmann's view about Pentecostal uniformity represents one extreme, other writers generalize about such common elements as an emphasis on asceticism, individualism, and prosperity; see Robbins, "The Globalization of Pentecostal and Charismatic Christianity."

50. Andre Droogers, "Globalisation and Pentecostal Success," in *Between Babel and Pentecost*, 41–61; see esp. 54.

51. Birgit Meyer, "'Praise the Lord': Popular Cinema and Pentecostalite Style in Ghana's New Public Sphere," *American Ethnologist* 31 (2004): 92–110; Meyer writes that Pentecostal churches in Africa encourage believers to "make a complete break with the past," and suggests that Pentecostalism "recasts modernity as a Christian project" and often finds itself in "marked opposition to state politics of identity" (93).

52. De Witte, "Altar Media's *Living Word*," 197. See also Birgit Meyer, "Christianity in Africa: From African Independent to Pentecostal-Charismatic Churches," *Annual Review of Anthropology* 33 (2004): 447–74.

53. Asonzeh Franklin-Kennedy Ukah, "Advertising God: Nigerian Christian Video-Films and the Power of Consumer Culture," *Journal of Religion in Africa* 33 (2003): 203–31; Asonzeh Franklin-Kennedy Ukah, "The Redeemed Christian Church of God (RCCG), Nigeria: Local Identities and Global Processes in African Pentecostalism" (Ph.D. diss., University of Bayreuth, 2003). See also Ruth Marshall-Fratani, "The Global and Local in Nigerian Pentecostalism," in *Between Babel and Pentecost*, 80–105, who also contrasts the newer churches with the more traditional ones, writing that "these new organizations place themselves firmly in the world. Typically young, upwardly mobile, relatively well-educated, their leaders privilege international contacts and experiences" (85).

54. Ibid.

55. David B. Barrett and Todd M. Johnson, *World Christian Trends, A.D. 30–A.D. 2200: Interpreting the Annual Christian Megacensus* (Pasadena, Calif.: William Carey Library, 2001), 73.

56. Graddol, *The Future of English?*

57. R. Stephen Warner, "The Place of Congregation in the Contemporary American Religious Configuration," in *American Congregations: New Perspectives in the Study of Congregations*, vol. 2, ed. James P. Wind and James M. Lewis (Chicago: University of Chicago Press, 1994), 54–100; similar arguments about the convergence of diverse immigrant groups toward a common "congregational" style are found in R. Stephen Warner and Judith Wittner, eds., *Gatherings in Diaspora: Religious Communities and the New Immigration* (Philadelphia: Temple University Press, 1998), and Fenggang Yang and Helen R. Ebaugh, "Transformations in New Immigrant Religions and Their Global Implications," *American Sociological Review* 66 (2001): 269–88. These studies are discussed and critically examined in Wendy Cadge, "The De Facto Congregationalism of Post-1965 Immigrants to the United States: A Revised Approach" (unpublished paper, Department of Sociology, Harvard University, May 2005).

58. Gabriel A. Almond, R. Scott Appleby, and Emmanuel Sivan, *Strong Religion: The Rise of Fundamentalisms around the World* (Chicago: University of Chicago Press, 2003); note especially these authors' observation: "Are separatist fundamentalists really acting in relation to the outside world? Indeed, they are. The separatism of the enclave is an important mode of fundamentalism, and it is also a form of fundamentalist interaction with the outside world" (146). For a useful discussion of U.S. Christian fundamentalists' reactions to globalization, see Didi Herman, "Globalism's 'Siren Song': The United Nations and International Law in Christian Right Thought and Prophecy," *Sociological Review* 77 (2001): 56–77.

59. Christian Broda and David Weinstein, "Globalization: The Gains from Variety," *Federal Reserve Bank of New York Staff Report*, no. 180 (March 2004). The number of goods increased from 7,731 in 1972 to 16,390 in 2001 and the average number of exporting countries doubled from six to twelve. Thus, the fourfold increase in product variety was obtained by multiplying the two to obtain a sum of "country-good pairs." Broda and Weinstein build on the work of Paul R. Krugman, "Increasing Returns, Monopolistic Competition, and International Trade," *Journal of International Economics* 9 (1979): 469–79, and Paul R. Krugman, "Scale Economies, Product Differentiation, and the Pattern of Trade," *American Economic Review* 70 (1980): 950–59.

60. Eric Schossler, *Fast Food Nation* (New York: Houghton Mifflin, 2001), 47.

61. Craig J. Thompson and Zeynep Arsel, "The Starbucks Brandscape and Consumers' Anticorporate Experiences of Glocalization," *Journal of Consumer Research* 31 (2004): 631–42. The tendency for alternative coffee shops to locate in the vicinity of Starbucks may be one reason for the peculiar practice in some cities of Starbucks opening shops within a few hundred yards of another Starbucks.

62. Nneka Ijeoma Nwosu, "A Study of McDonald's Restaurants and Globalization" (senior thesis, Department of Sociology, Princeton University, 2005).

63. Christian Parker Gumucio, "Religion and the Awakening of Indigenous People in Latin America," *Social Compass* 49 (2002): 67–81. On the relationship of globalization to Catholicism and Pentecostalism in Chile, see Arturo Fontaine Talavera, "Trends toward Globalization in Chile," in *Many Globalizations: Cultural Diversity in the Contemporary World,* ed. Peter L. Berger and Samuel P. Huntington (New York: Oxford University Press, 2002), 250–95.

64. David Maxwell, "'Sacred History, Social History': Traditions and Texts in the Making of a Southern African Transnational Religious Movement," *Comparative Studies in Society and History* 43 (2001): 502–24; see also Norman Etherington, "Recent Trends in the Historiography of Southern Africa," *Journal of Southern African Studies* 22 (1996): 201–19.

65. Patricia A. Thornton, "The New Cybersects: Resistance and Repression in the Reform Era," in *Chinese Society: Change, Conflict and Resistance,* 2nd ed., ed. Elizabeth Perry and Mark Selden (New York: Routledge, 2004), 247–70; see also Patricia A. Thornton, "Unofficial Religions in China: Beyond the Party's Rules" (presentation at the Congressional-Executive Commission on China, May 23, 2005), online at www.cecc.gov.

66. This interpretation is emphasized in Andrew B. Kipnis, "The Flourishing of Religion in Post-Mao China and the Anthropological Category of Religion," *Australian Journal of Anthropology* 12 (2001): 32–46, who grounds his argument in larger debates about the constructed character of "religion." An alternative interpretation that emphasizes the Chinese authorities' over-response but attributes it to internal weakness is presented in Elizabeth J. Perry, "Challenging the Mandate of Heaven: Popular Protest in Modern China," *Critical Asian Studies* 33 (2001): 163–80. United States Congress, Congressional-Executive Commission on China, *Annual Report* (Washington, D.C.: Government Printing Office, 2004), online at www.cecc.gov, includes thirty-six references to Falun Gong, which it describes as a "spiritual group" but uses as the primary and most specific example of China's intolerance of religious "cults."

67. Roland Robertson, *Globalization: Social Theory and Global Culture* (Thousand Oaks, Calif.: Sage, 1992), 173–74. See also Roland Robertson, "Glocalization: Time-Space and Homogeneity-Heterogeneity," in *Global Modernities,* ed. Mike Featherstone, Scott Lash, and Roland Robertson (Thousand Oaks, Calif.: Sage, 1995), 25–44.

68. Ulf Hannerz, *Transnational Connections: Culture, People, Places* (New York: Routledge, 1996), 55; see also pp. 56–64, in which Hannerz examines arguments about the threat of homogenization and concludes that "the prognosis for cultural diversity is not that bad" (64).

69. Peter Worsley, *The Trumpet Shall Sound: A Study of Cargo Cults in Melanesia* (London: MacGibbon and Kee, 1957); Peter Lawrence, *Road Belong Cargo: A Study of the Cargo Movement in the Southern Mdang District, New Guinea* (Manchester, U.K.: Manchester University Press, 1964).

70. Birgit Meyer, "Christianity in Africa."

71. Arjun Appadurai, *Modernity at Large: Cultural Dimensions of Globalization* (Minneapolis: University of Minnesota Press, 1996), 42.

72. Jason Kindopp, "Fragmented yet Defiant: Protestant Resilience under Chinese Communist Party Rule," in *God and Caesar in China: Policy Implica-*

tions of *Church-State Tensions,* ed. Jason Kindopp and Carol Lee Hamrin (Washington, D.C.: Brookings Institution Press, 2004), 122–48; quotation is on p. 137. Additional examples are given in Carol Lee Hamrin, "Faith-Based Organizations: Invisible Partners in Developing Chinese Society" (presentation at the Congressional-Executive Commission on China, May 15, 2003), online at www.cecc.gov. On the interaction of globalization, Christianity, and local diversity in China, see especially Miwa Hirono, "Framing Interaction: Transnational Religious Actors and Ethnic Communities in China" (unpublished paper, Department of International Relations, Australian National University, 2005); Daniel H. Bays, "Chinese Protestant Christianity Today," *China Quarterly* 174 (2003): 488–504; and Ben Hillman, "The Rise of the Community in Rural China: Village Politics, Cultural Identity and Religious Revival in a Hui Hamlet," *China Journal* 51 (2004): 53–73. Benjamin C. Ostrov, "Something of Value: The Religious Response to De-Maoization in China," *Social Science Journal* 42 (2005): 55–70, offers a more subjective interpretation of recent Chinese religious developments but includes a useful literature review.

73. Bernice Martin, "From Pre- to Postmodernity in Latin America: The Case of Pentecostalism," in *Religion, Modernity and Postmodernity,* ed. Paul Heelas (Oxford: Blackwell, 1998), 102–46.

74. Paul Gifford, *Ghana's New Christianity: Pentecostalism in a Globalizing African Economy* (Bloomington: Indiana University Press, 2004), 35. Highlife was also influenced by British military marching music, Western harmony, and American jazz. For a broader discussion of the perhaps ironic ways in which "world music" is regarded as distinctly local and ethnic yet acquires this distinction only through global marketing, see John Connell and Chris Gibson, "World Music: Deterritorializing Place and Identity," *Progress in Human Geography* 28 (2004): 342–61.

75. "Music Record Industry: Sales Stats 1998," online at www.soc.duke.edu.

76. "Holy Hip Hop Radio," *New World Music Newsletter,* September 8, 2003; online at www.live365.com.

77. Dollar, "Globalization, Inequality, and Poverty since 1980," 2.

78. Ibid., 34.

79. Steger, *Globalization,* 105. The few studies by sociologists also suggest mixed relationships between globalization and inequality; for instance, see the literature reviewed in Glenn Firebaugh, "Empirics of World Income Inequality," *American Journal of Sociology* 104 (1999): 1597–1630, and Brian Goesling, "Changing Income Inequalities within and between Nations: New Evidence," *American Sociological Review* 66 (2001): 745–61. Also relevant is Roberto Patricio Korzeniewicz and Timothy Patrick Moran, "World-Economic Trends in the Distribution of Incomes, 1965–1992," *American Journal of Sociology* 102 (1997): 1000–1039.

80. Dollar, "Globalization, Inequality, and Poverty since 1980," 38.

81. World Bank, *World Development Report 2004,* online at wdsbeta.world bank.org.

82. For an especially useful methodological critique, see Martin Ravallion, "The Debate on Globalization, Poverty and Inequality: Why Measurement Matters," World Bank Policy Research Working Paper 3038 (April 2003), online at

www.econ.klte.hu. Another critique is Angus Deaton, "Is World Poverty Falling?" *Finance and Development* 39 (2002), online at www.imf.org. The view that globalization benefits everyone is presented in Jagdish Bhagwati, *In Defense of Globalization* (New York: Oxford University Press, 2004), but is longer on argument than evidence.

83. Xin Zhigang, "Dissecting China's 'Middle Class,'" *China Daily*, October 27, 2004, online at www2.chinadaily.com.cn. The national figures are from research conducted by the Chinese Academy of Social Sciences, while the urban figures are from China's National Bureau of Statistics. Dorothy Solinger, "Globalization and the Paradox of Participation: The Chinese Case," *Global Governance* 7 (2001): 173–96, provides a critical discussion of Chinese economic data and emphasizes China's policy of "selective globalization." The "managed" character of Chinese globalization is featured in Michael Webber, Mark Wang, and Zhu Ying, eds., *China's Transition to a Global Economy* (New York: Palgrave, 2002). See also Azizur Rahman Khan and Carl Riskin, *Inequality and Poverty in China in the Age of Globalization* (New York: Oxford University Press, 2001), who observe that China's leaders recognized that trade liberalization would likely increase domestic inequality, which it did, and that poverty reduction occurred more significantly prior to globalization in the 1980s than it did in the early 1990s (their research does not include data from the late 1990s). Further information on China's economic policies is presented in Ding Lu, "Industrial Policy and Resource Allocation: Implications of China's Participation in Globalization," *China Economic Review* 11 (2000): 342–60.

84. Gurcharan Das, "The Respect They Deserve," *Time Asia*, December 6, 2004, online at www.time.com; Dollar, "Globalization, Poverty, and Inequality," 106. However, Raghbendra Jha, "Reducing Poverty and Inequality in India: Has Liberalization Helped?" World Institute for Development Economics Research Working Papers, no. 204 (2000), observes "a sharp rise in rural and, particularly, urban inequality and only a marginal decline in poverty."

85. Dollar, "Globalization, Poverty, and Inequality," 106, 121.

86. World Bank, *Pro-Poor Growth in the 1990s: Lessons and Insights from 14 Countries* (2005), 83, online at www.worldbank.org.

87. Quoted from Bishop Saah of Action Faith Ministries on March 10, 2005, in J. Kwabena Asamoah-Gyadu, "Reshaping Sub-Saharan African Christianity" (unpublished paper, Trinity Theological Seminary, Legon, Ghana, 2005).

88. Gifford, *Ghana's New Christianity*, 80–82. Meyer, "Christianity in Africa," 459, writes of these churches: "Building huge churches to accommodate thousands of believers, making use of elaborate technology to organize mass-scale sermons and appearances on TV and radio, organizing spectacular crusades throughout the country—often parading foreign speakers—so as to convert nominal Christians . . . all create an image of successful mastery of the modern world." See also Paul Gifford, "Persistence and Change in Contemporary African Religion," *Social Compass* 51 (2004): 169–76. Gifford provides examples from Nigeria as well, such as the Winners' Chapel, founded in Lagos in 1983 and with four hundred branches nationwide by 2000, including an auditorium seating 50,400. One of the more useful discussions of the relationship between Pentecostalism and economic practices involving asceticism and consumerism is Bernice

Martin, "New Mutations of the Protestant Ethic among Latin American Pentecostals," *Religion* 25 (1995): 101–17.

89. De Witte, "Altar Media's *Living Word*," quotations on pp. 177 and 190; of the U.S. influence, De Witte writes that "much of the broadcasting format derives from American televangelism" (186). The corporation that underwrites the International Central Gospel Church's television ministry is Kingdom Transport Services, which in 1999 received a $1.07 million loan from the Blue Bird Corporation of Macon, Georgia, with assistance from the Export-Import Bank of the United States (www.exim.gov). Additional information about the church is presented in Asamoah-Gyadu, "Reshaping Sub-Saharan African Christianity," and Gifford, *Ghana's New Christianity*, 113–39 (other chapters of which describe Pentecostal churches that attract lower-income groups). Birgit Meyer, " 'Delivered from the Powers of Darkness': Confessions of Satanic Riches in Christian Ghana," *Africa* 65 (1995): 236–55, includes examples from Accra that demonstrate the incorporation and transformation of traditional concerns about evil, witches, and demon possession into Pentecostal discourse. Other helpful studies of the relationships between market expansion and Pentecostalism in Africa include David Maxwell, "The Durawall of Faith: Pentecostal Spirituality in Neo-Liberal Zimbabwe," *Journal of Religion in Africa* 35 (2005): 4–32; David Maxwell, " 'Delivered from the Spirit of Poverty?': Pentecostalism, Prosperity and Modernity in Zimbabwe," *Journal of Religion in Africa* 28 (1998): 350–73; and Rijk A. Van Dijk, "From Camp to Encompassment: Discourses of Transsubjectivity in the Ghanaian Pentecostal Diaspora," *Journal of Religion in Africa* 27 (1997): 135–59.

90. Chen Cunfu and Huang Tianhai, "The Emergence of a New Type of Christians in China Today," *Review of Religious Research* 46 (2004): 183–200; the term "boss Christians," these writers explain, derives from the term *laoban*, which "in Chinese has attained new connotations and has begun to be used all over the country to refer extensively to anyone who owns or has a position in a business of whatever scale" (190). The authors note that boss Christians have a "heartfelt dislike" of the government's official associations for Protestants and Catholics but are "pragmatic" (197). Additional discussion of the effects of globalization on churches in China is included in Jacqueline E. Wenger, "Official vs. Underground Protestant Churches in China: Challenges for Reconciliation and Social Influence," *Review of Religious Research* 46 (2004): 169–82.

91. These examples are discussed in R. Drew Smith, "American Evangelists and Church-State Dilemmas in Multiple African Contexts," in *Freedom's Distant Shores: American Protestants and Post-Colonial Alliances with Africa*, ed. R. Drew Smith (Waco, Tex.: Baylor University Press, 2006), chap. 7. I am grateful to Professor Smith for bringing this information to my attention.

92. Amy Reynolds, "Faith-Based Networks and the Central American Coffee Business" (unpublished paper, Princeton University Center for the Study of Religion, June 2005).

93. Enterprise Development International, *2005 Annual Report*, online at www.endpoverty.org, and interview with executive director Ken Wesche, December 2, 2005. Enterprise Development International's contribution is primarily technical assistance and seed grants, all of which totaled approximately

$944,546 in 2005. It is also worth noting that international trade and mutual membership in Christian organizations may reinforce each other. To my knowledge, no statistical evidence provides a basis from which to infer, for instance, that corporations in the United States prefer to trade with predominantly Christian countries or with Christian groups within countries. However, research does show that other kinds of cultural affinities are conducive to international trade. Language similarity is one and warmth of feelings toward another country, as measured in opinion polls, is another. The latter is especially relevant because research also shows that religious and ethnic similarities are among the most important factors influencing warmth of feelings; see Marcus Noland, "Affinity and International Trade," Institute for International Economics Working Paper, no. WP 05–3 (June 2005), quotations are from pp. 109, 122.

    94. World Bank, *Pro-Poor Growth in the 1990s,* 83.

    95. Xin, "Dissecting China's 'Middle Class.'"

    96. Fauzia Erfan Ahmed, "The Rise of the Bangladesh Garment Industry: Globalization, Women Workers, and Voice," *NWSA Journal* 16 (2004): 34–45; Lourdes Beneria, "Shifting the Risk: New Employment Patterns, Informalization and Women's Work," *International Journal of Politics, Culture and Society* 15 (2001): 27–53; Sandra E. Black and Elizabeth Brainerd, "Importing Equality? The Impact of Globalization on Gender Discrimination," *Industrial and Labor Relations Review* 57 (2004): 540–59; Jean L. Pyle, "Sex, Maids, and Export Processing: Risks and Reasons for Gendered Global Production Networks," *International Journal of Politics, Culture and Society* 15 (2001): 55–75.

    97. Giovanni Arrighi, Beverly J. Silver, and Benjamin D. Brewer, "Industrial Convergence, Globalization, and the Persistence of the North-South Divide," *Studies in Comparative Development* 38 (2003): 3–31. On local variations in the effects of globalization among African countries, a good source is Wim van Binsbergen and Rijk van Dijk, eds., *Situating Globality: African Agency in the Appropriation of Global Culture* (Boston: Brill, 2004). An excellent general source is Nancy Birdsall, "A Stormy Day on an Open Field: Asymmetry and Convergence in the Global Economy," *RBA Annual Conference Volume* (Sidney: Reserve Bank of Australia, 2002), online at www.rba.gov.au. Birdsall emphasizes that open markets are better for countries with ample than meager resources and shows that developing countries heavily dependent on commodity exports (nonmanufactured goods such as minerals and agricultural produce) did not benefit from trade liberalization; she also reviews evidence on the negative effects of market volatility and of the disadvantages experienced by unskilled workers. See also Nancy Birdsall and A. Hamoudi, "Commodity Dependence, Trade, and Growth: When 'Openness' Is Not Enough," Center for Global Development Working Paper No. 7, online at www.cgdev.org.

    98. Patrick Johnstone and Jason Mandryk's *Operation World* (Carlisle, U.K.: Paternoster, 2001), 510, reports 2,221 missionaries in Papua New Guinea, 1,228 from the United States. A resident of Port Moresby told a journalist in 1992 that "a lot of missionaries are rushing here, telling our people that Jesus will be here very soon, so you've got to be ready. They say if you don't believe in our God you will go to hell" (James Heer, "Papua New Guinea Up to Their Necks in Missionaries," *Toronto Globe and Mail,* June 6, 1992). The U.S. State

Department indicates that about 1 percent of the Papua New Guinea population is foreign, "most of whom are missionaries" (www.state.gov).

99. Eric Hirsch, "New Boundaries of Influence in Highland Papua: 'Culture,' Mining and Ritual Conversions," *Oceania* (June 2001), online at www.findarticles.com.

100. Betel nut is exported widely to East and South Asia, where it is chewed as a mildly euphoric stimulant.

101. Margaret Mase, "Development, Life-Modes and Language in Papua New Guinea," *Development Bulletin* 50 (October 1999): 67–69.

102. Hirsch, "New Boundaries"; Eric Hirsch, "Between Mission and Market: Events and Images in a Melanesian Society," *Man*, n.s., 29, 3 (1994): 689–711.

103. The Urapmin are a group of approximately 375 people living in the highlands of the West Sepik Province of Papua New Guinea.

104. Joel Robbins, "When Do You Think the World Will End? Globalization, Apocalypticism, and the Moral Perils of Fieldwork in 'Last New Guinea,' " *Anthropology and Humanism* 22, 1 (1997): 6–30; quotation is on p. 6; Joel Robbins, "On Reading 'World News': Apocalyptic Narrative, Negative Nationalism, and Transnational Christianity in a Papua New Guinea Society," *Social Analysis* 42, 2 (1998): 103–30; Joel Robbins, "Becoming Sinners: Christianity and Desire among the Urapmin of Papua New Guinea," *Ethnology* 37, 4 (1998): 299–316; Joel Robbins, "Secrecy and the Sense of an Ending: Narrative, Time, and Everyday Millenarianism in Papua New Guinea and in Christian Fundamentalism," *Comparative Studies in Society and History* 43, 3 (2001): 525–51; and Joel Robbins, *Becoming Sinners: Christianity and Moral Torment in a Papua New Guinea Society* (Berkeley and Los Angeles: University of California Press, 2004).

105. R. Andrew Chesnut, *Born Again in Brazil: The Pentecostal Boom and the Pathogens of Poverty* (New Brunswick, N.J.: Rutgers University Press, 1997); R. Andrew Chesnut, "Pragmatic Consumers and Practical Products: The Success of Pneumacentric Religion among Women in Latin America's New Religious Economy," *Review of Religious Research* 45 (2003): 20–31; see also Lieve Troch, "Ecclesiogenesis: The Patchwork of New Religious Communities in Brazil," *Exchange* 33 (2004): 54–72, who contrasts the Pentecostalism Chesnut observed with another style of Pentecostalism more common among the upwardly mobile in southern Brazil. Writing about Brazil more generally, Patricia Birman and Marcia Pereira Leite, "Whatever Happened to What Used to Be the Largest Catholic Country in the World?" *Daedalus* 129 (2000): 271–90, suggest that Pentecostalism attracted followers by associating worldly tribulations with the Devil and offering moral guidelines for overcoming adversity. Eric W. Kramer, "Spectacle and the Staging of Power in Brazilian Neo-Pentecostalism," *Latin American Perspectives* 32, 1 (2005): 95–120, offers a nice example of local traditions of exorcism being turned into a "transnational space" (96) through the use of broadcast media. Other studies of Central and South America that emphasize the relationships between social dislocation and developments in Christianity include Andre Corten, "Transnational Religious Needs and Political Delegitimisation in Latin America," in Corten and Marshall-Fratani, *Between Babel*

and Pentecost, 106–23; and Laennec Hurbon, "Pentecostalism and Transnationalisation in the Caribbean," in Corten and Marshall-Fratani, *Between Babel and Pentecost,* 124–41.

106. Birgit Meyer, "Commodities and the Power of Prayer: Pentecostalist Attitudes towards Consumption in Contemporary Ghana," *Development and Change* 29 (1998): 751–76. In "Delivered from the Powers of Darkness," Meyer writes: "The Ghanaian stories of satanic riches are part of a popular culture which might be referred to as a 'culture of poverty' in the sense that lack of money informs all human relations and forms of cultural expression. Those who tell them find themselves in a different economic situation and in family circumstances which generate dreams of 'big money.' The wealth that is denounced in the story of the satanic riches is at the same time people's great desire" (250). See also Birgit Meyer, *Translating the Devil: Religion and Modernity among the Ewe in Ghana* (Edinburgh: Edinburgh University Press, 1999).

107. Joseph Kahn, "Violence Taints Religion's Solace for China's Poor," *New York Times,* November 25, 2004; Matthew Forney, "Jesus Is Back, and She's Chinese," *Time Asia,* November 5, 2001, online at www.time.com. For a study of a different example, see Kenneth Dean, *Lord of the Three in One: The Spread of a Cult in Southeast China* (Princeton, N.J.: Princeton University Press, 1998).

108. Birdsall, "A Stormy Day," 82.

109. Whether people do in fact think of themselves as world citizens appears to be a relatively weak test of globalization; for instance, in surveys that asked which geographic entity people identified with first, an average of 8 percent of those polled in more than fifty countries said "the world," compared with 26 percent who said their nation and 55 percent who said their locality or town; Marlies Glasius, Mary Kaldor, and Helmut Anheier, eds., *Global Civil Society 2002* (Oxford: Oxford University Press, 2002), 353.

110. Brief accounts of previous "waves" of long-distance trade and migration are common in general introductions to globalization; see for example Steger, *Globalization,* 17–34, and Robertson, *Globalization,* 58–60. World system theory provides a more detailed historical account; see Immanuel Wallerstein, *The Modern World System* (New York: Academic Press, 1974), and Immanuel Wallerstein, *Geopolitics and Geoculture* (Cambridge: Cambridge University Press, 1991). The standard story about Bretton Woods and the formation of the International Monetary Fund and the World Bank can be found in numerous publications, including Eckes and Zeiler, *Globalization and the American Century.* From an anthropological perspective a good cautionary note is provided by Ulf Hannerz, *Cultural Complexity: Studies in the Social Organization of Meaning* (New York: Columbia University Press, 1992), 242, who writes: "The onslaught of transnational influences, as often described or hinted at, seems rather too sudden. In West Africa, such influences have been filtering into the coastal societies for centuries. . . . There has been time to absorb the foreign influence, to modify the modifications in turn, and to fit shifting cultural forms to developing social structures."

111. Thomas L. Friedman, *The World Is Flat: A Brief History of the Twenty-First Century* (New York: Farrar, Straus, and Giroux, 2005).

112. Young-Gi Hong, "Progress and Pitfalls: Globalization and the Korean Church" (paper presented at the International Association for Mission Studies Conference, Port Dickson, Malaysia, 2004), provides a valuable critique of the extent to which churches in Korea have been influenced by McDonaldization.

113. Cadge, "The De Facto Congregationalism of Post-1965 Immigrants."

114. Mauro F. Guillen, *The Limits of Convergence: Globalization and Organization Change in Argentina, South Korea, and Spain* (Princeton, N.J.: Princeton University Press, 2001). A study of organizational change in liberal arts colleges also casts doubt on the homogenization argument; see Matthew S. Kraatz and Edward J. Zajac, "Exploring the Limits of the New Institutionalism: The Causes and Consequences of Illegitimate Organizational Change," *American Sociological Review* 61 (1996): 812–36.

115. For a useful elaboration of this point, see Brian Howell, "Practical Belief and the Localization of Christianity: Pentecostal and Denominational Christianity in Global/Local Perspective," *Religion* 33 (2003): 233–48, who examines Baptists in the Philippines and Pentecostals in Jamaica and concludes that "interpretations must face the problem of an empirical reality in which both processes—of hegemony from afar and local relevance—are present and efficacious in the minds and lives of non-Western Christians" (246). Drawing on research in Cuba, Ana Celia Perera Pintado, "Religion and Cuban Identity in a Transnational Context," *Latin American Perspectives* 32, 1 (2005): 147–73, observes similarly that "the proliferation and relocalization of what were, until recently, strictly regional religious expressions, generate global connections where earlier there were none and introduce heterogeneity at the national level" (148).

116. See the influential discussion of Africa's awareness of and responses to globalized marginalization in Jean-Francois Bayart, "Africa in the World: A History of Extraversion," *African Affairs* 99 (2000): 217–67, and for an application to religion, Harri Englund, "Christian Independency and Global Membership: Pentecostal Extraversions in Malawi," *Journal of Religion in Africa* 33 (2003): 83–111.

117. Graddol, *The Future of English?*

118. Martin, "From Pre- to Postmodernity in Latin America," 126.

4. THE EVOLUTION OF TRANSNATIONAL TIES

1. William Carey, *An Enquiry into the Obligations of Christians to Use Means for the Conversion of the Heathens* (Leicester, U.K.: Ann Ireland, 1792), 67.

2. Henry Howe, *Adventures and Achievements of Americans* (New York: Geo. F. Tuttle, 1859), 511–20.

3. John K. Fairbank, "Introduction: The Many Faces of Protestant Missions in China and the United States," in *The Missionary Enterprise in China and America*, ed. John K. Fairbank (Cambridge, Mass.: Harvard University Press, 1974), 8.

4. Alexis de Tocqueville, *Democracy in America*, vol. 2 (New York: Vintage Books, 1945), 114.

5. "Benevolent Institutions," *American Almanac* (Boston: Gray and Bowen, 1836), 154; in addition to the sixty-three overseas mission stations, the Amer-

ican Board of Commissioners for Foreign Missions also sponsored thirty-two stations among Native Americans.

6. Ibid.

7. Sidney Ahlstrom, *A Religious History of the American People* (New Haven: Yale University Press, 1972), 423; although 1806 is the date typically cited for the so-called Haystack meeting at Williams College, some historians prefer 1808.

8. Joseph Tracy, *History of the American Board of Commissioners for Foreign Missions* (New York: M. W. Dodd, 1842), 32.

9. *Historical Statistics of the United States,* online at www.lib.umich.edu/govdocs/historiccpi.html; with 1967 as a base year equaling 100, the consumer price index for 1810 was 47 and for 2005, 565, or approximately twelve times higher.

10. These estimates are from unpublished histories of local congregations.

11. Rufus Anderson, *Memorial Volume of the First Fifty Years of the American Board of Commissioners for Foreign Missions* (Boston: American Board of Commissioners for Foreign Missions, 1861), 58–59.

12. *Connecticut Evangelical Magazine and Religious Intelligencer,* February 1810, 5.

13. Carey, *Enquiry,* 84.

14. Nathan O. Hatch, *The Democratization of American Christianity* (New Haven: Yale University Press, 1989), 25, observes that the number of newspapers grew from 90 to 370 between 1790 and 1810.

15. Charles A. Maxfield III, "The 'Reflex Influence' of Missions: The Domestic Operations of the American Board of Commissioners for Foreign Missions, 1810–1850" (Ph.D. diss., Union Theological Seminary, Richmond, Virginia, 1995), 8; Maxfield has not only provided a riveting account of Harriet Atwood Newell's heartbreaking story but also assembled an enormous volume of detail about the origins of the ABCFM, from which I have benefited greatly. The story of Harriet Atwood Newell is also recounted in Dana L. Robert, "The Influence of American Missionary Women on the World Back Home," *Religion and American Culture* 12 (2002): 59–89.

16. Theda Skocpol, "How Americans Became Civic," in *Civic Engagement in American Democracy,* ed. Theda Skocpol and Morris P. Fiorina (Washington and New York: Brookings Institution and Russell Sage Foundation, 1999), 27–80; quotation is on p. 47; see also Theda Skocpol, Marshall Ganz, and Ziad Munson, "A Nation of Organizers: The Institutional Origins of Civic Voluntarism in the United States," *American Political Science Review* 94 (2000): 527–46.

17. Quoted in James H. Hutson, *The Founders on Religion: A Book of Quotations* (Princeton, N.J.: Princeton University Press, 2005), 143–45.

18. From an unnamed critic quoted by Jeremiah Evarts in an 1813 address; quoted in ibid., 16; see also Anderson, *Memorial Volume,* 73–76.

19. Richard D. Brown, "The Emergence of Voluntary Associations in Massachusetts, 1700–1730," *Journal of Voluntary Action Research* 2 (1973): 64–73.

20. Carey, *Enquiry,* 84; emphasis in original.

21. From an 1826 sermon preached by Beriah Green; quoted in Maxwell, "The 'Reflex Influence' of Missions," 23; emphasis added.

22. Ibid., 80.

23. Samuel J. Baird, *History of the New School* (Philadelphia: Claxton, Remsen and Haffelfinger, 1868), chap. 19; online at www.americanpresbyterianchurch.org. Some of the acrimony toward the ABCFM is evident in Baird's concluding observation about its relationship with the Presbyterian General Assembly: "Thus, with paeans, was celebrated the finishing stroke of a policy, which, for a time, stripped the Presbyterian Church of every mission, which, with prayer and toil, she had established among the heathen; and transferred their control to a body over which the Church of God has not the slightest official authority."

24. John Clark Marshman, *The Life and Times of Carey, Marshman, and Ward: Embracing the History of the Serampore Mission,* vol. 1 (London: Longman, 1859), 22–43.

25. Similarities between the ABCFM command structure and that of the military should not be overdrawn, but ABCFM leaders were well aware of Napoleon's ventures and sometimes likened their own to an army campaign; see Clifton Jackson Phillips, *Protestant America and the Pagan World: The First Half Century of the American Board of Commissioners for Foreign Missions, 1810–1860* (Cambridge, Mass.: Harvard University Press, 1969), 266–68.

26. Michael P. Young, *Bearing Witness against Sin: The Evangelical Birth of the American Social Movement* (Chicago: University of Chicago Press, 2006); see also Michael P. Young, "Confessional Protest: The Religious Birth of U.S. National Social Movements," *American Sociological Review* 67 (2002): 660–88.

27. "Benevolent Institutions," *American Almanac.*

28. Edwin Scott Gaustad and Philip L. Barlow, *New Historical Atlas of Religion in America* (New York: Oxford University Press, 2001), 374.

29. Thomas Armitage, *A History of the Baptists: The American Baptists,* chap. 14; online at www.fbinstitute.com.

30. Kenneth Scott Latourette, *A History of the Expansion of Christianity,* vol. 4: *The Great Century in Europe and the United States of America, A.D. 1800—A.D. 1914* (New York: Harper & Brothers, 1941), 95.

31. Ben Primer, *Protestants and American Business Methods* (Ann Arbor, Mich.: UMI Research Press, 1978).

32. William R. Hutchison, *Errand to the World: American Protestant Thought and Foreign Missions* (Chicago: University of Chicago Press, 1987), 95.

33. Stephen Neill, *A History of Christian Missions,* rev. ed. (London: Penguin, 1986), 420.

34. Robert E. Sheridan, *The Founders of Maryknoll* (Maryknoll, N.Y.: The Catholic Foreign Mission Society of America, 1980).

35. Paul R. Rivera, " 'Field Found!' Establishing the Maryknoll Mission Enterprise in the United States and China, 1918–1928," *Catholic Historical Review* 84 (1998): 477–517.

36. James Eldin Reed, "American Foreign Policy, the Politics of Missions and Josiah Strong, 1890–1900," *Church History* 41 (1972): 230–45; quotation is on p. 232. This evidence of the continuing power of Congregationalism is especially

important to recognize in view of recently popular arguments in some quarters about the so-called vitality of upstart sects that focus solely on membership statistics.

37. Hudson Taylor Armerding, "The China Inland Mission and Some Aspects of Its Work" (Ph.D. diss., University of Chicago, 1948), 6–9.

38. Andrew F. Walls, "The American Dimension in the History of the Missionary Movement," in *Earthen Vessels: American Evangelicals and Foreign Missions, 1880–1980,* ed. Joel A. Carpenter and Wilbert R. Shenk (Grand Rapids, Mich.: Eerdmans, 1990), 1–25.

39. John Errett Lankford, "Protestant Stewardship and Benevolence, 1900–1941: A Study in Religious Philanthropy" (Ph.D. diss., University of Wisconsin, 1962).

40. Merle Curti, Judith Green, and Roderick Nash, "Anatomy of Giving: Millionaires in the Late 19th Century," *American Quarterly* 15 (1963): 416–35; quotation is on p. 424.

41. Dana Lee Robert, *Occupy until I Come: A. T. Pierson and the Evangelization of the World* (Grand Rapids, Mich.: Eerdmans, 2003), 130–32.

42. Bruce J. Evensen, *God's Man for the Gilded Age: D. L. Moody and the Rise of Modern Mass Evangelism* (New York: Oxford University Press, 2003).

43. Robert P. Wilder, *The Student Volunteer Movement: Its Origins and Early History* (New York: Student Volunteer Movement, 1935).

44. David M. Howard, *Student Power in World Missions* (Downers Grove, Ill.: InterVarsity Press, 1970).

45. Virginia Lieson Brereton, *Training God's Army: The American Bible School, 1880–1940* (Indianapolis: Indiana University Press, 1990).

46. Heui Yeol Ahn, "The Influence of the Niagara Bible Conference and Adoniram Judson Gordon on Malcolm Fenwick and Korean Baptist Missions" (Ph.D. diss., Southwestern Baptist Theological Seminary, 2002).

47. On the role of Bible-institute training among 1929 recruits for the China Inland Mission, see Joel A. Carpenter, "Propagating the Faith Once Delivered: The Fundamentalist Missionary Enterprise, 1920–1945," in his *Earthen Vessels,* 92–132.

48. Hutchison, *Errand to the World,* 101; see also Latourette, *History of the Expansion of Christianity,* 98.

49. Joel A. Carpenter, "Appendix: The Evangelical Missionary Force in the 1930s," in his *Earthen Vessels,* 335–42.

50. Pei-heng Chiang, *Non-Governmental Organizations at the United Nations: Identity, Role, and Function* (New York: Praeger, 1981); Peter Willetts, ed., *'The Conscience of the World': The Influence of Non-Governmental Organizations in the UN System* (Washington, D.C.: Brookings Institution, 1996).

51. Kathleen D. McCarthy, *American Creed: Philanthropy and the Rise of Civil Society, 1700–1865* (Chicago: University of Chicago Press, 2003), 126–32. One example was the Brainerd Mission school near Chattanooga, which the ABCFM opened in 1817 and closed in 1838. A monument on the grounds notes that the mission received funding from the federal government.

52. Joel R. Wuthnow, "The U.S. Sanitary Commission in the Civil War" (unpublished paper, Department of History, Princeton University, 1999).

53. Foster Rhea Dulles, *The American Red Cross: A History* (New York: Harper and Brothers, 1950); Patrick F. Gilbo, *The American Red Cross: The First Century* (New York: Harper & Row, 1981).

54. John F. Hutchinson, "The Nagler Case: A Revealing Moment in Red Cross History," *Canadian Bulletin of Medical History* 9 (2004): 177–90.

55. David E. Hamilton, "Herbert Hoover and the Great Drought of 1930," *Journal of American History* 68 (1982): 850–75.

56. Peter Dobkin Hall, "A Historical Overview of Philanthropy, Voluntary Associations, and Nonprofit Organizations in the United States, 1600–2000," in *The Nonprofit Research Handbook,* 2nd ed., edited by Walter W. Powell and Richard Steinberg (New Haven: Yale University Press, 2006).

57. The earlier Adventist efforts led to the formation of Seventh-Day Adventist Welfare Service in 1956, which became Seventh-Day Adventist World Service in 1973, and Adventist Development and Relief Agency in 1983.

58. Although the American Red Cross and religious charities were exempt from direct supervision by the War Relief Control Board, longstanding concerns about the misappropriation of charitable funds dating from World War I encouraged religious leaders to cooperate voluntarily with board regulations.

59. Kenneth Hackett, "From the Heart of America: PVOs Celebrate 50 Years of PL-480" (address to the USDA VI Export Food Aid Conference, Kansas City, Missouri, April 20, 2004).

60. Eileen Egan, *Catholic Relief Services: The Beginning Years* (New York: Catholic Relief Services, 1988); Christopher J. Kauffman, "Politics, Programs, and Protests: Catholic Relief Services in Vietnam, 1954–1975," *Catholic Historical Review* 91 (2005): 223–50.

61. Jonathan Goldman, *The Empire State Building Book* (New York: St. Martin's Press, 1980), 64–66; see also the firsthand account of Gloria Pall, "The Day a B-25 Bomber Crashed into the Empire State Building," *Van Nuys Aviation and Business Journal,* July 2001, online at www.gloriapall.com.

62. Editorial Staff, "Catholic Relief Services," *America* 189 (September 1, 2003), online at www.americamagazine.org; Kenneth Hackett, "From the Heart of America," Catholic Relief Services, staff interview, October 25, 2005.

63. Lutheran Immigration and Refugee Service, staff interview, March 19, 2005; Lutheran World Relief, staff interview, April 8, 2005; United Methodist Committee on Relief, staff interview, April 21, 2005; Episcopal Migration Ministries, staff interview, July 26, 2005; Episcopal Relief and Development, staff interview, May 24, 2005; "World Relief Celebrates 60th Anniversary," *Evangelical News,* February 24, 2004.

64. Tim Stafford, "Imperfect Instrument," *Christianity Today,* February 24, 2005, online at www.christianitytoday.com.

65. Graeme Irvine, *Best Things in the Worst of Times: An Insider's View of World Vision* (Wilsonville, Calif.: Book Partners, 1996).

66. Alan Whaites, "Pursuing Partnership: World Vision and the Ideology of Development—a Case Study," *Development in Practice* 9 (1999): 410–23.

67. Bryant L. Myers, *Walking with the Poor: Principles and Practices of Transformational Development* (Maryknoll, N.Y.: Orbis Books, 1999). I want to thank my former student Neil Ahlsten for his discussion of this history in his

"A Critical Analysis of International Evangelical Christian Development NGOs" (unpublished paper, Woodrow Wilson School, Princeton University, May 2005).

68. Brian H. Smith, *More Than Altruism: The Politics of Private Foreign Aid* (Princeton, N.J.: Princeton University Press, 1990), 294–98; Smith reports 1981 figurês inflated to reflect 1986 dollars; I have deflated these adjusted figures to reflect actual 1981 expenditures. The figures for overseas aid do not include other expenditures, such as for U.S.-based staff or fundraising.

69. Ibid.

70. Ibid., 64.

71. International Mission Board, staff interview, May 5, 2005, and online information at www.imb.org.

72. Assemblies of God World Missions, staff interview, May 4, 2005.

73. Presbyterian Church (USA), Worldwide Ministries Division, staff interviews, April 15, 2005, May 17, 2005, and July 13, 2005; and www.pcusa.org/wmd.

74. William J. Nottingham, "Origin and Legacy of the Common Global Ministries Board" (Forrest H. Kirkpatrick Lecture, Disciples of Christ Historical Society, Nashville, Tennessee, September 23, 2005).

75. Common Global Ministries Board, staff interview, June 29, 2005.

76. A. Scott Moreau, "Putting the Survey in Perspective," in *Mission Handbook 2004–2006*, ed. Dotsey Welliver and Minnette Northcutt (Wheaton, Ill.: Billy Graham Center, 2004), 11–59.

77. Robert A. Blincoe, "The Strange Structure of Mission Agencies, Part III: Desired Symbiosis: Church and Mission Structures," *International Journal of Foreign Missions* 19 (Fall 2002): 43–46; for a listing of Association of Lutheran Mission Agencies, see www.alma-online.org.

78. Moreau, "Putting the Survey in Perspective."

79. Wendy Murray Zoba, "Bill Bright's Wonderful Plan for the World," *Christianity Today*, July 14, 1997, 14–27.

80. Financial information as reported to Ministrywatch.com.

81. Information from foundation grants database provided by Foundation Search, Inc.

82. Figures reported as of July 1, 2005, online at www.jesusfilm.org.

83. SIM, staff interview, September 6, 2005.

84. The figures reported are from IRS 990 forms and auditors' reports for 2003.

85. Government funding is as reported by USAID and in a few instances by Ministrywatch.com.

86. Samaritan's Purse, staff interview, December 1, 2005.

87. DeMoss Group Web site: www.demossgroup.com.

88. "CBN Ministry Report: An Overview," CBN (November 1990), online at www.publiceye.org.

89. Chris Slone, "Robertson Shakes Up Empire," *Christianity Today*, July 14, 1997, 60.

90. Operation Blessing, staff interview, December 16, 2005.

91. "TV Preacher Uses Ministry Assets for High Living," *Church and State* (November 2004): 19; William Lobdell, "Pastor's Empire Built on Acts of Faith

and Cash," *Los Angeles Times,* September 19, 2004; William Lobdell, "TBN's Promise: Send Money and See Riches," *Los Angeles Times,* September 20, 2004; Chris McConnell, "Trinity: Praying and Paying," *Broadcasting and Cable,* May 18, 1988, 24–30; Randy Frame, "TBN: Growth Has Bred Criticism," *Christianity Today,* October 8, 1990, 56–59.

92. Latourette, *A History of the Expansion of Christianity* ("great century" is from the book's subtitle).

5. THE GLOBAL ROLE OF CONGREGATIONS

1. Pew Research Center, February 15, 2005; survey results available on Public Opinion Online, a service of Lexis-Nexis.

2. These figures are from the various denominational Web sites and online newsletters; see especially www.imb.org, www.umc.org, www.elca.org, and www.usaid.gov.

3. Because members of large congregations have a statistically greater chance of being selected at random in a national survey of this kind, it is important to bear in mind that the percentages reported here refer to the proportion of church members whose congregations sponsor particular activities, not to the proportion of congregations that do. For instance, if responses are adjusted to give congregations of varying size equal weight, then the proportion of congregations that have special humanitarian offerings is 66 percent.

4. The examples from churches and quotes from church leaders in this chapter are from qualitative interviews conducted during 2005 and 2006; additional detail is provided in the appendix.

5. United Nations High Commissioner for Refugees, *2005 Global Refugee Trends* (Geneva: UNHCR Population and Geographical Data Section, 2005), online at www.unhcr.ch.

6. David B. Barrett and Todd M. Johnson, *World Christian Trends, A.D. 30–A.D. 2200: Interpreting the Annual Christian Megacensus* (Pasadena, Calif.: William Carey Library, 2001), 421.

7. Among evangelical Protestants in congregations of a hundred people or less, 72 percent say their congregation supports a missionary working abroad, compared with only 54 percent of mainline Protestants and 45 percent of Catholics in congregations of the same size.

8. This conjecture emerges from considering the fact that 54 percent of the members of historically black denominations say their congregation emphasizes supporting missionaries (i.e., in general) a lot, whereas only 41 percent say their congregation currently supports missionaries working outside the United States.

9. For instance, among those who said their congregation provides any support, 26, 26, and 34 percent of evangelical, mainline, and black Protestants, respectively, say this support went to a missionary organization, compared with 48 percent of Catholics.

10. An appropriate summary measure of statistical association for ordinal-level variables such as the ones under consideration is the gamma statistic, which varies between minus-one, plus-one. Gamma for the overall relationship between supporting a missionary and an offering for hunger or relief in the past year was

.311, and this figure ranged between .321 and .481 among the various religious traditions and from .307 to .418 for congregations of varying size above 150 members. Although popular interest in recent years has focused on evangelical churches becoming more engaged in humanitarian as well as in missionary efforts, the statistics here indicate that the strongest relationship between humanitarian and missionary efforts is among mainline Protestants (gamma = .481), followed by Catholics (gamma = .403), and then by evangelicals (gamma = .354) and black Protestant denominations (gamma = .321).

11. Allen D. Hertzke, *Freeing God's Children: The Unlikely Alliance for Global Human Rights* (Lanham, Md.: Rowman and Littlefield, 2004), 301–2.

12. Barrett and Johnson, *World Christian Trends*, 229.

13. These activities include having an offering for overseas hunger or relief, sponsoring a missionary, holding a meeting at which issues of war and peace were discussed, and hosting a guest speaker from another country.

14. Drawing further from these responses, the best numeric estimate is that about 29 percent of church members perceive their congregations to be clearly involved in transcultural ministries, about the same proportion (27 percent) think their congregations are relatively uninvolved, and the remainder (44 percent) fall in between. I derived these estimates by creating an index that gave respondents a score of 2 if they said their congregation emphasizes helping people in other countries a lot, a score of 2 if they said the same about emphasizing international ministries, a score of 1 for each of these items if they said their congregation emphasizes it some, and a score of 0 for responses indicating less emphasis. I then added the scores to form an index ranging from 0 (low) to 4 (high) and then collapsed the index so that a score of 4 was considered "high," scores of 2 or 3 were "medium," and scores of 0 or 1 were "low."

15. The conclusions in this paragraph are supported by multiple regression analyses in which the three-category index of transcultural involvement is the dependent variable; congregation size, religious tradition, and respondent's frequency of church attendance are included as control variables; and the independent variables tested (in separate models) include (with their respective standardized regression coefficients) these activities: having a hunger and relief offering (.196), having such an offering at least monthly (.168), helping refugees (.137), sponsoring a missionary (.281), having a meeting about war and peace (.078), hosting a missionary speaker (.220), having a staff member responsible for overseas outreach (.124), and having a missions committee (.286). In short, sponsoring a missionary, hosting a missionary speaker, and having a missions committee have the strongest impact on whether members perceive their congregation as emphasizing international ministries. Sponsoring short-term mission trips (considered elsewhere) also had a significant impact (.296).

16. More specifically, 39 percent of the church members surveyed said their congregation had a committee that focuses on overseas missions or other international programs.

17. John Ridley is a pseudonym. To guard the confidentiality of the real interviewee, I have also altered the location and a few other identifying details; the same is true of the other interviewees described in this chapter.

18. In interviews conducted for this book, we found farmers and other members of rural or small town churches in the Midwest, for example, who, because of the seasonal nature of their work, had gone on short-term mission trips to other countries in the 1960s to help with agricultural projects.

19. One of the more valuable overviews of the history and recent literature about short-term missions is C. M. Brown, "Field Statement on the Short-Term Mission Phenomenon: Contributing Factors and Current Debate" (unpublished paper, Trinity International University, June 9, 2005), online at www.tiu.edu/tedsphd/ics_research.

20. Dale Buss, "Taste: Houses of Worship," *Wall Street Journal,* December 4, 2003, 19. Short-term missions among Catholic laity also appear to have grown during the 1980s and 1990s but on a smaller scale; see Joseph Berger, "Spreading Their Faith Wherever It Leads," *New York Times,* January 4, 1996.

21. These figures are from the Global Issues Survey and are responses to questions that asked active churchgoers if they had participated in a high school church group when they were younger; if they had, whether they had gone on a short-term mission trip; and if so, whether it had been in the United States or another country. The responses of course are not exact indicators of trends. They are subject to bias from faulty recall and from attrition (i.e., people who may have been in youth groups and gone on mission trips but who are no longer active church members).

22. "Freed Aid Workers Say Faith Gave Them Strength," *CNN,* November 16, 2001, online at archives.cnn.com/2001/World.

23. Ted Olsen, "Pilot's Evangelistic Efforts Freak Out Passengers, Country," *Christianity Today,* February 10, 2004, online at www.christianitytoday.com.

24. For a useful summary of the arguments for and against short-term missions, see Luis Bush, "The Long and Short of Mission Terms," *Mission Frontiers* 22 (2000): 16–19.

25. Roger Peterson, Gordon Aeschliman, and R. Wayne Sneed, *Maximum Impact Short-Term Mission: The God-Commanded, Repetitive Deployment of Swift, Temporary, Non-Professional Missionaries* (Minneapolis, Minn.: STEM Press, 2003). As I was drafting this part of the chapter in late 2007, Roger Peterson and I were in communication. I am grateful for his insights about short-term missions and anticipate the next edition of *Maximum Impact.*

26. Other popular guidebooks include Tim Dearborn, *Short-Term Missions Workbook: From Mission Tourists to Global Citizens* (Downers Grove, Ill.: InterVarsity Press, 2003); Leon H. Greene, *A Guide to Short Term Missions: A Comprehensive Manual for Planning an Effective Mission Trip* (Waynesboro, Ga.: Gabriel Publications, 2003); and Martha VanCise, *Successful Mission Teams: A Guide for Volunteers* (Birmingham, Ala.: New Hope Publishers, 2004).

27. Peterson et al., *Maximum Impact,* 252.

28. Ken Walker, "Agencies Announce Short-Term Missions Standards," *Christianity Today,* September 30, 2003, online at www.christianitytoday.com.

29. Fifty-four percent of the members of evangelical Protestant congregations said their church had sponsored a mission trip abroad in the past year, 46 percent of mainline Protestant members said so, as did 31 percent of Catholics and 29 percent of black Protestants.

30. Peterson et al., *Maximum Impact*, 28; emphasis added.

31. Ibid., 255.

32. For members in the survey, the mean size of congregations was 784, which, when divided into the estimated total number of active church members in the United States and multiplied by the proportions of members estimating various numbers of participants from their congregation, yields a total national figure of between 1.5 million and 1.8 million.

33. "Value of Volunteer Time," Independent Sector, online at www .independentsector.org.

34. This figure is considerably lower than the 30 percent in a national survey of teenagers who said they had gone on a religious missions team or service project; Christian Smith, *Soul Searching: The Religious and Spiritual Lives of American Teenagers* (New York: Oxford University Press, 2005), 53. However, mission teams and service projects are such broad categories that almost anything—from going with the youth choir to another church to helping at a soup kitchen—could qualify.

35. Of those surveyed who had gone on a mission trip in the past year, 55 percent were men, 79 percent were white, 69 percent were married, 60 percent were college graduates, 64 percent were age thirty through fifty-nine, 66 percent had no children, 64 percent worshiped in communities with few residents belonging to religions other than Christianity, 57 percent lived in a suburb, 64 percent lived in the South or Midwest, 55 percent were affiliated with an evangelical church, 81 percent had been a member of their congregation more than three years, 92 percent attended religious services every week, and 57 percent held a leadership position.

36. Leadership positions among those surveyed were as common among women as among men.

37. These results are from the Religion and Diversity Survey I conducted in 2003 among 2,910 nationally representative adults. Among those who had traveled or lived outside the United States, 14 percent of men and 8 percent of women had been in a Middle Eastern country, such as Israel or Egypt, and 24 percent of men and 14 percent of women had been in India, China, Japan, or another part of Asia.

38. Although the typical mission trip participant had no children living at home, women who had one child living at home were significantly less likely than women who had no children living at home to have participated, whereas this was not the case among men.

39. Among persons age eighteen through thirty in the survey, 4.3 percent had gone on a mission trip in the past year, compared with 2.1 percent among persons age thirty-one through sixty-four (and only 0.6 percent among persons age sixty-five and older).

40. Among college graduates, 3.2 percent had been on a mission trip in the past year, compared with 1.4 percent of those without college degrees.

41. David B. Barrett, George T. Kurian, and Todd M. Johnson, *World Christian Encyclopedia: A Comparative Survey of Churches and Religions in the Modern World*, 2nd ed. (New York: Oxford University Press, 2001), 658.

42. Dotsey Welliver and Minnette Northcutt, *Mission Handbook 2004–2006: U.S. and Canadian Protestant Ministries Overseas* (Wheaton, Ill.:

Billy Graham Center, 2004), 13; data assembled after 2004 suggests that full-time staff numbers were even higher, but raises questions about the accuracy of the reported number of volunteers.

43. The question in the Global Issues Survey was "During the past year, have you done volunteer work for an organization that is specifically concerned with helping people in other countries?" Although it is possible that a person who did any volunteer work at his or her church may have responded yes because the church included an international ministry, it does not appear that this was generally the case. Overall, 39 percent said they had done some kind of volunteer work in their community, significantly more than the 20 percent who said they did volunteer work for an organization concerned with helping people in other countries.

44. About half (49 percent) are in their forties or fifties, 65 percent live in the South or Midwest, and 75 percent attend church weekly; 63 percent are women, 56 percent have not graduated from college, and only 39 percent are from evangelical churches.

45. Robert Wuthnow, *Acts of Compassion: Caring for Others and Helping Ourselves* (Princeton, N.J.: Princeton University Press, 1991), 10.

46. These relationships are all statistically at or beyond the .05 level of probability (chi-square).

47. These conclusions are drawn from logistic regression models in which the items mentioned were the dependent variable, having gone on a mission trip was the test variable, and frequency of attendance, leadership position, congregation size, and religious tradition were included as control variables.

48. From logistic regression analysis; probability at or beyond the .05 level.

49. On the role of reflection and changes in self-identity, see Robert Wuthnow, *Learning to Care: Elementary Kindness in an Age of Indifference* (New York: Oxford University Press, 1995); see also Rebecca Anne Allahyari, *Visions of Charity: Volunteer Workers and Moral Community* (Berkeley and Los Angeles: University of California Press, 2000).

50. These and other practices are discussed in Glenn Schwartz, "How Short-Term Missions Can Go Wrong," *International Journal of Foreign Missions* 20 (Winter 2003): 27–34.

51. See especially the valuable discussion by Kurt Ver Beek and Robert Priest, "Do Short-Term Missions Change Anyone?" *Christianity Today*, July 6, 2005, online at www.christianitytoday.com.

6. FAITH AND FOREIGN POLICY

1. Esther Kaplan, *With God on Their Side: How Christian Fundamentalists Trampled Science, Policy and Democracy in George W. Bush's White House* (New York: New Press, 2005), 1–2.

2. Brian Urquhart, "Extreme Makeover," *New York Review of Books*, February 24, 2005, 4–5.

3. Susan Page, "Christian Right's Alliances Bend Political Spectrum," *USA Today*, June 14, 2005.

4. Tony Carnes, "The Bush Doctrine," *Christianity Today*, April 25, 2003.

5. Peter Waldman, "Evangelicals Give U.S. Foreign Policy an Activist Tinge," *Wall Street Journal,* May 26, 2004.

6. Paul Marshall, "Religion and Global Affairs: Disregarding Religion," *SAIS Review* 18 (1998): 13–18.

7. Blumhofer and Cizik are quoted in Todd Hertz, "Are Evangelicals the 'New Internationalists'?" *Christianity Today,* May 29, 2002.

8. R. Scott Appleby, *Religion's Role in World Affairs* (New York: Foreign Policy Association, 1998), online report available at www.fpa.org; see also R. Scott Appleby, "Religion and Global Affairs: Religious 'Militants for Peace,'" *SAIS Review* 18 (1998): 38–44, and Gabriel A. Almond, R. Scott Appleby, and Emmanuel Sivan, *Strong Religion: The Rise of Fundamentalisms around the World* (Chicago: University of Chicago Press, 2003).

9. Daniel Philpott, "The Challenge of September 11 to Secularism in International Relations," *World Politics* 55 (2002): 66–95.

10. Douglas Johnston, "Introduction: Beyond Power Politics," in *Religion: The Missing Dimension of Statecraft,* ed. Douglas Johnston and Cynthia Sampson (New York: Oxford University Press, 1995), 3–7; see also Douglas Johnston, ed., *Faith-Based Diplomacy: Trumping Realpolitik* (New York: Oxford University Press, 2003).

11. Eric O. Hansen, *Religion and Politics in the International System Today* (New York: Cambridge University Press, 2006).

12. For instance, see James W. Skillen, *With or Against the World? America's Role among the Nations* (Lanham, Md.: Rowman and Littlefield, 2005), and Jonathan Fox and Shmuel Sandler, *Bringing Religion into International Relations* (New York: Palgrave Macmillan, 2004).

13. Useful overviews include Michael C. Williams, *The Realist Tradition and the Limits of International Relations* (New York: Cambridge University Press, 2005); Bruce W. Jentleson, *American Foreign Policy: The Dynamics of Choice in the 21st Century* (New York: Norton, 2003); and the essays in G. John Ikenberry, ed., *American Foreign Policy: Theoretical Essays,* 6th ed. (New York: Longman, 2006).

14. Quoted in David D. Kirkpatrick, "In Secretly Taped Conversations, Glimpses of the Future President," *New York Times,* February 20, 2005.

15. Sheryl Henderson Blunt, "The Unflappable Condi Rice: Why the World's Most Powerful Woman Asks God for Help," *Christianity Today,* August 22, 2003, online at www.christianitytoday.com.

16. Gregg Zoroya, "He Puts Words in Bush's Mouth," *USA Today,* April 10, 2001, online at www.usatoday.com; Gretchen Passantino, "Barbara Walters to Interview Bush Advisor Karen Hughes," *Answers in Action,* March 26, 2004, online at answers.org.; Corrie Cutrer, "No Place Like Home," *Today's Christian Woman,* November/December 2004, online at www.christianitytoday.com.

17. David D. Kirkpatrick, "Club of the Most Powerful Gathers in Strictest Privacy," *New York Times,* August 28, 2004; Vicky Dillen, "The Council for National Policy: What It Is," July 5, 2001, online at www.seekgod.ca/cnp.htm.

18. Office of the Press Secretary, "President Bush Addresses the 51st Annual Prayer Breakfast," February 6, 2003, online at www.whitehouse.gov.

19. Office of the Press Secretary, *Memorandum for the Administrator of the United States Agency for International Development,* January 22, 2001, online at www.whitehouse.gov. On the structure and influence of the Fellowship, see D. Michael Lindsay, "Elite Networks as Social Power: New Modes of Organization within American Evangelicalism," *Sociology of Religion* 67 (2006), and D. Michael Lindsay, "The National Prayer Breakfast and the 'Christian Mafia': Religious Publicity and Secrecy within the Corridors of Power," *Journal of the American Academy of Religion* 74 (2006).

20. Julia Duin, "Evangelicals Urged to Vote and 'Shape Public Policy,' " *Washington Times,* June 22, 2004.

21. Michael Foust, "86 percent of Evangelicals Say Bush Has Their Vote," *B[aptist]P[ress] News,* June 7, 2004, online at www.bpnews.net.

22. CNN, "Election Results," November 3, 2004, online at www.cnn.com.

23. John C. Green, "The American Religious Landscape and Political Attitudes: A Baseline for 2004," August 9, 2004, online at www.pewforum.org.

24. As quoted in James Rusling, "Interview with President William McKinley," *The Christian Advocate,* January 22, 1903, 17.

25. Saul Landau, "From McKinley to Bush: Listening and Talking to God about Invading Other Countries," December 11, 2004, online at www.counterpunch.org

26. William Martin, "With God on Their Side: Religion and U.S. Foreign Policy," in *Religion Returns to the Public Square: Faith and Policy in America,* ed. Hugh Heclo and Wilfred M. McClay (Washington, D.C., and Baltimore: Woodrow Wilson Center Press and Johns Hopkins University Press, 2003), 327–59; the Dulles quote is on p. 350.

27. Bob Woodward, *Plan of Attack* (New York: Simon & Schuster, 2004).

28. Steven Waldman and John Green, "It Wasn't Just (or Even Mostly) the 'Religious Right,' " *Beliefnet,* 2004, online at www.beliefnet.com.

29. Lindsay, "Elite Networks as Social Power," and personal communication with Michael Lindsay; see also D. Michael Lindsay, *Faith in the Halls of Power: How Evangelicals Joined the American Elite* (New York: Oxford University Press, 2007).

30. Quoted in Esther Kaplan, "Follow the Money," *The Nation,* November 1, 2004, online at www.thenation.com.

31. Details about implications of the Mexico City policy can be found in Population Action International, *What You Need to Know about the Global Gag Rule Restrictions* (2001), online at www.populationaction.org.

32. Robert Wuthnow, *Saving America? Faith-Based Services and the Future of Civil Society* (Princeton, N.J.: Princeton University Press, 2004); Amy Black, *Of Little Faith: The Politics of George W. Bush's Faith-Based Programs* (Washington, D.C.: Georgetown University Press, 2004); and personal communication with Don Eberly.

33. Green, "The American Religious Landscape."

34. Martin, "With God on Their Side."

35. For an interesting discussion of the use of this phrase and other instances of religious language by President George W. Bush, including commentary

by E. J. Dionne Jr., Richard Cizik, and others, see "The Jesus Factor," online at www.pbs.org.

36. George Lakoff, "Nailing the Frames of the Republican National Convention," *University of California at Berkeley News,* September 3, 2004, online at www.berkeley.edu/news. A lengthier discussion is found in George Lakoff, *Whose Freedom? The Battle over America's Most Important Idea* (New York: Picador, 2007), and for an alternative to the argument at the 2004 Republican National Convention, see Paul Starr, *Freedom's Power: The True Force of Liberalism* (New York: Perseus, 2007).

37. Office of the Press Secretary, "President's Remarks at the 2004 Republican National Convention," September 2, 2004, online at www.whitehouse.gov.

38. On the metaphoric and narrative construction of redemption in American culture, see especially Dan P. McAdams, *The Redemptive Self: Stories Americans Live By* (New York: Oxford University Press, 2006); on the unencumbered self, see Michael Sandel, *Democracy's Discontent: America in Search of a Public Philosophy* (Cambridge, Mass.: Harvard University Press, 1996).

39. Steve Brouwer, Paul Gifford, and Susan D. Rose, *Exporting the American Gospel: Global Christian Fundamentalism* (New York: Routledge, 1996), 3.

40. George Soros, *The Bubble of American Supremacy* (New York: Public Affairs, 2004), 10.

41. Quoted in James Davison Hunter, *Culture Wars: The Struggle to Define America* (New York: Basic Books, 1991), 111.

42. Quoted in Tim Stafford, "Good Morning, Evangelicals! Meet Ted Haggard, the NAE's Optimistic Champion of Ecumenical Evangelism and Free-Market Faith," *Christianity Today,* November 4, 2005, online at www.christianitytoday.com.

43. Randall Balmer, *Blessed Assurance: A History of Evangelicalism in America* (Boston: Beacon Press, 1999), 11.

44. Wyndy Corbin, "The Impact of the American Dream on Evangelical Ethics," *Cross Currents* 55 (Fall 2005), online at www.crosscurrents.org/corbin2005.htm.

45. On the core meanings of the American Dream, see Jennifer Hochschild, *Facing Up to the American Dream: Race, Class and the Soul of the Nation* (Princeton, N.J.: Princeton University Press, 1995), and on changing meanings of the American Dream, see Robert Wuthnow, *Poor Richard's Principle: Recovering the American Dream through the Moral Dimension of Work, Business, and Money* (Princeton, N.J.: Princeton University Press, 1996), and Cal Jillson, *Pursuing the American Dream: Opportunity and Exclusion over Four Centuries* (Lawrence: University of Kansas Press, 2004).

46. Christian Smith, *American Evangelicalism: Embattled and Thriving* (Chicago: University of Chicago Press, 1998), 202; see also Michael Emerson and Christian Smith, *Divided by Faith: Evangelical Religion and the Problem of Race in America* (New York: Oxford University Press, 2000).

47. Robert Wuthnow, *The Crisis in the Churches: Spiritual Malaise, Fiscal Woe* (New York: Oxford University Press, 1997), 211.

48. David Martin, *Pentecostalism: The World Their Parish* (Oxford: Blackwell, 2002), 171.

49. "Samburu Samplings," International Mission Board, Southern Baptist Convention (2005), online at www.imb.org.

50. Joel Robbins, "When Do You Think the World Will End? Globalization, Apocalypticism, and the Moral Perils of Fieldwork in 'Last New Guinea,'" *Anthropology and Humanism* 22, 1 (1997): 6–30; quotations are on pp. 10, 11.

51. Among evangelicals, 74 percent agreed that promoting trade helps reduce hunger, as did 77 percent of mainline Protestants and 77 percent of Catholics; among black Protestants, 78 percent agreed. The percentages saying that solving problems by promoting international trade is a good reason, were, respectively, 44, 49, 54, and 54. Protecting jobs of American workers was regarded as a very important priority by 84, 79, 80, and 93 percent, respectively; and 56, 54, 51, and 55 percent, respectively, said they would be bothered a lot by a large company moving to another country. Analysis of some other questions in the Global Issues Survey can be found in Robert Wuthnow and Valerie Lewis, "Religion and Altruistic U.S. Foreign Policy Goals: Evidence from a National Survey of Church Members," *Journal for the Scientific Study of Religion* 47 (2008): 176–89.

52. Church World Service, *Churches in the U.S. and Just Trade: The Free Trade Area of the Americas (FTAA)*, 2004, online at www.cwa.org.

53. General Assembly of the Presbyterian Church (USA), Overture 03–33, 2003, online at www.pcusa.org.

54. Rich Ufford-Chase, "Empire and Church: Pitfalls and Priorities for the Presbyterian Church in a Time of Globalization" (speech to the Presbyterian Peace Fellowship Breakfast, 215th General Assembly, Denver, May 28, 2003), online at www.pcusa.org.

55. New York Labor-Religion Coalition; information from www.labor -religion.org.

56. General Accounting Office, *Budget of the United States for Fiscal Year 2006* (Washington, D.C.: Government Printing Office, 2005), 46.

57. These figures are from national polls conducted in the years indicated by the Gallup organization and reported on Public Opinion Online (available through Lexis-Nexis). The exact question was "Next, I'm going to read a list of possible foreign policy goals that the United States might have. For each one please say whether you think it should be a very important foreign policy goal of the United States, a somewhat important goal, not too important a goal, or not an important goal at all. How about . . . promoting and defending human rights in other countries?"

58. Elisabeth Bumiller, "Evangelicals Sway Bush on Foreign Policy," *New York Times*, October 26, 2003.

59. Allen D. Hertzke, *Freeing God's Children: The Unlikely Alliance for Global Human Rights* (Lanham, Md.: Rowman and Littlefield, 2004).

60. Nicholas D. Kristof, "Bleeding Hearts of the World, Unite!" *New York Times*, November 6, 2005.

61. Waldman, "Evangelicals Give U.S. Foreign Policy an Activist Tinge."

62. Bumiller, "Evangelicals Sway Bush on Foreign Policy."

63. Letter dated August 6, 2004, online at www.nae.net.

64. Alan Wisdom and Erik Nelson, "Churches Repeating Past Mistakes on Human Rights—and Making New Ones," *Faith & Freedom* (Winter 2005): 10–11; quotes are on p. 11.

65. Hertzke, *Freeing God's Children,* 225–27.

66. Ibid., 205.

67. Albert Pennybacker, "Testimony before the House Subcommittee on International Operations and Human Rights," February 15, 1996, online at www.ncccusa.org.

68. Theodore E. McCarrick, "Statement on the Fiftieth Anniversary of the Adoption of the Universal Declaration of Human Rights," United States Conference of Catholic Bishops, December 8, 1998.

69. Elenora Giddings Ivory, "Religious Freedom Bill Revised," *Washington Report to Presbyterians* (March/April 1998), online at www.pcusa.org.

70. The percentages who said their congregation should emphasize the problem of religious persecution in other countries "a lot" were 45 among evangelical Protestants, 37 among mainline Protestants, 33 percent among black Protestants, and 37 percent among Catholics.

71. Executive Committee of the High Commissioner's Programme, "UNHCR Annual Programme Budget," United Nations General Assembly, 2006.

72. Through their cooperative Asylum and Immigration Grant Program, the two agencies made awards totaling $254,000 in 2005.

73. The overall budget of Presbyterian Disaster Assistance in 2005 was approximately $6 million.

74. "How Trafficking Works," *Refugee Reports* 23 (April 2002), online at www.refugees.org.

75. U.S. State Department, *Trafficking in Persons Report* (Washington, D.C.: Government Printing Office, 2003).

76. "Different Faiths, Different Messages: Americans Hearing about Iraq from the Pulpit, but Religious Faith Not Defining Opinions," Pew Research Center, March 19, 2003.

77. Corwin E. Smidt, "Religion and American Attitudes toward Islam and an Invasion of Iraq," *Sociology of Religion* 66 (2005): 243–61.

78. On this possibility, see Michael Lind, "How Neoconservatives Conquered Washington—and Launched a War," *Antiwar.com,* April 10, 2003, and Chip Berlet and Nikhil Aziz, "Culture, Religion, Apocalypse, and Middle East Foreign Policy," *Rightweb.com,* December 5, 2003.

79. The survey was conducted by the Harris Poll in 2002 and this question was asked of 1,023 respondents; my analysis is of the electronic data file, which I obtained through Firestone Library at Princeton University.

80. Lower support for superior military power in the 2005 Global Issues Survey than in the 2002 Council on Foreign Relations poll reflected a decline in support in the public at large. For instance, a 2005 Gallup poll of the nation showed that 56 percent regarded maintaining superior military power worldwide as a very important foreign policy goal, down from 68 percent in 2002; comparable figures were 50 percent in 1995, 59 percent in 1998, and 59 percent in 2001 be-

fore 9/11. These figures are from Public Opinion Online (available through Lexis-Nexis).

81. Daniel Yankelovich, "Poll Positions," *Foreign Affairs*. September/October 2005, online at fullaccess.foreignaffairs.org.

82. "51 Protestant, Orthodox, Catholic, Evangelical Leaders Petition President Bush to Reconsider Iraq Invasion," *News from the National Council of Churches*, September 12, 2002, online at www.ncccusa.org.

83. Todd Hertz, "Opinion Roundup: Is Attacking Iraq Moral?" *Christianity Today*, September 4, 2002, online at www.christianitytoday.com.

84. Quoted in Charles Duhigg, "Evangelicals Flock into Iraq on a Mission of Faith," *Los Angeles Times*, March 18, 2004.

85. "Faith-Based NGOs and International Peacebuilding," United States Institute of Peace, October 22, 2001, online at www.usip.org.

86. Case studies of many of these conflict resolution and interreligious diplomatic efforts are included in Johnston, *Faith-Based Diplomacy.*

87. "CRS and Iraq—the Human Face of Suffering in the Current Crisis," Catholic Relief Services (2003), online at www.catholicrelief.com.

88. Tom Coipuram Jr., "Iraq: United Nations and Humanitarian Aid Organizations," *CRS Report for Congress*, June 27, 2005, online at www.crs.org.

89. Lester Kurtz and Kelly Goran, "Love Your Enemies? Protestants and Foreign Policy in the United States," in *The Quiet Hand of God: Faith-Based Activism and the Public Role of Mainline Protestantism*, ed. Robert Wuthnow and John Evans (Berkeley and Los Angeles: University of California Press, 2002), 364–80.

90. David Beckmann, "Debunking Myths about Foreign Aid," *Christian Century*, August 1–8, 2001, 26–28.

91. Jeff M. Sellers, "How to Spell Debt Relief," *Christianity Today*, May 21, 2001, online at www.christianitytoday.com.

92. Bill Nichols and Barbara Slavin, "Foreign Aid Hike Pushed," *USA Today*, February 19, 2001.

93. Mary E. McClymont, "Testimony on U.S. Foreign Assistance after September 11th: Major Changes, Competing Purposes and Different Standards—Is There an Overall Strategy?" Committee on International Relations, U.S. House of Representatives, January 28, 2004.

94. Bradley Graham and Glenn Kessler, "Rice Explains Aid Restructuring to USAID Employees," *Washington Post*, January 20, 2006.

95. Conference Report, *Sphere in Practice* (Geneva, Switzerland, 2004), online at www.sphereproject.org.

96. "Foreign Aid," Council on Foreign Relations, online at cfrterrorism.org.

97. "Commitment to Development Index," Center for Global Development, online at www.cgdev.org.

98. Peter J. Schraeder, Steven W. Hook, and Bruce Taylor, "Clarifying the Foreign Aid Puzzle: A Comparison of American, Japanese, French, and Swedish Aid Flows," *World Politics* 50 (1998): 294–323.

99. Gallup polls conducted between 1974 and 2003 as reported in Public Opinion Online (available through Lexis-Nexis).

100. Ben Mitchell, "Why Southern Baptists Should Not Support the ONE Campaign," *Florida Baptist Witness,* June 30, 2005, online at www.floridabaptistwitness.com.

101. Kurtz and Goran, "Love Your Enemies?"

102. The different positions were outlined by participants at a symposium entitled "Can Food Aid Be a More Effective Development Tool?" Washington, D.C., Institute for International Economics, December 9, 2005; at the "Strengthening the Food Aid Chain," USDA and USAID Export Food Aid Conference VII, Kansas City, Missouri, May 3–5, 2005; and in *Food Aid Briefing,* World Vision, December 2005.

103. Lilia Tse, "International Leaders Launch the Micah Challenge," *Ecumenical Press,* October 18, 2004.

104. Quoted in Jeffrey K. Hadden and Anson Shupe, *Televangelism: Power and Politics on God's Frontier* (New York: Holt, 1988), online at www.lib.virginia.edu.

Selected Bibliography

Abrahamsen, Rita. "African Studies and the Postcolonial Challenge." *African Affairs* 102 (2003): 189–210.

Adorno, Theodor W. *Culture Industry.* New York: Routledge, 1991.

Ahlstrom, Sidney. *A Religious History of the American People.* New Haven: Yale University Press, 1972.

Ahmed, Fauzia Erfan. "The Rise of the Bangladesh Garment Industry: Globalization, Women Workers, and Voice." *NWSA Journal* 16 (2004): 34–45.

Ahn, Heui Yeol. "The Influence of the Niagara Bible Conference and Adoniram Judson Gordon on Malcolm Fenwick and Korean Baptist Missions." Ph.D. diss., Southwestern Baptist Theological Seminary, 2002.

Alba, Richard D., and Victor Nee. *Remaking the American Mainstream: Assimilation and Contemporary Immigration.* Cambridge, Mass.: Harvard University Press, 2003.

Allahyari, Rebecca Anne. *Visions of Charity: Volunteer Workers and Moral Community.* Berkeley and Los Angeles: University of California Press, 2000.

Almond, Gabriel A., R. Scott Appleby, and Emmanuel Sivan. *Strong Religion: The Rise of Fundamentalisms around the World.* Chicago: University of Chicago Press, 2003.

Ammerman, Nancy Tatom. *Bible Believers: Fundamentalists in the Modern World.* New Brunswick, N.J.: Rutgers University Press, 1987.

———. *Pillars of Faith: American Congregations and Their Partners.* Berkeley and Los Angeles: University of California Press, 2005.

Anderson, Gerald H. "World Christianity by the Numbers: A Review of the *World Christian Encyclopedia*, Second edition." *International Bulletin of Missionary Research* 26 (July 2002): 128–30.

Anderson, Rufus. *Foreign Missions: Their Relations and Claims.* Boston: Congregational Publishing Society, 1874.

————. *Memorial Volume of the First Fifty Years of the American Board of Commissioners for Foreign Missions.* Boston: American Board of Commissioners for Foreign Missions, 1861.

Appadurai, Arjun. *Modernity at Large: Cultural Dimensions of Globalization.* Minneapolis: University of Minnesota Press, 1996.

Appleby, R. Scott. "Marching as to War." *New York Times,* May 12, 2002.

————. "Religion and Global Affairs: Religious 'Militants for Peace.'" *SAIS Review* 18 (1998): 38–44.

————. *Religion's Role in World Affairs.* New York: Foreign Policy Association, 1998.

Armerding, Hudson Taylor. "The China Inland Mission and Some Aspects of Its Work." Ph.D. diss., University of Chicago, 1948.

Arrighi, Giovanni, Beverly J. Silver, and Benjamin D. Brewer. "Industrial Convergence, Globalization, and the Persistence of the North-South Divide." *Studies in Comparative Development* 38 (2003): 3–31.

Asamoah-Gyadu, J. Kwabena. "'Christ Is the Answer: What Is the Question?' A Ghana Airways Prayer Vigil and Its Implications for Religion, Evil and Public Space." *Journal of Religion in Africa* 35 (2005): 93–117.

Baird, Samuel J. *History of the New School.* Philadelphia: Claxton, Remsen and Haffelfinger, 1868.

Baldwin, David A., ed. *Neorealism and Neoliberalism: The Contemporary Debate.* New York: Columbia University Press, 1993.

Balmer, Randall. *Blessed Assurance: A History of Evangelicalism in America.* Boston: Beacon Press, 1999.

Barber, Benjamin R. *Jihad vs. McWorld.* New York: Ballantine Books, 1996.

Barrett, David B. *World Christian Encyclopedia: A Comparative Survey of Churches and Religions in the Modern World A.D. 1900–2000.* Oxford: Oxford University Press, 1982.

Barrett, David B., and Todd M. Johnson. *World Christian Trends, A.D. 30— A.D. 2200: Interpreting the Annual Christian Megacensus.* Pasadena, Calif.: William Carey Library, 2001.

Barrett, David B., Todd M. Johnson, and Peter F. Crossing. "Missiometrics 2005: A Global Survey of World Mission." *International Bulletin of Missionary Research* 29 (January 2005): 27–30.

Barrett, David B., George T. Kurian, and Todd M. Johnson. *World Christian Encyclopedia: A Comparative Survey of Churches and Religions in the Modern World,* 2nd ed., 2 vols. Oxford: Oxford University Press, 2001.

Bashford, J. W. *World Missionary Conference,* vol. 9. Cambridge: Henry Martyn Centre, 1910.

Bayart, Jean-Francois. "Africa in the World: A History of Extraversion." *African Affairs* 99 (2000): 217–67.

Beckmann, David. "Debunking Myths about Foreign Aid." *Christian Century,* August 1–8, 2001, 26–28.

Bediako, Kwame. "Africa and Christianity on the Threshold of the Third Millennium: The Religious Dimension." *African Affairs* 99 (2000): 303–23.

————. *Jesus and the Gospel in Africa.* Maryknoll, N.Y.: Orbis, 2004.

Beneria, Lourdes. "Shifting the Risk: New Employment Patterns, Informalization and Women's Work." *International Journal of Politics, Culture and Society* 15 (2001): 27–53.

Berger, Joseph. "Spreading Their Faith Wherever It Leads." *New York Times,* January 4, 1996.

Berger, Julia. "Religious Nongovernmental Organizations: An Exploratory Analysis." *Voluntas: International Journal of Voluntary and Nonprofit Organizations* 14 (2003): 15–39.

Berger, Peter L. "Four Faces of Global Culture." *National Interest* 49 (1997): 23–29.

Beyer, Peter. *Religion and Globalization.* Thousand Oaks, Calif.: Sage, 1994.

Bhagwati, Jagdish. *In Defense of Globalization.* New York: Oxford University Press, 2004.

Birman, Patricia, and Marcia Pereira Leite. "Whatever Happened to What Used to Be the Largest Catholic Country in the World?" *Daedalus* 129 (2000): 271–90.

Black, Amy. *Of Little Faith: The Politics of George W. Bush's Faith-Based Programs.* Washington, D.C.: Georgetown University Press, 2004.

Black, Sandra E., and Elizabeth Brainerd. "Importing Equality? The Impact of Globalization on Gender Discrimination." *Industrial and Labor Relations Review* 57 (2004): 540–59.

Blincoe, Robert A. "The Strange Structure of Mission Agencies, Part III: Desired Symbiosis: Church and Mission Structures." *International Journal of Foreign Missions* 19 (2002): 43–46.

Blunt, Sheryl Henderson. "The Unflappable Condi Rice: Why the World's Most Powerful Woman Asks God for Help." *Christianity Today,* August 22, 2003.

Boli, John, Thomas A. Loya, and Teresa Loftin. "National Participation in World-Polity Organization." In *Constructing World Culture: International Nongovernmental Organizations since 1875,* edited by John Boli and George A. Thomas, 50–79. Stanford: Stanford University Press, 1999.

Boli, John, and George A. Thomas, eds. *Constructing World Culture: International Nongovernmental Organizations since 1875.* Stanford: Stanford University Press, 1999.

Bosch, David J. *Transforming Mission: Paradigm Shifts in Theology of Mission.* Maryknoll, N.Y.: Orbis, 1991.

Bowen, Kurt. *Evangelism and Apostasy: The Evolution and Impact of Evangelicals in Modern Mexico.* Montreal: McGill-Queen's University Press, 1996.

Brereton, Virginia Lieson. *Training God's Army: The American Bible School, 1880–1940.* Indianapolis: Indiana University Press, 1990.

Brouwer, Steve, Paul Gifford, and Susan D. Rose. *Exporting the American Gospel: Global Christian Fundamentalism.* New York: Routledge, 1996.

Brown, Richard D. "The Emergence of Voluntary Associations in Massachusetts, 1700–1730." *Journal of Voluntary Action Research* 2 (1973): 64–73.

Bruce, Steve. *God Is Dead: Secularization in the West.* Oxford: Blackwell, 2002.

Brusco, Elizabeth. *The Reformation of Machismo: Evangelical Protestantism and Gender in Colombia.* Austin: University of Texas Press, 1995.

Bumiller, Elisabeth. "Evangelicals Sway Bush on Foreign Policy." *New York Times,* October 26, 2003.

Bush, Luis. "The Long and Short of Mission Terms." *Mission Frontiers* 22 (2000): 16–19.

Buss, Dale. "Taste: Houses of Worship." *Wall Street Journal,* December 4, 2003.

Carey, William. *An Enquiry into the Obligations of Christians to Use Means for the Conversion of the Heathens.* Leicester, U.K.: Ann Ireland, 1792.

Carnes, Tony. "The Bush Doctrine." *Christianity Today,* April 25, 2003.

Carpenter, Joel A. "Appendix: The Evangelical Missionary Force in the 1930s." In *Earthen Vessels: American Evangelicals and Foreign Missions, 1880–1980,* edited by Joel A. Carpenter and Wilbert R. Shenk, 335–42. Grand Rapids, Mich.: Eerdmans, 1990.

———. "The Christian Scholar in an Age of Global Christianity." Paper presented at conference on Christianity and the Soul of the University, Baylor University, March 25–27, 2004.

———. Preface. In *The Changing Face of Christianity: Africa, the West, and the World,* edited by Lamin Sanneh and Joel A. Carpenter, vii–ix. New York: Oxford University Press, 2005.

———. "Propagating the Faith Once Delivered: The Fundamentalist Missionary Enterprise, 1920–1945." In *Earthen Vessels: American Evangelicals and Foreign Missions, 1880–1980,* edited by Joel A. Carpenter and Wilbert R. Shenk, 92–132. Grand Rapids, Mich.: Eerdmans, 1990.

Carpenter, Joel A., and Wilbert R. Shenk., eds. *Earthen Vessels: American Evangelicals and Foreign Missions, 1880–1980.* Grand Rapids, Mich.: Eerdmans, 1990.

Casanova, Jose. "Religion, the New Millennium, and Globalization." *Sociology of Religion* 62 (2001): 415–41.

Chaves, Mark. *Congregations in America.* Cambridge, Mass.: Harvard University Press, 2004.

———. "Secularization as Declining Religious Authority." *Social Forces* 72 (1994): 749–74.

Chen Cunfu and Huang Tianhai. "The Emergence of a New Type of Christians in China Today." *Review of Religious Research* 46 (2004): 183–200.

Chesnut, R. Andrew. *Born Again in Brazil: The Pentecostal Boom and the Pathogens of Poverty.* New Brunswick, N.J.: Rutgers University Press, 1997.

———. "Pragmatic Consumers and Practical Products: The Success of Pneumacentric Religion among Women in Latin America's New Religious Economy." *Review of Religious Research* 45 (2003): 20–31.

Chiang, Pei-heng. *Non-Governmental Organizations at the United Nations: Identity, Role, and Function.* New York: Praeger, 1981.

Cleveland, Harlan. *The Art of Overseasmanship.* Syracuse, N.Y.: Syracuse University Press, 1957.

Cnaan, Ram A., and Stephanie C. Boddie. "Philadelphia Census of Congregations and Their Involvement in Social Service Delivery." *Social Service Review,* December 2001, 559–80.

Coakley, John W., and Andrea Sterk, eds. *Readings in World Christian History.* Maryknoll, N.Y.: Orbis, 2004.

Coipuram, Tom, Jr. "Iraq: United Nations and Humanitarian Aid Organizations." *CRS Report for Congress,* June 27, 2005.

Connell, John, and Chris Gibson. "World Music: Deterritorializing Place and Identity." *Progress in Human Geography* 28 (2004): 342–61.

Coote, Robert T. "Finger on the Pulse: Fifty Years of Missionary Research." *International Bulletin of Missionary Research* 24 (July 2000): 98–105.

Corbin, Wyndy. "The Impact of the American Dream on Evangelical Ethics." *Cross Currents* 55 (Fall 2005).

Corten, Andre. "Transnational Religious Needs and Political Delegitimisation in Latin America." In *Between Babel and Pentecost: Transnational Pentecostalism in Africa and Latin America,* edited by Andre Corten and Ruth Marshall-Fratani, 106–23. Bloomington: Indiana University Press, 2001.

Corten, Andre, and Ruth Marshall-Fratani, eds. *Between Babel and Pentecost: Transnational Pentecostalism in Africa and Latin America.* Bloomington: Indiana University Press, 2001.

Curti, Merle, Judith Green, and Roderick Nash. "Anatomy of Giving: Millionaires in the Late 19th Century." *American Quarterly* 15 (1963): 416–35.

Cutrer, Corrie. "No Place Like Home." *Today's Christian Woman,* November/ December 2004.

Das, Gurcharan. "The Respect They Deserve." *Time Asia,* December 6, 2004.

Dawkins, Richard. *The God Delusion.* New York: Houghton Mifflin, 2006.

Dean, Kenneth. *Lord of the Three in One: The Spread of a Cult in Southeast China.* Princeton, N.J.: Princeton University Press, 1998.

Dearborn, Tim. *Short-Term Missions Workbook: From Mission Tourists to Global Citizens.* Downers Grove, Ill.: InterVarsity Press, 2003.

Dennett, Daniel C. *Breaking the Spell: Religion as a Natural Phenomenon.* New York: Penguin, 2006.

Dennis, James S. *Centennial Survey of Foreign Missions.* New York: Fleming H. Revell, 1902.

———. *Christian Missions and Social Progress,* 3 vols. New York: Fleming H. Revell, 1897–1906.

De Witte, Marleen. "Altar Media's *Living Word:* Televised Charismatic Christianity in Ghana." *Journal of Religion in Africa* 23 (2003): 172–202.

DiMaggio, Paul J., and Walter W. Powell. "The Iron Cage Revisited: Institutional Isomorphism and Collective Rationality in Organizational Fields." *American Sociological Review* 48 (1983): 147–60.

Ding Lu. "Industrial Policy and Resource Allocation: Implications of China's Participation in Globalization." *China Economic Review* 11 (2000): 342–60.

Dollar, David. "Globalization, Inequality, and Poverty since 1980." Washington, D.C.: World Bank Development Research Group, November 2001.

Douglas, Ann. *The Feminization of American Culture.* New York: Knopf, 1977.

Douthat, Ross. "The Christian Future." *Policy Review* 117 (February–March 2003): 89–94.

Droogers, Andre. "Globalisation and Pentecostal Success." In *Between Babel and Pentecost: Transnational Pentecostalism in Africa and Latin America,* edited by Andre Corten and Ruth Marshall-Fratani, 41–61. Bloomington: Indiana University Press, 2001.

Duhigg, Charles. "Evangelicals Flock into Iraq on a Mission of Faith." *Los Angeles Times,* March 18, 2004.

Duin, Julia. "Evangelicals Urged to Vote and 'Shape Public Policy.'" *Washington Times,* June 22, 2004.

Dulles, Foster Rhea. *The American Red Cross: A History.* New York: Harper and Brothers, 1950.

Eckes, Alfred E., Jr., and Thomas W. Zeiler. *Globalization and the American Century.* New York: Cambridge University Press, 2003.

Ecklund, Elaine Howard, and Wendy Cadge. "Immigration and Religion." *Annual Review of Sociology* 33 (2007): 17.1–17.21.

Egan, Eileen. *Catholic Relief Services: The Beginning Years.* New York: Catholic Relief Services, 1988.

Emerson, Michael, and Christian Smith. *Divided by Faith: Evangelical Religion and the Problem of Race in America.* New York: Oxford University Press, 2000.

Engel, James F., and William A. Dyrness. *Changing the Mind of Missions: Where Have We Gone Wrong?* Downers Grove, Ill.: InterVarsity Press, 2000.

Englund, Harri. "Christian Independency and Global Membership: Pentecostal Extraversions in Malawi." *Journal of Religion in Africa* 33 (2003): 83–111.

Escobar, Samuel. *The New Global Mission: The Gospel from Everywhere to Everyone.* Downers Grove, Ill.: InterVarsity Press, 2003.

Etherington, Norman. "Recent Trends in the Historiography of Southern Africa." *Journal of Southern African Studies* 22 (1996): 201–19.

Evensen, Bruce J. *God's Man for the Gilded Age: D. L. Moody and the Rise of Modern Mass Evangelism.* New York: Oxford University Press, 2003.

Fairbank, John K. "Introduction: The Many Faces of Protestant Missions in China and the United States." In *The Missionary Enterprise in China and America,* edited by John K. Fairbank. Cambridge, Mass.: Harvard University Press, 1974.

Firebaugh, Glenn. "Empirics of World Income Inequality." *American Journal of Sociology* 104 (1999): 1597–1630.

Forney, Matthew. "Jesus Is Back, and She's Chinese." *Time Asia,* November 5, 2001.

Foucault, Michel. *The Archaeology of Knowledge and the Discourse on Language.* London: Tavistock, 1972.

———. *The Order of Things: An Archaeology of the Human Sciences.* New York: Random House, 1970.

Foust, Michael. "86 Percent of Evangelicals Say Bush Has Their Vote." *B[aptist]P[ress] News,* June 7, 2004.

Fox, Jonathan, and Shmuel Sandler. *Bringing Religion into International Relations.* New York: Palgrave Macmillan, 2004.

Frame, Randy. "TBN: Growth Has Bred Criticism." *Christianity Today,* October 8, 1990.

Friedman, Thomas L. *The World Is Flat: A Brief History of the Twenty-First Century.* New York: Farrar, Straus, and Giroux, 2005.

Froehle, Bryan T., and Mary L. Gautier. *Global Catholicism: Portrait of a World Church.* Maryknoll, N.Y.: Orbis, 2003.

Gaustad, Edwin Scott, and Philip L. Barlow. *New Historical Atlas of Religion in America*. New York: Oxford University Press, 2001.

Gifford, Paul. *Ghana's New Christianity: Pentecostalism in a Globalizing African Economy*. Bloomington: Indiana University Press, 2004.

———. "Persistence and Change in Contemporary African Religion." *Social Compass* 51 (2004): 169–76.

Gilbo, Patrick F. *The American Red Cross: The First Century*. New York: Harper & Row, 1981.

Giving USA Foundation. *Giving USA 2006*. Glenview, Ill.: American Association of Fundraising Counsel, 2006.

Glasius, Marlies, Mary Kaldor, and Helmut Anheier, eds. *Global Civil Society 2002*. Oxford: Oxford University Press, 2002.

Goesling, Brian. "Changing Income Inequalities within and between Nations: New Evidence." *American Sociological Review* 66 (2001): 745–61.

Goldman, Jonathan. *The Empire State Building Book*. New York: St. Martin's Press, 1980.

Goodsell, Fred Field. *You Shall Be My Witnesses*. Boston: American Board of Commissioners for Foreign Missions, 1959.

Goodstein, Laurie. "More Religion, but Not the Old-Time Kind." *New York Times,* January 9, 2005.

Graddol, David. *The Future of English? A Guide to Forecasting the Popularity of the English Language in the 21st Century*. London: The British Council, 1997.

Graham, Bradley, and Glenn Kessler. "Rice Explains Aid Restructuring to USAID Employees." *Washington Post,* January 20, 2006.

Green, John C. "The American Religious Landscape and Political Attitudes: A Baseline for 2004." Pew Forum for Religion and Public Life, August 9, 2004.

———. "Evangelical Protestants and Civic Engagement: An Overview." In *A Public Faith: Evangelicals and Civic Engagement,* edited by Michael Cromartie, 11–30. Lanham, Md.: Rowman and Littlefield, 2003.

Greene, Leon H. *A Guide to Short Term Missions: A Comprehensive Manual for Planning an Effective Mission Trip*. Waynesboro, Ga.: Gabriel Publications, 2003.

Grimes, B. F. *Ethnologue: Languages of the World*. Dallas, Tex.: Summer Institute of Linguistics, 1996.

Guder, Darrell L., ed. *Missional Church: A Vision for the Sending of the Church in North America*. Grand Rapids, Mich.: Eerdmans, 1998.

Guillen, Mauro F. *The Limits of Convergence: Globalization and Organization Change in Argentina, South Korea, and Spain*. Princeton, N.J.: Princeton University Press, 2001.

Gumucio, Christian Parker. "Religion and the Awakening of Indigenous People in Latin America." *Social Compass* 49 (2002): 67–81.

Gunther, Wolfgang. "The History and Significance of World Mission Conferences in the 20th Century." *International Review of Mission* 92 (2003): 521–37.

Guzzini, Stefano. "A Reconstruction of Constructivism in International Relations." *European Journal of International Relations* 6 (2000): 147–82.

Hacking, Ian. *The Social Construction of What?* Cambridge, Mass.: Harvard University Press, 1999.

Hadden, Jeffrey K., and Anson Shupe. *Televangelism: Power and Politics on God's Frontier.* New York: Holt, 1988.

Hall, Douglas John. *The Cross in Our Context: Jesus and the Suffering World.* Minneapolis, Minn.: Fortress Press, 2003.

Hall, Peter Dobkin. "A Historical Overview of Philanthropy, Voluntary Associations, and Nonprofit Organizations in the United States, 1600–2000." In *The Nonprofit Research Handbook,* 2nd ed., edited by Walter W. Powell and Richard Steinberg, 32–65. New Haven: Yale University Press, 2006.

Hamilton, David E. "Herbert Hoover and the Great Drought of 1930." *Journal of American History* 68 (1982): 850–75.

Hannerz, Ulf. *Cultural Complexity: Studies in the Social Organization of Meaning.* New York: Columbia University Press, 1992.

———. *Transnational Connections: Culture, People, Places.* New York: Routledge, 1996.

Hansen, Eric O. *Religion and Politics in the International System Today.* New York: Cambridge University Press, 2006.

Hanson, Mark. "The Ligaments and Landscapes of Ecumenism." *Dialog: A Journal of Theology* 42 (Winter 2003): 366–67.

Hatch, Nathan O. *The Democratization of American Christianity.* New Haven: Yale University Press, 1989.

Hays, Daniel H. "Chinese Protestant Christianity Today." *China Quarterly* 174 (2003): 488–504.

Hearn, Julie. "The 'Invisible' NGO: U.S. Evangelical Missions in Kenya." *Journal of Religion in Africa* 32 (2002): 32–60.

Heer, James. "Papua New Guinea Up to Their Necks in Missionaries." *Toronto Globe and Mail,* June 6, 1992.

Held, David, and Anthony McGrew, eds. *The Global Transformations Reader: An Introduction to the Globalization Debate,* 2nd ed. Cambridge: Polity, 2003.

———. *Globalization and Anti-Globalization.* Cambridge: Polity, 2002.

Herman, Didi. "Globalism's 'Siren Song': The United Nations and International Law in Christian Right Thought and Prophecy." *Sociological Review* 77 (2001): 56–77.

Hertz, Todd. "Are Evangelicals the 'New Internationalists'?" *Christianity Today,* May 29, 2002.

———. "Opinion Roundup: Is Attacking Iraq Moral?" *Christianity Today,* September 4, 2002.

Hertzke, Allen D. *Freeing God's Children: The Unlikely Alliance for Global Human Rights.* Lanham, Md.: Rowman and Littlefield, 2004.

Hillman, Ben. "The Rise of the Community in Rural China: Village Politics, Cultural Identity and Religious Revival in a Hui Hamlet." *China Journal* 51 (2004): 53–73.

Hirsch, Eric. "Between Mission and Market: Events and Images in a Melanesian Society." *Man,* n.s., 29, 3 (1994): 689–711.

————. "New Boundaries of Influence in Highland Papua: 'Culture,' Mining and Ritual Conversions." *Oceania,* June 2001.

Hochschild, Jennifer. *Facing Up to the American Dream: Race, Class and the Soul of the Nation.* Princeton, N.J.: Princeton University Press, 1995.

Holland, Thomas P., and William L. Sachs. *The Zacchaeus Project: Discerning Episcopal Identity at the Dawn of the New Millennium.* New York: Cornerstone, 1999.

Holley, Marietta. *Josiah Allen's Wife as a P.A. and P.I.: Samantha at the Centennial.* Hartford, Conn.: American Publishing Co., 1893.

Howard, David M. *Student Power in World Missions.* Downers Grove, Ill.: InterVarsity Press, 1970.

Howe, Henry. *Adventures and Achievements of Americans.* New York: Geo. F. Tuttle, 1859.

Howell, Brian. "Practical Belief and the Localization of Christianity: Pentecostal and Denominational Christianity in Global/Local Perspective." *Religion* 33 (2003): 233–48.

Hsu, Becky Yang, Amy Reynolds, Conrad Hackett, and James Gibbon. "Estimating the Religious Composition of All Nations: An Empirical Assessment." Princeton, N.J.: Princeton University, Center for the Study of Religion, 2005.

Hunter, James Davison. *Culture Wars: The Struggle to Define America.* New York: Basic Books, 1991.

Huntington, Samuel P. *The Clash of Civilizations and the Remaking of World Order.* New York: Simon & Schuster, 1998.

Hurbon, Laennec. "Pentecostalism and Transnationalisation in the Caribbean." In *Between Babel and Pentecost: Transnational Pentecostalism in Africa and Latin America,* edited by Andre Corten and Ruth Marshall-Fratani, 124–41. Bloomington: Indiana University Press, 2001.

Hutchinson, John F. "The Nagler Case: A Revealing Moment in Red Cross History." *Canadian Bulletin of Medical History* 9 (2004): 177–90.

Hutchison, William R. *Errand to the World: American Protestant Thought and Foreign Missions.* Chicago: University of Chicago Press, 1987.

Hutson, James H. *The Founders on Religion: A Book of Quotations.* Princeton, N.J.: Princeton University Press, 2005.

Ikenberry, G. John, ed. *American Foreign Policy: Theoretical Essays,* 6th ed. New York: Longman, 2006.

Irvin, Dale T. "A Review of *The Next Christendom: The Coming of Global Christianity* by Philip Jenkins." *Journal of Pentecostal Studies* 13 (2005): 273–80.

Irvin, Dale T., and Scott W. Sunquist, eds. *History of the World Christian Movement: Earliest Christianity to 1453.* Maryknoll, N.Y.: Orbis, 2001.

Irvine, Graeme. *Best Things in the Worst of Times: An Insider's View of World Vision.* Wilsonville, Calif.: Book Partners, 1996.

Ivory, Elenora Giddings. "Religious Freedom Bill Revised." *Washington Report to Presbyterians,* March/April 1998.

Jaffarian, Michael. "The Statistical State of the Missionary Enterprise." *Missiology* 30 (January 2002): 15–32.

Jenkins, Philip. "After the Next Christendom." *International Bulletin of Missionary Research* 28 (January 1, 2004): 20–22.

———. "A New Christendom." *Chronicle Review,* March 29, 2002.

———. *The New Faces of Christianity: Believing the Bible in the Global South.* New York: Oxford University Press, 2006.

———. *The Next Christendom: The Coming of Global Christianity.* New York: Oxford University Press, 2002.

———. "The Next Christianity." *Atlantic Monthly* 290 (October 2002): 53–68.

Jentleson, Bruce W. *American Foreign Policy: The Dynamics of Choice in the 21st Century.* New York: Norton, 2003.

Jillson, Cal. *Pursuing the American Dream: Opportunity and Exclusion over Four Centuries.* Lawrence: University of Kansas Press, 2004.

Johnson, Todd M. *Countdown to 1900: World Evangelization at the End of the 19th Century.* Hamilton, Mass.: Center for the Study of Global Christianity, 2002.

———. "Demographic Futures for Christianity and the World Religions." *Dialog: A Journal of Theology* 43 (Spring 2004): 10–19.

Johnson, Todd M., and Sun Young Chung. "Tracking Global Christianity's Statistical Centre of Gravity, AD 33–AD 2100." *International Review of Mission* 93 (April 2004): 166–81.

Johnson, Todd M., and Sandra S. Kim. "Describing the Worldwide Christian Phenomenon." *International Bulletin of Missionary Research* 29 (April 2005): 80–82.

Johnston, Douglas, ed. *Faith-Based Diplomacy: Trumping Realpolitik.* New York: Oxford University Press, 2003.

———. "Introduction: Beyond Power Politics." In *Religion: The Missing Dimension of Statecraft,* edited by Douglas Johnston and Cynthia Sampson, 3–7. New York: Oxford University Press, 1995.

Johnstone, Patrick, and Jason Mandryk. *Operation World.* Carlisle, U.K.: Paternoster, 2001.

Kahn, Joseph. "Violence Taints Religion's Solace for China's Poor." *New York Times,* November 25, 2004.

Kaplan, Esther. "Follow the Money." *The Nation,* November 1, 2004.

———. *With God on Their Side: How Christian Fundamentalists Trampled Science, Policy and Democracy in George W. Bush's White House.* New York: New Press, 2005.

Kauffman, Christopher J. "Politics, Programs, and Protests: Catholic Relief Services in Vietnam, 1954–1975." *Catholic Historical Review* 91 (2005): 223–50.

Kauffman, Richard A. "Scholars Uncovering Church's Hidden History." *Christianity Today,* July 13, 1998, 22–23.

Kearney, A. T. "Measuring Globalization: The Global Top 20." *Foreign Policy,* May–June 2005, 52–60.

Keller, Catherine, Michael Nausner, and Mayra Nivera, eds. *Postcolonial Theologies: Divinity and Empire.* New York: Chalice Press, 2004.

Kelley, Dean M. *Why Conservative Churches Are Growing: A Study in Sociology of Religion,* rev. ed. Macon, Ga.: Mercer University Press, 1986.

Khan, Azizur Rahman, and Carl Riskin. *Inequality and Poverty in China in the Age of Globalization.* New York: Oxford University Press, 2001.

Kindopp, Jason. "Fragmented Yet Defiant: Protestant Resilience under Chinese Communist Party Rule." In *God and Caesar in China: Policy Implications of Church-State Tensions,* edited by Jason Kindopp and Carol Lee Hamrin, 122–48. Washington, D.C.: Brookings Institution Press, 2004.

Kipnis, Andrew B. "The Flourishing of Religion in Post-Mao China and the Anthropological Category of Religion." *Australian Journal of Anthropology* 12 (2001): 32–46.

Kirkpatrick, David D. "Club of the Most Powerful Gathers in Strictest Privacy." *New York Times,* August 28, 2004.

———. "In Secretly Taped Conversations, Glimpses of the Future President." *New York Times,* February 20, 2005.

Kondracke, Mort, and Fred Barnes. "Interview with Philip Jenkins." *Fox News,* December 21, 2002.

Korzeniewicz, Roberto Patricio, and Timothy Patrick Moran. "World-Economic Trends in the Distribution of Incomes, 1965–1992." *American Journal of Sociology* 102 (1997): 1000–1039.

Kraatz, Matthew S., and Edward J. Zajac. "Exploring the Limits of the New Institutionalism: The Causes and Consequences of Illegitimate Organizational Change." *American Sociological Review* 61 (1996): 812–36.

Kramer, Eric W. "Spectacle and the Staging of Power in Brazilian Neo-Pentecostalism." *Latin American Perspectives* 32 (2005): 95–120.

Kristof, Nicholas D. "Bleeding Hearts of the World, Unite!" *New York Times,* November 6, 2005.

———. "Where Faith Thrives." *New York Times,* March 26, 2005.

Krugman, Paul R. "Increasing Returns, Monopolistic Competition and International Trade." *Journal of International Economics* 9 (1979): 469–79.

———. "Scale Economies, Product Differentiation, and the Pattern of Trade." *American Economic Review* 70 (1980): 950–59.

Kuhn, Thomas S. *The Structure of Scientific Revolutions.* Chicago: University of Chicago Press, 1962.

Kurtz, Lester, and Kelly Goran. "Love Your Enemies? Protestants and Foreign Policy in the United States." In *The Quiet Hand of God: Faith-Based Activism and the Public Role of Mainline Protestantism,* edited by Robert Wuthnow and John Evans, 364–80. Berkeley and Los Angeles: University of California Press, 2002.

Lakoff, George. "Nailing the Frames of the Republican National Convention." *University of California at Berkeley News,* September 3, 2004.

———. *Whose Freedom? The Battle over America's Most Important Idea.* New York: Picador, 2007.

Langham, Thomas C. "Review of *The Next Christendom.*" *Sociology of Religion* 65 (Spring 2004): 95–97.

Lankford, John Errett. "Protestant Stewardship and Benevolence, 1900–1941: A Study in Religious Philanthropy." Ph.D. diss., University of Wisconsin, 1962.

Larkin, William J. "The Contribution of Luke-Acts to Missionary Moves of the

Christian Religion in 21st Century Post-Modern Global Context." *Global Missiology* (January 2004): 1–9.

Latourette, Kenneth Scott. *A History of the Expansion of Christianity*, vol. 4: *The Great Century in Europe and the United States of America, A.D. 1800— A.D. 1914*. New York: Harper & Brothers, 1941.

———. "Missionaries Abroad." *Annals of the American Academy of Political and Social Science* 368 (1966): 21–30.

Lawrence, Peter. *Road Belong Cargo: A Study of the Cargo Movement in the Southern Mdang District, New Guinea*. Manchester, U.K.: Manchester University Press, 1964.

Lawton, Kim A. "Faith without Borders: How the Developing World Is Changing the Face of Christianity." *Christianity Today* 41 (May 19, 1997): 38–49.

Lazerwitz, Bernard, J. Alan Winter, and Arnold Dashefsky. "Localism, Religiosity, Orthodoxy, and Liberalism: The Case of Jews in the United States." *Social Forces* 67 (1988): 229–42.

Lehmann, David. "Review of David Martin, *Pentecostalism: The World Their Parish*." *Journal of Religion in Africa* 3 (2003): 120–22.

———. *Struggle for the Spirit*. Cambridge: Polity, 1995.

Leiper, Henry Smith. *The Ghost of Caesar Walks: The Conflict of Nationalism and World Christianity*. New York: Friendship Press, 1935.

———. *World Chaos or World Christianity: A Popular Interpretation of Oxford and Edinburgh*. New York: Friendship Press, 1937.

Lindner, Eileen W. *Yearbook of American and Canadian Churches 1998*. Nashville: Abingdon Press, 1998.

———. *Yearbook of American and Canadian Churches 2005*. Nashville: Abingdon Press, 2005.

Lindsay, D. Michael. "Elite Networks as Social Power: New Modes of Organization within American Evangelicalism." *Sociology of Religion* 67 (2006).

———. *Faith in the Halls of Power: How Evangelicals Joined the American Elite*. New York: Oxford University Press, 2007.

———. "The National Prayer Breakfast and the 'Christian Mafia': Religious Publicity and Secrecy within the Corridors of Power." *Journal of the American Academy of Religion* 74 (2006).

Lobdell, William. "Pastor's Empire Built on Acts of Faith and Cash." *Los Angeles Times*, September 19, 2004.

———. "TBN's Promise: Send Money and See Riches." *Los Angeles Times*, September 20, 2004.

Longenecker, Dwight. "Christianity Is Not on the Wane in the World, It's Just Reshaping and Relocating." *The Times (London)*, March 22, 2003.

Lott, Jeremy. "The Faith of the Global South." *Touchstone*, 2002.

MacLeod, Alex. "A New Reformation Is Happening in Global Christianity." *Presbyterian Record* 128 (February 2004): 44–45.

Marcuse, Herbert. *One-Dimensional Man: Studies in the Ideology of Advanced Industrial Society*, 2nd ed. Boston: Beacon Press, 1991.

Marshall, Paul. "Religion and Global Affairs: Disregarding Religion." *SAIS Review* 18 (1988): 13–18.

Marshall-Fratani, Ruth. "The Global and Local in Nigerian Pentecostalism." In *Between Babel and Pentecost: Transnational Pentecostalism in Africa and Latin America*, edited by Andre Corten and Ruth Marshall-Fratani, 80–105. Bloomington: Indiana University Press, 2001.

Marshman, John Clark. *The Life and Times of Carey, Marshman, and Ward: Embracing the History of the Serampore Mission*, 2 vols. London: Longman, 1859.

Martin, Bernice. "From Pre- to Postmodernity in Latin America: The Case of Pentecostalism." In *Religion, Modernity and Postmodernity*, edited by Paul Heelas, 102–46. Oxford: Blackwell, 1998.

———. "New Mutations of the Protestant Ethic among Latin American Pentecostals." *Religion* 25 (1995): 101–17.

Martin, David. *Pentecostalism: The World Their Parish*. Oxford: Blackwell, 2002.

———. *Tongues of Fire: The Explosion of Protestantism in Latin America*. Oxford: Blackwell, 1990.

Martin, William. "With God on Their Side: Religion and U.S. Foreign Policy." In *Religion Returns to the Public Square: Faith and Policy in America*, edited by Hugh Heclo and Wilfred M. McClay, 327–59. Washington, D.C., and Baltimore: Woodrow Wilson Center Press and Johns Hopkins University Press, 2003.

Marty, Martin E. "The True Believers." *New York Times*, May 8, 1994.

Marx, Karl, and Frederick Engels. *The German Ideology*. New York: International Publishers, 1947.

Mase, Margaret. "Development, Life-Modes and Language in Papua New Guinea." *Development Bulletin* 50 (October 1999): 67–69.

Masuzawa, Tomoko. *The Invention of World Religions*. Chicago: University of Chicago Press, 2005.

Maxfield, Charles A., III. "The 'Reflex Influence' of Missions: The Domestic Operations of the American Board of Commissioners for Foreign Missions, 1810–1850." Ph.D. diss., Union Theological Seminary, Richmond, Va., 1995.

Maxwell, David. "'Delivered from the Spirit of Poverty?': Pentecostalism, Prosperity, and Modernity in Zimbabwe." *Journal of Religion in Africa* 28 (1998): 350–73.

———. "The Durawall of Faith: Pentecostal Spirituality in Neo-Liberal Zimbabwe." *Journal of Religion in Africa* 35 (2005): 4–32.

———. "'Sacred History, Social History': Traditions and Texts in the Making of a Southern African Transnational Religious Movement." *Comparative Studies in Society and History* 43 (2001): 502–24.

McAdams, Dan P. *The Redemptive Self: Stories Americans Live By*. New York: Oxford University Press, 2006.

McCarthy, Kathleen D. *American Creed: Philanthropy and the Rise of Civil Society, 1700–1865*. Chicago: University of Chicago Press, 2003.

McConnell, Chris. "Trinity: Praying and Paying." *Broadcasting and Cable*, May 18, 1988, 24–30.

McConnell, Francis John. *Human Needs and World Christianity*. New York: Friendship Press, 1929.

McCullum, Hugh. "Healing and Reconciliation Theme." *Conference on World Mission and Evangelism News*, 2005.

McGrath, Alister E. *The Future of Christianity*. Oxford: Blackwell, 2002.

Meyer, Birgit. "Christianity in Africa: From African Independent to Pentecostal-Charismatic Churches." *Annual Review of Anthropology* 33 (2004): 447–74.

———. "Commodities and the Power of Prayer: Pentecostalist Attitudes towards Consumption in Contemporary Ghana." *Development and Change* 29 (1998): 751–76.

———. "'Delivered from the Powers of Darkness': Confessions of Satanic Riches in Christian Ghana." *Africa* 65 (1995): 236–55.

———. "Powerful Pictures: Popular Christian Aesthetics in Southern Ghana." *Journal of the American Academy of Religion* 76 (2008): 82–110.

———. "'Praise the Lord': Popular Cinema and Pentecostalite Style in Ghana's New Public Sphere." *American Ethnologist* 31 (2004): 92–110.

———. *Translating the Devil: Religion and Modernity among the Ewe in Ghana*. Edinburgh: Edinburgh University Press, 1999.

Meyer, John W. "Globalization: Sources and Effects on National States and Societies." *International Sociology* 15 (2000): 233–48.

Meyer, John W., John Boli, George A. Thomas, and Francisco O. Ramirez. "World Society and the Nation-State." *American Journal of Sociology* 103 (1997): 144–81.

Meyer, John W., John Boli-Bennett, and Christopher Chase-Dunn. "Convergence and Divergence in Development." *Annual Review of Sociology* 1 (1975): 223–46.

Miller, Basil. *William Carey: The Father of Modern Missions*. Minneapolis, Minn.: Bethany House, 1985.

Miller, Donald E., and Tetsunao Yamamori. *Global Pentecostalism: The New Face of Christian Social Engagement*. Berkeley and Los Angeles: University of California Press, 2007.

Mitchell, Ben. "Why Southern Baptists Should Not Support the ONE Campaign." *Florida Baptist Witness*, June 30, 2005.

Moe-Lobeda, Cynthia D. *Healing a Broken World: Globalization and God*. Minneapolis, Minn.: Augsburg Fortress, 2002.

———. "Journey between Worlds: Economic Globalization and Luther's God Indwelling Creation." *Word & World* 21 (2001): 413–23.

Moreau, A. Scott. "Putting the Survey in Perspective." In *Mission Handbook 2004–2006*, edited by Dotsey Welliver and Minnette Northcutt, 11–59. Wheaton, Ill.: Billy Graham Center, 2004.

Morrison, Charles Clayton. "The World Missionary Conference." *Christian Century*, July 7, 1910.

Mortensen, Viggo. "What Is Happening to Global Christianity?" *Dialog: A Journal of Theology* 43 (Spring 2004): 20–27.

Myers, Bryant L. *Walking with the Poor: Principles and Practices of Transformational Development*. Maryknoll, N.Y.: Orbis Books, 1999.

Nash, David. "Reconnecting Religion with Social and Cultural History: Secularization's Failure as a Master Narrative." *Cultural and Social History* 1 (2004): 302–25.

Ndaywel E Nziem, Isidore. *Les Langues Africaines et Creoles Face a Leur Avenir*. Paris: L'Harmattan, 2003.

Neill, Stephen. *A History of Christian Missions*. London: Penguin, 1964.

————. *A History of Christian Missions*, rev. ed. London: Penguin, 1986.

Newbigin, Leslie. *Foolishness to the Greeks*. Grand Rapids, Mich.: Eerdmans, 1986.

Nichols, Bill, and Barbara Slavin. "Foreign Aid Hike Pushed." *USA Today*, February 19, 2001.

Noll, Mark A. "Review of *World Christian Encyclopedia: A Comparative Survey of Churches and Religions in the Modern World*." *Church History* 71 (2002): 448–54.

Norris, Pippa, and Ronald Inglehart. *Sacred and Secular: Religion and Politics Worldwide*. Cambridge: Cambridge University Press, 2004.

Olsen, Ted. "Pilot's Evangelistic Efforts Freak Out Passengers, Country." *Christianity Today*, February 10, 2004.

Ostrov, Benjamin C. "Something of Value: The Religious Response to De-Maoization in China." *Social Science Journal* 42 (2005): 55–70.

Padilla, C. Rene. "The Future of Christianity in Latin America: Missiological Perspectives and Challenges." *International Bulletin of Missionary Research* 23 (July 1999): 105–11.

Page, Susan. "Christian Right's Alliances Bend Political Spectrum." *USA Today*, June 14, 2005.

Passantino, Gretchen. "Barbara Walters to Interview Bush Advisor Karen Hughes." *Answers in Action*, March 26, 2004.

Perry, Elizabeth J. "Challenging the Mandate of Heaven: Popular Protest in Modern China." *Critical Asian Studies* 33 (2001): 163–80.

Peterson, Roger, Gordon Aeschliman, and R. Wayne Sneed. *Maximum Impact Short-Term Mission: The God-Commanded, Repetitive Deployment of Swift, Temporary, Non-Professional Missionaries*. Minneapolis, Minn.: STEM Press, 2003.

Phillips, Clifton Jackson. *Protestant America and the Pagan World: The First Half Century of the American Board of Commissioners for Foreign Missions, 1810–1860*. Cambridge, Mass.: Harvard University Press, 1969.

Philpott, Daniel. "The Challenge of September 11 to Secularism in International Relations." *World Politics* 55 (2002): 66–95.

Pintado, Ana Celia Perera. "Religion and Cuban Identity in a Transnational Context." *Latin American Perspectives* 32 (2005): 147–73.

Portes, Alejandro, and Ruben G. Rumbaut. *Immigrant America: A Portrait*, 3rd ed. Berkeley and Los Angeles: University of California Press, 2006.

Powell, Walter W., and Paul J. DiMaggio, eds. *The New Institutionalism in Organizational Analysis*. Chicago: University of Chicago Press, 1991.

Primer, Ben. *Protestants and American Business Methods*. Ann Arbor, Mich.: UMI Research Press, 1978.

Putnam, Robert D. *Bowling Alone: The Collapse and Revival of American Community*. New York: Simon & Schuster, 2000.

Pyle, Jean L. "Sex, Maids, and Export Processing: Risks and Reasons for Gendered Global Production Networks." *International Journal of Politics, Culture and Society* 15 (2001): 55–75.

Ravallion, Martin. "The Debate on Globalization, Poverty and Inequality: Why Measurement Matters." World Bank Policy Research Working Paper 3038 (April 2003).

Reed, James Eldin. "American Foreign Policy, the Politics of Missions and Josiah Strong, 1890–1900." *Church History* 41 (1972): 230–45.

Richard, Pablo. *Death of Christendoms, Birth of the Church: Historical Analysis and Theological Interpretation of the Church in Latin America.* Maryknoll, N.Y.: Orbis, 1987.

Ritzer, George. *The McDonaldization of Society,* rev. ed. Thousand Oaks, Calif.: Pine Forge Press, 2004.

Rivera, Paul R. " 'Field Found!' Establishing the Maryknoll Mission Enterprise in the United States and China, 1918–1928." *Catholic Historical Review* 84 (1998): 477–517.

Robbins, Joel. "Becoming Sinners: Christianity and Desire among the Urapmin of Papua New Guinea." *Ethnology* 37 (1998): 299–316.

———. *Becoming Sinners: Christianity and Moral Torment in a Papua New Guinea Society.* Berkeley and Los Angeles: University of California Press, 2004.

———. "The Globalization of Pentecostal and Charismatic Christianity." *Annual Review of Anthropology* 33 (2004): 117–43.

———. "On Reading 'World News': Apocalyptic Narrative, Negative Nationalism, and Transnational Christianity in a Papua New Guinea Society." *Social Analysis* 42 (1998): 103–30.

———. "Secrecy and the Sense of an Ending: Narrative, Time, and Everyday Millenarianism in Papua New Guinea and in Christian Fundamentalism." *Comparative Studies in Society and History* 43 (2001): 525–51.

———. "When Do You Think the World Will End? Globalization, Apocalypticism, and the Moral Perils of Fieldwork in 'Last New Guinea.' " *Anthropology and Humanism* 22 (1997): 6–30.

Robert, Dana L. "The Influence of American Missionary Women on the World Back Home." *Religion and American Culture* 12 (2002): 59–89.

———. "Shifting Southward: Global Christianity since 1945." *International Bulletin of Missionary Research* 24 (2004): 50–58.

Robert, Dana Lee. *Occupy until I Come: A. T. Piersoon and the Evangelization of the World.* Grand Rapids, Mich.: Eerdmans, 2003.

Robertson, Roland. *Globalization: Social Theory and Global Culture.* Thousand Oaks, Calif.: Sage, 1992.

———. "Glocalization: Time-Space and Homogeneity-Heterogeneity." In *Global Modernities,* edited by Mike Featherstone, Scott Lash, and Roland Robertson, 25–44. Thousand Oaks, Calif.: Sage, 1995.

Rockwell, Norman. *Walking to Church. Saturday Evening Post,* April 4, 1953, cover.

Roof, Wade Clark. *Community and Commitment: Religious Plausibility in a Liberal Protestant Church.* New York: Elsevier, 1978.

———. *Spiritual Marketplace: Baby Boomers and the Remaking of American Religion.* Princeton, N.J.: Princeton University Press, 1999.

Ruggie, John Gerard. *Constructing the World Polity.* New York: Routledge, 1998.

———. "What Makes the World Hang Together? Neo-Utilitarianism and the Social Constructivist Challenge." *International Organization* 52 (1998): 855–85.

Rupert, Mark. *Ideologies of Globalization: Contending Visions of a New World Order.* New York: Routledge, 2000.

Rusling, James. "Interview with President William McKinley." *The Christian Advocate,* January 22, 1903, 17.

Said, Edward W. *Culture and Imperialism.* New York: Vintage, 1993.

Sandel, Michael. *Democracy's Discontent: American in Search of a Public Philosophy.* Cambridge, Mass.: Harvard University Press, 1996.

Sanneh, Lamin. "Global Christianity and the Re-education of the West." *Christian Century,* July 16, 1995, 715–18.

————. *Whose Religion Is Christianity? The Gospel beyond the West.* Grand Rapids, Mich.: Eerdmans, 2003.

Schmidt, Leigh Eric. "Mixed Blessings: Christianization and Secularization." *Reviews in American History* 26 (1998): 637–43.

Schossler, Eric. *Fast Food Nation.* New York: Houghton Mifflin, 2001.

Schraeder, Peter J., Steven W. Hook, and Bruce Taylor. "Clarifying the Foreign Aid Puzzle: A Comparison of American, Japanese, French, and Swedish Aid Flows." *World Politics* 50 (1998): 294–323.

Schwartz, Glenn. "How Short-Term Missions Can Go Wrong." *International Journal of Foreign Missions* 20 (Winter 2003): 27–34.

Sebastian, Mrinalini. "Mission without History? Some Ideas for Decolonizing Mission." *International Review of Mission* 93 (January 2004): 75–96.

Sellers, Jeff M. "How to Spell Debt Relief." *Christianity Today,* May 21, 2001.

Sheridan, Robert E. *The Founders of Maryknoll.* Maryknoll, N.Y.: The Catholic Foreign Mission Society of America, 1980.

Siermon-Netto, Uwe. "Surprise: Resilient Christianity." *World & I* 18 (July 2003): 29–31.

Skillen, James W. *With or Against the World? America's Role among the Nations.* Lanham, Md.: Rowman and Littlefield, 2005.

Sklair, Leslie. *Globalization: Capitalism and Its Alternatives,* 3rd ed. New York: Oxford University Press, 2002.

Skocpol, Theda. "How Americans Became Civic." In *Civic Engagement in American Democracy,* edited by Theda Skocpol and Morris P. Fiorina, 27–80. Washington and New York: Brookings Institution and Russell Sage Foundation, 1999.

Skocpol, Theda, Marshall Ganz, and Ziad Munson. "A Nation of Organizers: The Institutional Origins of Civic Voluntarism in the United States." *American Political Science Review* 94 (2000): 527–46.

Slone, Chris. "Robertson Shakes Up Empire." *Christianity Today,* July 14, 1997.

Smidt, Corwin E. "Religion and American Attitudes toward Islam and an Invasion of Iraq." *Sociology of Religion* 66 (2005): 243–61.

Smith, Brian H. *More Than Altruism: The Politics of Private Foreign Aid.* Princeton, N.J.: Princeton University Press, 1990.

Smith, Christian. *American Evangelicalism: Embattled and Thriving.* Chicago: University of Chicago Press, 1998.

————. *Moral, Believing Animals: Human Personhood and Culture.* New York: Oxford University Press, 2003.

———, ed. *The Secular Revolution: Power, Interests, and Conflict in the Secularization of American Public Life.* Berkeley and Los Angeles: University of California Press, 2003.

———. *Soul Searching: The Religious and Spiritual Lives of American Teenagers.* New York: Oxford University Press, 2005.

Smith, R. Drew. "American Evangelists and Church-State Dilemmas in Multiple African Contexts." In *Freedom's Distant Shores: American Protestants and Post-Colonial Alliances with Africa,* edited by R. Drew Smith, chap. 7. Waco, Tex.: Baylor University Press, 2006.

Solinger, Dorothy. "Globalization and the Paradox of Participation: The Chinese Case." *Global Governance* 7 (2001): 173–96.

Soros, George. *The Bubble of American Supremacy.* New York: Public Affairs, 2004.

Stackhouse, Max L., Don S. Browning, and Peter J. Paris, eds. *God and Globalization,* vol. 2: *The Spirit and Modern Authorities.* Philadelphia: Trinity Press International, 2001.

Stackhouse, Max L., and Diane B. Obenchain, eds. *God and Globalization,* vol. 3: *Christ and the Dominions of Civilization.* Philadelphia: Trinity Press International, 2002.

Stackhouse, Max L., and Peter J. Paris, eds. *God and Globalization,* vol. 1: *Religion and the Powers of the Common Life.* Philadelphia: Trinity Press International, 2000.

Stafford, Tim. "Good Morning, Evangelicals! Meet Ted Haggard the NAE's Optimistic Champion of Ecumenical Evangelism and Free-Market Faith." *Christianity Today,* November 4, 2005.

———. "Imperfect Instrument." *Christianity Today,* February 24, 2005.

Stark, Rodney, and Roger Finke. *Acts of Faith: Explaining the Human Side of Religion.* Berkeley and Los Angeles: University of California Press, 2000.

Starr, Paul. *Freedom's Power: The True Force of Liberalism.* New York: Perseus, 2007.

Steger, Manfred B. *Globalism: The New Market Ideology.* Lanham, Md.: Rowman and Littlefield, 2002.

———. *Globalization: A Very Short Introduction.* New York: Oxford University Press, 2003.

Stevens, Joann. "Clerics Differ in Reaction to Pope's Visit." *Washington Post,* October 11, 1979.

Stoll, David. *Is Latin America Turning Protestant? The Politics of Evangelical Growth.* Berkeley and Los Angeles: University of California Press, 1990.

Talavera, Arturo Fontaine. "Trends toward Globalization in Chile." In *Many Globalizations: Cultural Diversity in the Contemporary World,* edited by Peter L. Berger and Samuel P. Huntington, 250–95. New York: Oxford University Press, 2002.

TeSeele, Gene. "Scholars Look at Religion in Society." *Witherspoon on the Web,* November 26, 2003.

Thomas, George A., and John W. Meyer. "The Expansion of the State." *Annual Review of Sociology* 10 (1984): 461–82.

Thompson, Craig J., and Zeynep Arsel. "The Starbucks Brandscape and Consumers' Anticorporate Experiences of Glocalization." *Journal of Consumer Research* 31 (2004): 631–42.

Thornton, Patricia A. "The New Cybersects: Resistance and Repression in the Reform Era." In *Chinese Society: Change, Conflict and Resistance,* 2nd ed., edited by Elizabeth Perry and Mark Selden, 247–70. New York: Routledge, 2004.

Thumma, Scott and Dave Travis. *Beyond Megachurch Myths: What We Can Learn from America's Largest Churches.* San Francisco: Jossey-Bass, 2007.

Tocqueville, Alexis de. *Democracy in America.* New York: Vintage Books, 1945.

Tomlinson, John. *Globalization and Culture.* Chicago: University of Chicago Press, 1999.

Tracy, Joseph. *History of the American Board of Commissioners for Foreign Missions.* New York: M. W. Dodd, 1842.

Troch, Lieve. "Ecclesiogenesis: The Patchwork of New Religious Communities in Brazil." *Exchange* 33 (2004): 54–72.

Tse, Lilia. "International Leaders Launch the Micah Challenge." *Ecumenical Press,* October 18, 2004.

Turner, Victor. *The Ritual Process: Structure and Anti-Structure.* Ithaca, N.Y.: Cornell University Press, 1969.

Ukah, Asonzeh Franklin-Kennedy. "Advertising God: Nigerian Christian Video-Films and the Power of Consumer Culture." *Journal of Religion in Africa* 33 (2003): 203–31.

———. "The Redeemed Christian Church of God (RCCG), Nigeria: Local Identities and Global Processes in African Pentecostalism." Ph.D. diss., University of Bayreuth, 2003.

United Nations. *Forging a Global South.* New York: United Nations Development Programme, 2004.

———. *Human Development Report: 2004.* New York: United Nations, 2004.

U.S. State Department. *Trafficking in Persons Report.* Washington, D.C.: Government Printing Office, 2003.

Urquhart, Brian. "Extreme Makeover." *New York Review of Books,* February 24, 2005, 4–5.

Urry, John. *Global Complexity.* Cambridge: Polity, 2003.

van Binsbergen, Wim, and Rijk van Dijk, eds. *Situating Globality: African Agency in the Appropriation of Global Culture.* Boston: Brill, 2004.

Van Cise, Martha. *Successful Mission Teams: A Guide for Volunteers.* Birmingham, Ala.: New Hope Publishers, 2004.

van Dijk, Rijk A. "From Camp to Encompassment: Discourses of Transsubjectivity in the Ghanaian Pentecostal Diaspora." *Journal of Religion in Africa* 27 (1997): 135–59.

Vasquez, Manuel A., and Marie Friedmann Marquardt. *Globalizing the Sacred: Religion across the Americas.* New Brunswick, N.J.: Rutgers University Press, 2003.

Ver Beek, Kurt, and Robert Priest. "Do Short-Term Missions Change Anyone?" *Christianity Today,* July 6, 2005.

Verstraelen, F. J. *Missiology: An Ecumenical Introduction, Texts and Contexts of Global Christianity.* Grand Rapids, Mich.: Eerdmans, 1995.

Waldman, Peter. "Evangelicals Give U.S. Foreign Policy an Activist Tinge." *Wall Street Journal,* May 26, 2004.

Waldman, Steven, and John Green. "It Wasn't Just (or Even Mostly) the 'Religious Right,'" *Beliefnet,* 2004.

Walker, Ken. "Agencies Announce Short-Term Missions Standards." *Christianity Today,* September 30, 2003.

Wallerstein, Immanuel. *Geopolitics and Geoculture.* Cambridge: Cambridge University Press, 1991.

———. *The Modern World System.* New York: Academic Press, 1974.

Walls, Andrew. "Culture and Coherence in Christian History." *Evangelical Review of Theology* 9 (1984): 215–24.

———. *The Missionary Movement in Christian History: Studies in the Transmission of Faith.* Maryknoll, N.Y.: Orbis, 1996.

Walls, Andrew F. "The American Dimension in the History of the Missionary Movement." In *Earthen Vessels: American Evangelicals and Foreign Missions, 1880–1980,* edited by Joel A. Carpenter and Wilbert R. Shenk, 1–25. Grand Rapids, Mich.: Eerdmans, 1990.

Walls, A[ndrew] F. "World Christianity, the Missionary Movement and the Ugly American." In *World Order and Religion,* edited by Wade Clark Roof, 147–72. Albany: State University of New York, 1991.

Warner, R. Stephen. "The De-Europeanization of American Christianity." In *A Nation of Religions: The Politics of Pluralism in the United States,* edited by Stephen Prothero. Chapel Hill: University of North Carolina Press, 2005.

———. *New Wine in Old Wineskins: Evangelicals and Liberals in a Small-Town Church.* Berkeley and Los Angeles: University of California Press, 1988.

———. "The Place of Congregation in the Contemporary American Religious Configuration." In *American Congregations: New Perspectives in the Study of Congregations,* vol. 2, edited by James P. Wind and James M. Lewis, 54–100. Chicago: University of Chicago Press, 1994.

Warner, R. Stephen, and Judith Wittner, eds. *Gatherings in Diaspora: Religious Communities and the New Immigration.* Philadelphia: Temple University Press, 1998.

Webber, Michael, Mark Wang, and Zhu Ying, eds. *China's Transition to a Global Economy.* New York: Palgrave, 2002.

Weber, Max. *The Protestant Ethic and the Spirit of Capitalism.* New York: Scribner, 1952.

Weinstein, Michael M., ed. *Globalization: What's New?* New York: Columbia University Press, 2005.

Welliver, Dotsey, and Minnette Northcutt. *Mission Handbook, 2004–2006: U.S. and Canadian Protestant Ministries Overseas.* Wheaton, Ill.: Billy Graham Center, 2004.

Wendt, Alexander. "Constructing International Politics." *International Security* 20 (1995): 71–81.

Wenger, Jacqueline E. "Official vs. Underground Protestant Churches in China:

Challenges for Reconciliation and Social Influence." *Review of Religious Research* 46 (2004): 169–82.

Whaites, Alan. "Pursuing Partnership: World Vision and the Ideology of Development—a Case Study." *Development in Practice* 9 (1999): 410–23.

Wickeri, Philip L. "Mission from the Margins: The *Missio Dei* in the Crisis of World Christianity." *International Review of Mission* 93 (April 2004): 182–98.

Wilder, Robert P. *The Student Volunteer Movement: Its Origins and Early History.* New York: Student Volunteer Movement, 1935.

Willetts, Peter, ed. *'The Conscience of the World': The Influence of Non-Governmental Organizations in the UN System.* Washington, D.C.: Brookings Institution, 1996.

Williams, Michael C. *The Realist Tradition and the Limits of International Relations.* New York: Cambridge University Press, 2005.

Winter, Ralph D. "Review of Philip Jenkins, *The Next Christendom.*" *Mission Frontiers,* January–February 2003, 14–15.

Wisdom, Alan, and Erik Nelson. "Churches Repeating Past Mistakes on Human Rights—and Making New Ones." *Faith & Freedom,* Winter 2005, 10–11.

Woodward, Bob. *Plan of Attack.* New York: Simon & Schuster, 2004.

World Council of Churches, Central Committee. "Major Features of Globalization Affecting the Church." *Ecumenical Review* 54 (October 2002): 483–94.

Worsley, Peter. *The Trumpet Shall Sound: A Study of Cargo Cults in Melanesia.* London: MacGibbon and Kee, 1957.

Wuthnow, Robert. *Acts of Compassion: Caring for Others and Helping Ourselves.* Princeton, N.J.: Princeton University Press, 1991.

———. *America and the Challenges of Religious Diversity.* Princeton, N.J.: Princeton University Press, 2005.

———. "Beyond Quiet Influence? Possibilities for the Protestant Mainline." In *The Quiet Hand of God: Faith-Based Activism and the Public Role of Mainline Protestantism,* edited by Robert Wuthnow and John Evans, 381–404. Berkeley and Los Angeles: University of California Press, 2002.

———. *The Crisis in the Churches: Spiritual Malaise, Fiscal Woe.* New York: Oxford University Press, 1997.

———. *Learning to Care: Elementary Kindness in an Age of Indifference.* New York: Oxford University Press, 1995.

———. *Poor Richard's Principle: Recovering the American Dream through the Moral Dimension of Work, Business, and Money.* Princeton, N.J.: Princeton University Press, 1996.

———. *Saving America? Faith-Based Services and the Future of Civil Society.* Princeton, N.J.: Princeton University Press, 2004.

Wuthnow, Robert, and John H. Evans, eds. *The Quiet Hand of God: Faith-Based Activism and the Public Role of Mainline Protestantism.* Berkeley and Los Angeles: University of California Press, 2002.

Wuthnow, Robert, and Valerie Lewis. "Religion and Altruistic U.S. Foreign Policy Goals: Evidence from a National Survey of Church Members." *Journal for the Scientific Study of Religion* 47 (2008): 176–89.

Wuthnow, Robert, and Steve Offutt. "Transnational Religious Connections."
    Sociology of Religion 69 (2008): 110–21.
Xin Zhigang. "Dissecting China's 'Middle Class.'" *China Daily*, October 27, 2004.
Yang, Fenggang, and Helen R. Ebaugh. "Transformations in New Immigrant Re-
    ligions and Their Global Implications." *American Sociological Review* 66
    (2001): 269–88.
Yankelovich, Daniel. "Poll Positions." *Foreign Affairs*, September/October
    2005.
Young, Michael P. *Bearing Witness against Sin: The Evangelical Birth of the
    American Social Movement.* Chicago: University of Chicago Press, 2006.
———. "Confessional Protest: The Religious Birth of U.S. National Social
    Movements." *American Sociological Review* 67 (2002): 660–88.
Zoba, Wendy Murray. "Bill Bright's Wonderful Plan for the World." *Christian-
    ity Today*, July 14, 1997, 14–27.
Zoroya, Gregg. "He Puts Words in Bush's Mouth." *USA Today*, April 10, 2001.

Index

Text: 10/13 Sabon
Display: Sabon
Compositor: Binghamton Valley Composition, LLC
Indexer: Kevin Millham
Printer and Binder: Maple-Vail Book Manufacturing Group